Who Made Me
A Refugee

Jinnah, Gandhi, Nehru, Mountbatten

"No man is good enough to rule another man, and no nation is good enough to rule another nation. For a man to rule himself is liberty; for a nation to rule itself is liberty. But for either to rule another is tyranny. If a nation robs another of its freedom, it does not deserve freedom for itself, and under a just God it will not retain it."

Abraham Lincoln

"It may be that the public mind of India may expand under our system till it has outgrown that system: that by good government we may educate our subjects into a capacity for better government; that, having become instructed in European knowledge, they may, in some future age, demand European institutions. Whether such a day will come I know not. But never will I attempt to avert or retard it. Whenever it comes it will be the proudest day in English history. To have found a people sunk in the lowest depths of slavery and superstition, to have so ruled them as to have made them capable and desirous of all the privileges of citizens, would indeed be a title to glory all our own".

Lord Macaulay, Minute on Indian Education, 1835

Who Made Me
A Refugee

Jinnah, Gandhi, Nehru, Mountbatten

Jagdish Mitter Sarin

&

Brig. Parmodh Sarin

Manas Publications

New Delhi-110 002 (INDIA)

MANAS PUBLICATIONS

(Publishers, Distributors, Importers & Exporters)
4858, Prahlad Street,
24, Ansari Road, Darya Ganj,
New Delhi - 110 002 (INDIA)
Ph.: 23260783, 23265523 (O); 23842660 (R)
Fax: 011 - 23272766
E-mail: manaspublications@vsnl.com
Website: www.manaspublications.com

© Brig. Parmodh Sarin

2006

ISBN 81-7049-296-3

Rs. 595/-

Typeset at
Manas Publications

Printed in India at
Salasar Imaging Systems, Delhi
and Published by Mrs Suman Lata for
Manas Publications, 4858, Prahlad Street,
24, Ansari Road, Darya Ganj,
New Delhi - 110 002 (INDIA)

Contents

Glossary

Ahimsa	non-violence
Akali	Sikh zealot who strictly follows the dictates of the Gurus
Amir	Muslim prince or counsellor
Arya Samaj	a reformist Hindu sect founded by Dayanand Saraswati
Ashram	a place of Hindu religious retreat
Azad, Azadi	free, freedom
Bagh	a garden
Babu	a clerk-honorific for an educated Bengali
Bande Matram	'Hail to thee, Mother', the first Indian national anthem
Bania	member of the Hindu merchant class
Bapu	father, affectionate term for Gandhi
Begum	a Muslim noble woman of high rank, term is also used for royal consort
Bhadralok	'gentlefolk', the intellectuals of Bengal
Bhagwad Gita	'Song of the Blessed one': Krishna's discourse to Arjuna,
Brahmin	a Hindu priest
Caliph (or Khalifa)	Deputy of Allah, Commander of the faithful
Charkha	simple spinning wheel, popularised by Gandhi
Dewan	Revenue Collector, also a Mughal Viceroy

Dharna	a peaceful protest against an injustice
Feringhee	a foreigner, usually a White person
Ghadr	rebellion
Goonda	a gangster, hoodlum, hired thug
Gurudwara	a place of Sikh worship
Guru	teacher
Harijan	an Untouchable, (literally: 'child of God')
Haj, Hajji	the Muslim pilgrimage, individual pilgrim
Hartal	the closing of shops and business as a mark of protest or mourning
Jai Hind	victory to India
Jats	race of peasant farmers and warriors of Punjab and United Provinces
Khadi	cotton cloth spun and woven by hand
Khalsa	'the pure': the Sikh army of the pure
Khan	a tribal leader in the northern frontier region
Khilafat	a Muslim movement dedicated to the Caliphate of Turkey
Khudai Khidmatgars	organisation led by Abdul Gaffar Khan (literally 'servants of God)
Kotwali	a police post
Kirpan	a curved sword, carried by Sikhs
Lathi	wooden staff, when metal tipped used by police
Maha	prefix meaning large or great
Mahant	head of a Hindu/Sikh religious organisation or establishment
Mahatma	literally great soul, a title popularly applied to Gandhi
Maidan	open space separating blocks of houses
Masjid	Mosque
Mela	a fair, normally a small town affair

Maulana	an honorary title given to Muslims versed in scriptures
Mofussil	country districts, particularly in Bengal
Munshi	variously, a teacher or scribe, a native secretary
Naik	non-commissioned sepoy officer in the army
Namaz	prayer, obligatory for Muslims five times a day
Nawab	a title conferred on an Indian governor by the Mughal emperor
Neta ji	Leader (Bengali)
Nizam	title of the ruler of the Deccan
Pandit	an honorary title given to Hindus versed in scriptures
Panchayat	an elected body of local elders acceptance of whose rulings was mandatory
Pindaris	a band of marauders
Puja	ritual of Hindu worship
Quaid-i-Azam	'Great Leader': title bestowed on Jinnah by Muslim League
Raj	rule, government (commonly British rule in India)
Ryot, raiyat	peasant, any 'tenant of the soil' who worked the land
Sabha	a Committee or a group coming together
Sadhu	a Hindu holy man
Samadhi	a small mausoleum, usually built where holy men are buried
Sardar	leader or chief, usually of a tribe
Sati	the immolation of a surviving Hindu wife with the dead husband
Satyagraha	policy of passive resistance, developed by Gandhi
Shashtra	law-books and sacred texts of Hindus
Sheikh	Muslim religious or tribal leader, a person known for his piety

Shia	a major sect of Islam
Shuddhi	a movement for reconversion from Islam
Swadeshi	home spun cloth, or not imported, Indian product
Swaraj	self-government
Syed	a direct descendant of the Holy Prophet
Ulama	the community of Muslim learned men
Vakil	an advocate or lawyer, a court pleader
Zamindar (Zemidar)	a landowner, also a revenue collecting landlord

Preface

The freedom that our country enjoys today is the product of a great historical process. India's fight for freedom had to overcome narrow communalism, racial and linguist separation inherent to our society; factors that were engrained far too deep in the Indian psyche over centuries. But then, why were we enslaved in the first place? The boundaries of India standing on its apex like a gigantic triangle are protected in the north by the mighty Himalayas. Western, Eastern and Southern boundaries are protected by the Arabian Sea, and the Bay of Bengal of the Indian Ocean. So why was it that with such a natural protection available India through the ages had been open to invasion, right from the times of Alexander the Great who invaded India in 327 B.C? Thereafter, there has been many number of adventurers who came from the north, eventually subjugating the country, setting up dynasties and then withering away. Chinese travellers were mostly on the mission of peace and were not any threat to the rulers of those times. It was only the European seamen looking for fresh outlets for their trade who took the 'Sea route' in the fifteenth century who found India to be a lucrative market. The French, the Dutch, the Spaniards; and of course, the British; just about every power in Europe decided to explore India with a view to establish their trade with a country that was seen as full of all kinds of riches. Even America was discovered by default in the process. For a variety of reasons the British eventually succeeded in farming out India as their territory for trade. Finally, they got to rule over the country for over hundred years and built an Empire in the process. But they were reluctant and unwilling rulers in the beginning, no invasion like many that had come from the land routes preceded establishment of this Empire.

The British Empire, the school children were taught in the earlier part of the twentieth century, was so powerful and so beneficent to the rest of the world, particularly the weak and poor people of the countries under British rule, that it could be regarded as likely to last forever; because the underprivileged of these countries would want it to. We even then knew that there were powerful and meaningful disagreements to this premise, but that is what the 'Whites' thought. So what happened that made the Empire disappear before the century was half-way through; more importantly, why did they lose India, euphorically described as the 'jewel in the crown', a source of endless pride to the British and a key factor in the formulation of all major policies concerning the Empire?

Several accounts of the Indian Freedom Movement have been written and published over the years. This fascinating subject has long employed the diligence of historians, both Indian and foreign. Almost all of these accounts have been well researched and documented. Most of the key players of this saga have also written their memoirs, autobiographies and narrated those events (from their perspective) that changed the course of the Indian history. It will be churlish on my part to even try to negate or contest their valuable work, even if their opinions have been far too diverse from each other. So, is it appropriate to produce yet another account when I have absolutely no claim to be associated with any event that has shaped India's history, except for the fact that I was a five years old 'refugee' from Lahore when the country got divided? What is worse I have never been a student of History; except for studying Military history and personalities who fought wars, shaped events and destinies of different countries right through the ages.

I had sentimental reasons for taking on this project. This book is based on long drawn research done by my late father, Mr. Jagdish Mitter Sarin who wanted to obtain his PhD degree by presenting a study on India's freedom movement. His research confined itself to the period 1909 to 1920. This, apparently, was the most epoch-making and definitive era that finally led to the disappearance of the Raj. It was in 1909 that the British government had agreed to undertake some kind of 'reforms' that could give the Indians some hope for the future. Concurrently, in consonance with the theory of 'divide and rule' the rulers had also been able to identify a potential ally in the form of the Aga Khan who was keen to ensure that the Muslims retained their separate identity. A new Muslim political party (All India Muslim League) came into being with apparent blessings of the administration as a counterpoise to the rising (and predominantly Hindu) unrest against foreign domination in the country. Resultantly, any possibility of the Hindus and the Muslims jointly fighting against the British receded and made the task of the separatists easier.

This period also saw emergence of a lawyer from South Africa, one Mohandas Karamchand Gandhi, anointed as 'Mahatma' in due course of time and accepted as the 'Father of the Nation' notwithstanding his personal fads and fancies, taking control of the freedom movement with no one contesting his claim to guide this country's destiny. For millions of Indians, Gandhi was almost a divine being. He conformed to the established religious idea of saintly leader and as such mixed an essentially a political demand with a moral fable where the lowly confronted the highest to teach them how the affairs of the state should be settled. He taught how nationalism and cultural self-awareness were inextricably bound together. It was during this period that the 'moderates' among our leaders turned into 'pragmatists' under Gandhi's guidance and the non-revolutionary sentiments of the existing leadership was given a turn towards result-oriented agitationism.

The period also was a witness to another, and much more charismatic and successful lawyer, Mohammad Ali Jinnah, converting from a strong nationalist to a proponent of 'two nation' theory', demanding a separate homeland for the Muslims leading to the partition of the country. Intelligent people do not change their fundamental stand on the issues of such great importance, issues like break up of one of the most ancient civilisations unless there are strong compulsions for them to do so: that, Jinnah was one of the most intelligent and charismatic personalities of those times is obvious. So why did he elect to seek a separate 'homeland' for Muslims is one question that has been rankling me. I am sure that in the wake of recent controversy generated by the (former) BJP President Mr L K Advani on the subject there are many more Indians who are equally inquisitive.

Numerous accounts of India's freedom movement available have generally intrigued a lay reader like me with regard to certain other aspects of the entire saga. How did Tilak and Gokhale, with tremendous and mass following of their own, the two had been working hard at awakening the Indians from their slumber of slavery got sidelined when Gandhi arrived on the scene? Why is it that intellectuals like C Rajagopalachari, C R Das, and Motilal Nehru who did not necessarily agree with Gandhi's approach to the freedom movement fell in line with the Mahatma's strategy?

On hindsight the Mahatma's game plan was seemingly simple. Majority population, that is, Hindus were not temperamentally into picking up arms for the purpose of attaining freedom; unlike Russian and French revolutions it would have been far too cumbersome to organise an armed revolution, then that kind of approach to the problem of getting rid of the British was also not in consonance with the Mahatma's philosophy of life; there would have been a moral contradiction for him if he had contemplated recourse to violence of any kind. This had to be a non-violent movement awakening the national consciousness encompassing every section of the Indian society. How did he manage to do all this when his adherence to 'Ahimsa' and other fads had not yet gained in popularity in the country? There were revolutionaries who propounded political theories of different hues and took to arms while challenging the might of British Empire; concurrently people like Gokhale and Lajpatrai who wanted to, and tried to, reason with the British to leave India were also in the thick of things. All the three had the same aim but different methodology and ideology to dislodge the Raj, but rarely agreed to form a joint front for the purpose. What confounds the confusion for a young reader is that historians from Pakistan would tell you that the Muslim leaders were honourable and undemanding and the Congress counterparts were wily, grasping and unscrupulous. Was it really so? These and some other issues, which will emerge during this narration, also worked on my mind.

One could always simplify and say that, 'Politically, Gandhi solved a dilemma which had been agitating the minds of Indian nationalists for over a generation. Should they adopt constitutional methods of opposing the British, confining themselves to making speeches on the subject of freedom, or should they side with those who were increasingly picking arms against the foreign rulers. To them there was no immediate future in sight in either method. Gandhi came up with his formula of 'unconstitutional but non-violent opposition' by asking the Indians to violate the law as imposed by our foreign rulers, boycott British goods, and resign jobs in the government in order to show solidarity with those who sought to liberate the country. Operative clause was that at no stage and under no circumstances should anyone be physically hurt. The idea was to hinder working of the government in every possible manner so that the British should get fed up of the whole thing and leave India.' How did he manage to bring a vast majority in this country to accept his way to be the right way for gaining independence? Clearly, Gandhi has been an enigma for those who may have not been well versed with the saga of India's freedom movement.

Gandhi, after all, had spent most of his adult life abroad, he had no power base in India, controlled no political organisation, did not enjoy support of any social or politically savvy community, so how did he become leader of the freedom movement in no time at all. He, then went on to become Father of the Nation, a status, that has remained unchallenged to date, in spite of political parties with different leanings and varying ideologies emerging over the years, with most of them not particularly enamoured, either with Gandhi, or with his philosophy of life. As we go along the narrative, we will observe that one secret of Gandhi's success was that he turned Congress party from a group of middle class intellectuals into a mass movement. Indian peasantry soon swelled Congress ranks because the poor and the underprivileged could identify with Gandhi's native common sense and apparent simplicity.

The subject of Indian independence movement has had a tremendous impact on the history of the third world. For far too long I have wanted to collect, collate and present the subject to our present generation. As said earlier, this account of the country's freedom movement is based on the research done by my late father over an extended period of time. It was supposed to have been his thesis for the PhD degree. Something that he wanted to achieve in his lifetime but did not live long enough to realise his dream. I thought that it was only appropriate that I undertook the task of bringing his years of labour to light. In the process I have also updated his research and also taken the subject to its logical conclusion—the emergence of a 'partitioned' but a free India. This became necessary because a fairly large number of 'official papers' have been declassified during the last thirty-five years; that is, since my father's death in 1971. Of particular importance has been the publication in 1992 of the records kept by Christopher Beaumont, who was the secretary to Sir Cyril Redcliffe, Chairman of the Boundary Commission. Redcliffe was appointed on 6th July 1947. Beaumont's conclusion is that Gandhi, Jinnah and Nehru must share the blame for the misery and mayhem that followed. "Transfer of Power" declassified and published in ten volumes in 1980 cleared a lot of fog on the subject. (Note—Now there are twelve volumes with the thirteenth being still classified). A reappraisal of the eventful years preceding India's partition merit repeated reading. Largely, my theme for the terminal phase of the freedom movement is to find if Mountbatten inflicted on India 'a grave injustice which amounted to a breach of faith by the British'.

I could have also chosen to take the route of a historical novel instead of a pure research work in order to enhance marketability of the end product, but then I realised that a thesis cannot become a thriller without unsubstantiated garnishing of facts. That the history of India's fight for freedom is far too serious a subject to be taken lightly was another reason for me to keep the details of the events, issues and the personalities involved at their proper level. Messrs Larry Collins and Dominique Lapparie have done enough damage to this glorious saga by trivializing both, events and people who led Indian masses at the time. They were obviously egged on to do so by Mountbatten who could say whatever he wanted to because all the major players of the movement for freedom were dead. There was no fear of contradiction. Throughout

'Freedom at Midnight' there is an insufferable, ignominious and pervading air of a condescending and patronising approach towards the poor Indians. All set and done, and to my mind, the ambiguities and paradoxes of our struggle for freedom do demand a concurrent look. There will always be some angle, some distinct character, or a specific chain of events that did not receive an appropriate or adequate representation in a particular treatise dealing with our freedom movement. I had no choice but to put across this account because I felt that one more book on the subject will only enrich the literature already available.

Having worked on the manuscript for a long time one is always tempted to make it as broad-based as possible. But then with the facts mostly and generally known to most of the potential readers I had to, perforce, confine myself by limiting the number of personalities involved. Clearly, it has not been possible to include many of the people who strutted across the stage of Indian history from 1909 onwards, and even before. Most of them did make their mark in one way or the other, I have chosen to delve on those who either illustrate the deep-rooted contrast that existed between those playing a major part in the course of events, or those whose actions changed the course of Indian history.

With so much literature available on the subject I couldn't restrain myself from delving into those intractable realities of India's society, its culture and its people who were at the centre stage during the Raj, and who formulated the destiny of this sub-continent. A more serious reader of the Indian history might find that at some places I have deviated from the main course. That becomes inevitable when you want to inform the present generation about the harsh realities of a hard won but expensive freedom; expensive in terms of loss of human lives and expensive in terms of permanent problems that came in the wake of freedom. And the tragedy is that all this loss could have been avoided if our leaders at the time had been more circumspect, more mature and more adjusting while dealing with their peers. Compromises and concessions at the right time and to the right people could, perhaps, have saved this country from the agony of an unnatural divide.

There is no vision better than 'hindsight'. While working on this book I had all the advantages that could be had by anyone interested in clearing his own cobwebs. This is my effort to do so, through a study of lives of those who contributed towards India's freedom, we can retrospectively learn that the present grew out of the past as its inevitable outcome. Any penetrating analysis of the Indian situation under the British would reveal what was unconventional about their rule. Simply put, mouthing platitudes on democracy and voice of the people they were always qualifying these remarks with a rider that all this did not apply to India. "Why not?" is the first question that would come to a reader's mind. With trained lawyers like Gandhi, Jinnah and both the Nehrus, father and son, guiding the destiny of this country and scrutinising acts of the British over the years gone by, they could easily discern how the legal and historical traditions of the constitutional state had been abrogated.

During the last three hundred years we had been pitted against the world's craftiest imperialism that could practice to perfection the adage of using the opponent's weaknesses, real or imaginary, to its advantage and to thrive on situations that were tailormade for exploitation. There is no history without contradictions and there is no way, as Lenin once said, of stepping out of history. Good, bad or ugly, we have to accept contribution, negative or positive, of all those who strived to give shape to this country's destiny from the time the Westerners started exploring India to the time they settled down to rule and to the time they were finally ejected out against their wishes.

The difficulties, the dilemmas, even the delusions encountered during India's struggle for a dignified place in the comity of independent nations will, for a long time test the diligence of historians and the intellectuals. I have no claim to any such eminence. Simply put, in this account of India's struggle for freedom, I have kept the today's generation as my target reader. Perhaps, the new generation has been unaware of the sacrifices made on their behalf and thus immune to the sufferings that subjugation to a foreign ruler involved. Therefore, another, and more topical motive has been to engage their attention, most of whom are not really aware of the sacrifices made by those who made it possible for our generation of Indians to breath the air of freedom.

With a project of this nature, I would have made little progress without the support of people more knowledgeable than myself. I will be eternally grateful for the advice, guidance, encouragement and moral support that I got during the time I was working on this book. If I list my well-wishers individually I might miss out on some, therefore, and to be on the safe side I prefer to be generic in acknowledging the kindness, the understanding and enthusiastic support given to me by anyone and everyone I approached.

I am also grateful to the members of the staff at British Library in London for allowing me to go through the "Transfer of Power" papers and the assistance provided in scanning microfilms pertaining to the subject at hand.

Brig Parmodh Sarin (Retd)

Prologue

Organised power having broken down, the field was left open to adventurers and new claimants for dominion. Among these...the British, and the British alone at the time, possessed many of the qualities necessary for success. Their main disadvantage was that they were foreigners coming from a far country. Yet that very disadvantage worked in their favour, for no one took them seriously or considered them as possible contestants for the sovereignty of India...

Jawaharlal Nehru—*The Discovery of India*

No other country discovered by Europeans has been the object of such varying opinions as India. It resounded with illusive characteristics, created false impressions, or became what the visitor wanted it to be in his imagination. The Portuguese, helped by their considerable skills in navigation and exploration in the late fifteenth and sixteenth centuries, had been the first among the Europeans to have a permanent settlement in India. Level of ignorance of these European travellers was such that in 1498 Vasco da Gama came to Calicut and mistook a Hindu temple for a Christian church resplendent with sculptural adornments representing the Virgin Mary. These first arrivals did try to establish their business in India, hoping to expand in due course of time. The French, and the Dutch soon followed them and sundry other upstarts came looking for lucrative trade. But navigational abilities alone were not enough for any one of them to sustain for too long, they lacked logistical and administrative infrastructure to build on to the toe-hold they had established, except for the French in some coastal areas and the Portuguese in Goa.

Earliest arrivals from England, France, Portugal and other European countries were more interested in developing trading equation with the Indians. The total land mass was too big, and people too diverse in their dress, language and even ethnicity for these traders to even contemplate anything else. None of them (seemingly) had any inclination to subjugate the country as such. The 'mysterious East' euphemistically but aptly conveyed the confused feelings and impressions of travellers. Wanderlust brought in many such travellers and the tales of the exotic land that they carried back made India an outstanding example of the attraction of far-off lands where one could find an alternative to the mundane existence of home, where differences in culture and the distance from traditional authorities of own civilisation offered a unique amount of freedom and a chance to be on one's own.

Like every other country in Europe, Britain too had its quota of adventurous and restless souls who wanted to venture out of the narrow confines of their 'Island' nation, and create riches for themselves. To such India offered an ideal destination. They could go to the newly discovered America, but the journey was hazardous and natives hostile to the 'white man', or the 'pale face' as they called them. On the contrary, the Mughal rulers impressed foreigners with their courtesy, worldly wisdom and natural charm; they were richer and obviously far more civilised than many in Europe. To the intellectuals and thinkers who were looking for sources of evidence outside the Holy Writ, India offered answers to their queries because it was as yet untouched by the Gospel. India, naturally offered the best opportunity to all such seekers. In 1613, the English received permission from the Great Mughal rulers to found a trading station in India.

The British conquest of India began from Calcutta in the late 18th century, the primary urge being lust for profits by employees of the East India Company, a trading concern chartered by the British Crown. In due course of time the company acquired some of the characteristics of a government, more by default rather than by design because when they arrived India was not a country but a land ruled by kings, princes, and sundry warlords who had each taken control of a segment of the land and had declared themselves as the rulers of the areas under their control. A shrinking Mughal Empire was still the biggest and strongest entity on this land. But the Rathores of Rajasthan, and the Marathas of Deccan were challenging the Mughals. The Sikhs had carved out a kingdom centred around Lahore. In 1739, the Persians, coming through the Khyber Pass, invaded India, defeated the Mughals and plundered Delhi. Among the ashes of one dying Empire, another could now rise. Any outsider who could play his cards right had a chance of expanding his influence because the internecine fights amongst various Indian rulers had reached a stage where 'foreign help' was actively sought for improving one's hold on land, particularly if the Mughals could be embarrassed in the process then that help was more than welcome. The situation was ripe for a more advanced and articulate agency to take advantage and win favours from the local rulers for expansion of its 'trading interests'. The situation was far too tempting for ambitious British traders.

India was a strange mixture of chaos and inertia to these early English businessmen. The vast spaces, slow communication between different parts of the country and between India and England, the variety of customs and peoples soon suggested to these traders that here was a place where the pre-established European standards need not apply. To them the country was an entrepreneur's dream where fortunes could be made if one had confidence in himself, was shrewd enough to know the ways of the world, and was willing to take risks. Roughly till the middle, of the 18th century, India was not behind the West in its economic strength. Robert Clive in 1757 saw Murshidabad" as extensive, populous and rich as the city of London.[1]

The East India Company, which was formed as a trading establishment, started thriving purely on account of British dominance of the seas, but it could not curtail the temptation of private trade among its own servants. No amount of moralising by occasional chaplains and straight-laced chief merchants could stop the rogue elements from thriving: most of the Company's servants were in search of a fortune, not salvation. The formal, if remote, rule of the Mughals and the native princes gave the fortune-hunters a protective covering for their shady dealings. The Company jealously preserved its monopoly of all trade to and from Britain; but the country trade, from India to Asian and African ports and within India itself, was open to any servant of the Company. In the early period of the Company's existence, many of its officials gained vast personal fortunes for themselves, and returned home to Britain with the purchasing power of a present day multi-millionaire.

The Britons had arrived in India to expand their trade. They had no specific goal of taking control of the country. Initially they were reluctant imperialists. Circumstances, and the need to protect their own turf against their European rivals, and hugely divided Indian society created situations where they kept getting deeper and deeper into local affairs. One fine day they found that they were in virtual control of most of India. Collapse of the Mughal Empire, duly hastened by internecine warfare and its inability to withstand the foreign invasions from the north-west had created a sort of vacuum which the British were able to fill; their economic and military power, especially at sea, outpacing that of its European rivals, saw them founding the Indian Empire. British ascendancy was 'an exception to all ordinary rules, a standing miracle in politics'.[2] In that, Britain remained in India, accepted the burden of ruling others and the mounting criticism of the ruled, without having a very clear or consistent idea of why it was there, what it aspired to do, or what advantages it gained.

The British government tended to curb the excesses of the Company's employees, and in the first half of the 19th century, the professed aim of the East India Company was to provide fair government to those sections of India it had conquered and to conduct trade with Indians. However, emergence of the French, the Portuguese and certain other powers on the Indian scene made the Company take steps to safeguard its turf and its territories. Making deft use of differences between various rulers of a large number of Indian states, these mercenaries went on to control considerable real estate with all its assets. This was against the express wishes of the headquarters located in London because the cost of these military operations was throwing East India Company into heavy debt. But then the communications were poor, and it could take anything up to two years for a sailing ship to transmit an order from London to India and to get a reply from the man on the spot. In the interim, the local officials acted on their own initiative. Native rulers, not in the same league as the English or the French, fell prey to their own greed and to that of these foreign traders. The Company eventually bested the French as well a large number of rulers of Indian states. The reason for this state of affairs was simple: where lower levels of its staff indulged in self-aggrandizement, those who were elected to head the organisation were generally men with vision. In addition to enhancing the trade, they were in their own way concerned with the social environment, and as culture of their country of origin prescribed duties of a government also delved into improving the conditions of the general population living in their ever expanding domain.

The British rule over India began with the famous battle of Plassey in 1757 where Robert Clive was clever enough to exploit the differences between the Nawab and his rivals for power. The battle was no more than a skirmish, the British losses were seven Europeans and sixteen native soldiers killed; thirteen Europeans and thirty-six native soldiers wounded. The victory established the British supremacy over Bengal, leading to their control over Bihar, Orissa and the East Coast of India. The consolidation of British power after 1765 was made possible by a persistent willingness to engage in war against Indian states. The spoils of war in India were considerable; the defeated enemy was often made to pay the costs of war, and lost land or financial power. (Lala Lajpatrai recorded in his book 'Unhappy India', "The beauty of the English conquest of India lies in the fact that from the first to the last not one single penny was spent by the British on the conquest. India was conquered by the British with Indian money and Indian blood." *Unhappy India,* p. 343).

This process of conquest had its own momentum. When a province had been conquered, its troops were enlisted to conquer another one. Indians, and their perpetual infighting made it essential for the Company to get involved in local affairs, primarily to safeguard its commercial interests. Various Governor Generals appointed by the Company, carried out their own agendas to further the cause of their employers. In the process they were able to consolidate the hold of the government on a territory in which the King of England was not initially interested. A large tract of land and a wide variety of chieftains, particularly in Calcutta, Madras, and Bombay subjugated themselves to British interests because they had scores to settle with their 'native' peers. The British played along and suddenly found themselves in control of more than half of India. Some kind of government was set up by the Company in areas under its direct control, but it was understood that this government was necessarily autocratic, unpopular, and not directly responsible to the people of India. A new revenue system was introduced superseding the existing one and the traditional ownership rights. A new class of landowners was created in the process, which owed its loyalty to the conquerors. Under the "Ryotwari" system, the individual cultivator became owner of the land he tilled, and a village no longer remained as a unit of land assessment and revenue generation. With the establishment of private property, and individual's right to its disposal, the agricultural land got consolidated in fewer hands. This landed gentry owed its riches to the British and were naturally loyal and staunch supporters of the foreign rulers.

Where Indian industry was concerned, its decay was hastened by a rapid influx of cheap and machine made goods from Britain rendering traditional artisans jobless. They now became either labourers working for the rich landlords or started eking out miserable existence as paupers. It was for the first time that the rural population was experiencing the impact of a Rule that was alien to them. Hither to fore, no political upheaval had, had any kind of impact on their daily existence. In short, the new system introduced over the conquered territory was totally divorced from the ground realities and it was heavily loaded in favour of the British industry and trade. Indians, meaning the civil population of the conquered territories with its centuries of culture and history, resented this. Native rulers, even though despotic and cruel, were seen to be sons of the soil and therefore preferable to these outsiders who neither understood India, nor Indians. We can, therefore, say that the history of India's freedom movement had been a developing process, concurrent to the expansion of the Empire.

The process of converting the East India Company into a delegated political authority was completed in 1833. The Governor General was now empowered to make and regulate laws affecting all British India, though Parliament retained overall control. Successive defeats of various Indian rulers and consequent British consolidation of territory gave the latter broader opportunities to scrutinise the people now under their jurisdiction. An Indian Law Commission was formed to survey existing policies and judicial procedures and report on ways in which India might obtain a codified and well-define system of law and justice. This was not something to which the Indian princes, various rulers and for that matter, even commoners were used to. Obviously, there was resentment and disenchantment against the foreign rulers, and the Mughals were particularly upset on having lost their Empire to these undeserving foreigners.

To be fair to the earlier Governor Generals appointed by the Company, these worthies did try to rid India of some of those ugly facets of the Indian, or more appropriately, the Hindu society of some of its decadent customs like "Sati" wherein the wife was required to be burnt on the funeral pyre of her husband. Of the Western powers, the Portuguese under Viceroy Albuquerque were the first to prohibit this practice in Goa as early as 1510. Initially the British refused to imitate the Portuguese in this as well as in other matters, maintaining a policy of non-interference in Hindu social customs. It was only after the conquest of Bengal that their reticence was roused where the prevalence of "Sati" seems to have been most widespread in the eighteenth and the early nineteenth century. Progressive forces were already at work under the redoubtable Raja Ram Mohan Roy in the state. Roy was an intellectual and a reformer. After an intensive research, he had in 1815, produced his own translations of the Vedas into Bengali, and began a personal campaign to demonstrate how the Brahmins had hidden the true religion in a Sanskrit fog, and how the ancient Hindu religion had been corrupted by idolatry. To awaken the Hindus from their dreams of error he produced a dissertation against "Sati". He was soon able to win a large number of signatories repulsed by this inhuman custom. Lord William Bentinck's government prohibited the practice of "Sati" in 1829.

The orthodox ranks of the natives protested loudly against this order and even appealed to the Privy Council in England with a plea to have the orders of the Governor Generals countermanded. In due course of time wise counsel prevailed and between 1837 and 1841 this practice was abolished in almost all Indian states. Slavery, another institution that was thriving in some parts of India, was finally abolished when Warren Hastings, who as the governor general took up the matter in his hands. But it took a long time for the British to rid India of this practice when the Charter Act of .1833 provided for the ultimate extinction of slavery; and Act V of 1842 made holding of slaves, illegal. Indian Penal Code of 1860 prohibited all trade in and possession of slaves. Where the perennial problem of the "caste system" is concerned, the British started with the passing of the Caste Disabilities Removal Act (XXI of 1850). This Act aimed at giving legal equality to converts into Christianity, but intended to prohibit their right of inheritance. It impaired the authority of the "caste panchayats", and did create a lot of resentment among the orthodox Hindus who took it as an unwarranted interference in their centuries old customs by the foreign rulers. Female infanticide, then prevalent in the northern belt more prominently than the rest of India was another issue that needed action, but considerations of military exigencies and political interests prevented the British from actively seeking reform in this field. However, when they were firmly in saddle, a special legislation was passed in 1870 to abolish this practice. That the practice continues to this day in some parts of the country is another matter.

There were frequent risings — many violent — against the British administrative system that was being superimposed on the conquered territories in the early nineteenth century. This process found its culmination in the revolt of 1857, which was pre-eminently directed against the continuation of foreign rule in India. The failure of this mass uprising to throw out the British militarily marked the end of any large scale and violent opposition to their rule for a considerable length of time. It was so because once having got to rule a country like India the opinion in London was that, "to retain power in India we must sweep away every political establishment and every social usage which may prevent our influence from being universal and complete."[3] Harriet Mariner, a thinker of the time in England wrote, "In India the theory of government must be simple despotism. The only choice for us is between a despotism of brute force and one of reason and justice." That the second option given by the intellectual was not even considered by the powers that be is a fact of history. "The loss of his old world, with no gain of a new one," wrote Karl Marx in one of its famous letters on India (10 June 1853), "imparts a peculiar type of melancholy to (India's) present misery." India did not reconcile to the foreign rule even after the 1857-58 revolt had been crushed. Some historians, mostly from the 'Whites Community' stipulate that British responsibility was ultimately justifiable because Indians were not yet ready or able to manage themselves when the Queen took over reigns of the country after the revolt of 1857. The rebels took up the sword against the British to wrest power from their hand and to force them to leave the shores of India. We could now term the revolt as the 'first war of independence' because it is politically convenient to say so, but it was nothing of the kind. The native soldiers were hurt and antagonized by their British officers because they tended to treat them far below their own level of understanding and intellect. That the Indians were not as dumb as the British thought them to be was one reason, the other obviously was their trying to fiddle with the religious sentiments of the Indian soldier. That the British were not welcome as far back as 1857 is a historical fact. Also the indigenous laws and customs had not been sufficiently integrated when the Raj was in its infancy. Justice and right had been construed according to the laws of England as early as 1726. The British, with their total lack of awareness of the country's culture tried to superimpose their ideas in a diverse range of fields then considered important by European standards as important and relevant for development and growth of a society. For them ignorance of the English language in itself was a sign of backwardness. One would concede that education in English language was the hallmark of British rule from the very beginning, even when the Empire itself had not taken any concrete shape. By invitation, selected Indians were to be shown the ways of political leadership and responsibility so that they could some day far in future govern themselves, was the 'stated' aim of this exercise. According to John Stuart Mill: "English was to be the torch that welded the political liberalism of the left to a revived Hindu tradition, from which Indian nationalism took its origin."

On 21 May 1857, the celebrated journal "*Hindoo Patriot*" wrote: "It is no longer a mutiny but a rebellion...there is not a single native of India who does not feel the full weight of the grievances imposed on him by the very existence of British rule in India...grievances inseparable from subjection to foreign rule." There are any number of reasons for the failure of that effort. Mainly, it was lack of coordination, communication and absence of a leader under whom various, and widely differing, elements could unite for a common cause. Lack of preparation – as Gandhi termed his later day forays in the arena of India's struggle for freedom – was the main reason for the failure of this endeavour. Had the Indians united in their effort to dislodge the British, this revolt would surely have been the end of the expanding Empire. The princes of India were divided and quarrelling among themselves. Most of them preferred to have individual and separate treaties with the British, rather than dealing amicably with their own race. There was no middle class in India; and poor peasantry was too absorbed in eking out a living, which could retain it above starvation level. The rulers, even when they knew that their population was in a bad way, were generally too despotic to care one way or the other. There were some exceptions to this thesis, and rulers like Laxmibai of Jhansi, Tantya Tope and some others did lead from the front, fighting for throwing out the British, but there were too few of them to make a difference in the long run. In any case, assuming that if the revolt had succeeded one can't see any of these rulers accepting an aging and reluctant rebel (Bahadur Shah Zafar) lording over them from Delhi. Political vacuum, absence of a common strategy and absolutely no preparation before challenging the British allowed them to gradually and systematically regain control. As each mutinous regiment was subdued, the rebellion too died away.

The result of the mutiny was to put India under a much stronger grip of the British and on a permanent basis. The Crown took over the government from the East India Company, the effective authority going to the British Cabinet with the appointment of a Secretary of State for India. The Governor General, hither-to-fore a representative of the Company, acquired the title of 'Viceroy of India'. British system of administration was now made applicable in the country. Indian Civil Service was created, and the British Legal system was implemented. Calcutta, wherefrom the East India Company had been operating, was now declared as the capital of India. About forty battalions of the British regular army with supporting troops were eventually stationed in India, basically to prevent a recurrence of 1857. The main responsibility for internal security rested with these units and they were spread all over the country.

All these arrangements were not enough to sustain the Raj for far too long because India was not one of those impoverished, backward (or even aboriginal) and illiterate countries of Africa, Australia or America where the white man could easily dominate and settle down for good. This country was far too ancient a civilisation for any foreign power (particularly Western) to hope for a permanent rule. So the struggle for political emancipation had through-out been manifesting itself into spasmodic outbursts, though never a continuous affair. The 'White' shadow of imperialism that spread all over India was clearly resented by the majority of Indian population. That it was so with a variegated people peculiarly inured to endurance and hardships caused by present evil because of their cycle of Karma and therefore had to be endured since life is transitory and that there will be compensations for good behaviour as promised in the cycle of existence, has to be attributed to a total lack of understanding of the Indian psyche by our foreign rulers.

Effectively speaking, the wheels to throw the British out were churning almost concurrently with the expansion of the Raj. Unlike the upper layers of the society who made their peace with the conqueror and then became so fascinated by British that subjugation lost its sting, the common man never really acquiesced and never applauded white man's supposed superiority. By and large, British rule was accepted, but never with pleasure. Between 1757 and 1857 there never was a time when our people, somewhere or other in India, were not fighting stubbornly to seek freedom from this foreign intruder, or were clinging on to their independent status. Sir Thomas Munro, a famous thinker of the time, observed in 1814: "our situation in India has always been precarious...we might now be swept away in a single whirlwind. We are without roots." That the British could hang on for almost a hundred years after the revolt of 1857 is one of those travesties of history, which can easily be attributed to the problems of religion, caste and economic backwardness of the masses that have always created fissures in the Indian society; and sadly, continue to do so. But the suppression of the revolt did not signify liquidation of all resistance to British authority, or willing submission of the people of India to this alien domination. The battle was gradually taken over by the new and emerging intellectual class, which now provided leadership.

The character of the struggle became non-violent, constitutional and gained in popularity when the masses were slowly drawn into its fold. The freedom movement then transcended its political limits and became comprehensive to include various facets of national life, all of which showed signs of vitality and desire to be rid of the foreign rulers. The mode of political operation adopted by the western educated community initially was to render petitions and appeals for reforms in administration so that grievances of the local populations could be addressed. They genuinely believed that the defects of government and consequent hardships of the people would be remedied if the higher authorities, both in India and England were apprised of the situation. They were naive enough to think that the liberty-loving English people would ever knowingly permit a system that was unjust and tyrannous. Unfortunately for them, the administration could not rise above corruption but took more and more the character of a police state; in their scheme of things welfare of the people came just about at the bottom of the ladder where their priorities were concerned. Consequently, the administration grew more and more unresponsive and rigid in its attitude towards the Indians.

The process of India's struggle for freedom can be divided into three distinct phases. Phase one was when the soldiers showed their resentment in 1857, phase two coincides with the emergence of people who were intellectuals, successful, and fiercely independent in their thinking that India needed no outsiders to evolve as a nation. In the earlier parts of the 20th century they had come together to take India towards its road to freedom. Lala Lajpatrai put up India's case for freedom before the American Foreign Relations Committee through a counsel. Tilak put up his petition for the same purpose before the 'League of Nations'. But nothing came off these efforts because Britain was seen as an ally of the Americans. There was just about nobody who could challenge the might of the 'White' rulers in the rest of the world. The third and conclusive phase could logically be said to have started with the Jallianwala Bagh Massacre and the widespread resentment and riots that followed.

Footnotes

1. JR Seeley, *The Expansion of England*, pp 217-218.
2. *The Times*, 29 June 1857.
3. *The Times* , 29 June 1857.

1

Beginning of the End

Our Empire can hardly be called old, but seems destined to be short-lived.

Sir Charles Metcalfe, 11 October 1829

Way back in 1821, when the Raj had not even taken any kind of shape, Thomas Munro, an important functionary of the Company had written to the Governor General, "I have no faith in the modern doctrine of the rapid improvement of the Hindus...they should be now encouraged to take charge of their own affairs until, in the fullness of time, Britain could withdraw from an enlightened and independent India."

An odd Governor General of the East India Company did realise that the natives were far too intelligent to be subjugated for long, but the ruling classes in the country had too many differences among themselves; and their mutual distrust and rivalry allowed Britain to consolidate its hold on India. So the British were generally content to ensure that like machinery item the administration moved in a direction that could only perpetuate the Raj.

The story of India's fight for freedom effectively started with the revolt of 1857 when Mangal Pandey of the Bengal Infantry lighted the flame. The rebels, who were nursing a wide range of grouses against their British officers for their cruelty and inhuman treatment of the Indian soldier, gained control on practically the whole of India. The British had failed to realise that the native soldier was capable of strongest religious excitement, and very sensitive to disrespect of their persons or infringement of their customs. Not many British officers appreciated the fact that the Indian soldiers could be persuaded to do miracles, to fight against tremendous odds, to triumph over dangers of all kinds, provided they could trust in the absolute respect of their officers for traditional customs and beliefs, no matter how irrational or illogical it might appear to a European. This lack of sensitivity created a climate of mutual distrust, duly aggravated by introduction of new cartridges using beef or pork tallow; and required to be stripped by mouth; a situation unacceptable to both Hindus and Muslims.

In the aftermath of the 1857 revolt and taking over the running of the country by the Imperial government from the East India Company, the freedom struggle was confined to the intelligentsia who were the product of modern education imparted in the new institutions established by the British in India during the nineteenth century. Exposure to the English language created awareness among the educated Indians who gradually became disaffected towards the government. Now that they had imbibed the knowledge of western history, political and social theories, they grew conscious of their rights and wished to have their own democratic institutions in place of an irresponsible, and often insensitive, bureaucratic administration controlled by a foreign power. Totally consisting of Whites, the bureaucracy had failed to see the general awareness and evolution. It had become inaccessible and invisible to the common man. One could easily comprehend that between the ruler and the ruled—who did not speak the same language, and ignored each other— the least misunderstanding could cause exasperation. Lord Curzon went on to expound the theory that a "despotically paternal government is the only one suited to India, and that the only thing necessary for the happiness of the people of India was sound administration of justice." He was convinced that the justification for the British rule was the well being of Indians. His theme was "there has never been anything so great in the world's history as the British Empire, so great as an instrument for the good of humanity." He and his senior bureaucrats laughed off any suggestion that he should consult Indians before taking any major decision affecting the native population, while at the same time paying lip-service to the "respect which must be paid to the feelings generated by differences of religion, of nation and of caste". The Indians were despondent, resentful and angry at the administration. Struggle for freedom then going on in different parts of the world also fired the imagination of the Indian youth. Events and happenings in Ireland, Hungary, Poland, Egypt and the Balkan States were studied with interest, Indian national movement thus attained maturity in the process. Italy had freed herself from foreign rule only a little earlier, and examples of Mazzini were the guiding stars for Indian nationalism. Emergence of Japan as a great power built on the foundations of intense patriotism and zealous nationalism was another beacon to be followed. The entire East was in ferment and the West was facing a threat from expanding socialism.[1] It was in this environment and the context of the world developments that

Indian nationalism was being nurtured and a new ideology, having its roots in traditional Indian culture and ethical values was developing.

The 'seventies' and 'eighties' of the nineteenth century were a period of massive disquiet in the country. In Maharashtra, Bengal, Punjab and elsewhere, it was the revolutionaries who started giving Indians back their pride and some kind of self-belief. There was a great deal more to their movement than a desperate gamble and a hope to liberate the country by resorting to use of 'arms'. Waking up to the ground realities the government did try to apply the instrument of reforms and legislations in order to assuage the feelings of hurt nurtured by the Indians; but it refused to depart from the trodden path. Liberalism could survive for a few years, the Minto-Morley diplomacy to separate the Muslims from the fight for freedom paid some dividend for a while, but the Balkan wars, participation of Turkey on the side of Germany in the Great War and the alienation of Arab lands from the Turkish Empire at the end of the war which Germany and her partners lost, made the Muslims no less bitter against the British. The failure of Morley-Minto Reforms to lead to responsible government and the denial by the Crown and the Company that Self-Government was never even considered while defining these so-called Reforms, only intensified discontent and activated political movement further. The stage was set for a new struggle, where new and more durable leaders with vision, intelligence, and competence that were no less than the best that the Empire could produce, took the centre stage. Concurrent to these developments was the emergence of those revolutionaries who had come to the conclusion that a repressive regime required a dose of its own medicine. From the late 'nineties' of the nineteenth century till almost the nineteen thirties, the history of India's freedom movement is strewn with bold, brave and courageous sons of the soil who had taken deliberate decision to sacrifice their all for the cause.

Emergence of Nationalist Leaders

The seeds of disenchantment with the British sown by the leaders of the times, led to revival and emergence of a set of visionaries who held good of India closest to their heart. The apostles of this new creed were Tilak, Gokhale, Lajpatrai, Bipin Chandra Pal and Aurbindo Ghose and many other intellectuals. The ground for them was prepared by the stalwarts of an earlier era when men like Swami Dayanand and Swami Vivekanand strode on the national scene. They provided the religious setting for Indian nationalism. These new leaders were no professional politicians or agitators. They urged redress of acknowledged grievances of the people and demanded practical and workable reforms. They, seemingly, did not desire to subvert the British rule or substitute another in its place; in fact, early generation of 'nationalists' took pride in their membership of an Empire on which the sun never set. This new leadership desired a radical change, a revolution, in the system of government which was expressed by progressively using terms like "Swaraj", Self-Government, Home Rule—which they now demanded and which became the goal of Indian political progress in late eighteen eighties and earlier part of the twentieth century. This breed of current leadership stood for change in every sphere of the national life. Indian nationalism was being nurtured and a new ideology having its roots in the traditional Indian culture, values and ethics was developing. The government took to repression to suppress this new spirit, but the blood of those who got killed in the process only strengthened the resolve of these leaders and the foundations of the new edifice.

In the beginning, the struggle for freedom was confined to the intelligentsia who were the product of modern education imparted in newly established institutions when the British were still consolidating their hold on the country. Setting up in Bengal of the British India Society in 1843 and then the Indian Association in 1875, to be followed by similar organisations in Bombay and Madras were clear indications that the educated Indians were evidently inspired by western ideals of liberty and freedom. They were looking forward to creating an All India political organisation that could provide direction to the masses in their search for freedom from a foreign rule.

Establishment of Indian National Congress

By eighteen eighties it was becoming clear that educated Indians needed a platform to present their views on matters that affected Indians in any way. Surendranath Banerjee's 'Indian Association', in spite of all its schemes and plans remained largely a Bengali set up and therefore, ineffective where issues of national relevance were concerned. Finally it was left to a retired English official, Allan Octavian Hume to give some kind of a semblance to the concept of an Indian organisation that could create an environment for growth of Indian nationalism. Hume was the product of a British system that grew up by accident rather than design. It encouraged officials in the field to identify themselves with their territories and to feel emotional loyalty to the people over whom they ruled on behalf of the Queen (Queen Victoria). Hume had joined the East India Company's civil service in 1849. He saw action during the 1857 revolt and was decorated for bravery. He was, perhaps, the only British official who insisted on scrupulously fair trials of the rebels. He showed a marked reluctance to impose the death penalty. He hanged only seven mutineers, and even then designed a new form of gallows to make their end as quick and as painless as possible. Now he felt that he had to do something for the Indians that would make the natives responsive to political progression. He sent the following letter to all the living graduates of Calcutta University:

"There are aliens, like myself, who love India and her children...but the real work must be done by the people of the country themselves...If fifty men cannot be found with sufficient power of self-sacrifice, sufficient love and pride in their country, sufficient genuine and unselfish patriotism to take the initiative and if need be to devote the rest of their lives to the Cause-then there is no hope for India. Her sons must and will remain humble and helpless instruments of foreign rulers." (Philips Mason)

There is a school of thought that subscribes to the theory that Hume had been encouraged by the then Viceroy, Lord Dufferin, to undertake such an exercise because the government felt that the restless masses could conjure something akin to the events of 1857, fed up as they were with the hopelessness of their situation, and were "going to do something and stand by each other" and "that something meant violence"—also that a "terrible revolution" might ensue since a "certain small number of the educated classes would join the movement, assume here and there the lead, give the outbreak cohesion and direct it as a national revolt." (W Wedderburn, Alan Octavian Hume, 1913, pp 80-81, 101). The official sponsoring of the Congress was expected to be an insurance against an armed revolt.

Hume found not fifty men but seventy-two—including 39 lawyers, 14 journalists and one doctor—who met in Bombay on 28th December 1885 for the first session of the 'Indian National Congress'. It was a small beginning, but one Briton at least recognised its significance: Florence Nightingale sent a goodwill message from England saying, "We are watching the birth of a new nationality in the oldest civilisation in the world". In the early sessions of the Congress, the main demand used to be for separation of executive from judiciary because the judiciary was not really independent, there was a clear bias when a 'white' was on trial against the 'native'. The British 'colour bar' and arrogance was manifested far too often even if the crime committed by the white was far too heinous to warrant any mercy; this was not to be expected from a fair judge. Equal opportunities in the competitive examinations for the public services were also sought so that the Indians could gain experience and expertise in administration so as to be ready when the country gained independence. Now Dufferin was worried because the potential of the Congress as the leader of the masses in the independence struggle soon became apparent. He started ridiculing the organisation because it was not delivering on the expected lines; that is, contrary to his belief that the organisation would be effectively controlled by the British and would thus remain subservient to the administration, was not happening. His animosity made no difference to the Congressmen because they had now been able to form a forum that could help furthering the aim of the nationalists. It had become a platform for the educated Indians to seek some kind of participation in the governing of the country. At that point of time all that they wanted was an element of Self-Government under the British as had been given to Canada in 1867. Lord Dufferin was annoyed no end over such an ambition being nurtured by the Indians.

His successor, Lord Ripon, was not averse to allowing educated Indians to look after primary schools, drains and towns etc, being equally firm in his opinion that Administration should not be given to Indians. Even then he did try to introduce a Bill, which intended that Indian judges should be enabled to try 'white' men. Animosity of Anglo-Indians and Europeans to any such thought did not allow him to proceed in this direction. There was some talk in educated circles of 'moral hostility' to the British— a forerunner of later day boycotts and strikes. If the Congress had come up as a part of the imperialistic game plan then the Indian's ability to absorb knowledge and education had not been factored into the scheme of things. A judge of the Calcutta High Court spoke for most of his compatriots when he wrote to 'The Times' that the government of the British in India was "essentially an absolute government, founded, not on consent, but on conquest. It could not represent the native principles of life or of government." Till the Minto-Morley Reforms of 1909, an odd crumb here and there was thrown the way of Indians so as to prevent any serious agitation. For example, Act of 1892 made it possible for the Indians to be members of central and local councils, they could discuss the budget, ask questions, which may or may not be answered; to make it worse they were not allowed to vote on a budget that had a direct impact on the country's population. The ideology adopted by the Congress in those initial stages was largely Hindu in coloration, partly due to insignificant Muslim representation and largely due to the fact that Hindus did form the majority population of the country, but there definitely was no conscious antagonism towards the Muslims, or their culture, in the party.

Muslims in Congress

Besides Hume, Sir William Wedderburn and Sir Henry Cotton, both of whom were to be elected president twice also attended the inaugural session. However, only two Muslim graduates attended this session. One reason for this poor Muslim participation was the fact that the Muslims were at least fifty years behind the Hindus where western education was concerned. This lack of education was not entirely the doing of Muslims: In 1843, Governor General Lord Ellen Borough in a feedback report had informed London, "I cannot close my eyes to the belief that the race (Mohammedans) is fundamentally hostile to us and our true policy is to conciliate the Hindus." Even earlier, on 4th October 1842, while writing to the Duke of Wellington after the fall of Kabul and Ghazani, the Governor General had observed, "I could not have credited the extent to which the Mohammedans desired our failure in Afghanistan, unless I heard here circumstances which prove that the feeling pervaded even among those who are entirely dependent on us ... The Hindus, on the other hand are delighted. It seems to me most unwise, when we are sure of the hostility of one-tenth, not to secure the enthusiastic support of the nine-tenths which are faithful." It was clearly in the interest of the British to ensure that, as far as possible, the Muslims were denied opportunity to advance in life and prosper. If they remained poor and ignorant, they were less likely to give any trouble to the expanding British Empire. Not unnaturally, at that time against 3,155 Hindu graduates in the whole of India there were only 57 Muslims.

A member of Bengal Civil Service-Henry Harrington Thomas-explained why the Mohammedans deserved the wrath of Englishmen in 1858.

"I have stated that the Hindus were not the contrivers or the primary movers of the (1857) rebellion; and I shall now attempt to show that it was the result of a Mohammedan conspiracy, which had been in agitation for a longer period than was generally suspected, though it was developed somewhat sooner than the authors had intended ...But the question is, who planned and organised this combined movement for the murder of every Christian man, woman and child throughout the country? Left to their own will and their own resources, the Hindus never would, could, have compassed such an undertaking... No: it is amongst the Mohammedans not the Hindus we must look for the real originators of this terrible plot! ... But, in order to comprehend in their full force the motives which induced the Mohammedans, more particularly than our other Indian subjects, to lay their plot for our extermination, it will be necessary to consider the character and tenets of the Mohammedans in general. They have been uniformly the same from the times of the first Caliphs to the present day, proud, intolerant and cruel, even aiming at Mohammedan supremacy by whatever means and ever fostering a deep hatred of Christians. They cannot be good subjects of any government, which professes another religion: the precepts of Koran will not suffer it. They deem themselves placed in a false position under any but a Mohammedan dynasty. For this reason, no favours or honours can conciliate them, but they can dissimulate to perfection, until their opportunity presents itself; and then their true character becomes manifest.... But in India the Mohammedans had other motives for seeking our destruction, besides their rooted anti-Christian feeling. They could not forget that they had been masters of the country for many generations, and they never ceased to persuade themselves, that if the British power were thoroughly destroyed they would recover their lost position, and once more lord it over the Hindus. They perceived the disaffection, which had been spreading among the native regiments and fanned the flame by their intrigues. Well aware that no decisive blow could be struck without the cooperation of the Hindu troops, and the surest means of urging them to desperate measures was to convince the Brahmins, in the first place that their religion was in danger, the Mohammedans artfully circulated a report which was echoed by the Brahmins, that the British government was undermining the Hindu faith, with the covert intention of converting the Hindus to Christianity. In their determined character, their education and mental capacity, the Mohammedans are vastly superior to the Hindus, who comparatively speaking are mere children in their hands. The Mohammedans, moreover, on account of their higher qualification for business, have been more generally taken into public employ, which afforded them facilities for becoming acquainted with the measures of government and gave weight and importance to their assertions...the Mohammedans planned and organised this rebellion (or rather revolution) for their own aggrandizement alone, and that the Hindu Sepoys of the Bengal Army were their dupes and instruments."[2] Sir James Outran said about 1857 that it was a "Mohammedan conspiracy, making capital of Hindu grievances".

Naturally, getting the Muslims to cooperate with the British was just as difficult as getting the British to trust Muslims, convinced as they were that it were the Muslims who had tried to restore the glory of Mughal Empire in 1857 and thus had caused all the troubles for the East India Company. This assessment of the British ignored the fact that more prominent leaders of the mutiny; that is, Rani of Jhansi, Tantya Tope or for that matter Mangal Pandey whose refusal to use newly introduced cartridges because of application of Beef Tallow for sealing the cartridge had actually triggered the soldier's revolt were all Hindus.

This writer gives yet another reason for the antipathy, that is, the impossibility of converting the Mohammedans to Christianity: "The missionary seldom convinces a Mohammedan; the very fact of his Christianity militates against his success. In general the Mohammedan avoids discussion with the missionaries and he listens with impatience to their arguments, if he does not wholly turn a deaf ear to them. Of a nature less stern and obdurate, the Hindus are frequently touched by the preaching of the missionaries." Hunter's analysis, though alarmist, was more or less accurate. From Siraj-ud-daula to Tipu Sultan, Muslims had been among the most dangerous enemies of Britain; therefore it was not too difficult to attribute the mutiny to the Muslim hostilities to the infidel British. In India of those times, Islam confronted Christianity like a reproach. Consequently, the Muslim community was differentiated socially, culturally and even religiously.

The above-referred mindset of the British towards the Muslims was not ignored by more articulate and educated among the Muslims. One Sir Syed Ahmed Khan, even though a great advocate of the western education for Muslims, was publicly urging them to stay away from the Congress. He founded in 1875, United India Patriotic Association with considerable encouragement and support of the government, largely because the British rulers felt that the time had come to counter-balance the growing Hindu presence on the national scene. Sir Syed, even otherwise, had very strong reasons for doing so. His Association's additional aim was to strengthen the British rule in India, and to remove the feelings of distrust the British had for the Muslims due to their role in the 1857 revolt. "After the mutiny," Sir William Hunter, a British civil servant, wrote in 1870, "the British turned upon the Mussalmans as their real enemies; therefore, the failure of the revolt was much more disastrous to them than the Hindus."[3] The administration decided to ensure that the Muslims should be so treated that they were left with neither time nor resources to think of another revolt against the British. Traditionally, upper class Muslims had made their living as landlords, administrators or soldiers. But one by one these three pillars had been knocked out from under them. Muslims lost their place in the administration when English replaced Persian as the language of the government and the law. Everywhere, doors were being closed to them. For the next quarter of a century they would be forced to live apart and be cut off from the mainstream of India's affairs.

In the later years of the nineteenth century, and with the constant propaganda of the likes of Sir Syed, Muslims also grew in confidence. Also grew alongside tension between the two communities. Racially the Muslims and the Hindus are practically the same and there is no definite linguistic division between them. Strains between Hindus and Muslims had existed for generations. Riots between different Indian communities, like natural calamities, periodically swept India in varying degrees of ferocity. The differences and disputes between the two communities were not just doctrinal, like those between the Catholics and Protestants in Ireland. They extended also into social life over such matters as the sacredness of the cow. The rank and file on both sides was volatile in defending their faiths and it was part of the common pattern of India for riots and murders to flare out of trivial disputes between the two faiths. During the Raj there was no clear geographic boundary either between the two communities.

Congress went to great lengths to allay all the fears and forebodings of the Muslims and other minorities. After the Hindu Bannerjee and the Parsi Dada Bhai Naoroji, the third president of the Congress was Justice Badrudddin Tyabji, India's first Muslim high court judge. In his presidential address, Tyabji spoke out for integration of various races and communities and for the people to work shoulder to shoulder for the common good. But Tyabji was a member of the minority Shiite Khoja sect. Therefore, for all his pleadings, most Muslims listened to Sir Syed, and stayed away from the Congress and its approach for gaining a democratic set up in the country. Sir Syed was not an anti-Hindu as such. He had a large circle of Hindu friends and worked closely with Hindu social workers. In spite of his having stressed the separate identity of the Muslims in India, he was at the same time, credited with such sayings as that Hindus and Muslims were the 'two eyes' of Mother India, and if one was damaged, the other would also be. In his opinion, there was a possibility of the two coming together, if there was a good enough movement, a strong enough movement, and a properly conducted enough movement. He, however, believed and propagated that "Hindus and Muslims were two different nations even though they drank from the same well and breathed the same air from the city." It was a prophetic statement, the first public airing of the two nations idea that was to bedevil the final years of the Raj, ultimately leading to a bloody and messy division of the country—a painful culmination of 'Divide and Rule' principle and policy. The seeds of separation, and therefore of two nation theory were unwittingly sown even before the Indians had taken their first step towards organising themselves into a country or a community that wanted to throw away the foreign yoke. The British found it convenient to let Sir Syed and his like carry on with their propaganda on these lines because by now they had also come to the conclusion that 'Divide and Rule' was their best option and weapon.

Historically, the Muslims had been the ruling community, which had made converts from the Hindus. In the early years of the British rule, when there were no special considerations for the Muslims, the Hindus had become better educated and economically more prosperous and enterprising. Apart from historical antipathies and jealousies there were all kinds of day-to-day conflicts. If the Muslims wanted peace and tranquillity for their evening prayers, the Hindus needed all kinds of musical instruments for their evening prayers, with the temple gongs informing everyone in the vicinity that the prayers were on. The Muslim practice of slaughtering cows during their religious festivals was a regular source of conflict. For Hindus, killing a cow could be considered a sin greater than killing a man—even a Brahmin. For Muslims, sacrificing a cow rather than a sheep or goat was a matter of prestige. Many Muslims leaders, including Sir Syed, tried to dissuade their followers from hurting religious sentiments of the Hindus prevailing upon them to give up the practice of cow slaughter. But old customs, particularly when these involve pride, do not die away that easily. Hindus formed cow protection societies but surprisingly took no offence when the white rulers merrily went about killing and eating cows.

Sir Syed feared that if Muslims got involved with the Indian National Congress and its agitationist approach it would revive the mistrust of the British, something he had been trying to dispel for almost 25 years. In addition, he feared that if the representative democracy as propagated by the Congress came about then the majority rule would imply a Hindu Rule as the Hindus were more than four times in number. During the 1920s Gandhi and Congress leadership had gone out of their way to conciliate the Muslims; there had been five Muslim Presidents of the Congress in ten years. "Hindu-Muslim unity is no less important than the spinning wheel; it is our breath of life," said Gandhi. Nevertheless by sheer weight of numbers the Hindus dominated the Congress and it was easy for Muslim communalists to propagate that the Congress was a Hindu organisation. Consequently, the Muslims were much less active than the Hindus in pursuing civil disobedience movement. When the 'All India Muslim League' was formed in 1906, due to pragmatism of leaders like Jinnah and Motilal Nehru, both Congress and the League worked in close cooperation. Jinnah remained an active member of the Congress for a long time, and it was on his initiative that the League started holding its annual session to coincide with that of the Congress and in the same location. At Lucknow in 1916, the Congress and the League came together and concluded a pact of friendship. The purist Hindus, who had their own organisation, 'the Hindu Mahasabha', repudiated the idea of building a secular India and wanted a definitely Hindu regime to replace the British. It was not without reason that during the 1920s the Congress and the Muslim League started following independent policies, drifting apart, and were generally hostile to each other.

By the time the 'nationalists', all prominent Hindus, started gaining ground and following, the British had to quickly come up with something that could neutralise their impact on the country. The British also needed a counter-balance to the growing strength of the Hindus: 'Divide and Rule' was never officially acknowledged as a policy, but as a strategy it was too valuable to ignore.[4] So the British only utilised the division between the two communities, they did not invent it. Sir John Maynard, a retired senior member of the Executive Council of Punjab was candid enough to admit, "It is, of course, true that British authority could not now maintain itself but for a fissiparous tendency, of which the Hindu-Muslim antagonism is one manifestation. It is also true that the mass rivalry of the two communities began under the British rule". As David Page puts it, "In the consolidation of interests around communal issues, the Imperial Power played an important role. By treating the Muslims as a separate group, it divided them from other Indians. By granting them separate electorates, it institutionalised that division. This was one of the most crucial factors in the development of communal politics. Muslim politicians did not have to appeal to Muslims. This made it very difficult for a genuine nationalist to emerge". (Page-Prelude to Partition, p.260)

Persecuting rulers had made their appearance from time to time in the pre-British era, levying tribute on unbelievers or punishing with fanatical zeal all those who proclaimed superiority of their religion in the face of Islam. But it is also true that the Hindu and Muslim masses— before they had eaten off the tree of knowledge and became religion conscious—worshipped peacefully side by side. As if to reiterate the same theme Lord Olivier, secretary of state for India in the Ramsay Macdonald government, observed, "No one with a close acquaintance with Indian affairs will be prepared to deny that on the whole there is a predominant bias in British officialdom in favour of the Muslim community, partly on the ground of closer sympathy but more largely as a make-weight against Hindu nationalism." Sir Fuller, a governor of Curzon created province of East Bengal, in an oft-quoted address picturesquely referred to the British government in India as having two wives, Hindu and Muslim, of which the Muslim wife was the 'favourite' wife. The official philosophy, apparently was, "Our endeavour should be to uphold in full force the (for us fortunate) separation which exists between different religions and races, not to endeavour to amalgamate them. In the first and consolidation phase of the Raj the Muslims were to be suppressed, and now with emergence of Hindu nationalism, it was essential to win them over so as to counter-balance the growing dissent against the British. Consequently, the last two decades of the nineteenth century witnessed this swing of the pendulum.

This change of heart of the British is somewhat difficult to comprehend because after the 'revolt' the official conclusion was that the 'Muslims' cannot be good subjects of any government which professes another religion: 'the precepts of Koran will not suffer it'. Now they were apparently trying to build Muslim loyalty within the precepts of Koran. So here the question was: whether Muslims could remain good Muslims and yet become good subjects of the Empire. What also helped Muslims regain their standing was their religion's uncomplicated dictates. There were too many versions, branches and sides to the Hindu religion for an uninitiated to understand. Fresh arrivals from Britain could not fathom the implications of the Hindu Caste System, nor could they comprehend various versions of the religion, to them Muslim faith was more comprehensible than Hinduism. There was another reason for this bias in the British towards the Muslims by the turn of the century: demand for army recruitment was growing due to fears of Russian invasion through Afghanistan and there were not many volunteers other than Muslims. This was largely instinctive; the Muslims formed the backbone of the 'then' Indian Army, and as a largely peasant community were more willing than middle class Hindus to adopt an attitude of respect towards the British. Clearly, the Muslim opposition to an emerging organisation that had a predominantly Hindu slant was the best card the British had in their hand, and they were all set to exploit it to the hilt.

The nationalists blamed the British for fomenting trouble between the two communities, claiming that, before they came Hindus and Muslims had lived like brothers, happily intermingling with each other. This does not seem to be a valid statement because the Muslim rulers, particularly after Akbar, had made the life difficult for the Hindus, leading to creation of The Sikhs, who took arms to defend their faith against the Mughals. Welded into a militant community under the leadership of their Gurus in the 17th and the 18th centuries, the Sikhs had stubbornly resisted Muslim oppression. Establishment of their hegemony over Punjab in the 19th century under Maharaja Ranjit Singh was the culmination of their endeavour. In 1920s when some Muslim leaders started advocating a separate electorate and building a purely Muslim constituency so as to safeguard the interests of the community the Sikhs started feeling uncomfortable with these developments. Their resentment over the issue took the shape of Akali (Followers of the Eternal Faith) Movement. Beginning as a puritanical upsurge, the Akalis soon clashed with the government because they had started using congregations in the Gurudwaras for reviving the Sikh pride in freedom. Their non-violent agitation to wrest control of cash-rich Gurudwaras from 'Mahants' who were pro-government and therefore, open to manipulation by officials of the Raj soon took a nationalistic turn and gave a big fillip to a dying down non-cooperation movement in the rest of India. The government was worried over these developments because the Sikh agitation was also affecting morale of the Sikhs in the army.

Uneasy Punjab

Unlike other conquerors, who came to India through the north and consolidated their hold on the country from that direction, Punjab was the last province to be added to the British Empire. Having come through the Arabian Sea and Bay of Bengal the English had no other option. Russian threat through Afghanistan was a worrying prospect and from time to time effort was made to subjugate that country but no success was met. The terrain was too inhospitable, and people too proud and brilliant fighters to let the British in. This hardiness was also built into the Punjabis, especially the Sikhs. French advisers and some others were egging Maharaja Ranjit Singh to take on the British who were in the process of retreating from Kabul, but Ranjit Singh was too astute a tactician to fall for such advice. He had the examples of the Marathas and Tipu Sultan before him, he was careful not to fall out with John Company. It was only after his death the Sikh chieftains fell to quarrelling, and the Khalsa re-emerged to become the arbiters of peace or war, the vibrant energy of the state got dissipated; firstly, in fighting among themselves to gain supremacy and then taking on the British without adequate and sound preparation. Two bloody wars, in 1845 and 1849 saw the British taking control of the state.

The British knew that without Punjab they will never be safe and secure, its annexation was essential from political and economical point of view. It is not as if the British had not been trying to capture Punjab; after Delhi this was a logical expansion plan besides securing their northern flank. Two famous battles and decline of the Ranjit Singh's empire after his death allowed the British to get a toehold in the province. But in typically Punjabi spirit, the people were up and about no sooner than the state was added to the Raj. Had the Punjab not been conquered, then the British fate in 1857 would have been catastrophically different. In 1857 itself "Mar Firangi" was the clarion call that did make the British hearts aflutter with trepidation. Cleverly, they used the Muslim-Sikh rivalry and mutual hate to their advantage while suppressing the rebellion. Swadeshi might have originated in Bengal, but the 'Kukas', brave Sikhs of the times had much earlier decided to boycott even the railways, postal services, and no Kuka ever visited a practitioner of the western medical system. The sufferings of Guru Ram Singh, whom the Sikhs revered as the reincarnation of Guru Gobind Singh, and his band of selfless and highly disciplined followers occupied the imagination of rural Punjab. The Guru had been imprisoned in remote Rangoon after the British had been able to suppress the Kuka rebellion of 1863-72, but the tradition of anti-imperialist militancy generated by the Kukas led to a situation where Punjab played a major role in India's struggle for freedom.

In the north, particularly in Punjab, the rural population was getting restless with new laws relating to land and its acquisition that were being formulated by the government. The government now wanted Punjab to be prosperous province of the British Raj, with Sikh warriors converted to contented peasants turning in a revenue surplus. To this end various laws were passed for land consolidation and revenue generation, not all were common farmer friendly.

The urban Sikhs were shown the path to freedom by Sardar Dyal Singh Majithia who, realizing the power of the press, in addition to starting schools and colleges, started '*The Tribune*' in Lahore. Another concurrent, and equally powerful, establishment was the "Arya Samaj" propagating the thoughts of Swami Dayanand. The Arya Samaj was founded in Bombay in 1875 to reassert Hindu orthodoxy in the face of westernising tendencies. This, Dayanand Anglo Vedic or DAV for short, was a movement that captured the imagination of the Punjabi Hindu in a big way. DAV created a new and vibrant class of intelligentsia led by the likes of Lala Lajpatrai, Bhai Parmamand, and Mahatma Hansraj. The movement of Arya Samaj gained so much of momentum that the government started branding every Arya Samaj member as a potential threat to its existence. The organisation itself was considered to be seditionery.

Lala Lajpatrai was one of the very few leaders who attained a national stature virtually in no time. Lajpatrai was the son of a poor Urdu and Persian teacher in Delhi; he belonged to the first generation of English-educated Punjabis. The boyhood years of poverty made it natural for him to identify with the needs and sufferings in the country. "I have deeply felt the degradation of my country and the humiliation of my countrymen has sunk deep into my soul," he had observed. In 1896, he published biographies of 'fighters like Garibaldi and Shivaji'. These were distributed freely to all those who could read. This was in keeping with the clever ruse (earlier used by Tilak) of invoking heroes of the past to supply a contemporary message to the youth of India, and yet avoid any official censor. In 1897 he founded the 'Hindu Orphan Relief Movement for the young victims of the raging famine.

\Books about those who had fought oppression and had tried to unite their country did have a positive message for the target readership, but the government was not able to decipher as to what all this was leading to. To be on the safe side, the Home Department opened a file on him, in due course his books were labelled seditious, and he was put under a scanner. Unconcerned, Lalaji went about his way to awaken the youth of India and particularly that of Punjab. By 1908 the Movement was expanded to encompass general relief to anyone in need of succour. But the government put even this movement under surveillance lest the money raised for relief was used for political purposes. In the meanwhile charges on land revenue and water were raised, causing a great deal of resentment in Punjab. A bill proposing that irrigable land could only be sold to 'agricultural tribes' was proposed, causing a great deal of resentment amongst the Hindus who saw it as another ruse of the administration to prevent them from buying land in their own state. Lajpatrai led an agitation on the issue because he felt that uplifting of the poor and the economic strength of the masses only could help India get out of its problems. When unrest grew in the newly formed district of Lyallpur due to upward revision of revenue and shortage of water, which compounded the problems of the poor farmers, Lajpatrai rushed along with his immediate deputy—Sardar Ajit Singh. The new governor of Punjab, one Denzil Ibbertson, decided to act firmly because he felt that people were being incited without sufficient cause. Lajpatrai was arrested on his orders and after a sham trial, was deported to Mandalay under Regulation III of 1818, which precluded trial or legal defence. Even Secretary of State—Morley observed on this deportation of Lajpatrai: "Nothing could be thinner than what they call evidence in the instant case." The youth of Punjab showed its resentment over this misdemeanour of the governor by taking to arms. Earlier, on the 28th of August 1906, *The Pioneer*-which was the chief 'Anglo-Indian' mouthpiece, wrote apropos of a Russian terrorist outrage: "the bomb is the only method of fighting left to the people who are at war with despotic rulers." It is certain that this profound observation of *The Pioneer* was not lost; and who knows if the bomb a useful and legitimate weapon against the Tsars, did not then appear to some Indian youths as the weapon indicated and justified by '*The Pioneer*' against the despotism of a "white and insensitive bureaucracy." It was a Punjabi who threw a bomb on the Viceroy's procession in Delhi. It appears that, led by Punjab and Bengal, at that point of time the revolutionary movement was the most assertive political force in the country. But the biggest contribution of Punjab was the formation of 'Ghadr Party" on 10 May 1913 in America by Lala Hardyal.

Footnotes

1. "The Imperialism could not solve the internal economic problems. It created 'two nations' between whom there could be no intercourse or sympathy; the Rich and the Poor"—Benjamin Disraeli A former Prime Minister of England in a parliamentary speech.

2. *The Late Rebellion in India and Our Future Policy*, pp 13-17.

3. WW Hunter The Indian Mussalmans published in 1870.

4. British Rule in India was established by playing Hindus against the Muslims and native states and Principalities against each other. International Study Club Bulletin No 2, Tokyo 1905.

2

Restive India 1905-1908

The year 1905 symbolizes the watershed of British rule in India. During that year two important events occurred: Curzon's resignation and Japan's victory over Russia. Lord Curzon, the then Viceroy of India had a penchant for deriding and slighting the educated Indian opinion leading to a bitter reaction to him and to British rule among the most modern regions and classes of Indian society. Where Japan's victory over Russia was concerned, it was seen as a victory of the so-called barbarians and uncivilised Asians over a major European power. The speeches and writings of Indian politicians and opinion-makers from 1905 onward repeated the theme that Japan was an appropriate example for India. Educated Indians increasingly felt that they did not need to slavishly model their institutions after those of Britain: they now had an Asian text to follow. To them Japan had clearly demonstrated that the technical and organisational prerequisites of nationhood were not confined to Caucasians alone. Indians, with their history, culture and now education might also move toward greater independence; they could be confident that they possessed— or would soon possess— the necessary skills. This new exuberance and confidence, which had been slowly building, affected Indians of all political persuasions, but was evident in the activities of revolutionaries and more traditional leadership, particularly that of Bal Gangadhar Tilak.[1]

Tilak was a Sanskrit scholar, popular journalist and a radical in Indian politics. Tilak's political philosophy and background were strongly traditional; a brilliant journalist, he used his native Marathi language to carry his message of Hindu patriotism to the lower middle classes in Deccan towns and villages through his newspaper 'Kesri' (The Lion). Born to a prosperous Chitpavan Brahmin family in 1856, Tilak received a western education at the Deccan College in Poona. He went on to found a number of schools where western sciences were restated in traditional Hindu terms. In many ways, Tilak's schools were a counterpart to the educational work of Syed Ahmed Khan among the Muslims, but unlike Sir Syed, Tilak was concerned with undermining the British rule and not with its continuation in India. In his typical style, he bemoaned the fact that the British were willing to share everything with Indians except power. (To Home Member, HH Cradock Tilak appeared as a man who was 'impelled by a venom and hatred against everything British'—so the animosity between him and the British was mutual). He created or revived two major Hindu festivals in Maharashtra, one commemorating the birth of Lord Shiva's son, 'Ganesh', and the other honouring the Maratha hero, 'Shivaji', founding father of Maratha nation against all odds, including long drawn war with the Mughals. He attacked the factory of the East India Company in Surat in the first fight between the English and natives. He founded an empire, reorganised civil institutions, and was a devout orthodox Hindu. He was an ideal example of bravery, orthodoxy and self-sufficiency that Tilak thought would stimulate national idealism. Through these festivals Tilak was able to achieve the desired end of infusing the people with a religious and national fervour.

Both the festivals were noisy; some called them even 'chauvinistic' designed to alienate the Muslims because the total Hindu bias of these celebrations created a situation where Muslims started feeling threatened. Tilak was given the title 'Lokmanya' (revered by the nation) –but the nation concerned remained (largely) a Hindu nation. The British kept an eye on his activities. So far he hadn't done anything that could be termed seditious; but with his kind of deep-rooted animosity for the Raj he was to give a chance to the administration to react to his activities, which was not too late in coming. In 1897, bubonic plague spread from Bombay to Poona. British doctors lead by a Mr. Rand, the assistant collector of Poona, took immediate and somewhat brutal measures to contain the epidemic. This included isolating people in camps and destroying crops and property that was believed to be contaminated. In the process, even those who had not been infected were taken away, their houses damaged and looted by some of the soldiers. Instances of molestation of women, disrespect to places of worship, wanton destruction of property, and general mistreatment, made the search parties of the Government more feared by the native than the plague. Rand did nothing to stop this official loot.

Tilak took strong umbrage over this insensitive and rash act describing it as a monumental example of arrogance and insensitivity. His 'Kesri' carried editorials and articles on the subject, in a way inciting people to stand up against, what he called, a vast engine of oppression. On 27th

June of the same year Rand and his assistant were shot dead. Tilak was arrested for sedition, and charged with incitement to murder British officials. After a trial, which was just going through the motions, he was sentenced to 18 months imprisonment. It was a big mistake made by the British. Tilak was now not only a Hindu martyr but also a national hero. He emerged from the prison adopting a new slogan: '*Swaraj is my birthright, and I will have it*!' Swaraj (meaning self-rule) was a demand originally made by Shivaji two centuries ago. He was demanding it from the Mughals: Tilak now demanded it from the British for India as a whole, and was prepared to fight for it. Tilak's efforts at broad-basing the movement against foreign rule were praiseworthy, progressive and even radical. But the slogans on which the whole thing was planned to build a mass movement were self-defeating. Resultantly, any possibility of Hindus and Muslims jointly struggling against the British receded, making the task of the 'separatists' that much easier. The Muslims had found no reason to be associated with the festivals concerning either Ganesh or Shivaji. No lessons were learnt from these developments. Later, when Gandhi emerged on the national scene and took control of the freedom movement he also took recourse to only those issues, which had a definite Hindu angle. Although, Gandhi was influenced by various cultures and beliefs, he remained predominantly a Hindu and a strong protagonist of the Hindu ways of life. His call for 'cow protection,' 'Hindi Prachar', 'Harijan Seva', and the like was essentially Hindu in character. Slogans like 'Swaraj and Ram Raj' were open to misinterpretation by those Muslim leaders who were not particularly enamoured with Gandhi. Naturally, most of the Muslims viewed him with suspicion and never fully trusted him; they were convinced that his calls for unity implied not equality but ultimately subjugation to the Hindu majority. Over the years Gandhi's Hinduism, his ways of relating anything and everything to a Hindu way of life, kept on widening the gap between the two communities, finally leading to the demand for and partition of India.

Another Chitpavan Brahmin, Gopal Krishna Gokhale, who was a protégé of Justice Ranade, contrasted Tilak's firebrand style. Born into a poor family in 1866, Gokhale was an outstanding intellectual and had a fine grasp on economics. He relied on sweet reason and detailed logical arguments when making his point. Like Tilak, Gokhale edited a newspaper, '*Sudharak*', but unlike Tilak, who looked back nostalgically to a golden past of Maratha glory and demanded rights, Gokhale politely sought concessions, admiring the British and embracing western ideas. Tilak wanted Swaraj now, Gokhale believed India would not be ready for independence until it made those social and religious reforms that would allow all its people to live together in harmony. While Tilak created Hindu festivals and the militant cult of Shivaji, Gokhale founded the Servants of India Society, a select, quasi-monastic band of workers dedicated to selfless service to the motherland and its people, regardless of caste or creed. By the end of the nineteenth century, though older leaders like Ranade, Dadabhai Naoroji, Surendranath Bannerjee and Pherozeshah Mehta were still around, Gokhale and Tilak had become the acknowledged leaders of the two wings of the Congress. The wings were known simply as the Moderates and the Extremists. Congress, in the meanwhile, had worked its way to passing of the Indian Council's Act of 1892. The act envisaged the extension of the Viceroy's council and that of the Governors of Madras and Bombay to include 'elected' representatives of the Indians for the first time. The act, though considered to be the first big step towards self-government, did little to improve position of the Congress in the eye of the British, who still regarded it at best with suspicion and at worst with derision. Division between the Moderates and the Extremists were forever widening, weakening the organisation from within. So much so, Lord Curzon, who arrived as Viceroy in 1899, declared: "The Congress is tottering to its fall, and one of my greatest ambition while in India is to assist it to its peaceful demise." It is a paradox of history that George Nathaniel Curzon, due to his deeds while Viceroy of India, actually revived the fortunes of a moribund Congress, restoring its respectability and turned it into a forceful organisation.

On the face of it no one was better qualified to be the Viceroy of India than 39 years old George Curzon. He had spent most of his life preparing himself for the job, having decided as a boy that there were only two worthwhile goals in the life of a deserving 'leader' of men: to be Viceroy of India and Prime Minister of Great Britain. All through he had been too full of himself. He was convinced that he was better informed, better educated, more extensively travelled, more industrious and more often right than his colleagues, rivals and opponents. He saw no reason why he should not achieve both of his aims, using one as a stepping-stone to the other. An out and out imperialist, his stated aim was 'to rivet the British rule more firmly on to India and to postpone the longed-for day of emancipation.' He had a poor view of his own countrymen. "All these gentlemen state their worthless views at equal length," he remarked of his departmental chiefs, and the result is a sort of literary bedlam. Of only one of his provincial governors could he say that "it is such a Godsend in this pigmy-ridden country to find a man who al least has mental stature. Otherwise, the government of India is a mighty and miraculous machine for doing nothing." One positive was that Curzon had a deep love for India's people and their culture. With all his faults he seemingly had a genuine regard for Indians, considering them to become someday the greatest partners of the Empire. He would, often advise his officers, "Authority should not make Indians feel they are a conquered people, exercise it kindly and not offensively." While refusing to send 20,000 Indian indentured labourers for railway construction in South Africa, he said, "many Indians found the concept of British empire disreputable because in practice it means to India a full share of the battles and burdens of the Empire, but uncommon little of the privileges and rights." An Indian lawyer in Durban South Africa, a certain M K Gandhi, who was fighting for the rights of Indians in that racist land at the time, couldn't have put it better.

Curzon did a lot to improve the economy of India by creating a Department of Commerce and Industry. He created a separate Department of Agriculture with a modern research station and pushed through large irrigation projects in the arid and semi-desert regions. It was during his time that the railways added 6,000 miles of track to the existing network. His proposals for reforms of the police and the administration, though came into effect after his departure, paved the way to provincial self-government. He drove through education reforms increasing primary and secondary schooling. He accepted that Hindi, as the language of the majority, should be officially recognised. Muslim objections he just ignored saying, "spleen of a minority from whose hands are slipping away the reigns of power." His most memorable and durable act was to revitalise the archaeological department, in the process he discovered some of the lost treasures and rescued many known monuments, which were otherwise destined to permanent decay and disappearance. Taj Mahal, Fatehpur Sikri, the Pearl Mosque in Lahore, the palace in Mandalay, and the temples at Khajuraho owe their revival to Lord Curzon. Whereas his successes were of the highest order, his blunders were of equally high order. Curzon pacified the Pathan and Afghan frontiers by creating a new province to administer the region. This province (North-West Frontier) was cast out of the then Punjab creating widespread agitation and resentment. Curzon was convinced that Russia's national ambition was dominance in Asia, and ultimately conquest of India. Pathologically suspicious of Russia, like most of his predecessors, he sent out a military expedition under the command of a friend, Major Francis Younghusband, who elected to go through a defence-less Tibet on this mission. The mission was bound to be a monumental failure because neither the logistics of such an adventure, nor manpower requirements had been worked out in any realistic manner.

Home government did not approve of this misadventure and totally disowned any responsibility for this act of Curzon: London accepted

Russian disclaimers of any interest in India. Not to be flustered by any such setback to his plans, and believing firmly that Afghanistan offered the shortest route to India, Curzon now elected to cow down the Afghans by trying to interfere in their affairs. He apparently, had not read his history; else he would have known that the Afghans made most formidable enemies and their country allowed them all kinds of protection against a foreign invasion. After considerable loss of life and limb Curzon's temporary replacement, when the Viceroy was away on home leave, managed to calm down the Afghans. It wasn't Curzon's fault that he had wanted to consolidate the Empire against a Russian invasion through Afghanistan. Even in 1874, Lord Lawrence, had warned the Secretary of State that if an effort was made to position British agents in that country they wouldn't last long enough to play any meaningful role in negating the Russian threat to the Empire. This advice was ignored, a British Residence was 'permanently' established at Kabul, just to teach a lesson to Lawrence; and of course to tell the Russians how protective was Britain where its Asian acquisitions were concerned. Lawrence was right in his assessment, a British Residency established in Kabul was put to sword, and a garrison of 25 was all dead within weeks of having taken station in Afghanistan.

Curzon's lack of political savvy caught up with him on his return for the second term when his 'handpicked commander-in-chief Lord Kitchner locked horns with the Viceroy. Kitchner, whose ego was as monumental as that of Curzon, was not the one to let the Viceroy get away with control over the Indian Army. He was further miffed when he found that where he himself was merely an ex-officio member of the Viceroy's executive council, a subordinate officer sat on it as military member. It had always been like this, but Kitchner took it as a personal insult and affront. In an increasingly and bitter row developing over the issue Kitchner had the support of the Prime Minister, the King and the Secretary of State, St John Broderick. Broderick and Curzon had gone to the same school and were together later at Oxford but they were never friends. In addition, Broderick had always resented the insulting and rude attitude of Curzon. For that matter Curzon had lost the friends he needed in high places by his well-known opinions on their limited competence. Once he became the Secretary of State, Broderick technically became Curzon's superior and gladly joined hands with Kitchner in his row with Curzon.

Partition of Bengal

The fight with Kitchner and Broderick was no match for the mess Curzon was concurrently in the process of landing in—he was actively into dividing Bengal. Besides historic Bengal, the province included Bihar, Orissa and Chota Nagpur. It was, undoubtedly too big for one Governor to rule. For over twenty years, the civil servants had been throwing up the idea of dividing this cumbersome state and to make it more convenient to manage. Nothing had, however, been done so far because the administration feared a Bengali backlash and unrest over the issue. No such consideration ever worried Curzon. He felt that time to stop talking and to act had come. In April 1902, he wrote to the Secretary of State about possible boundary changes. He pointed out that the eastern districts of Bengal had long been neglected and that the province of Assam was, in contrast to its giant neighbour too small. The plan was to create two new provinces, West Bengal and East Bengal, by a line drawn down the centre of the old one just east of Calcutta and the Hoogly River. Assam was to be added to the eastern half. Western Bengal would include Bihar, Chota Nagpur and Orissa. In spite of all his professed or manifest compassion for the Indians, Curzon did not feel that there was any need for him to consult the locals. He, in any case, had a lot of disdain for the Bhadralok of Bengal. Where he was concerned this division was a logical and efficient solution to a longstanding administrative problem.

The moment plans to divide leaked there was a massive outcry not only in Bengal but the whole of India. The Hindus of Bengal were not at all impressed with this division of their state. They saw it as a ploy to destroy their power base, as they would be reduced to a minority in East Bengal, which would have 18 million Muslims and only 12 million Hindus. To make matters worse, in the West Bengal, 17 million Bengalis would be vastly out-numbered by 37 million speaking Hindi or Oriya. It is hard to believe that Curzon was unaware of the ramifications of this act of his. He contemptuously dismissed the suggestion that he was pursuing the policy of 'Divide and Rule', in spite of the fact that some of his advisers (particularly HH Risley, the Home Secretary) did try to tell him that "Bengal united is power...and Bengal divided will pull in several different ways". Risley also said that the Congress leaders feel that this division of the state was done with a view to weaken their power base. Curzon ignored all these protests and advice given by more mature civil servants. All that he subscribed to was the theory that the damage the partition would do to the Congress was merely a convenient side-effect. Curzon had read his history lessons carefully and had drawn inspiration from the thinkers of earlier times who had advocated that," Motto of British Administration, over time our policy should be to play off race against race and caste against caste." The tidal waves of protest against this division were totally ignored by him. Bengalis, he observed loftily, "Howl until a thing is settled and then they accept it." This time, however, they did not accept it and the howls did not die away after the partition was put into effect on 16th October 1905.

Partition of Bengal came like a political gift from heaven for Congress, which was fading fast under an ineffectual and moderate leadership. Gokhale, elected president in 1905, seized the opportunity to rally his members in his opening address at that year's session in Benaras. A cruel wrong has been inflicted on our Bengali brethren, and the whole country has been stirred to its deepest depths in sorrow and resentment", he thundered. But he was factually not totally correct. Muslims of East Bengal were delighted.

While the Hindus were mourning the day of partition with "Hartals" in Calcutta, the Muslims in Dacca were celebrating with prayers of thanks giving. Ninety per cent of Bengali Muslims were poor peasants who had converted to Islam from the lowest orders of Hinduism in earlier times, hoping that they would gain equality with the main community. But caste Hindus still despised them. Having got a state where they were in majority they felt that now they would be spared the repression at the hands of caste Hindus. In a visit to Dacca before partition Curzon had promised Muslims that they would soon have 'preponderating voice' in the state, and their city would be converted from a sleepy backward town into a thriving provincial capital, and Chittagaon would emerge from the giant shadow of Calcutta to become an important port in its own right, serving the trade needs of the new province. The issue of partition of Bengal transformed Congress from an elite Brahmin club into a national political movement. As one East Bengal provincial Congress leader, Abdul Rasul—one of the very few Muslims— put it: "What we could not have accomplished in 50 or 100 years, the great disaster, the partition of Bengal, has done for us in six months. It has given an impetus to the "Swadeshi" movement."

Swadeshi, which literally means 'of our own country', was a new and powerful weapon fashioned by Tilak and his Extremists. The theme had originally been adopted by the Chinese who had boycotted American goods as a protest against US domination of the Chinese economy and mistreatment of Chinese immigrants in America. The movement began in Bengal with a boycott resolution passed at a public meeting in Calcutta Town Hall on 7, August 1905. Where Gokhale was keen to restrict the movement to Bengal, Tilak took it to Poona and Bombay, and Lala Lajpatrai, leader of the Hindu revivalist organisation Arya Samaj, took it to his native Punjab. Even moderates like Surendranath Bannerjee toured the country urging people to boycott Lancashire cloth and Liverpool salt. The normally passive Indian middle class felt no harm in supporting the Swadeshi movement because it involved no riots, no violence and no damage to the property as such. Mill owners and industrialists were thrilled no end over this development because boycott of foreign goods meant greater demand for their products. Throughout India, people made bonfires of their British material and clothing, while Indian-owned cotton mills in Bombay, Ahmedabad and Nagpur worked flat out trying to meet unprecedented demand for Swadeshi cloth. The boycott also led to the revival of the old cottage industry of hand spinning and weaving. Wearing home-produced cottons, even though they were of poorer quality than imported fabrics, became a badge of pride. Swadeshi soon expanded to include other imports like sugar, soap, chemicals, glassware, shoes, matches and metal hardware. Indigenous replacements were often of poor quality, and the manufacturers and the middlemen were making huge profit as the production couldn't suddenly cope up with the demands, but nobody seemed to mind this profit-making because it was being made by the Indians and money was remaining within the country and not being taken to England.

Swadeshi caught the imagination of the Hindu population as nothing had before. Those sections of the community who had never earlier evinced any interest in the affairs of the country suddenly found something to show their solidarity with the movement. Washer-men refused to wash clothes made of foreign material, cobblers wouldn't touch foreign made shoes, priests wouldn't accept temple offerings made from British sugar, even women came out of the shelters of their homes and refused to wear foreign-made bangles in a spirit of solidarity with the movement. This new spirit of nationalism was further spurred on by the news that an Asian nation Japan, had inflicted a crushing defeat on a European power, Russia, killing 200,000 Russian soldiers in a great land battle at Mukden, Inner Mongolia on 10th March 1905. They had wiped out the Russian Navy in the straits of Tsushima on 28th May of the same year. That the Asians could defeat the Europeans caught the fancy of the youth.

G D Birla, founder of the Birla commercial empire, recalled later, "India did not escape the surge, ambition of seeing India free began to excite me." (G D Birla-*In the Shadows of the Mahatma*). While Birla was dreaming the dreams of the youth, India's other great industrial dynasty, the TATA family was in the process of building India's first iron and steel works on a rural site in west Bengal. They named the town that grew around the plant 'Jamshedpur' after the founder of the dynasty, Jamshed N TATA, another pearl from the remarkable Parsi community. Jamshed Tata had made his fortune from cotton mills in Bombay and Nagpur and had died in 1904. The family seeing the Swadeshi spirit catching on decided to diversify. In this they were encouraged by the leaders of Congress. The British gave them no help in setting up the plant; in fact, certain members of the government tried to put all kinds of impediments in their desire to see the project fail. Tatas took technical and other help from the Americans instead and went ahead to successfully complete the plant with American equipment and encouragement of the leaders like Tilak and Gokhale. From that moment the TATA family became the main financial supporters of the Congress. Later, G D Birla also joined them in giving a boost to the Swadeshi movement.

As the Swadeshi movement gathered momentum, it came more and more under the control of Tilak and the extremists. Its character became more Hindu than a national movement where Muslims and others could also share their feelings. The Bengali festival of 'Durga Puja', always one of the highlights of the Hindu calendar year, was celebrated in 1905 with greater intensity than ever. Durga, the malevolent Kali, and the demoness Durga are both forms of the mother goddess, consort of the Hindu God Shiva, the creator and destroyer of life. People swore never to buy British goods, never to have anything to do with them, and the priests exhorted each batch of worshippers to swear to serve their motherland. They asked them to offer their lives in the service of their motherland and to worship "Bharat Mata" ahead of any other deity.

The idea of the motherland as a deity to be worshipped was anathema to the Muslims: their holy Qur'an dictated worship only of one true god—Allah. This conflict of perception between the Hindus and Muslims lead to a situation where Muslims felt that the Hindus were trying to dictate them what to do and what not to do. Gradually they refused to support what they saw as a Hindu boycott and insisted to continue to buy and sell British goods. The Hindus tried to stop them, inevitably leading to arguments, fights and much more. Instead of the agitation becoming one against the British, it became more of a Hindu—Muslim fight leading to a lot of violence and bloodshed. The partition of Bengal certainly worked to drive a blow home at the heart of Bengali patriotism, and to push the Hindus and the Muslims against each other, for the third party to gain from this whole exercise. It is another matter that when the agitation seemed to be going out of hand no one wished to acknowledge authorship of this partition. Even Lord Curzon discovered in his notes, as late as 1908, that he had never desired it, and that the Secretary of State and one Lord Ampthill plotted it in his absence. But the later repudiated this charge, and no one really believed in this tardy discovery of Lord Curzon.

The partition had succeeded in driving a wedge between the Hindus and Muslims of Bengal, and that seemingly was the aim of the whole exercise at that time. For, if the question was only of simplifying administration differently, a more feasible and workable territorial readjustment could have been worked out. The partition of Bengal gave a deep and penetrating wound to the patriotic sentiment of the people-something that the rulers had not believed to be so much alive. The British game plan went awry because this division created a situation where all the rancour, all the distrusts, and the discontentment with the foreign rulers, which had been generally confined to the elite till then, manifested themselves in the common man. Now old-fashioned Hindus, privileged Brahmins, merchants, landlords, villagers and even lowly coolies unanimously joined in protesting against what the rulers had done to their beloved Bengal. Aga Khan, the leader of the Muslims in India during his visit observed, "I arrived in the capital of India towards the middle of last December (1905), and at once became aware of a remarkable change—all my friends, Hindus and Muslims, who did not concern themselves with politics, and whom I freely questioned, including a number of men in the street most of whom were Bengalis by race, and they all appeared to have their hearts broken and bleeding owing to the partition of their province. I had never seen, and I would not have been able to think of a sentiment as universal and as profound as that of the popular masses against this partition of Bengal. Clearly, some of the Muslim leaders were seeing certain advantages in this partition of the state but the common man was not privy to any gain to himself."

By this time, Lord Minto had replaced Curzon. A Tory landowner, Minto was more into usual pursuits of the landed gentry of the time. His great-grandfather had been the Governor General of India from 1807 to 1813. Minto had been Governor General of Canada before coming to India. That was too soft a posting for him to prepare for a country that was awakening to the reality of slavery and all that it entails. At the age of sixty, Minto, with all his pragmatism and honesty of purpose, was not up to the situation. Therefore Minto, in his endeavour to lead a peaceful life elected to leave running of the country to Kitchner and the bureaucrats. Unfortunately for him, and the Empire, only thing where the ICS and Kitchner agreed was the strategy of brute force and repression while dealing with a political agitation of this magnitude. To add to the problems of India, Minto's boss in London the Secretary of State was a seventy years old intellectual, Morley.

Formation of the Muslim League

When Morley in his Budget speech expressed his desire to consider the proposal for reforming the Legislative Council and Minto appointed a committee to look into the matter and suggest some reforms, the Muslim leaders saw red. They apprehended that unless the Muslim position was also taken into account by the government, they could very well be left out of any new dispensation. The people were already seeing these developments as a great success achieved by the Congress.

It was against a well-established background of social differences between Hindus and Muslims that in October 1906, a delegation of 35 Muslim princes and nobles from various parts of India, led by the young Aga Khan, went to Simla to meet the Viceroy, Lord Minto. Fearing that the Congress president might have created a pro-Hindu bias in the mind of Secretary of State and liberalization could give Hindu majority an upper hand, they thought it prudent to counter balance any such thought nursed by the British government. Their theme was that the Muslims were totally different from Hindus, in their religious pursuits, their culture and their customs. They demanded, with exquisite courtesy, reserved positions for Muslims in the service, courts and administration, and reserved seats in any elected councils. Their main demand was creation of a separate electorate for the Muslims with only Muslim voters electing candidates from their own religion. Hearing this Minto's advisers virtually rubbed their hands in glee. They didn't have to 'Divide and Rule'; a section of Indians was, itself, demanding it. The British were always ready to manipulate, manoeuvre, and exploit such divisive ideas that helped sustenance of the Empire. Way back Lord Elphinstone, Governor of Bombay, in a minute dated 14th May 1859 wrote: "Divide Et Empera was the old Roman Motto and it should be ours". Sir John Strachey, an eminent British Indian Civilian and writer on India had said, "The existence, side by side of hostile creeds among the Indian people, is one of the strong points in our political position in India.)" With so much of political wisdom from the past guiding the Viceroy, Minto heartily, welcomed these proposals.

Dr Ambedkar points out in his book '*Partition of India*' that in the memorandum it was also stipulated that if the British Government did not do something to appease the discontent, something serious might happen as the young Muslims were getting discontented and would join united agitation. As keeping the two communities divided was in the best interest of the Raj, an added impetus was provided towards accepting the Muslim demands by such an assertion about the intentions of the Muslim youth.

Flushed with their success in Simla, the Muslim leaders decided to set up a political organisation of their own, so as to counter-balance Congress. That year, Aligarh's Muhammadan Educational Conference was purposely held at Dacca, a Muslim stronghold, where the city's leading landowner, Nawab Salimullah Khan, suggested that a 'Muslim All-India Conference' should be convened at the same time. On 30th December 1906, All-India Muslim League was founded at Dacca's Shah Bagh (Royal Garden) with the following manifesto:

- To promote among the Muslims of India feelings of loyalty to the British Government and to remove any misconceptions that may arise as to the intentions of the Government with regards to any of its measures.

- To protect and advance the political rights and interests of the Muslims of India, and respectfully represent their needs and aspirations to Government.

- To prevent the rise among Muslims of India of any feelings of hostility towards other communities without prejudice to other objects of the League.

(Pirzada—Foundations of Pakistan, pp6)

Formation of the League was not favourably received in London, and to a great extent it went unnoticed. '*The Times*', in an editorial on 2nd January 1907, subscribed to the theory that it was an inevitable outcome of the Congress movement and an exposure of the hollowness of the Congress pretensions to speak for India, and expressed doubts whether the formation of League would actually lead to a more peaceful atmosphere, despite the pacific language of the founders. The new party was well received by the Muslims of India. Very soon branches were set up at various places. Syed Amir Ali headed one branch opened in London. In due course of time, this branch played a very important role in projecting the Muslim viewpoint in various forums.

The League, originally, was an elite club, restricting its membership to just four hundred conservative aristocrats and wealthy landed gentry. There were a few lawyers, journalists and academics to lend it a multi-discipline culture. For having bankrolled the project Aga Khan was made president for life. It is not that all Muslims subscribed to the League's charter. Some were actively opposed to its aims and objectives. According to Humayun Kabir, "Founded in 1906 by a group of well-to-do and aristocratic Muslims, it was intended to keep the Muslim intelligentsia and middle class away from the dangerous politics into which the Indian National Congress was just then embarking."[2] One man in particular, the Aga Khan, complained later, "came out in bitter hostility towards all that I, and my friends, had done and were trying to do. He was the only well-known Muslim to take this attitude…He said that our principle of separate electorates was dividing the nation against itself". The man the Aga Khan described as 'our doughtiest opponent in 1906', was a rising new star of the Congress. His name was M A Jinnah.

Mohammad Ali Jinnah

Born Mohammad Ali Jinnah in Karachi, the first child of Jinnahbhai, a leading light of his community and a member of the Shiite Khoja sub-sect, the family was disciples of the Ismaili Aga Khan. The Khojas were a mercantile community, far more outgoing and adaptable than most Indian Muslims. With a sharp eye for business and generally keen intelligence, many of the Khojas built up considerable fortunes through trade. Jinnah elder built up a thriving export-import business handling a wide range of products—raw cotton, wool, hides, oil-seeds, gram and so on going out and cotton piece goods from Lancashire, metal ware from Birmingham, refined sugar from Liverpool and London, coming in, had made him a very rich man. But he was not very happy with his son's academic progress. As a child M A Jinnah was more into usual childhood pranks—playing marbles and guli danda (tip-cat) with his friends rather than spending his time on brushing up the multiplication tables. His teachers conceded that Mamad (as Jinnah was known as a child) was an exceptionally gifted and intelligent child, but the environment did not seem to be conducive to his academic pursuits. In order to remove him from the bad influence of his playmates, when Jinnah was nine years old, the family decided to send him to Bombay to live with elder sister of Jinnahbhai. Mamad found Bombay to be too exciting and interesting. The sheer energy of the place seemed to have mesmerised him. He was, however, recalled home after six months because his mother, pining for her son, had fallen ill.

Back in Karachi, Mamad found the place to be far more boring than ever. He was re-registered in his old school. But the usual life of a student of that school and his penchant developed during his Bombay sojourn for high energy living and the academic pursuits of someone naturally gifted did not jell with his environment. He started missing classes and often absented himself totally from the school because teachers, whom he considered to be far below his ability were obviously reluctant to grant him his due as someone who was a nature's gift because such an admission would have gone against the accepted norms. Eventually, Mamad's name was struck off the school register, because of his 'long absences' when he was fifteen years old.

Jinnahbhai, totally in despair over his son's wayward conduct, discussed the matter with an English friend, Sir Fredrick Leigh Croft, who was general manager of Douglas Graham and Company, Karachi's leading British managing agency, with which Jinnahbhai's own firm had close connections. Sir Fredrick, who liked the quick-witted and intelligent boy, felt that he did have potential. He came up with a radical suggestion. He could arrange to send the boy to their head office in London for a three-year commercial apprenticeship. After that he would be suitably qualified to assist his father in his ever-expanding business.

London sounded more exciting than Bombay, and not withstanding the pleadings of his heart-broken mother who was definitely more upset over losing her son for three years in the far away capital of the Empire, and perhaps, full of all kinds of vice-dens; strong willed Mohammad Ali Jinnah overruled all her pleadings and objections. He, however, agreed to get married to a girl selected by his parents before sailing for the West as a special concession to his mother, who thought that bad influences of the London could lead her son to marry an English girl, not considered appropriate for a boy from a religious Muslim family. He was married to a 14 years old Emibai—a Khoja girl from another eminent family of the community. A few days after the marriage Mamad sailed for England, never to see either his wife or mother again. His father deposited enough money in a London Bank for his son's three years stay.

After initial feelings of loneliness, natural in totally foreign and different environments, teenaged Mamad settled down to enjoy his new found freedom in London. A restless spirit by nature, he quickly became anglicised, shortened his name to 'Jinnah' from Jinnahbhai, and discarded his traditional long yellow Sindhi coat for the first of his many Seville Row suits, stiff-collard shirts and silk neckties, he became the very model of sartorial elegance. Round about the same time he came under the influence of Dadabhai Naoroji, who had just become a member of the British parliament. He imbibed the philosophy of secular liberal nationalism propagated by Naoroji. His other great hero was the future Secretary of State for India 'John Morley'. Morley was the most trusted lieutenant of the Prime Minister Gladstone and a disciple of John Stuart Mill, another famous thinker and writer. It did not take long for Jinnah to be actively involved in the future of India.

Jinnah had been bitten by the political bug, and began to sit in the gallery of the House of Commons whenever he could. On weekends, he joined the throng at 'Speakers Corner' in Hyde Park, where orators of different hues ventilated their opinion on anything and everything under the sun. He, in any case, was finding the clerical work at the Graham's office to be too boring and irksome. Much to the chagrin of his father, he abandoned his training, but instead of wasting his time and his father's money, this time he elected to take up the study of law. He had realised that to succeed either in politics or other walks of life available to the likes of him back home in India, status as a lawyer was a big step forward. He applied for admission to the Inns of Court, passed the entrance examination on 25th May 1893, and enrolled at Lincoln's Inn, the Alma Mater of his mentor John Morley.

Back home Jinnahbhai's business collapsed, and he beseeched his son to return and help restoring the same. But M A Jinnah ignored all such entreaties and immersed himself into serious study of law. He was called to the bar on 11th May 1896. Concurrently he had also got interested in theatre and applied for a role in an amateur presentation of Shakespeare's Romeo and Juliet. Extremely handsome and with a grand presence, he was immediately accepted and contracted by the theatre company. His father was shattered at this yet again wayward behaviour of his, now grown up, son. He wrote him a long letter asking him to change his mind and not to bring a bad name to the family by appearing on the stage, something done only by the lower strata of the Indian society at that time. Seemingly, the same letter also contained the shattering news of the death of his wife and mother. According to Jinnah himself, one phrase in his father's letter—"Do not be a traitor to the family"—achieved what had always been impossible with headstrong Mohammad Ali; he backed down from pursuing a theatrical career, persuaded the manager to release him from the contract, and packed his bags to return to India. On 16th July 1896 he sailed home, heading not for Karachi where his father was eagerly awaiting the return of his son, but for Bombay—a city he had fallen in love with when he was barely nine years old.

In Bombay, he enrolled as a Barrister in the High Court. For the first three years, he did little more than deal with litigation that had started against his father following the liquidation of his business. Gradually, however, Jinnah began to build a reputation. When an influential friend introduced him to the advocate general, so impressed he was with this 22 years old lawyer that he gave him a job in his office. Jinnah was on a roll; he was now at the centre stage of Bombay law scene. He eventually quit, became a magistrate for a while and then again resumed independent practice. Jinnah began to thrive as a barrister, impressing just about everyone with the sharpness of his legal mind and dazzling courtroom performances. He came under the influence of Tyabji, worked for a while under the legendary Pherozeshah Mehta, who had also been a protégé of Dadabhai Naoroji while studying for the bar in London in the 1860s. With the backing of such stalwarts, Jinnah was able to create a solid support base for his political career. By 1904, when Congress met in Bombay, he was ready to make his presence felt. Although that year's president was an Englishman, Sir Henry Cotton, Mehta was the power behind the throne. Mehta made sure that every delegate knew who Jinnah was.

During the next two years, Jinnah worked to establish himself in Congress. He declared that his aim was to become 'the Muslim Gokhale'.

He had met Gokhale for the first time during the 1904 session, and the two had become firm friends. Both believed in Indian rather than Hindu or Muslim nationalism. By 1906, the gulf between the Moderates and the Extremists in Congress had widened so much as to bring the Party virtually to a break up. Gokhale, Mehta and the Moderates vetoed the idea of Tilak being anointed as the President of the Congress. The split was avoided by drafting in the 81 years old Naoroji as that year's president, to whom not even Tilak could object. The old man was too weak even to make his presidential speech himself. It was read for him by Gokhale—but it had been largely written by his 'political secretary' Mohammad Ali Jinnah, who celebrated his thirtieth birthday on the platform. The speech strongly condemned the division of Bengal. It called the division as 'a bad blunder for England'. The speech exhorted all Indians to sink or swim together, all differences between people and communities must be given up. The efforts, the speech announced, were to be directed towards a new goal: no longer merely a share in running the country but "self- government' or "Swaraj" like that of the United Kingdom or the Colonies. When his own time to address the session came, Mohammad Ali Jinnah thundered," If they do not leave peacefully, the British should know that Bombay will become another Boston, in an apparent reference to the revolt of the American Colonies against the Empire, but this time it would not be chests of tea thrown into the sea but cartloads of live British."

Jinnah did not know it at the time but another lawyer, again from Gujarat, was then awakening Indians in South Africa, his name was Mohandas Karam Chand Gandhi.

Footnote

1. Humayun Kabir, *Muslim Politics* 1906-1942 12 RP DUA, *The Impact of the Russo-Japanese War on Indian Politics.*

3

Raj Awakens to Indian Needs

"Liberty will not descend to a people. People must raise themselves to liberty. It is a blessing that must be earned before it can be enjoyed."

Chiselled on the portals of The South Block, New Delhi

Ever since it had come into existence, the Indian National Congress had been clamouring for some kind of Indian participation in governing the country. The British parliament finally agreed to set up a committee to examine all the issues involved and make suitable recommendations that would ensure continuation of the Empire as well as give Indians a sense of involvement in the country's affairs. The Secretary of State for India had been supportive in helping India's cause along. He made draft proposals keeping all aspects and issues involved in his perspective and sent them to the Viceroy, Lord Minto for a detailed study at his end.

As a Secretary of State John Morley was politically a good choice. He had a genuine concern for India, and in his very first speech as the Secretary of State he announced in the parliament in London his determination to bring about meaningful reforms, which would allow Indians to play a greater role in governing the country. In 1906, he invited Congress President Gokhale to London for discussions vis-à-vis affairs of India. A former president of Congress RC Dutt, who was then teaching Indian History at University College, London, was also asked to join in. Gokhale was happy that at last some one in London, the seat of British power, was actually listening to what Indians had to say about the affairs back home. But the talks, lengthy though they were, had hardly any reason to succeed: Morley had no mandate to offer anything concrete to the Indian leader.

By the spring of 1907, Minto and his officials had completed their report on Morley's reform proposals, which was to form the basis for a New Indian Councils Act. Morley overruled some of the reservations of Minto and his team, but the proposals did fall short of what the Indians were hoping for. Gokhale was 'seemingly' satisfied with the proposals; he had helped draft these while he was in London to have discussions with the Secretary of State. Being a Moderate, he was sure that self-rule could not be achieved in one go; it had to come in stages. He believed that the new Act would be a significant advance towards eventual self-rule, as indeed it proved to be. But Tilak and his hardliners were in no way mollified; instead, the gulf between the Moderates and the hardliners further widened, leading to a virtual break up of the party with the hardliners under Tilak calling themselves the 'New Party'. It was led by the 'Lal, Bal and Pal' as the militant students liked to chant. Lal referred to Lala Lajpatrai, the Arya Samaj leader from the Punjab, Bal was a reference to Tilak, and Pal stood for Bipin Chandra Pal, a militant Bengali youth leader.

The work of Tilak, amongst the educated Indians, who were greatly agitated over cumbersome, expensive, irresponsible and inefficient system of administration, was the mainspring of the liberation movement in India. The Government was regarded as the entrenched citadel of officialdom, the incarnation of all that was bad in the bureaucratic regime. Added to these were the handicaps and hardships the people of India as a whole faced on account of a system akin to that of absentee landlordism in the form of nominal, shadowy, unreal, and a largely unacceptable form of parliamentary control on Indian affairs (*The Awakening of India* by J Ramsay Macdonald). There is no doubt that the three contributed a certain depth and militancy to the people's consciousness. Unfortunately, it was unavoidable for them to link national feelings with Hindu mysticism and therefore, retard extension of the social base of the awareness they were trying to create.

The New Party wanted total boycott of everything British. In addition to giving up British made goods, they now wanted every Indian to resign from British India jobs as well. Situation soon went out of control of the leaders and there was widespread violence and riots in Punjab, East Bengal and certain other parts of the country. Newly appointed Lt Governor of Punjab, one Sir Denzil Ibbetson, was clearly out of his depth. With Minto's hawkish advisers like Kitchner telling him that 'strong medicine' was the only cure for the malady, he arrested Lala Lajpatrai along with a Sikh friend of his, one Sardar Ajit Singh. Just three days before the fiftieth anniversary of the great revolt of 1857, the two were whisked away to prison in far away Mandalay in Burma. Morley was horrified over these developments; but Minto, now convinced that some kind of revolt was again building up and to forestall any violent reaction, invoked the repressive Police Act of 1861. Troops were ordered into Lahore, the streets were cleared, and the agitators were imprisoned for two years without any trial for unspecified 'reasons of state'. The editor and proprietor of Lahore's most popular Indian paper, The *'Punjabee'*, were also arrested for sedition and sentenced to two years and six months of 'rigorous imprisonment'.

The government had been able to bring some semblance of peace in the state of Punjab, but the price had been high. Throughout the rest of 1907, the threat of trouble loomed constantly all over India. It was further accentuated when leader of the British Parliamentary Labour Party, James Keir Hardie visited India in September and October of that year for a first hand study of the situation. He publicly accused Britain of running India 'like the Czar runs Russia'. This note of sympathy from the prominent opposition leader further encouraged the 'students' to take to the streets. Riots raged through Calcutta for two days with police and students fighting running battles all over the city. A week later, Minto imposed a nationwide ban on all public meetings.

By December 1907, as the annual meeting of the Congress approached, Lala Lajpatrai was back in circulation again. He had been released from the prison and had by now become some kind of a national hero because of his exile and imprisonment. The New Party wanted him to be the next president of Congress that year and the moderates did not have any grand old man now to counter the threat of take-over of the Congress by the hardliners. All that the Moderates could do was to hold the 1907 Congress session in Surat—a seaport in Gujrat— and a stronghold of the Moderates. The Moderates proposed the name of a distinguished Bengali educationist, Dr Rash Behari Bose. Tilak would have none of it. As soon as Dr Bose rose to make his statement Tilak rushed to the rostrum, intending to announce Lajpatrai's candidacy. The young 'ceremonial guards' stopped him. Someone threw a shoe, which hit first Surendranath Bannerjee and then Mehta. A free for all soon followed. Turbans and hats were trampled in the melee, chairs were damaged, the huge Pandal was pulled down and the police had to be called in to restore order. The Surat session of Congress was abandoned. The long-threatened divide in the party had come about in such an undignified manner that it would take almost ten years before any kind of reconciliation could take place. Minto, in the meanwhile, was thrilled no end over this turn of events. He gleefully cabled Morley in London with the news, "The Congress collapse", he said, "was a great triumph for us". The reconciliation had to await the arrival on the scene, of the lawyer from South Africa, one Mohandas Karamchand Gandhi.

Congress Break-up and its After Effects

Tilak just as much as Gokhale regarded the split as a catastrophe for the nationalist movement. He tried for a rapprochement and agreed to accept Dr Ghose as president and promised to work for the unity of the party. But it was too late: Mehta and other Moderates were glad to be rid of the troublemakers. A strong supporter of Mehta, one H A Wadya wrote,' the union of these troublemakers with the Congress will be like union of a diseased limb with a healthy body. And the only remedy is surgical severance if the Congress is to be saved from death by 'blood poisoning'.

The New Party losing its clout within the Congress had its rippling effect. The youth, particularly in Bengal, turned to violent means, picking up guns and bombs. They started targeting those British bureaucrats who were known to be (or assumed to be) cruel and harsh where it concerned Indians. It was decided to throw a bomb on a railway compartment, in which a district judge—Douglas Kingford, known for flogging dissenting Indians—was believed to be travelling on 30, April 1908. One Khudiram Bose and Prafulla Chaki undertook the mission. Unfortunately, two innocent English women, who died in the blast, occupied the compartment, targeted judge was not there. British newspapers screamed for vengeance. A region-wise hunt was launched with full force. During the search for the conspirators the police found huge cache of arms and ammunition in Calcutta on 2nd May 1908, leading to further outcry, both in India and England. The young terrorists were extremely unhappy over what they had done, even by default. Full of remorse over this terrible mistake of killing innocent women, Chaki shot himself. Khudi Ram Bose was caught, tried and hanged. Tilak tried to save him by taking cudgels on his behalf, stipulating in *'Kesri'* that Khudiram Bose was sad and sorry over avoidable killing of the family of one Mr. Kennedy having died in an attack meant for cruel Douglas Kingsford. The young revolutionaries of Bengal, he said, had adopted the tactics of the Russian anarchists 'not for the sake of self-interest but owing to the exasperation produced by the autocratic exercise of power by the unrestrained and powerful white official class.' The Raj, he concluded, had brought destruction on itself. The only solution according to him was for the British to leave India immediately, granting the long cherished Swaraj.

Tilak's Call for Swaraj

Initially, the authorities ignored Tilak's statements. But when he continued with his tirade describing the bomb as 'magic', 'a sacred formula' and an 'amulet', exhorting the extremists to take on the might of the Empire, the authorities could take it no more because Tilak was a powerful politician and his opinions and ideas carried a lot of weight where influencing young Indians was concerned. He was arrested for sedition and held without bail. Tilak retained Jinnah as his defence lawyer. This choice reflected the growing stature of Jinnah within the Congress and his open-mindedness in taking up the case of a political opponent who had virtually wrecked the party. In the court, however, Tilak elected to defend himself. Just as well, because, turning to Hindu belief of Karma and Dharma—the line of defence he took was that as a newspaper editor it was his 'Dharma' to speak freely on public events, without fear or favour. He also pointed out that it was the Dharma of a jury to defend the 'freedom of the press'. The defence offered by Tilak did not impress the jury consisting of seven Europeans and two Parsis. He was sentenced to serve six years imprisonment in Mandalay, a place where there were too few Hindus to be influenced or impressed by Tilak.

With Tilak out of the way, the iron hand of the British authorities clamped even tighter norms on the dissidents. New laws suspended trial by jury, increased the penalties for sedition, and gave magistrates further powers to close down newspapers, seize their presses. Holding of 'meetings' by Indians were further restricted. Hundreds of suspected terrorists were rounded up all over the country; leaders with extremist inclinations were deported. Bipin Chandra Pal and Lala Lajpatrai escaped to London, with the later moving further on to New York. Here he founded the Indian Home Rule League and edited a newspaper called 'Young India' to explain harsh realities of the British rule and Indian nationalism. He wrote an open letter, banned in India, to Lloyd George, the Prime Minister of Britain, in 1917 with a bitterness that encapsulated the thinking of educated and concerned Indians of the time.

In spite of all the measures adopted by the British to stifle increasingly loud voice of the Indians seeking freedom from the foreign rulers, the government could not totally prevent public meetings and speeches by the local leaders. In Madras, a respected local leader-Chidambaram Pillay—was sentenced to transportation for life; the judge observing that there was neither any reason nor occasion for making a political speech. The Anglo-Indians were happy, but Morley in London was upset. He apparently believed in the saying that,' when you use force to silent someone he is inclined to use force to make himself heard'. In this he was right, because the India youth, particularly in Punjab and Bengal did whatever that they could to restore the pride in their brethren. They cheerfully went to the gallows when caught and did leave their footprint for the likes of Bhagat Singh to follow in the later years.

Sporadic terrorist activity continued in spite of all the repressive measures adopted by the government. There were attempts on the lives of important British officials, some successful and some failures. Minto's comment after the first attempt on his life seems to be a masterpiece of British sang-froid: 'I hope that the public opinion won't take the unreasonable view that the deeds of a few anarchists are proof of the disloyalty of all India.'(Mason pp281). Minto, however, did not fail to realise that the growth of education and political awareness had created aspirations in India which could not be ignored, and that it was urgently necessary to associate Indians with 'an administration which our military alone guarantees.'

Concurrently, with turbulence rising in India, Morley was pressing on with his plans for reforms. In this, he was ably supported and assisted by his Parliamentary undersecretary, Edwin Montagu, who shared his master's passionate concern for India. That Montagu was a genuine India lover and had a passion to improve the lot of Indians not withstanding aberrations caused by various Indian and British hardliners is clear from the speech that he made on 6 July 1910, while discussion on the budget for India was being examined by the parliament. He said, "We must remember, however, that the yeast necessary to leaven a loaf is very small; when the majority have no ideas or views, the opinion of the educated minority is the most prominent fact in the situation. How much earnest thought and hasty judgment centres on the word 'unrest'. Of course, there is unrest...And when we undertook the government of the country, when further, we deliberately embarked on a policy of educating the people on Western lines, we caused the unrest because we wished to colour Indian ideals with Western aspirations." Expressing his unhappiness over the conduct of administration in India he said, "The officials administrate and do not govern. They refuse to explain themselves...they misuse power." Too bad that the Indians did not have Montagu sufficiently high up in hierarchy to take up cudgels on their behalf in a way that could mould the thinking of decision makers in London.

In 1908, while the Indian Councils Act was still being drafted, Morley managed to get an Indian appointed as law member of the Viceroy's Executive Council. He also hoped that the 'reformed' legislative council in India would serve the latter as a whetstone. Kitchener resented intrusion of an Indian into the haloed precincts of the Council. He told the Viceroy that he was much more concerned about outrages committed by Punjabis because 'they are the fighting classes from which we draw our Army' and because, in an emergency, they would be more difficult to cow. Instead, he pressed for the rigorous prohibition of all obnoxious public meetings and seditious publications as well as for the infliction of the death penalty upon anyone who attempted to tamper with the loyalty of his soldiers, which was in fact never, at any period, in serious doubt (*Kitchner-Portrait of an Imperialist* by Philip Magnus).

Morley ignored Kitchner's reservations on the subject; and when Minto tried to endorse Kitchner's opinion he told him that he was convinced that conciliation, not repression, was the right policy. "Reforms," he wrote to Minto, "may not save the Raj, but if they don't nothing else will." To these remarks, Minto replied, "if reforms do not save the Raj nothing else will", I am afraid I must utterly disagree. "The Raj will not disappear in India as long as the British race remains what it is, because we shall fight for the Raj as hard as we have ever fought, if it comes to fighting, and we shall win as we have always won"(Minto Papers M 1007 and 8 May 1907).

Morley emphasised the two-fold purpose of the legislative reforms in his final dispatch to Minto on 27 November 1908. "It was to enable Government to realise the wants, interests, and sentiments of the governed; and, on the other hand to give the government a better chance of understanding, as occasion arises, the case for the government, against the misrepresentation of ignorance and malice".[1] Seasoned politicians that these two were, they were not willing to take a long-term perspective of the whole issue: "If we can hatch some plan and policy for half a generation that will be something, and if for a whole generation, that would be better. Only I am beset, as you assuredly are, on doing nothing to 'loosen the bolts'." (Morley to Minto 17 April 1907). British Parliament was equally disinclined to take a long-term view. Lord Crewe, a senior and seasoned parliamentarian spoke for most of his contemporaries when he remarked in the House of Lords on 24 February 1909: "What will be the future of India fifty, sixty, or a hundred years hence need not, I think, trouble us. It is on the knees of the gods. And all we have got to do is to provide; as best as we can for conditions of the moment, having, of course, an eye to the future, but not troubling ourselves about what may happen in days when to use Sheridan's words—all of us are dead and most of us are forgotten".

The King-Emperor was not happy with this turn of events where Indians were allowed to sit on such an important Council. Edward VII voiced his opinion on this Minto-Morley proposal thus: ' Having given a deep and detailed thought to the proposal, His Majesty views this development as a step that is fraught with the greatest danger to the maintenance of British Empire under British rule.' He agreed, however, with very bad grace, noting petulantly: 'Morley knows how strong my views are on the subject and so does Minto, but they don't care what I say.' But Morley was very clear in his mind as to what needed to be done for making Indians friends of the Raj. 'I am more and more convinced that our policy has been right. It may be that the notion of cooperation between foreigners and alien subjects is a dream, very likely: then the alternative is pure repression and the naked sword, he told some of his well-meaning friends. "The only chance", he (Morley) wrote to Minto, "be it a good chance or a bad chance, is to do our best and make English rulers friends with Indian leaders, and at the same time to do our best to train them in habits of political responsibility".[2]

Opposition to the appointment of an Indian member to the Viceroy's Council was intense. The British Cabinet was also greatly influenced by the opposition of Lords Ripon and Elgin, they were concerned that the Indian member would be privy to secrets pertaining to military and foreign relations and that could be dangerous where British interests were concerned. Vested interests, largely led by Anglo-Indians, whipped up a controversy over the issue. A correspondent in a letter to *The Englishman*' dated 1 April 1907 expressed—what could be termed as the view of majority of Englishmen and the Anglo-Indians—thus; "There is a fear that there were great possibilities 'to hand us over to those English speaking Babus', he appealed to the English Press, the Anglo-Indian Defence Association and such other public bodies to stir themselves to protect us before it is too late." Minto thought of it to be a narrow view based almost entirely on assumption that it is impossible to trust a native in a position of great responsibility: he decided to ignore all these reservations and protests. He recognised the necessity of keeping the loyal and moderate men among the educated class on the side of the government. He was certain that all the adverse reactions on the issue will gradually subside; and decided that this first shot in the campaign for the native participation will be a good education of the sort of things that were to be expected; to his credit, he decided to brave the storm.

Morley wanted to display the 'moral strength' of the British. He felt that this strength could only be derived through association of Indians in the administration of their country. In the House of Lords, Morley said, "Military strength, material strength, we have in abundance. What we still want to acquire is moral strength...in guiding and controlling the people of India in the course of which we are now launching them. The bitter cry against the Indian Member grows more and more shrill—reinforced by our 'Muslims'. But if I once make the recommendation, the cry will drop." The Muslims wanted that there should be two and not one Indian Representative and one of these should be a Muslim. The community even sent a delegation to England to seek redress, but the Secretary of State curtly turned their plea down because in his opinion two Indians at one go could be counter-productive. Morley was

aware of likely Hindu reaction if the majority community was equated
with the minority Muslims. Jinnah took no notice of the Muslim sentiment
over the issue. He was busy convincing the selected candidate (Lord
Sinha—a top flight lawyer) to sacrifice his huge income in the interest of
the country.

Earlier, Curzon had dismissed the idea with his usual airs of white
man's misplaced notion of superiority. He had said that in the whole of
Indian continent there was no Indian who could be considered as
capable of being appointed to that post. He had rejected the idea out
of hand. The prime minister overruled him and a decision to find a
suitable Indian was taken. The man chosen for this role by Minto and
Morley was a Moderate Congressman and a highly successful lawyer,
Satyendra P Sinha (later Lord Sinha, under secretary of state for India).
There was another candidate, P M Mukherjee— scion of a prominent
Bengali Zemindar family. Minto rejected Mukherjee, saying that 'Sinha
is comparatively 'white' and Mukherjee is as black as my hat'. Sinha
turned down the offer, much to the chagrin of Minto. His reason was
that by accepting such an appointment he would be losing approximately
ten thousand pounds a year that he was earning as a Barrister. The
Congress leadership dispatched Gokhale and Jinnah to persuade Sinha
to change his mind. It was a long drawn effort but Jinnah finally managed
to convince Sinha when he drew his attention to the fact that Gokhale,
in his bid to help Indian cause, had voluntarily limited his income to a
beggarly sum of Rs 75 per month. That he himself had cut down on a
flourishing legal practice in order to work for the party was another
argument offered by Jinnah.

Sinha believed that due to the British presence in India his country
was quiet, otherwise there would have been chaos, anarchy and disorder
that would have taken them back to the black days of misrule by an
Aurangzeb or loot by Nadir Shah. If the English left, he said in a
conversation during official dinner, "We would have to telegraph to
Aden to get them to return, else India would be in a turmoil." The
whites had clearly chosen a right 'poodle' to further their cause in the
country when the intelligentsia was waking up to the injustice of a
foreign rule.

Morley-Minto Reforms

The Indian Council Act, more commonly known as the Morley-Minto
reforms, was passed by the Parliament on 25th May 1909. Membership
of the Imperial Legislative Council was increased from 25 to 60, in addition
to the eight ex-officio members of the Executive Council. Thirty-six were
officials, and five were nominated non-officials, thus ensuring a permanent

majority over the remaining 27 members who, for the first time ever, were to be elected. The electorate was very select and limited only to graduates of long-standing, rich land-owners and those who had been paying municipal and other taxes for a specific duration. There were reserved seats for the minorities, particularly six seats for the Muslims to be elected only by Muslim voters. In addition, Minto also promised to nominate two Muslims, if none of the other special constituencies elected them. Effectively it meant that out of the twenty-seven elected members eight would be Muslims. It was also decided that to qualify as a voter, a Muslim needed to have a taxable income of Rs 3000 only, a Hindu required an income of Rs thirty thousand. A Hindu graduate needed to have been a graduate for thirty years and a Muslim only for three years. The scheme was hedged around with safeguards where British interests were concerned. Viceroy and provincial governors were given powers to override legislatures and ministerial councils whenever they felt necessary in the 'public interest'. The franchise qualifications, based on income and education, were stringent. Out of a population of over 300 million only five million were qualified to vote for provincial legislatures and only one million for the central legislature.

There were similar changes in the provincial legislators as well. But the important difference was that they were all to have a majority of elected members. And in all the councils, both central and provincial, members were allowed to debate and vote on proposed legislations and budgets. Gokhale, Surendranath Bannerjee, and Motilal Nehru an upcoming and a brilliant lawyer, were among the prominent Congressmen elected to the Council. Jinnah, though, he thoroughly disapproved the concept of separate electorate, was elected as Muslim member from Bombay. One of the first acts of these Congressmen was to move a resolution prohibiting the recruitment of Indian indentured labourers for South Africa, as the whole of India had been shocked by news of the violent repression of peaceful protesters led by M K Gandhi.

Divide and Rule-Its Manifestation

Minto made the official stand clear in his very first address to the Reformed Council when he said, "this representative Government in its Western sense is totally inapplicable to the Indian Empire and would be uncongenial to the traditions of Indian populations—that the safety and welfare of this country must depend on the supremacy of British administration—and that supremacy can, in no circumstances, be delegated to any kind of representative assembly."

India owes to Lord Minto the system of 'Communal Representation', observed Sir Surendranath Bannerjee. Jinnah was more vociferous in expressing his opinion, and in keeping with his penchant for subtle and piercing rhetoric where the issue involved concerned hapless Indians, was more than eloquent in denouncing the goings on in that distant land just because, the British administration had ignored to protect the interests of its subjects. Minto considered Jinnah's language to be intemperate while speaking on the resolution, and he tried to reprimand him. Jinnah rebuffed him with a stinging retort: "My Lord, I should feel much inclined to use much stronger language. But I am fully aware of the constitution of this Council, and I do not wish to trespass for one single moment," Minto was struck dumb. There were others who described the whole exercise as socially heinous, malignant and oppressive in the columns of the national press. Those who think that Lord Minto had merely to concede what was thrust upon him by the Muslims would do well to ponder over the words of the prominent Muslim leader, Mr. Muhammad Ali, who in his address at the Indian National Congress had said, "Some months previously a Muslim deputation had waited at Simla on the Viceroy, Lord Minto, to place before him and his government a statement of the Muslim demands in connection with the Minto-Morley Reforms. There is no harm in saying that the deputation's was a command performance! It was clear that the government could no longer resist the demands of educated Indians and, as usual, it was about to dole out a morsel that would keep them gagged for some years. Hither to fore, the Mussalmans had acted very much like the Irish prisoners in the docks who, in reply to the judge's enquiry whether he had any counsel to represent him in the trial, had frankly replied that he had 'friends in the jury'. Lord Morley, joint author of the Minto-Morley reforms evidently took the same view while formulating the so-called reforms when it sought to divide the electorate on communal lines."

Minto-Morley Reforms was an exercise to put power not into the hands of those who demanded reform but into the hands of those on whose cooperation the Raj had long relied. Chiefly making local self-government bodies the electorates for council seats did it. The Reforms Act of 1909, conferred upon the Muslims constitutional safeguards and weightage, as a protection against the majority. Introduction of separate electorates for Muslims and other minorities effectively set in motion the sequence of events which eventually snowballed into break up of India. May be such a legislative provision was required to balance the two main communities in term of their representation but it certainly was a British ploy to prolong their Raj. 'Divide and Rule' might not have been an intention but no effort was made by the government to educate the Indian leaders or the masses with regard to the desirability of such a classification.

As this narrative will establish in due course this apparent neglect first sowed seeds of distrust between Hindus and Muslims, and then destroyed, the unity and integrity of India. But it would be unfair to blame only the British. Native leaders, particularly men of the stature of Dadabhai Naoroji, Tilak and Gokhale also made no effort in that direction. Mohammad Ali Jinnah, who had joined Congress only in 1906, though hailed as harbinger of Hindu Muslim unity, was too new in 1909 to be taken seriously either by Hindus or Muslims. The Act, thus, was not so much a stepping-stone in the direction of responsible government; it was a disintegrating factor that ultimately broke this country up.

The reluctant trader who had become ruler of India by default had by now tasted enough blood to start working on schemes and making plans that could ensure continuation of the Raj and also give the natives a sense of having achieved something. Consequently, it is not surprising that when Montagu-Chelmsford, and later Parliamentary Committees sat down to shape the 1919, Reforms the very idea of India vanished from the Bill, to be replaced instead by a plethora of sundry headings, like Hindu, Muslim, Sikh, Maratha, Brahmin, non-Brahmin, Indian-Christian, Anglo-Indian, English and other such divisive sub-divisions of the Indian Nationality. The Government of India insisted that special conditions prevailing in the country required creation of class, communal and special electorates. The white rulers were bent upon injecting the germs of 'special class representation' into the body politics of India. In the absence of any such distinction they really had no chance to hope for continuation of the Raj for long. Luckily for them, some Indian leaders, lacking in vision and understanding of their own divisive culture, fell into the trap of the British. They coveted the propinquity to power that their status gave them.

Gokhale soon realised that the Indian Councils Act of 1909, had not been enacted with a view to transfer any power or responsibility to the Indians. Instead, it had been more of a charade carried out in order to win over the more conservative elements in India. There was never any plan to democratise Indian Institutions in the foreseeable future. (Till then, Gokhale was strongly of the opinion that, " They (educated Indians) frankly and loyally accepted British rule because they were convinced that that rule alone could secure in the country the peace and order which were necessary for slowly evolving nation out of the heterogeneous elements of which it was composed, and ensuring to it a steady advance in different directions."—(Speeches of Gopal Krishna Gokhale p 1006). Being a Moderate, Gokhale could not envisage radical changes in the proposals. He did want to have 'provincial autonomy' introduced as a first step towards the ultimate goal of freedom. For the present, he was happy to leave the overall control of the country with central authorities; he wanted the Council to be renamed as the Legislative Assembly of India, which would be freed from the control of Secretary of State. He also wanted Indians to be considered for the grant of commission in the army. His detailed plan for the purpose of Reforms got to be known as "Gokhale's Political Testament." Morley perhaps did have some kind of an idea to provide limited latitude to the Indians but neither the government in London, nor in India was enthusiastic about doing anything of the kind. Kitchner and his ICS coterie would have none of this. In their opinion continuing with the status quo could only ensure the permanency of the Raj. With a non-effective Minto at the helm in India, guided by his hardliners, Morley could not stop the sabotage of his efforts at liberalization. That the narrow and factional approach of some of the Indian leaders of the time was helpful to the Raj was purely by default.

Morley stepped down from the India Office on 7 November 1910, handing over charge to Lord Crewe, who had previously been the colonial secretary. Minto's tenure was also at an end. As a final service to the Indians, Morley blocked Lord Kitchner's bid (which was rather a burning desire with him) to become Viceroy of India, and appointed Lord Hardinge of Pinehurst instead. Like Minto, Hardinge also had India in his blood, as his grandfather had been Governor General from 1844 to 1848.

Re-unification of Bengal

One of the first acts of Hardinge was a to announce re-unification of Bengal, because he felt that a great injustice had been done to the Bengalis by reducing them to a minority in both the provinces. George V, who had succeeded to the British throne by then, supported all the moves made by Hardinge that could pacify the Indians. George V had visited India as a crown prince and had carried fond memories of the country and its people.

The decision to reunify Bengal, and at the same time create a new province of Bihar and Orissa, was one of the best-kept secrets in British imperial history. King George had expressed a desire to celebrate his coronation as king-emperor with a grand Durbar in Delhi. The re-unification would be announced at the Durbar, as a surprise boon to the Bengalis. So too, would a second boon, suggested by the home member of Hardinge's Executive Council, Sir John Jenkins; the removal of the seat of government from Calcutta to the old Mughal capital, Delhi. It was expected to act as a 'tonic' for the Indians. Moving the seat of power out of ever-restless Bengal had been contemplated for a long time, as neither the climate, nor the geographical location suited efficient running of the Country, but the 'powerbrokers' of Calcutta in the form of British businessmen were always trying to influence official decisions to suit their commercial interests, and were doing just about anything to prevent such a move that could have an adverse effect on their expansion plans.

On 12 December 1911, the king-emperor stood under a golden dome in the royal pavilion at the center of the Durbar ground and made the announcement. The estimated crowd of over 10,000 people stood silent for a moment and then the enormity of the announcement sank in. There were spontaneous cheering and celebrations. Simultaneously, the announcement was also made in Calcutta. If the move of the Capital was expected to be a snub to Bengali Hindus it failed miserably to excite any negative reaction. With all their intelligence, the power of understanding and typical British supercilious air of superiority, the British had not, even after over a hundred years in the country understood that to a Bengali Hindu, Calcutta was the centre of the universe. So where the government went and where the Viceroy took his residence next was totally immaterial to him.

The Muslims said little about Delhi—they were too deeply shocked by the decision to reunify Bengal. Morley had assured them that such a thing would never happen. Surendranath Bannerjee led the celebrations on reunification as he had led the agitation on the subject; he claimed it to be 'the triumph of the British justice and the vindication of constitutional methods used to settle political controversies'. The Muslims saw the whole thing differently. 'No bombs, no boons', was the new slogan coined, bewailing the fact that the concessions were only achieved through terrorism.

With this one move the British had alienated their main support base in India, the Muslims no longer believed that their future was aligned with the continued presence of the British in the country. Muslim leaders and intellectuals started several newspapers in 1911 and 1912 to propagate their views on the subject of majority rule per se. More prominent among these were 'Comrade', founded by Muhammad Ali, and 'Al-Hilal', founded by Abul Kalam Azad. Both of them saw themselves as more of religious leaders rather than anything else. Both were entitled to the honorific title 'Maulana', signifying a man of great Quranic learning. Maulana Azad, twenty five years old son of a famous Muslim family of saints and scholars, had adopted the name 'Azad' signifying 'Free', to show that he now belonged to no sect or orthodox religious doctrine. Although born in Mecca, he was raised in Calcutta where he had become closely involved with revolutionary politics, even though these were almost entirely dominated by Hindus. Initially, Azad had reservations about Hindu dominance, he gave call for formation of an 'Islamic State', calling upon Muslims to organise themselves into "Hizbullah" – the party of God—an entity in which Britons and Hindus will have no place. Azad was later to become president of Congress, but at that stage in his thinking, he condemned Muslim cooperation with any Hindu dominated organisation, calling instead for a jihad, a holy war for independence.

Leaders of Muslim organisations were trying hard to enrol those Muslims who had a definite standing in different walks of life. Towards this end in view, in 1912 at Bankipur, the council of the ultra-loyalist Muslim League changed the aims stated in its original constitution to include: 'The attainment of a form of self-government suitable to India...through constitutional means—by promoting unity and fostering public spirit among the people of India, and by cooperating with other communities for the said purpose.' (Pirzada 'Foundation of Pakistan'). This new clause had been added on being urged by Mohammad Ali Jinnah, whom the League leaders had been persuading for a long time to join hands with them. Jinnah had made inclusion of such a clause as a condition for joining Muslim League. He did join in 1913, on the condition that his loyalty to it and to Muslim interests 'would in no way and at no time imply even a shadow of disloyalty to the larger national cause to which his life was dedicated.'

Elsewhere, Hardinge got busy with his plans for building a new capital, which was to be a symbol of British power and permanence of Raj. It was the eighth city to be built in the area by various rulers over the centuries, in clear defiance of an old Indian prophecy that, whoever builds a new city in Delhi will lose it. It was to be designed by Sir Herbert Baker and Sir Edward Lutyens, the most celebrated British architect of his day. Hardinge had expected the new capital to be built immediately or at least during his tenure, but it took almost twenty years to be completed. The capital, however, had moved from Calcutta immediately after the decision to move to Delhi was taken. It functioned from temporary offices and the buildings of the old Mughal Empire.

To formally celebrate the setting up of the capital in Delhi, Hardinge decided to lead a procession into the old city, riding in state on the back of an elephant with his wife beside him, acknowledging the cheers of a happy crowd. As he entered the great boulevard of Chandni Chowk—literally meaning 'Silver Street'—an unknown terrorist, never caught or identified in spite of a reward of ten thousand pounds, threw a bomb into the howdah. The man holding the ceremonial umbrella over the Viceroy was killed outright. Hardinge survived, but he suffered serious injuries, which took a long time to heal. Above everything else, he was seriously demoralised by this turn of events and became more and more erratic in his behaviour.

The Round Table Group-A new Concept about Governance

Some young men started the Round Table Group in South Africa shortly after the Boer War. These energetic and obviously well meaning men were helping Lord Milner in his reconstruction work in South Africa. They undertook a campaign of political education of the natives, their efforts finally led to the formation of the Union of South Africa in 1910. Soon after this success they conceived the revival of a more ambitious project for creation of Imperial Federation, a scheme, which actually had been lying dormant for a long time. For this purpose, the leader of the group, one Lionel Curtis visited Canada, Australia, New Zealand and some other colonies of the Empire. The group started publishing a house journal 'Round Table' in London with a view to exchange information on the project. In 1912, Sir William Harris and Lord Weston, both of whom belonged to the Indian Civil Service and were members of the Round Table Group first made the first suggestion that India should also be admitted to the group. Mr. Curtis approved the suggestion and in the autumn of 1915 gathered a group of eminent people who were interested in and were acquainted with the problems of India. The first conclusion the group arrived at was the same as some prominent Indians had been saying for a long time; that is, 'a further advance on the path marked the Minto-Morley Reforms was a step over the precipice and a plunge towards anarchy; and if, responsible government was to be at all introduced, no doubt, gradually and with due regard to the safety and security—there was no alternative to "Dyarchy"—the creation of two governments in one area, one responsible to the British electorate and the other to the India electorate to be formed in various localities. Curtis then urged that one of the members of the group, with lifelong experience of Indian conditions, should assume the position of a technical expert and evolve a suitable scheme for the future of India. Sir William Duke, a former governor of Bengal took up the task on behalf of the Group and produced an approach paper for consideration by the Round Table. After consultations and appropriate changes the paper was printed in May 1916 for private circulation, Lord Chelmsford, the Viceroy asked for and was provided with a copy of the report by Curtis. It contained the first statement of the theory of 'Dyarchy' i.e. dual government in the provinces; this finally found its place as an essential feature of the Montague-Chelmsford plan of Reforms. Curtis had also advocated that the British Commonwealth could not survive unless British subjects in the self-governing Dominions were on an equal footing with those in the United Kingdom and shared its supreme responsibilities.

The Indian leadership was not very enthusiastic about these developments as the proposals fell far too short of expectations. What made it even worse were two events of tremendous magnitude: one, passage of Rowlett Act providing for preventive detention, and the second was the brutal massacre of innocent Indians who had only collected to celebrate a traditional harvesting festival at Jallianwala Bagh in Amritsar. This was done on the orders of General Dyer who wanted to create a situation of fear and terror into the hearts of those who wanted to be free of the British. Proper working of the Government of India Act, 1919, was also seriously hampered when Gandhi launched his non-violent, non-cooperation movement in the wake of these two events. In 1920, on his appointment as the President of the Home Rule League in place of Mrs. Besant, Gandhi changed the mission of the League—henceforth, it was going to be complete 'Swaraj'—freedom from all ties with the British, instead of 'self-government' within the British Empire.

Footnotes

1. Proposals of the Government of India and Dispatch of the Secretary of State 4426(1908).
2. Morley to Minto 2 April 1909, Minto Papers M 1009, No. 22.
3. William Archer India and the Empire, London (1917), p. 295.

4

Mohandas Karamchand Gandhi

Born on 2 October 1869 to the Dewan of a tiny state—Porbandar in Gujarat—Mohandas Gandhi had been brought up in a strict religious environment. The family were devout Hindus, but not rigidly orthodox. Members of all faiths and leanings were welcome to the Karamchand (his father's) household, be they Parsis, Muslims, or of any other leaning. Jainism was a more prominent sect in Gujarat, and Jain Monks were regular visitors. Jainism is an ascetic religion, based on the belief that everything in nature, even a rock or a stone, has a soul, and it is wrong to destroy life in any shape or form. The greatest Jain influence on Gandhi was its central doctrine of "Ahimsa"—non-violence. Though, ahimsa has definite interpretation in all other variations of the Hindu religion, Gandhi invested it with the more positive Jain interpretation of not simply refraining from physical violence, but of actively returning good for evil.

Mohandas wasn't a particularly bright student. He managed to pass his matriculation examination but failed in college. The family decided to pool its, not so liberal, resources and sent him to England to obtain an English legal qualification. Gandhi learned more than law during his time in London. This was his first taste of an alien environment and culture. Having come away from his native Porbandar for the first time he started seeing himself as an Indian rather than a Gujarati. He also became a member of the London Vegetarian Society. Fellow members introduced him to the works of radical thinkers like John Ruskin and Count Leo Tolstoy. An exposure to these two and their works had a tremendous impact on young Gandhi as their philosophy of life generally jelled with his earlier understanding of Jainism. The Russian writer, who was also more of a social reformer, preached the doctrine of brotherly love, non-violent acceptance of evil, and renunciation of wealth; Ruskin, the English art critic and moralist, was a stern critic of the industrial society. Equally important to Gandhi's development was Madame Blavatsky's Theosophical Society. He never joined the Theosophists, but had several friends who were active members. Through them he got to discover roots of Hindu religion when he was given an English translation of Bhagwad Gita, one of the most sacred Hindu texts, which forms part of the great classic, the Mahabharata. The Theosophists also introduced him to Sir Edwin Arnold's 'The Light of Asia', an account of the teachings of Buddha. Gandhi now wanted to learn more and more about various other religions of the world, particularly Christianity. Even though he found the Old Testament to be too difficult to grasp its nuances, the New Testament seemed to have added to what all he had imbibed from various religions till then. Concurrently, he also continued with his studies of law.

On his return to India in 1891, he found that it was not all that easy to establish himself as a lawyer in Bombay. He neither had the money, nor connections needed to set up a legal practice; what was worse, he had no knowledge of Indian law. Finally, when a case in Bombay's small causes court did come his way he found himself too nervous and timid to get up and cross-examine the witnesses. The client was visibly upset with his England trained lawyer. Gandhi had to handover the case, and his small fee to another lawyer. Despairing over this failure in his chosen field of profession, he returned to Rajkot, and started scraping a living drafting legal documents.

If the fate had ordained differently, this might have been the last that anyone heard of Mohandas Karamchand Gandhi—a failed lawyer, with hardly any social or financial standing, trying to bring up his children like any lower middle class family man, who not having succeeded in life, takes out his frustrations on his wife and children and then fades away. This was not to be so. After about one year of drudgery, a Memon Muslim merchant from Porbandar, Dada Abdullah Sheth offered Gandhi an assignment in South Africa, where he had various legal problems connected with his business. With hardly any other option available, Gandhi accepted the assignment with alacrity. He sailed from Bombay in April 1893, a struggling 24-year-old lawyer with an uncertain future, and not so distinguished a present.

Gandhi in South Africa

Gandhi found Natal a totally different kind of atmosphere. He was just about the only Indian who could talk to the rulers in their own language. Even the wealthy Muslim merchants hardly had any formal education, and had only a smattering of spoken English, barely enough to get by with their day-to-day business. The vast majority of 60,000 or so Indians were peasants with no education. They had all been shipped as indentured labour for the sugar plantations and coalmines of Natal.

Until his arrival in South Africa, Gandhi had never faced racial discrimination. In England, he had been accepted as any other Law student, and had been enrolled at the Inner Temple with other Whites, with hardly anyone making a racist comment. He had been accepted on an equal footing. Yet within a few days of his arrival in South Africa, he came face to face with naked prejudice. Travelling from Durban to Pretoria, where he was to appear in court, he was thrown off the train after a white passenger refused to share a first class compartment with him. He spent the night shivering in the waiting room of a wayside station, too timid to ask the stationmaster for the warm coat locked away with his luggage. But, that shiver in the night in a foreign and apparently hostile land seems to have definitely awakened some inner strength in him. Mohandas suddenly found himself totally transformed. His habitual timidity was replaced by a fearlessness and strength of character that became his hallmark during the rest of his life. There were further humiliations when no hotel would give him a room, ostensibly due to non-availability, but effectively because of the colour of his skin.

The humiliations heaped upon him during that traumatic journey served only to strengthen his resolve to tackle the issue of racial discrimination in South Africa. Immediately on arrival in Pretoria, he called a meeting of the Indian population, drew their attention to insults heaped by the Whites, and urged them to organise themselves in a manner that could make the government take note of their plight. Gandhi's political life had begun. By the time he finished with the legal works of Dada Abdullah Sheth he had been able to create the 'Natal Indian Congress'. He was able to persuade the Natal government to reduce a prohibitive poll tax imposed on Indians, so as to deter them from settling in South Africa once their indentures were over. By the by, he was also able to establish the rights of Indians to travel first or second class on South African trains, provided they were properly attired. Thereafter, he planned to return to India.

Vastly impressed by the relief that Gandhi had been able to obtain from the local government, the Indian community requested him to stay a while longer and help them contest a controversial racist bill denying Indians the right to vote. He agreed to extend his stay by one month. The month eventually became twenty years, during which Gandhi came to India just twice. The first of these trips was in 1896, to collect his family and take them to South Africa. On his return he was almost killed by a White mob trying to stop 600 Indians landing at Durban. The wife of the superintendent of police rescued him. Disguised as a police constable he was smuggled out of the police station and taken to safety. Typical of the man, he refused to either identify his attackers or to bring any charges against them.

Now that he had taken on the responsibility of improving the lot of the Indians in South Africa, Gandhi immersed himself totally in this task. He campaigned continuously and vigorously for the rights of the India community, brandishing the proclamation of Queen Victoria as their 'Magna Carta'. The queen had issued a proclamation when the British government had taken over the task of ruling over India from the East India Company, after the revolt of 1857 wherein certain rights were guaranteed to the Indian subjects.

Proclamation of Queen Victoria: "It is Our earnest desire to stimulate the peaceful industry of India, to promote utility and improvements, and to administer the government for the benefit of all Our subjects resident therein. ....We declare it to be Our royal will and pleasure that none be in any wise favoured, none molested or disquieted, by the reason of their religious faith or observance, but all shall alike enjoy the equal and impartial protection of the law; and We do strictly charge and enjoin all those who may be in authority under Us that they abstain from all interference with the religious belief or worship ....Our subjects, of whatever race or creed, be freely and impartially admitted to office in Our service, the duties of which they may be qualified by their education, ability, and integrity duly to discharge."(Mason pp 10-11)

Where Gandhi was concerned the rights of Indians were clearly defined by the Queen in her proclamation. The governments in England and in India generally supported the fight that he had taken up on behalf of the Indians in South Africa, because apartheid wasn't really appreciated by the powers that be, and the authorities in England couldn't really do much to rein in the brutally repressive government in Pretoria. This tacit support made him a firm believer in the fairness of the British, seeing their rule over India as a divinely sanctioned force for India's good. So much so, he celebrated queen's diamond jubilee in 1897, by planting a tree and distributing souvenirs and sweets to Indian children. When the Boer War started in 1899, he did his duty to Britain by raising and leading an ambulance corps of 1100 Indians, which performed valiantly in and near the frontline. He even earned a decoration for his services to the Empire. Surprisingly, and oddly, the oppression suffered by the Blacks in South Africa did not seem to have caused any serious concern to Gandhi. Perhaps, he never considered them to be equal to his fellow Indians, who he believed came from a superior culture. One theory is that he shared the White man's fear of being overrun by the Black majority population if they were given any kind of liberty.

By 1901, Gandhi, feeling that others could now carry out his work in South Africa returned to India, setting up legal practice in Bombay. He was no longer the timid Mohandas who had failed miserably in his earlier effort to become a successful lawyer. What all he had done in South Africa for the Indians had already made Gandhi's name well known in India. His experiences in a wide and diverse range of fields in South Africa had given him enough self-confidence to lock horns with the best of legal brains in Bombay. Soon enough he was able to live in considerable style with a large bungalow in the fashionable suburb of Santa Cruz. But by now, he had also become aware of a need to participate in the affairs of the country. He attended the December 1901 session of Congress in Calcutta. He made an impassioned plea on behalf of the 100,000 Indians suffering all kinds of humiliations in South Africa. He managed to get a resolution passed supporting the move for civil rights of Indians in that far off-land. His intensity, apparent honesty of purpose and general demeanour so impressed Gokhale, that he immediately took this new recruit to the Indian cause under his wing as a personal protégé. However, before Gandhi could start making any political headway in India, he received a telegram from the Indians in South Africa, begging him to return and plead their case before the Secretary of State, Joseph Chamberlain, who was about to pay a visit to South Africa for an 'on the ground' assessment of the situation. Gandhi immediately rushed to Johannesburg to take up cudgels on behalf of the hapless Indian community in that far off-land.

Chamberlain did give a patient hearing to Gandhi, but refused to intercede on behalf of Indians on the premise that the imperial government, as a matter of policy, did not interfere in the internal affairs of self-governing colonies. Gandhi was dismayed with this reaction of the Secretary of State, particularly when the new regulations were found to be much more harsher where Indians were concerned. He felt that whereas back home in India there were other leaders to take up issues with the government, Indians in South Africa had nobody who could get them a just and fair deal. He decided to stay back and start all over again his fight for getting the Indian population of South Africa their legal rights. He could see a long struggle ahead, and sent for his wife and children to join him. He did anticipate a long, hard grind for the task he had taken up, but never did he think that it would take him over twelve years before he could even think of returning to India. During that time, the (now) prosperous lawyer in his stiff white collars and snazzy silk ties would totally alter his personality, and would gradually grow into the legendary Indian sage—he would become to be known as "Mahatma" Gandhi.

Once again, works of John Ruskin acted as the catalyst. Gandhi read his 'Unto This Last' during a journey from Johannesburg to Durban. According to Gandhi himself, he felt that some of his deepest convictions were strongly reflected in that book where the author speaks of the ill-effects of capitalism, property and modern society. He agreed with the author when he propounds the moral and redemptive values of physical labour. Soon enough, Gandhi was putting the author's ideas into practice with his first experiment in community living. Paying 1,000 Pounds for a 100 acre for a fruit farm at Phoenix, 14 miles out of Durban, he moved in with his family, friends and some admirers. The staff of his newly started 'Indian Opinion' also shifted base to this farm. Gandhi announced that he intended to retire from law and live a simple life at Phoenix. All the tasks, including menial, like cleaning of toilets- were to be performed by the individuals themselves. His wife Kasturba Gandhi and family joined in this experiment of his, not necessarily voluntarily; but for Gandhi democracy had no place in his view of the family. The wife had to sell off her treasured gold jewellery to help fund the Natal Indian Congress. By some accounts he, at times, was unnecessarily harsh with his own children.

Gandhi, himself, renounced every family tie, every comfort and started devoting himself entirely to public service. This decision of his was triggered by the harshness of war, when he, yet again, led a team of stretcher bearers during the Zulu Rebellion, where again he was awarded a medal for his selfless and fearless devotion to duty. He and his men tended both British soldiers and Zulu rebels whom no white man would touch due to a notion of racial superiority. The misery all around him, the uselessness of war, and utter waste of so many young men, convinced Gandhi that he had to follow a path of total 'non-violence' in all his endeavours. The doctrine of "Satyagraha" had started taking shape in his mind. In his scheme of things Satyagraha was not passive but an active method of seeking justice and redress. He described it as either 'soul force' or truth force'; the method of securing rights by personal suffering; "it is a reverse of resistance by arms", he declared.

The theory was soon put to test when in 1906, the Transvaal government introduced a bill designed to clear Indians out of the colony by stopping immigration and harassing those already there. Indian residents were to be finger printed and given registration certificates, which they had to carry at all times. The Indians protested strongly. This time, led by Gandhi, they registered their objection to the law by closing their shops in a "Hartal", organising mass petitions, pickets and representations, but to no avail. In any case, all Indians were not with Gandhi. Indian Christians and Tamils in South Africa, in particular, totally dissociated themselves from the agitation and branded Gandhi an agitator who was misleading the masses. This lack of unity among the affected people encouraged the government to ignore the agitation. The legislature passed the act.

Having full faith in the fairness of the British law, Gandhi went to England to plead on behalf of the suffering Indians. He met with the Secretaries of State for the colonies and for India, Lords Elgin and Morley respectively. Gandhi returned to Johannesburg with the assurance that the act would not receive royal assent. But this was mostly a usual British way of misleading the natives. A while later Transvaal became a self-governing colony. It was no longer required to refer its legislation to London for royal approval. The bill was promptly reintroduced, together with another restricting clause that debarred people from entering South Africa with a purpose of settling down unless they knew at least one European language. It became a law on 1st July 1907. Gandhi and his followers refused to register, and formed what was to be known as 'Satyagraha Association' to fight the establishment. Volunteers courted arrest in a big number to express solidarity with the Association.

Gandhi was arrested and sentenced to two months in jail with hard labour; this led to further unrest among the Indian community. General Jan Smuts, the Transvaal's colonial secretary, seeing the situation to be getting out of hand, met Gandhi and offered to repeal the act if Gandhi and his followers agreed to register voluntarily. Taking it as his moral victory, Gandhi agreed to lift the Satyagraha. A large number of Indians, who were uncomfortable with the provisions incorporated in the act resented his action and took it to be betrayal of the cause. In fact, when he came to sign the agreement, some Pathans set upon him, beating him virtually to death. When Smuts asked him to lodge a formal complaint against his attackers, he refused to do so, on the grounds that he was trying to protect the rights of Indians and did not want to cause any trouble to those who were not convinced with the correctness of his action.

To further cause a split in the Indian population Smuts reneged on his promise. This annoyed Gandhi no end. In order to register his protest, he along with over 2000 followers symbolically burnt the registration certificates in the grounds of 'Hamidia Mosque' in Johannesburg. Gandhi, along with his immediate colleagues was arrested. But the arrest did not deter his followers from resuming their Satyagraha with a renewed vigour. People crossed the border between Natal and Transvaal without permit, courting arrest in the process. Originally, Gandhi was wary of going to jail, as he felt that it might be difficult for him to survive the hard and harsh conditions. But soon enough his latent strength of character emerged, he quickly worked out a regime of cooking, exercise, prayer and study. He utilised his time in translating John Ruskin's works in his native Gujarati, spent time in imbibing teachings of the Qur'an, Gita and various other Hindu scriptural writings. Works of Bacon, Emerson, Huxley, Tolstoy, Plato and many other thinker philosophers allowed him to widen his horizon while doing his jail terms.

In 1909, various South African provinces were set to form a union, Gandhi again went to London to plead on behalf of Indians, but the effort was in vain because no body of consequence listened to him. The Union of South Africa retained all its racist laws. Gandhi returned a disappointed man. On the return voyage, he gathered his thoughts into a long essay under the title "Hind Swaraj" (Indian Home Rule). Gandhi, having lost faith in the fairness of the British system, now wanted India to discard everything foreign. He, even, opposed the use of English as the language of government and the law. What the Indian people could not make for themselves, he said, they could do without as their ancestors had done. Total boycott of imported goods was his latest call to his countrymen.

"Hind Swaraj" wasn't a definitive assessment of the situation and the Indian's appropriate response to the Raj, it was to be further refined and fine-tuned so as to be acceptable to different segments of the society. Gandhi devoted himself for the next five years in living out his ideas as expressed in Hind Swaraj. A large commune was set up on an 1100-acre farm near Johannesburg. Naming the new settlement Tolstoy Farm, Gandhi welcomed his followers there. Home was provided to the wives and children of those who were serving jail sentences for having taken part in Satyagraha. Everybody lived together as an extended family with Gandhi himself showing the way.

Gandhi started putting his theories to the test. His attitude to basic human needs like food became more rigorous, he started fasting regularly, sometimes for a week at a time: at first as a means of self-purification, and then as a penance for the misdeeds of others. At Tolstoy Farm everything was home grown, to put Gandhi's ideas on self-sufficiency into practice, everybody walked—Gandhi himself trudged 21 miles to Johannesburg everyday to attend court where he had a legal practice, no doctor was ever consulted. The sick were treated with diet and hydropathy. The various creeds, castes, and ethnic groups lived together in harmony.

In 1912, Gandhi's mentor, Gokhale, visited South Africa at the behest of the Viceroy, Lord Hardinge, to talk to Smuts and Prime Minister General Louis Botha, about the condition and position of the Indian immigrants. They both promised to repeal main anti-Indian laws.

Gokhale was given tremendous respect and dignity by the South Africa government. Wherever he went every reception in his honour was presided over by the local mayor and was attended by hundreds of white South Africans in addition to the 'coloured' population. The Government put at his disposal a state railway saloon. (*Jinnah—A Corrective Reading of Indian History* by Asiananda). In mid-November, he was received by General Botha and General Smuts, Gokhale got the assurance that an Asiatic Relief Bill will be introduced and would become Act settling all Indian grievances. Seemingly, with the help of Gokhale, Gandhi had achieved what he had set out to do for the Indians in South Africa. Gokhale tried to persuade him to return to India and to now join the main battle: That is, the one, he and other moderates were waging for India's freedom. However, before Gandhi could make up his mind on the subject, Smuts and Botha, both reneged on the promises they had made to the Viceroy's representative. In fact, more harsh laws were introduced to restrict entry of Indians into South Africa. A new act was passed effectively barring all future Indian immigration. A supreme-court judge ruled that only marriages performed under Christian rites were legal in South Africa. There was wide spread resentment among Indians over this ruling. Gandhi launched a fresh Satyagraha, calling all Indians to court arrest over this blatant violation of their religion and customs. The non-recognition of Indian marriages awakened the women folk also to take the plunge and under the leadership of Kasturba Gandhi, they started deliberately violating various laws and courting arrest. The coal-mining town of Newcastle employed over 5000 Indians and they all struck work. The managements of these mines tried to break the strike using brute force, throwing women and children out of company owned houses, denying them food and water, but they all held firm. Gandhi, who had personally taken charge of this agitation, could not find any way of feeding such a large number of people. Only course open to him was to get them all arrested and put up in jails—described by him as 'His Majesty's Hotels'. He personally led 2000 men, women and children across the border to Transvaal to court arrest. The authorities there arrested him along with some other leaders. Twice he was arrested and released, but third time he was dragged to court in manacles and sentenced to nine months of hard labour. His followers were not deterred and continued with their agitation. Fed up of the whole thing the authorities arrested them, and put the whole lot back on a train to Newcastle, where they were imprisoned inside the compounds of mines and forced to dig coal, with the supervisors becoming more and more brutal in order to break their spirit. When the news of this harsh action reached rest of the Indian community spread in different parts of South Africa, everywhere they struck work. Over 50,000 workers downed tools in sympathy with their countrymen agitating in Newcastle.

Gandhi, in the meanwhile, had kept leaders in India informed of the developments, he had been regularly sending cables and statements to various newspapers in England and India. The agitation, its aftermath, and cruel handling of the situation by the Botha government made headlines all over the world. Gokhale toured India rousing the public opinion on the issue. Lord Hardinge was equally upset over the insensitive behaviour of the South African government. He supported Gokhale's call for a 'commission of inquiry'. Pretoria finally agreed to set up a commission, but there was a fresh heartburn because all the members were White, with most of them being notorious for their 'anti-Indian' bias. Gandhi planned a fresh protest march on the issue, but he called it off when 'White' railway workers threatened to go on a strike, not because of the harsh treatment of Indians, but for some reason of their own. The Botha government found its survival under threat over this development, in addition to the Indian agitation gaining momentum. Botha, in his hour of distress turned to Gandhi and issued an appeal to him that the government's troubles had now increased beyond an acceptable limit. According to Gandhi's dictum, a Satyagrahi did not take advantage of the opponent's weakness; he withdrew his agitation. It was a move that totally disarmed his opponents, and threw them in utter confusion; for it was unfathomable for a White ruler not to take advantage of a situation when the adversary was down. Gandhi's followers were equally confused but most of them retained their faith in the wisdom of his action.

Gandhi held no official position, but seeing his tremendous hold on the immigrant population, in June 1914 Smuts called him for negotiations. The poll tax, registration, passes, and the system of indentured labour was all to be abolished, and Indian marriages were to be recognised. It was no more than a partial victory for Gandhi, because restrictions on immigration remained, so did the permit system for movement between provinces. But this was a big stride ahead, and considering his mission in South Africa accomplished, Gandhi decided to return to India (via England), much to the relief of Smuts. When Gandhi sailed homewards, Smuts declared, 'The saint has left our shores, I sincerely hope for ever.'

Gandhi arrived in England to a hero's welcome on 6 August 1914, just two days after Britain had declared war on Germany. But he was a very sick man. The strain of Satyagraha, jail terms in South Africa, and the innumerable fasts he had undertaken as penance for moral lapses by members of the Phoenix community were all catching up with him. What made matters worse was his insistence on treating himself with diet alone, and other natural means of debatable merit. The British government was concerned about his response and reaction to the war effort, which England couldn't have sustained without a wholesome contribution from India in the form of men and material. To their relief, Gandhi issued the following message to the people of India: "We are, above all, citizens of the great British Empire. Fighting as the British people are at present in a righteous cause for the good and glory of human dignity and civilisation...our duty is clear to do our best to support the British, fight with our life and property."

His followers and admirers were genuinely confused over this call to arms by someone of his stature who was so dedicated to the practice of non-violence. When questioned about this apparent conflict between his professed principles of non-violence and supporting a war, his response was typically Gandhian: the path to ahimsa was rarely an easily discernible one, he told them, since men were inevitably involved with violence simply for survival. Moreover, it would be cowardly for a Satyagrahi such as himself not to take part in a war he had done nothing to prevent, particularly since in London he enjoyed the protection of British arms. Typical of the man, he again volunteered to raise an Indian field ambulance corps.

Some 80 men volunteered, and all went well until the British army appointed a Colonel R J Baker, a former member of the Indian Medical Service, as commanding officer. He refused to accept Gandhi as the unofficial but de facto leader of these volunteers. Typically again, Gandhi launched a personal Satyagraha against Baker, leading to some kind of breakdown in the Army's chain of command; the members of this voluntary unit had come forward because Gandhi had asked them to do so. There was no way they were going to allow a mere colonel to annoy their leader. The India Office managed to effect a compromise, and the unit went into action nursing a contingent of wounded Indian troops brought over from France, due to poor health Gandhi was no longer available to lead this unit. Gandhi was now suffering from a severe attack of pleurisy, friends and doctors advised him to leave the cold and damp of the London winter and seek a warmer climate. Gentle persuasion of Kasturba Gandhi, other members of his inner circle and leaders like Gokhale, finally readied Gandhi to sail for India.

5

India and the First World War

The struggle for freedom was gaining intensity with more and more intellectuals and moderates joining either the League or the Congress. The government in London was also shaken by the goings on in India. There was a definite feeling that the loyalty of the subject race could not be taken for granted any longer. During the whole of 1913 and early 1914 when the war clouds were building, up the government in London was not averse in concluding that the moment England gets into any serious trouble elsewhere India, in its present temper, would burst into a 'Blaze of Rebellion'.[1] Germany too seemed to have counted on such a possibility. Therefore, in August 1914 when Hardinge informed the Indians that the country was at war with Germany, the overwhelming and spontaneous response of the people supporting the cause against Germany surprised both the Viceroy and the King-emperor. Even the Germans, who had been hoping that the Indians like Irish rebels would rise against Britain, were shocked at the reaction, that they were severely disappointed would be an understatement. The British had every reason to be nervous. This was a perfect opportunity for the 'virtually dormant' nationalist movement to reassert itself after three years of quiet. Instead, both Congress and the Muslim League declared their total loyalty and support to Britain in this war effort. Even Tilak, released recently, from his Mandalay gaol, cabled the King-emperor swearing his loyal support, and turned his oratory and writing skills in exhorting people to come forward and help in this 'fight for democracy'.

Renouncing his earlier hostility, Tilak went out of his way to reassure both his compatriots and the British about his honesty of purpose. On 27th August 1914, he wrote: "The reforms introduced during the administration of Lord Morley will show that the government is fully alive to the necessity of progressive change, and desire to associate people more and more in the work of the Government...this indicates a marked increase of confidence between the Ruler and the Ruled." He went on to state: "We are trying in India, as the Irish Home rulers have been doing in Ireland, for a reform of the system of administration and not for the overthrow of the Government." Acts of violence, he now felt, had retarded rather than hastened the pace of political progress. (Wolpert-*Tilak and Gokhale*, pp245-246). The American writer Fred B Fisher observed: "India rose to the support of the Allies with a spontaneous loyalty which stirred even the British pulse in those early days of the war, when glowing messages of support flooded into London from every corner of the Empire. Even erstwhile 'extremists', men like Tilak and Pal, preached cooperation with the government in the war effort." Contrary to official apprehensions, Tilak called upon his countrymen to support and assist His Majesty's Government, as it was the duty of every Indian to ensure that Germany did not win the war. Mrs. Besant also chipped in, but the theme of her utterances was that only a free India could defend the interests of the British Empire. The fate of the Empire, she said, "hinges on the fate of India, and therefore it is but wise and prudent to keep India contented by granting her freedom; a Home Ruled India was an asset to the Empire in its struggle against German militarism."[2] She had put on the garb of a radical Indian patriot in order to keep the country, as far as possible, on the safe track of constitutional agitation. She also hoped to disentangle the Nationalist extremists from their compromising alliance with the revolutionaries and to bring them closer to the Moderates within the Congress.

Within weeks, 290,000 fully trained and equipped troops, 210,000 of them Indians were on their way to France and Egypt. The first Indian Expeditionary Force, 28,500 Indians and 16,000 British troops reached the western front in Flanders just in time to hold the line against a furious German assault at the first Battle of Ypres. During the month long battle, they suffered over 7, 000 casualties. All told, during the war 1,440,437 Indians volunteered for service—even Bengalis and other groups who had been banned from the army since 1857—flocked to the recruitment centres when the situation compelled the authorities to lift ban. The Indian industry also pitched in a big way. The factories set up during the anti-British Swadeshi movement now found themselves serving Britain. The Tata Iron and Steel Works, which had come up despite all kinds of hurdles put by the British when the plant was being set up, seized upon this chance to grow, dramatic expansion soon went into overdrive. By the time the Second World War came around the TaTa's were the largest steel producers in the whole of British Empire.

As an often-used metaphor would have it, the Punjab and other traditional recruiting grounds constituted the 'sword arm of India'. "The rest of India had to be protected from this 'sword arm' by the continued presence of the British in the sub-continent, and the sword arm itself had to be protected from politicians and nationalists who were eager to blunt its keen edge," was the official refrain. British officers argued that it was easier to keep military uncontaminated if its recruiting base was narrow and if only reliable and trustworthy classes were taken in. One of the early casualties of World War I was the system of recruiting the martial races theory. Although the war verified the warlike characteristics of the classes designated as 'martial', with twenty two Victoria Crosses won by Punjabis in various battles, there was no other conclusion to arrive at; the war also demonstrated that other classes—given adequate training and leadership—performed equally well.

The greatest problem was the recruitment of the Jat Sikhs. Although there were fewer Sikhs recruited from the Punjab than Muslims—that was pursuant to build up the Muslim bulwark against Hindus/Sikhs, the Sikhs had been contributing a higher percentage of their manpower to the army. They were experiencing important social changes by way of militant Akali reform movement in the early part of the twentieth century, and were regarded as one of the more pugnacious classes. The Jat Sikhs had been the target of early nationalist propaganda and many were impressed by the news before World War I that several retired Sikh soldiers had destroyed their medals and discharge certificates in a wave of anti-British sentiment in America and Canada. Restrictions on Indian immigration to Canada and the Kamagata Maru incident fed conspiratorial sentiment. Copies of revolutionary newspapers filtered back to villages of the Punjab. The revolutionaries themselves leading to acts of violence followed these papers. Injured and disabled soldiers who returned from the World War had seen the way other colonial powers like France treated their subjects. The British had been found wanting in this regard, thus leading to considerable restiveness and bitterness. This bitterness was gradually transferred to other members of the community, thus leading to a fall in recruitment to the army. (For the government view on the Sikh unrest, see Major A E Barstow "*Sikhs*", Calcutta Government of India Publications Branch, 1928). The favouritism of many British officers towards the martial races was actually intensified by the nationalist movement.

Sir Michael O'Dwyer, Lieutenant Governor of Punjab, toured the countryside exhorting the Sikhs to come forward. His theme was that India's cause was that of Britain: therefore India, especially Punjab, should contribute to the war effort. In his speech in the Punjab War Conference, he explained his programme:—"I want two hundred thousand men for the regular army, voluntary if possible, conscription if necessary; twice the number of men we have been asked to supply". The Government of India had fixed an Indian quota of five lac soldiers for the whole country, but Sir Michael wanted his contribution to be forty per cent, knowing fully well that the population of the state, including that of the Princely states was not even fifteen per cent of the country's population. All means, legal, illegal and repressive were used to attain the target he had set for his state. There was widespread resentment in certain parts of Punjab, but Sir Michael knew how to make his plan work. He attempted to stir Jat Sikhs by pointing to the rise in Mazabhi (untouchable) Sikh recruitment. Then he played the card of Muslims versus the rest where recruitment figures were concerned. All this did have an impact on the rural belt of the state, unemployed youth and poverty ridden landless farmers thronged recruitment centres, particularly when other benefits like jobs for relations, admission to professional colleges etc were made easier for the kin of the soldiers.

All was not as honky-dory as some of the historians would have us believe. There were instances of dissent, often violent, against Indians being made cannon-fodder in a war that had nothing to do with India as such. Such agitations were immediately suppressed, but couldn't really be totally put out. Questions were soon being raised about the invulnerability of the British army and the superior qualities of the British race. The rancour was largely justified; there was hardly a Punjab village, which did not have its dead and permanently disabled. And none of these losses of life and limb had been incurred in defence of any Indian interest. In England, the *Manchester Guardian* told its readers that Indians "were sick and tired of being a subject race." There was a total disillusionment where Indians, be they Hindu, Muslim or Sikhs were concerned. Consequently, The Ghadr movement and pan-Islamism surfaced alongside this war effort.

The Ghadr Movement

The movement centred on the Sikhs of Punjab who had arrived in North America just about the time the war began in Europe. This movement, though had nothing to do with the war as such, it was a manifestation of people who would try just about anything to better their lot. It was started by a young Hindu from Delhi, Lala Hardyal, one of the many Indian activists driven abroad by British crackdown on dissent. A revolutionary socialist who dismissed Marxism as irrelevant nonsense, Hardyal, a brilliant student, had won a government scholarship to Oxford, but gave it up for political reasons before sitting for his final exams. In 1911 he moved to San Francisco, where for a time he taught Indian philosophy at Stanford University. The *Ghadr*, which literally means revolution, took shape when Hardyal observed the pitiable condition of the Indians, mostly from Punjab, who had been migrating to Canada and North America since 1904, basically to look for a future that was expected to be better than the past that was full of misery and poverty they had left behind in their native Punjab. As they were willing to work long hours on wages that were pittance when compared with the white man's salary they were welcomed whole-heartedly. However, soon their number increased to a level that was not acceptable to the local population as the balance between the whites and the browns was seen to be tilting towards the later. Consequently, the welcomes started turning hostile. A well-attended meeting of Indians living in Canada and America took place in Stockton sometime in the summer of 1913 to decide on their future course of action. Ostensibly to protect fellow Indians, Hardyal set up an organisation, which he called the Hindustani Workers of the West Pacific Coast with Sohan Singh Bhakana, a lumber mill worker, as the president and Hardyal as its secretary. Hardyal was extremely critical of the treatment given to the Indians in British Columbia and North America, and was particularly resentful of the restrictions that were being imposed on immigration from India. The 'Worker's Union' eventually got to be known as 'Ghadr Party'. Hardyal began publishing a newspaper, *Ghadr* (Rebellion), with its Mast emblazoned with the legend 'Enemy of the British Government', the first editorial declared: "Today there begins in foreign lands, but in our country's language, a war against the British Raj". Within a matter of months the paper was circulating in Indian expatriate communities all over the world. It was published in a number of Indian languages but predominantly "Gurmukhi" became the main script because the largest number of its readers were Sikhs and other Punjab migrants to foreign lands. Wherever there were Sikhs, there was *Ghadr*. However, with its mostly populist agenda, which concerned Indians intimately the paper caught interest of almost entire immigrant population of Indian origin. Right from the Pacific Coast to places as far away as Hong Kong, Shanghai and Singapore, the Ghadr Party and its mouthpiece had caught the Indians imagination.

On 25th March 1914, Hardyal was arrested by the San Francisco police and charged with anarchist activities. Released on bail he slipped out of America, and out of the movement he had started. But he had succeeded in igniting the Indian (particularly Sikh) minds. The Ghadr Party in Canada decided to test the government's tough entry restrictions against Indian immigrants. They chartered a Japanese ship, The *Kamagata Maru*, to bring 376 Sikhs, most of them former soldiers, from Hong Kong and the Far East to Vancouver. The ship was renamed "Guru Nanak Jehaz" for the duration of its charter for the purpose. Baba Gurdit Singh, who had chartered the ship, issued tickets to all the intending emigrants. Lure of the North American continent was such that a fairly large number of them had given up their steady and well-paid jobs in Hong Kong, Shanghai and elsewhere. There were problems in Hong Kong itself before the ship could finally leave that port for its ultimate destination. The police hauled up Baba Gurdit Singh and a large number of intending passengers were scared away. It was only after threatening the Hong Kong Government with a suit for damages and taking up this harassment of Indians with the local press which criticised the government for the whole episode that Gurdit Singh finally got clearance to leave Hong Kong. The ship kept collecting more and more passengers of Indian origin, not only from the Chinese Coastal cities but also from Yokohama, Singapore and Moji.

At last, on 21st May the S S Kamagata Maru anchored off Victoria where the port authorities demanded the clearance certificate from Yokohama and certain other documents. The captain of the ship claimed that the documents were missing from his cabin. The port authorities cabled Ottawa for instructions to send back the ship. The missing documents were found but the ship was quarantined; so much so, even hawkers who usually surrounded new arrivals were prevented from selling their ware to the passengers. In short, upon arrival they were refused permission to land, although they fulfilled the extraordinarily rigorous requirements set by the Canadian government. The local press went to town describing their arrival as an 'oriental invasion'. The *Pall Mall Gazette* editorially stated that the 'yellow races' are not wanted in Canada and cannot be introduced without endangering the livelihood of 'white settlers'. Sir Richard Mac Bride, the Prime Minister of British Columbia, declared that to admit them would lead to 'the extinction of the white peoples' in Canada, which he said must at all costs be preserved as a 'white man's country'. Only 22 men who could prove they were normally resident in Canada were allowed to land. The others had to remain on board the ship. The ship was escorted to Vancouver by the Immigration Department, and was instructed to lay anchors outside Canadian Waters. Baba Gurdit Singh was very upset with this turn of events. "What is done with this shipload of my people will determine whether we shall have peace in all parts of the British Empire," he announced. He also added that he was out to ascertain once and for all if Canada had any right to keep out British subjects while its allowed other aliens to land.

In India, nationalist leaders tried to arouse opinion in favour of their compatriots stranded in Canadian waters. In London, Mrs Annie Besant took up their cause in the British press. However, British, Indian and the Canadian governments refused to take any serious notice of the Indians marooned on a ship in those unfamiliar surroundings. The Viceroy,

Lord Hardinge, in a speech to his Council on 8th September 1914, said that the voyage of the ship to Canada had been undertaken without the cognizance or approval of the Indian government, and was in contravention of Canada's immigration laws. Considerable public opinion had been built up in favour of these hapless Indians but to no avail.

Kamagata Maru was ordered to clear Canadian waters at once, but by then the passengers had taken over its control from Captain Yamamoto and his crew. The immigration authorities prevailed upon the Japanese Captain of the ship to approach his government for rescue from rebellious passengers on the premise that the life of the Japanese crew was in serious danger. Two Japanese warships arrived and surrounded Kamagata Maru. Baba Gurdit Singh managed to approach the Japanese Consul through the Indians on shore and assured him that the passengers had no quarrel with the Japanese crew and the Captain was playing into the hands of the Canadian authorities. Convinced of the fact that there was no danger to the Japanese crew, the Consul approached the commanders of the warships with his reading of the situation. Both the warships then withdrew from the scene without creating any fuss. The immigration authorities, thereafter, tried all kinds of threats and pressure tactics, including stoppage of food and water being sent to the ship as this was thought to be suitable way of encouraging an early departure of the ship from their waters. But the sturdy Sikhs did not relent as they had resolved to have the issue settled their way. Protest rallies by Indians on shore had also started to cause law and order problem for the authorities. By now, it had assumed proportions of an agitation against discriminatory immigration laws of Canada. British Columbia Government was instructed to have the matter resolved quickly before it assumed more serious manifestation in the rest of the Empire. They decided to use force to have the ship moved away from Canadian jurisdiction.

When an armed Canadian police force of 120 odd men tried to forcibly take over the ship, the passengers, men, women and children, beat them back initially with coal from the engine room and wooden staves carved out of the ship's fittings. The Canadian authorities had clearly lost face: now it resolved to employ a sea-cruiser with over 150 heavily equipped commandos to not only show force but also to use it if the need arose. The fight had become totally unequal. Baba Gurdit Singh decided to take the ship out of Canadian waters. He had chartered the ship for six months and had collected his passengers at different ports—Hong Kong, Shanghai, Kobe and Yokohama. In the early hours of the morning of 23rd July 1914, the ship that had in two months become such an eye sore to the Canadian government silently slipped into the Pacific Ocean. But their hardships had not yet ended.

The Great War began while the Kamagata Maru was still at sea. The ship was not allowed to land passengers at Yokohama, its homeport, nor at Hong Kong or Singapore, where many of the men had their homes, but was directed on to Calcutta. There was a widespread apprehension that on hearing of the miserable plight of the Sikh passengers aboard Sikh Regiments located in those areas could revolt in protest. The ship, however, had been able to arouse emotions of Indians, and each time it reached port there were anti-British demonstrations by local Indians at every port of its call. British press had already labelled it as the 'Rebel Ship'. Finally the ship arrived at Budge-Budge, near Calcutta. Upon arrival in late September 1914, all the passengers were arrested as the Indian government planned to send all the men to the Punjab under police escort. Approximately, 300 Sikhs refused to comply and in the ensuing clash with the police and police firing twenty-one were killed. The rest were handcuffed and shipped to the Punjab by rail. After considerable hardship and two months in Canadian waters these brave Sikhs had returned to India, but not before showing the ugly face of the Empire. The whole episode was clearly a travesty of the famous, but selective, British 'fair play' and 'justice'. British subjects had been prevented from landing on the British soil because the colour of their skin was not compatible with that of the 'white man'. Rabindranath Tagore was so embittered over this whole episode that he declared that he would never set his foot in Canada on account of the manner in which the Canadians had treated his countrymen. True to his word, when he had been invited to visit Toronto and Montreal in 1916 he refused to go.

The Ghadr leaders in America, in the meanwhile, had decided that the outbreak of war was the opportunity they had been waiting for. Although they were totally unprepared and had no arms, they believed that they could overcome these minor difficulties by winning over Indian soldiers to their cause. Declaring war against the Raj, they called on their supporters around the world to return to India to join in an armed revolt. Many did return—along with thousands of loyal emigrants. Most of them were rounded up and by February 1915, 189 had been interned and 704 restricted to their villages, where they tried to instigate a rebellion among the local population. Local Punjabis were not impressed and in fact helped police in tracking them down. The religious leaders even went on to declare them as 'fallen Sikhs'.

In desperation, the Ghadrites called in as their leader the Bengali revolutionary, Rash Behari Bose, who claimed to be the man who had thrown the bomb at the Viceroy. Bose managed to bring some kind of an organisation to the movement. But the CID was watching every move of the Ghadrites. Soon they swung into action. All the Ghadr leaders were arrested, apart from Bose, whose instincts for self-preservation triumphed once again, and he disappeared from the scene. Forty-five revolutionaries were executed, and more than 200 sentenced to long terms of imprisonment.

The ruthlessness with which the dissent and the Ghadr movement were crushed was typical of the then Lt Governor of Punjab, Sir Michael O'Dwyer. O'Dwyer's harshness in the face of anything that he saw as a challenge to British authority was well known. This attitude of his, which was never questioned by the Viceroy or anybody superior to him, was to bear fruit four years later when the Jallianwala Bagh massacre took place, souring relations between the government and Indian leaders forever. In 1915, nobody cared to advise him regarding his, often unreasonable, harshness.

O'Dwyer, a spunky, clever and peppery Irishman, who never seemed to doubt his own judgment, believed, and perhaps understandably, that the Punjab had to be kept calm. Apart from being the bread-basket of India, which was exporting great quantities of wheat to Britain, the province was also the chief recruiting ground for the Indian army. Then O'Dwyer had his own reasons to be suspicious of Hindus. Before becoming Lt Governor, he had served in various assignments in Punjab. He had been a witness to the hatred, the Muslim peasantry had for the Hindu money-lenders. Wherever he looked he saw insurrection, real or imagined. The Ghadrites, predominantly a Hindu/Sikh organisation, instigated most of these agitations.

In truth, the Ghadr movement had never posed a serious, long-term threat to the Empire. What was more dangerous was pan-Islamism, which had been roused by Turkey's decision on 1st November 1914 to join Germany and the Central Powers against Britain, France and the Allies. A high proportion of the 16,000 Indian troops of the Poona Division's 16th Infantry Brigade, who had already been shipped to Bahrain, were Muslims. This raised a terrible conflict of loyalty for the great number of Muslims in the Indian army. Never before in history had Muslims fought alongside infidels against other Muslims. The British tried to resolve this difficulty by promising to respect the status of the Caliph and the holy places of Islam. Consequently, the Muslims largely remained loyal to their oath of allegiance and vigorously and bravely participated in various operations.

Back home in India, Maulana Azad and his friends did try their best to arouse Muslim passions, but their newspapers were closed down and their assets seized. Mohammad Ali and his brother Shaukat Ali were both held under house arrest right from the beginning of the war. Azad remained free for a while, but he too was finally held under the Defence of India Act. A fourth Muslim leader, Maulana Mahmood-ul-Hasan, went to Mecca to try through anti-British elements to persuade the Turkish government to invade India through Iran and Afghanistan now that it was depleted of British troops. The Turks had no resources to undertake a mission of such a huge dimension, and in due course of time the pan-Islamic threat to the Empire fizzled out as the Allies had also, in the meanwhile, gained an upper hand in the War.

During the first two years of the War, Congress was still divided deeply. Tilak, now 60 years old had, however, lost much of his steam, and was willing to join hands with the Moderates in their endeavour to seek self-government within the Empire 'by strictly constitutional means'. However, Mehta still strongly resented Tilak and no rapprochement was possible during his lifetime. Even Gokhale was not particularly keen on restoring friendly ties with Tilak. The hurt between the two stalwarts of the freedom movement was too deep to mend in a hurry. An Anglo-Irish lady Annie Besant, who had taken over the role of a 'firebrand' Congress worker tried her best to bring the two together, but could not succeed. It was only in late 1915, when both Mehta and Gokhale had died that Tilak could be re-admitted in Congress.

Annie Besant

Annie Besant at the age of 67 was full of irrepressible energy and drive. This estranged wife of an Anglican parson had been tried in England for immorality after she published a pamphlet on birth control. Her children had been taken away from her by a court order. She had eventually moved to India and soon became the President of the Theosophical Society. While Congress and the Muslim League had voluntarily put their political agitation on hold while the war in Europe was going on, Annie Besant felt that the war provided the right opportunity to increase pressure on Britain. The Irish Home Rule League was already creating problems for the Empire, and Annie Besant felt that the time for the Indians to do the same had come. The Congress support was not forthcoming for this venture of hers. So, in early 1915, she launched her own campaign through her two newspapers, *New India* and *Commonwealth* using the Theosophical Society's network to organise public meetings and conferences. However, before starting the 'Home Rule League' she did approach Gandhi to join hands with her. Gandhi did not agree and said: "Mrs. Besant, you are distrustful of the British and I am not. I will not help in any agitation against them during the War." (Dwarka Das – '*Through My Diary Leaves* pp10-11)

Tilak, now firmly entrenched in the Congress, and with the departure from the scene of stalwarts like Mehta and Gokhale, got busy in trying to restore his standing in the party. Seeing that Annie Besant was gaining in popularity he started his own version of the Home Rule League. However, before the rivalry could gain any intensity, by an unwritten compromise both Tilak and Annie Besant agreed to divide their respective areas of influence so as to avoid open conflicts. Tilak had a private interview with Mrs. Besant. They came to the conclusion the time was propitious for launching the Home Rule Movement rigorously. But they also realised that the Congress leaders would try to kill the movement if Tilak who, they believed, was in favour of terrorist activities, and had associated himself with these from the very beginning. They, therefore, decided that Mrs. Besant should win over Congress and adopt the movement before Tilak joins it. In the meantime, Tilak was to start a separate League, which would cooperate with Besant's League. That is how a separated league called the "Indian Home Rule League" came to be started by Tilak in Poona on 23 April 1916. Tilak's group based in Poona confined its activities to the Marathi speaking areas: Besant, who initially worked from Madras, operated in the rest of India. Only in Bombay did they overlap.

The Home Rule Leagues flourished for the rest of the war. They achieved nothing concrete but managed to create greater political awareness throughout India by means of public meetings and newspapers. The most influential of these was the national bi-weekly *Young India*, started in Bombay by the supporters of Annie Besant. The paper took its name from the 'Young Italy' and 'Young Ireland' freedom movements of the early nineteenth century. After a shaky start in 1916, the paper gradually built up its readership, until in 1919 it was taken over by Gandhi, who swiftly made it his mouthpiece.

The government did its best to crack down on the Leagues, imposing even more stringent restrictions on Tilak and Besant, banning them from several provinces and harrying their supporters. Mrs. Besant was prohibited from attending or taking part in any meeting, from delivering any lecture, from procuring or publishing any material composed by herself or any of her associates. She was also debarred from entering Madras. In fact, the authorities identified the districts where she could reside; she was not to leave those areas under any circumstances. On the eve of her internment, Annie Besant took leave of the public in a stirring farewell speech: "The real crime, she said, for which she was being punished was her having awakened the self-respect of the Indian people, which was fast asleep; of having roused them to a realisation that it was a disgrace, dishonour and moral turpitude to be a subject race". She taunted Great Britain for posing as the champion of liberty in Europe while revealing itself in India as autocratic, despotic and cruel rulers crushing aspirations of people who wanted only dignity, freedom and peace.

Tilak defined Home Rule in the following words, "I should be in my own country what an Englishman feels to be in England and in the colonies." In his speech delivered at Belgaum, he asserted, "We want some better arrangement for our Government. That is why we demand Swaraj, that is Home Rule...We see in India today that the people who govern us, who carry out our administration, come from England...But, however, good may be the law made by an alien people, it is not likely to win the approval of a nation which wants to decide its own destiny." On 23 July 1916, Tilak was arrested under section 108 of the Criminal Penal Code, the authorities charging him with 'having brought, or attempting to bring, into hatred and contempt for the government of India.' In plain language, his offence was that he had made three speeches on the subject of self-government. His theme was that a country in bondage was like a perpetually diseased man who was useless to himself and a nuisance to others, and that no political agitation could succeed unless it was a mass movement.

The case was heard on 7 August, before District Magistrate G W Hatch. Tilak again decided to rely on Jinnah to defend him. In spite of Jinnah's brilliant defence the court still found Tilak guilty, binding him over to be of good behaviour for a year, against a security or 20,000 rupees. Jinnah immediately lodged an appeal in the Bombay High Court, which effectively was his own turf. On 8 November, he won a stunning success. Tilak was found 'not guilty' and acquitted. 'A great victory has been won for the cause of Home Rule,' exulted the *Young India* banner headline. 'The Empire had tried to put chains on the struggle for Home Rule and has been thwarted in this attempt', said the editorial.

The efforts of the government to restrict the political activities of Tilak and Mrs. Besant, which were primarily confined to holding of public meetings and publication of leaflets etc., and demanding self-government had an effect that was contrary to what the administration had visualised. There were countrywide protests when the government tried to muzzle their voices. The press and the people derided use of 'Defence of India Act'. These leaders had not conspired with the enemy, nor had they done anything to subvert the British Government in India. They had not put any obstacles in the way of the vigorous prosecution of the War, or done anything to make the position of India or Indians unsafe; all that they had done was to use lawful means to bring about constitutional changes. The press, particularly *'The Hindu'* from Madras and some other papers in the North took up cudgels on behalf of these leaders. Jinnah and several other leading members of the Muslim League signified their protest by joining the Home Rule League. Jinnah called the internment of Besant as an 'attempt to intern the Home Rule or self-government scheme framed and adopted jointly by the Indian National

Congress and the Muslim League." In Allahabad a recruitment rally for the armed forces, scheduled to be held under the aegis of some prominent leaders, was cancelled. The atmosphere, wrote Pandit Nehru in his autobiography, "became electric and most of us young men felt exhilarated and expected big things in the future." Actions of the Government popularised the cause of the Home Rule League and it greatly influenced the thinking of the educated Indians; the Government was seen to be unnecessarily using harsh measures in suppressing the agitation for self-government. Seeing the way the wind was blowing, even Gandhi changed his stance vis-à-vis Mrs. Besant. He now wanted one hundred volunteers to walk with him from Bombay to Coimbatore (a distance of over one thousand miles) where Mrs. Besant was interned. But Gandhi's type of 'passive resistance' had not yet caught the public imagination so nothing came out of his call. Pandit Madan Mohan Malviya went to Calcutta to informally sound the Bangla leaders about a passive resistance oriented future course of action; but he could not find many takers for that line of action; ostensibly, during the anti-Bengal partition agitation people of the state had seen that passive resistance hardly had any impact on the Government.

The Home Rule movement kept on gaining momentum throughout 1916 and 1917, when Britain and Allies were suffering reverses in the war, not due to any superior German strategy, but due to sheer ineptness and incompetence of their own generals. A very large number of Indian soldiers died or were incapacitated in the process. Those returning home brought in the horror stories of how Britain had failed to look after the Indian volunteers and had not shied away from turning them into cannon fodder. The worst example was that of Mesopotamia, where the Indian army had been routed and thoroughly crushed by the tough Ottoman troops, disease and sheer bone headed military incompetence of their own commanders. The returning soldiers also told people back home how the British were indifferent to the 'subject races'. This further added to the resentment of the people, particularly that of Punjab, against their rulers. Main thing was the realisation that the British were not invincible; this further spurred the movement for gaining freedom.

Hindu-Muslim Unity

Due to untiring efforts of Jinnah, the December 1915 session of the Muslim League was held in Bombay, to coincide with the Congress session on at the same time, in the same city and a couple of miles away. At best it was a controversial decision, condemned both by the British authorities and local Sunni Muslims, who regarded Jinnah as a heretic if a Muslim at all. Over thirty thousand Sunnis attended the meeting, primarily to denounce both, Jinnah and the Muslim League.

Hordes of hecklers tried to disrupt the League's meeting. An opinion was that the governor of Bombay, Lord Willingdon, had organised this whole drama to embarrass the League leadership. The League, now presided over by a Muslim liberal—Mazhar-ul-Huq— saw through the charade; he simply adjourned the proceedings to be resumed next day at Taj Mahal Hotel in Bombay. Officially sponsored troublemakers now couldn't enter the premises. And there, on 1st January 1916, to loud cheers, Jinnah introduced his motion calling for a special committee to be formed to work in consultation with other political 'organisations', to formulate and frame a scheme of reforms...in the name of United India. (Pirzada—*Foundations of Pakistan*). The resolution was passed unanimously and Jinnah was praised for his sagacity and great work he had been doing for keeping the country united.

A committee of 71 members was appointed, representing every part of India, but the real spade work was undertaken by a nucleus of more active members: headed by Jinnah for the League and for Congress by an Allahabad lawyer who had gradually emerged as a leading Moderate, Motilal Nehru. Jinnah and Motilal immediately took to each other and became close friends. Both were highly sophisticated, brilliant lawyers, living thoroughly westernised lives in luxurious western style houses. Both were essentially secular, ignoring most of the dictates of their respective religions and enjoying the good things of life. More importantly, both were totally committed to Hindu-Muslim unity and to seeking self-government for India by strictly constitutional means.

Motilal was a highly successful lawyer of the Allahabad High Court. A larger than life character, Motilal spent money faster than he could earn it. British judges and lawyers liked and admired him. So much so, the Chief Justice of Allahabad High Court, Sir John Edge, had even wanted to propose him for membership of the 'Whites only' Allahabad club. Motilal courteously declined the offer. At that time Motilal was not into serious politics, and was rather keen to carry on with his thriving legal career. He was as angry over partition of Bengal as any other Indian, notably a Hindu. He did attend the Congress session in Benares, and later did go to the 1907 session in Calcutta; it took a lot of persuasion by the stalwarts of the party to have him agree to become actively involved in the affairs affecting India.

Like most moderates, Motilal had high expectations from the Minto-Morley reforms. He had expected the reforms to be the first step towards constitutional evolution towards dominion status and self-rule. Like many, he was also dismayed by the watered down final proposals. Reforms were becoming more and more British in their design, and therefore foreign; most of the major political leaders refused to be a party to any action that could connote that they were siding with the British. In spite of all his reservations, Motilal stood for a seat on the enlarged provincial council, and was elected. But he was soon disillusioned. Presided over by the lieutenant governor and packed with British officials, and lackeys of the Empire, not only was the council totally powerless but its Indian members were to show proper gratitude for the wise decisions taken on their behalf by British officials. Criticism of any kind or questioning of decisions taken, were not welcome. Undeterred by his provincial experience, however, Motilal also stood for election to the Imperial Legislative Council, taking his place in 1910 as a Congress representative in Calcutta alongside Sinha, Gokhale, Bannerjee and Jinnah.

Subsequent to the death of stalwarts like Mehta and Gokhale, Motilal was the natural choice to lead an important Congress committee to draft a pact with the Muslim League. He invited the Muslim representative— Jinnah— to come and stay with him at his palatial house (Anand Bhawan) at Allahabad. There during the summer heat of April 1916, the two sat down to draft what they chose to call 'Freedom Pact'. The pact that they drew up was in fact a set of proposals to take the Minto-Morley reforms further and provide a government structure acceptable to both major groupings. Both sides made concessions; and both Hindus and Muslims complained that too much was expected from their respective sides meaning that the pact was evenly balanced. As per the terms of the pact, the Hindus were to ensure that the Muslims got their one-third of all elected seats on the Imperial Legislative Council. This decision was taken in spite of the fact that the Muslims were not one-third but one-fourth of the country's population. They would, however, no longer be entitled to vote concurrently in general constituencies as well as their separate ones. However, in Bengal and Punjab, where Muslims held a majority, they would have no separate electorate and fewer seats than their proportion in population, on the grounds that they did not need special consideration in these states. The draft pact was discussed by a joint meeting of Congress and League leaders in Allahabad in October 1916, and approved unanimously. In December, it was presented to the annual sessions of both Congress and the League, which were held simultaneously in Lucknow. Jinnah was elected as the president of the League; this was also the occasion when Tilak was finally accepted back into the Congress fold after over ten years of wilderness. There were some reservations and opposition to the pact but when Tilak spoke forcefully in its favour the opposition simply faded away. At the League meeting Jinnah, in any case had no difficulty in carrying the motion through. The pact now was known as the 'Lucknow Pact'. In the absence of any alternative proposals on behalf of the government, the Congress-League scheme monopolized the political stage in India; and opinion began to crystallise fast in its favour. The

Home Rule League of Besant and Tilak started gaining fresh converts every day. Even the princes seemed to have developed some inclination towards the cause when in February 1917; the Maharaja of Bikaner publicly expressed the deep sympathy of the princes for 'the legitimate aspirations of our brother Indians.'

Lucknow Pact

Salient features of the Pact were:

- To ask for an enlarged legislative councils, both central and provincial, all with majorities by 'as broad a franchise as possible'.

- Half the members of the Viceroy's Executive Council should be Indians, elected by the elected members of the Imperial Legislative Council.

- The secretary of the state's council in London should be abolished.

- The cost of the India Office should be borne by Britain rather than India.

- Indians should be placed on a footing of equal status and rights of citizenship with other subjects of His Majesty the King throughout the Empire.

- Commissioned and non-commissioned ranks in the army and navy should be thrown open to the Indians, and adequate provision should be made for their selection, training and instruction in India.

Tilak, while supporting the Pact, and in spite of his clear pro-Hindu dominance leanings was more than sagacious during the discussions. He said," It has been propagated that we, Hindus, have yielded too much to our Muslim brothers. I am sure, I represent the majority of Hindu community all over India when I say that we could not have yielded too much. I would not care if the 'rights' of self-government were granted to the Muslim community only. I would not care if these rights are granted to the lower classes of the Hindu population either, because then the fight will not be triangular as it is at present."[3]

Lucknow Pact was the high water mark of the constitutional approach to the struggle for self-government, and of Hindu-Muslim cooperation. All was 'seemingly' well with the two communities. The leaders did not seem to realise that by arriving at this pact and adopting the same as a future policy, Syed Ahmed's two-nation theory was in fact being given acceptance. Jinnah and Motilal had unwittingly planted a time bomb, which would explode in due course of time, destroying the unity so painstakingly brought about by pragmatism and sagacity by these two learned and highly respected lawyers, and that too with the blessings of Bal Gangadhar Tilak.

The British government was not willing to accept the demands put forth by the League and Congress. So much so, when there was to be an Imperial Conference in 1917, to formulate policy both for the continuation of the war and for peace afterwards Indians were not asked to attend, whereas all 'white dominions' had been invited to send representatives. Indian leadership was legitimately hurt over this slight. India had contributed so much in the form of men and material that it had a right to be there. Even Lord Hardinge agreed with this, and supported this claim of the Indian leadership. But the war cabinet, which was dominated by Curzon and Kitchner—obviously still smarting form their bitter personal memories of the time spent in India—ignored his pleas on behalf of the Indians. Frustrated and weary of the goings on, which he felt were unfair to the Indians, Hardinge stepped down and returned to England. The Indians did not fail to notice this tendency amongst Englishmen to take Indian services for granted and even to rate them lower than those of the Dominions. "India figured rarely in the schemes for the future and it was feared that its services would be forgotten. Hardinge's Viceroyalty and the outbreak of the war had submerged old distrust and suspicions, but not eliminated them. And when in March 1915, the House of Lords rejected the proposal for creation of an Executive Council for the United Provinces, which had been recommended by the Legislative Council and the Lt. Governor of that province and was supported by the government of India and the Secretary of State, on the well-worn pleas that it was in the demand of a microscopic minority and that personal rule suited the East, members in the Imperial Legislative asked more in sorrow than in anger: 'Is this the first fruit of that change in the angle of vision which had been promised by a higher authority?" 'If this is the attitude of ex-Viceroys and ex-Governors towards us during the war, what will it be after the war? They have been paying us high and extremely flattering compliments upon our loyalty and devotion to the British crown, and yet in the same breath they tell us that we are in such a backward and primitive condition that even an Executive Council would be too good for us.' (KM Panikar-*Imperialism in Practice and Theory*) .

America Plays a Hand

In the heavily surcharged political atmosphere and due to suppressive measures adopted by the British, many men of political, legal and religious standings were moving towards those who were striving for Swaraj. One such man was Sir S Subramania, a respected leader in his own right. He elected to send an appeal to the President of America. On 24th June for

1917, in his letter to Woodrow Wilson, the American President he made a complaint against the British bureaucracy; he also brought home to him the awful situation prevailing in India, narrating the deplorable plight of Home Rule internees and resultant repressive measures by the British, which were causing unrest in the country. Mr. Subramania informed the President that an immediate promise of Home Rule Autonomy for India would surely result in an offer of five million men within in three months for service at the war-front and five million more in another three months.[4] The letter was delivered in Washington by hand through a Mr. and Mrs. Hotcher, editors, authors and lecturers on educational and humanitarian subjects, on or about 17th September 1917. The President forwarded the letter to his Secretary of State to look into the matter carefully and make his recommendations. Next day a printed copy of the letter was placed on the desk of 533 Senators and Congressmen. The letter virtually convulsed America from one end to another. A graphic account of the offer of ten million men was flashed all over the country by the press, leading to a great deal of sensation throughout. The American public began to support Home Rule for India as in Australia and Canada; pressure was applied on the British Government to consider the proposal favourably.

There naturally was a furore in London. Montagu declared in the House of Commons on 3rd June 1918: "Its (the letter's and American President's reaction) impropriety is all the more inexcusable because of the position of the writer. But the assertions in the letter are too wild and baseless to receive notice from any responsible authority." An official 'Rebuke' was issued to Sir Subramania for his 'indiscretion' in writing to the American President. The Chief Secretary of the Madras Government informed him, that, "His Excellency, the Viceroy and the Secretary of State have personally questioned and rebuked you for your conduct in this matter". Sir Subramania immediately announced his intention to renounce his title; saying, "He would prefer to renounce the Knight Companionship and return the insignia thereof, if the retention of the title and the insignia should in any way hinder the exercise of his right of citizenship to complain of wrongs and seek redress against consequences of mal-administration". So he decided to renounce both his titles as a protest against the most unbecoming, insulting and undignified language employed by the Secretary of State for India.

The whole episode did cause a lot of commotion in Britain. Lord Hardinge was able to shift a great part of the blame on the British War Office, yet Montagu vehemently condemned the existing system of Government in India. The issue of ill-treatment of the Indians, who had gone to fight and die for the Empire during the war, caught momentum and Austen Chamberlain had to resign from his post of the Secretary of State, and an Enquiry was ordered to look in the whole affair. Edwin Montagu, who had served as under secretary at the India Office, had visited the country in 1913, and had been utterly bowled over by it, replaced him. Being a Jew, he considered himself to be an 'oriental' and resolved to do everything in his power to help India and its people. In the House of Commons debate on the royal commission's report on Mesopotamia, he castigated the government of India. On 12th July 1917, in his famous speech he described the machinery of the Indian Government as "statute written, too wooden, too inelastic, too antediluvian to be of any use for the modern purposes we have in view, there is too much of a red tape in India and in India Office out here". He also observed that unless the century old and cumbrous machine designed to govern India was remodelled they would lose their right to control the destiny of the Indian Empire. Where he was concerned the Government of India was far too inefficient to represent the King Emperor. He called for recalling Hardinge at once. Mr. Chamberlain, the secretary of state for India resigned, and Montagu replaced him.

On 20th August 1917, Montagu made an authoritative statement on behalf of the British Cabinet highlighting the fact that a 'responsible' government in India was the goal of the British Government. He said, "The policy of His Majesty's Government with which the Government of India is in complete accord, is that of increasing the association of Indians in every branch of the administration and gradual development of self-governing institutions with a view to progressively realise a responsible government in India as an integral part of the British Empire...Ample opportunity will be afforded for public discussion of the proposals on the subject, which will be submitted to the parliament in due course of time." As a long awaited and welcome gesture of goodwill to the Indians, the new secretary of state removed the racial bar, which excluded the Indians from the King's Commission in the Army. That, the opening in the first instance was available only to the scions of the royal and rich families of Indians did create some kind of resentment amongst the commoners but that was not serious enough to cause any administrative problem. The extremists considered all these gestures of goodwill and good intentions falling too short of the people's aspirations. W R Smith, a thinker writer summed up the situation more aptly when he observed, "India was to be rewarded for its loyalty and at the same time to be bribed to keep quiet while the Empire was fighting for its survival." But all was not well where these pious intentions were concerned. Lord Curzon, the originator of the term 'responsible government', noted: 'When the Cabinet used the expression 'ultimate self-government' they probably contemplated an intervening period of five hundred years.' Birkenhead thought it 'frankly inconceivable that India will ever be fit for Dominion self-government'. Speaking in the House of Lords he pontificated, "To talk of India as an entity is as absurd as to talk of Europe as an entity." He also challenged the 'nationalists' to come up with an agenda that could evolve into a constitution acceptable along the length and breadth of the country. To his utter surprise, Motilal Nehru and a committee under his chairmanship did come up with a constitution that defined India as a 'dominion' having a federal structure where the government would be elected through universal suffrage with a strong centre having ultimate power over certain crucial aspects. Where this scheme or the draft constitution failed was its stipulation that the separate electorate be abolished. The vociferous element of the Muslim community led by Jinnah rejected the notion of one-man one vote on the premise that such a scenario would not allow the Muslims to share power because, they could never catch up with the Hindus in terms of numbers. Parity, or alternatively, reservation of thirty three per cent seats for the Muslims gained momentum. The British were quite happy to allow such differences between the two communities to grow because, only differences between Hindus and Muslims could ensure continuation of the Raj. In the twenties and thirties it was common for race, and by extension religion to define nationality. Luckily for the British, India was a place where the caste units and religious establishments had not shown any inclination to sink their differences in the larger interests of the country. Simon anticipated that the emergence of Indian nationhood would evolve a 'prolonged evolution'. (*Endgame of Empire* by R J Moore pp 34)

Though couched in terms like 'gradual development', 'progressive realisation' and 'responsible government' the Indian nationalists took Montague's pronouncement as a clear promise of the dominion status that they sought. In their opinion, no longer could their demand for Home Rule be considered seditious. Montague's stand on the issue of Home Rule was soon put to test. Earlier in June 1917, Annie Besant had been imprisoned by the government of Bombay along with two of her Home Rule associates for 'seditious journalism'. The arrest had led to massive protests and leaders like Malaviya, Bannerjee and Jinnah had picked cudgels on their behalf. In the wake of Montagu proclamation, Jinnah appealed to the Home Minister and Mrs. Besant was released. Later, in December, riding the tidal wave of emotion, she was elected president at the annual Congress session at Calcutta, which again coincided with the Muslim League session. In her presidential address, Mrs. Besant came out with an elaborate thesis on India's demand for freedom. She demanded, "A bill during 1918, establishing self-government in India on lines resembling those of the Commonwealth on a date to be laid down therein, preferably 1923, the latest 1928, the intermediate five or ten years being occupied with the transference of the Government from British to Indian hands, maintaining the British ties as in the dominion." The hopes of the Indians had been raised to such an extent about inevitability of freedom that even the issue of the National Flag was also formally raised during discussions and during the session at Calcutta. The Home Rule League had already adopted and popularised the 'Tricolour', but still a committee was appointed to recommend a design. The Committee never got to meet but the old Home Rule League flag eventually got adopted as the Congress flag with "Charkha" added in the center.

(In August 1917, Rabindranath Tagore wrote an article, "Thou Shalt Obey" wherein he said, "If a people have to crawl inch by inch, step by step, towards progress, Time itself would have to acknowledge defeat. No people on earth can be considered fit for freedom today if men have to prove their complete fitness before being entitled to opportunities for development." This was a retort to Montague's declaration of 1917, that India could progressively move towards self-government, every step having to be decided by Britain after examination of India's fitness for advance. In fact, Tagore issued a warning to England, which was widely published in the national press under the heading "Let England Leave India Alone", says Rabindra Nath Tagore. What the poet Laureate said was, "The problem of India is more complicated, but what I say to the British Government is that they should leave us alone, to our destiny, and let us solve our problems in the light of experiment and efforts and necessary suffering. We need the wisdom both of experience and initiative and must face reality in our own way so that we may exploit the full potentialities of our people. When others talk of our communal conflicts, linguistic differences and various social disharmonies, they conveniently forget that Europe also, even a short time ago, was in no better plight and yet it did not unman fully accept its limitations as inevitable. It has struggled through its dark periods at the cost of immense sufferings and sacrifice, which have been worthily rewarded by access to a people's eternal right to self-rule.

Spanish inquisitions, witch-burning, Catholic and Protestant Warfare, anti-scientific campaigns and fanaticism—you can go on adding to such unenviable activities of Europe till you come to the Great War when science and modernism only helped to intensify the savagery of fratricidal—combat.

Let the people of Asia profit by the lessons, which their brothers in the west have to teach us. Truth and freedom are for all, and we shall be proud to accept the gifts of modern western science, adapting them to the needs of our national genius, and our special traditions and circumstances.

India is on her path to self-realisation. It cannot afford to waste its priceless spiritual and intellectual resources in enforced emulation of ready-made ideals from outside. It must evolve its own civilisation unhampered by the dead past or her modern political slavery. (Quoted in 'The Vanishing Empire' by Chaman Lal - Sagar Publications, New Delhi)

Members of the Home Rule League continued with their propaganda work and political education of Indian masses. They also decided to extend their activities in England where an anti-Indian lobby had come up, and was creating adverse opinion about India and Indians in order to thwart the cycle of Reforms. This group was composed entirely of retired Anglo-Indians and other reactionaries. A deputation, composed of Tilak, Bipin Chandra Pal and some other intellectuals was organised to contact the 'Labour Party' leaders in England, and those other leaders who were sympathetic to India and its cause, were also identified. However, before the deputation could actually reach England their passports were cancelled and they were sent back without setting foot in England. The official reason for this treatment was that the country was at war and Indian affairs were likely to distract the administration during that sensitive phase of the World War. Seemingly, the War Cabinet at the behest of the General Staff took this action. Pal and Tilak were also debarred from entering Delhi and Punjab. All India Congress Committee met in Delhi on 23rd February 1918, to consider this ban on the two stalwarts of the Party and decided to send a deputation to the Viceroy for cancelling this order. The Viceroy refused to consider any such request. Working on the premise that 'England's calamity cannot be India's opportunity', Tilak continued to exhort young men to offer themselves for recruitment in the army. Only problem for the administration was that he also intermingled his political propaganda during his recruitment rallies. Therefore, in August 1918, he was served with an order prohibiting him from lecturing without previous permission of the District Magistrate.

The Mon-Ford Report

Lord Chelmsford, a former cavalry captain, who had climbed up the ladder due to family's influence, pulls and pressures, replaced Hardinge. Indians found him difficult to communicate with, and his own staff found him cold, distant and 'too much of a machine'. For all his lack of distinction, however, Chelmsford was no fool. Soon after taking over, he wrote to the Secretary of State for India, Austen Chamberlain, stressing the need to make a definite commitment to further constitutional progress of India. The members of his council, he reported, were increasingly becoming worried about the Home Rule movement, which was gaining momentum and was more and more vociferous and effective. Chelmsford recommended that India be given "the largest measure of self-government compatible with the maintenance of the supreme authority of British rule." (Bence Jones pp 221)

In the interim, Montagu was already on a visit to India in order to get first hand information and to interact with the Indian leaders. Montagu had come with a mission to do something, and in his own words "to do something big". Fearful of his enthusiasm; the official accompanying him and those from the Viceroy's staff kept him away from Calcutta, tying him down in Bombay and around. In a way their fears were well founded. Montagu had proclaimed at the start that, "My visit to India means that we are going to do something and something big. I cannot return home and produce something little or nothing, it must be epoch-making, or it is a failure; it must be the keystone of the future history of India." But he was virtually alone in his mission. Soon enough he discovered that just about nobody in the administration shared his enthusiasm. Neither the Viceroy, nor his staff, nor for that matter the Anglo-Indian population shared his concern for the Indians. Fact of the matter is that the Indians themselves, with their well-defined social strata and blatant racial discrimination, appeared to be too primitive by European standards. There were classes within classes. Soon enough he realised that to survive in India one had to conform; otherwise, regardless of social status one could be ostracised. The whites nearly all operated a strict colour bar; for them it was essential if the British were to continue to rule. They would work with Indians but never socialised with the natives. Educated and well to do Indians resented this attitude. To make matters worse, Montagu found Chelmsford and his government obsessed with files and regulations, far too rigid, lacking in appreciation of Indian political aspirations, and everything dominated by 'precedence, precedence and precedence.' In addition to all these handicaps, there were definite signs of resentment over Montagu's mission. Not known for giving up in a hurry, Montagu toured India meeting people, putting out feelers and seeking opinions. Among those he met was Sir Michael O' Dwyer—the Lieutenant Governor of Punjab—he was distrustful of Indians, detested the educated class and mistrusted just about anybody who was not white-skinned. In due course of time he became Montagu's personal albatross. To the majority of Anglo-Indians O'Dwyer was the epitome of the British Raj.

O' Dwyer, as an Irishman thought he had a nose for subversion. He wanted to 'sort out' foreign-educated intellectuals who were only intent on making trouble for the Raj. O' Dwyer's usual refrain was that common Indian was too poor to get involved in the affairs of the state. The fact is, he would say, as everyone, British or Indian, who understands the

East will, if honest, admit, that ninety per cent of the people do not care a brass farthing for the 'form of government.' Speaking in Imperial Legislative Council on 13th September 1914, he referred to India's claim for self-government in a very derisive manner. He said, "..In these days when we are in danger of being deafened by political harangues and of being blinded by the shower of political manifestoes, it is well occasionally to return to mother earth to clear up our minds of illusions, and to ask ourselves what will all this noise and talk do for the man on the soil, the man behind the plough, the man whose life is a long drawn question between a crop and another crop." He considered the farmer behind the plough to be the backbone of India, and he did have a genuine affection for the hard-working peasants of Punjab. In his Reforms Memorandum of 10th January 1918, he said, "Do anything to weaken or shake authority and you will be appalled to find how small is the margin of safety, how thin the partition that divides order from disorder...Place the interests of the silent masses before the clamour of the politicians, however, troublesome and insistent".

Clearly, O' Dwyer was not in favour of any Reforms, nor did he relish the idea of self-government for the Indians. He tried to put obstacles at each and every stage of the Reforms Commission's activities. Montagu complained to the Prime Minister Lloyd George of O' Dwyer's implacable hostility towards the Indians, and the way he was determined to maintain his position as the idol of the reactionary forces, and to try and govern by the iron hand.'—Montagu Report. Where O'Dwyer was clear about his line of action in keeping the Empire going, Chelmsford, fearful of criticism and failure, was too much of a vacillator and indecisive. "He never moves an inch without consulting his Council, never expresses an opinion without consulting his Council," Montagu later observed. Montagu had to take the lead and to assert himself to the utmost to make the government of India go as far as he possibly could. He impressed upon the Governors and Lieutenant Governors that 'our whole policy was to make India a political country, and it was impossible to associate that with repression.'

In spite of all the resistance from the Viceroy's inner circle and O'Dwyer and just about everybody's reluctance to cooperate, Montagu managed to come up with a 300-page report, 'Report on Indian Constitutional Reform', with a fairly large number of inputs from the 'Lucknow Pact'. The report was published in June 1918, and was presented to the British Parliament. The powers that be found his enthusiasm and the report to be too far ahead of its time and, even radical. Curzon and other die-hard imperialists like Winston Churchill shot it down in spite of the fact that the Prime Minister Lloyd George did want to have it considered in a proper and serious manner. That the Empire was too far and seriously involved in the War was the standard excuse of the Imperialists. Basic contents of the report, which came to be known as Montagu-Chelmsford Report, were:

- Give as far as possible complete popular control in local bodies with a measure of responsibilities to the Indians at once.

- Complete responsibilities be given once the locals have gained sufficient experience.

- Two bodies should replace Viceroy's Imperial Legislative Council, a Legislative Assembly with 106 elected and 40 nominated members, 25 of whom would be officials. There should be an 'Upper House'—the Council of States with 61 members to represent the larger landed gentry.

- Above these bodies should be the Viceroy's Executive Council with six members. Three of them should be Indians, besides Viceroy himself and the commander-in-chief.

All these bodies were to be strictly consultative. The Viceroy was not to be answerable to any one of them. As a vital step towards self-government, which was accepted as the ultimate goal but for the most hardened imperialists, the franchise base was to be considerably widened, with property and tax liability as the main but by no means the only qualifications. The provinces were also to be given a great deal of autonomy, with a view to train them for self-governance in due course of time.

The proposals were liberal, but were unacceptable to a fairly large number of Indians. The first reaction of the Congress leaders was to reject the proposals. Some, like Annie Besant, regarded the proposed reforms as 'unworthy of Britain to offer and India to accept', and wanted to reject them out of hand. But she didn't seem to be very sure of herself and changed her mind several times before finally advocating acceptance. A joint Congress-League committee was set up to examine the subject thoroughly and come up with recommendations, and to coordinate their official response. After four days of deliberations the Congress re-affirmed the principles of Reforms contained in the Congress-League Scheme, and declared that nothing less than Self-Government within the Empire would satisfy legitimate aspirations of the Indians. Gandhi did not attend this session because he held the view that the proposals were within the ambit of immediate ambitions of the country, Moderates agreed with him, but the Congress was eventually split between the Moderates and the hard-liners on this issue. The Experts Committee formed jointly by the League and the Congress recommended a qualified acceptance; in that, the proposed reforms be treated as a 'transitional stage', because these were at least a step in the right direction. Jinnah, whom Montagu regarded as the most outstanding of Indian national leaders, chaired the committee. So impressed was Montagu with Jinnah, his knowledge of the law and articulation, that he noted in his diary, "Chelmsford tried to argue with him, and was tied up into knots. Jinnah is a very clever man, and it is, of course, an outrage that such a man should have no chance of running the affairs of his own country", he added in his report.[5] Writing on 28th February 1918, Montagu claimed that even if he had not succeeded in evolving an agreed scheme, he had done something for which the Cabinet at Home ought to be grateful to him. "I have kept India quiet for six months at a critical period of the War; I have set the politicians thinking of nothing else but my mission." He had, however, done much more. He had rallied around him a batch of Indian leaders who were willing, rather pleased to lend him their full support. Salient features of the proposals were:-

- There should be as far as possible, complete popular control in local bodies.

- In order to facilitate introduction of responsible government in the provinces, the devolution of powers from the centre was to be extended.

- System of 'Dyarchy' be introduced in the states, so that complete responsibility could be given to the Indians as soon as possible. Under this various subjects dealt by the government were divided in two groups, transferred and reserved. The former included things like local government, public health, education, agriculture, and public works excluding major irrigation projects. The reserved group comprised of finance, law and order, land revenue, and police.

- The Central Government was to remain responsible to the Secretary of State, with the 'Lower House' to be known as 'the Legislative Assembly of India' representing the interests of the whole country, two-third of the members to be elected. Second Chamber to be known as the 'Council of States' will have twenty-one elected and twenty-nine nominated members.

- While retaining special dispensations for the Muslims given during the Minto-Morley Reforms it was also proposed to extend this concession to the Sikhs for service rendered in the armed forces.

- The Report also recommended creation of permanent 'Council of Princes'.

The proposals were definitely leading to the right direction where ambitions of Indians were concerned, but these fell far short of popular expectations. Mrs. Besant went to the extent of calling these proposals as a "line beyond which its authors cannot go—these indicate a scheme for permanent slavery and would need a revolution to rectify the situation", she stated. *The Modern Review*, a respected and well-read journal in its issue of August 1918, termed the proposals as a mixture containing five per cent milk and ninety per cent water mixed with powdered rice. The periodical called it 'a rough estimate and not result of any chemical analysis.' Mr. Vithalbhai Patel was more candid when he expressed his opinion on the Report when the Congress met on 29th August 1918, to consider all the implications of the proposals. He said, "Every proposed Reform is hedged round with so many safeguards that it looks as if a system of barbed wire fencing had been set up to keep out interlopers or an enemy." Jinnah while reacting to the proposals said, "I have no doubt that 'responsible government' in this country is bound to come, it must come, it is only a question of time. At present the only difference between the government in England and the Indians is that of 'speed'. We say that these proposals do not go far enough. The Government wants to proceed slowly, we want to go faster." Not withstanding all the disillusionments of the Indians and reservations of the Anglo-Indians and other pro-English people there were those who hailed the final report. Some Liberal newspapers went to the extent of calling the Montagu-Chelmsford Report as the most important document in Imperial history since the publication of Lord Durham's report on Canada in 1839. Conservative press, in turn, was equally critical of the report.

Lord Chelmsford had been more than circumspect about the whole thing. On 4th October 1918, he wrote to the King, "We have here an educated class. Ninety five per cent of whom are inimical to us, and I venture to assert that every student in every university is growing up with a hatred for us. These are, of course, at present a mere fraction of the population, but each year sees the number augmented, and it may well be imagined that their potentialities for mischief are infinite. If we can win these men over to our side, I am convinced that we can only do it by inviting and enlisting their cooperation". (Quoted by Hector Bolitho from Herald Nicholson's *King George V, His Life and Reign* p 503)

Eventually, Montagu's far-seeing and far-reaching plans, devised with active help of Chelmsford, were unfortunately not allowed to mature with the swiftness, which the swiftness of the changing environment of India demanded. On 2nd June 1919, while introducing the Bill in the House of Commons Montagu made an impassioned plea for acceptance and early passage of Government of India Act. In his speech he said, "I cannot believe that Parliament is going to afford any obstacle to the partnership of India in the British Empire. We have been so sympathetic to the national aspirations of Arabs, of Czechs, of Serbs, of Croat and of Slovenes. Here is a country desirous of achieving nationality once again, I repeat, an original member of the League of Nations, developed under our protecting care, imbued to a greater and greater degree with our political thought. Let us pass this Bill and start it, under the aegis of the British flag, on the road which we ourselves have travelled, despite all the acknowledged difficulties of area, of caste, of religion, of race and education."

The Government of India Act, when finally passed fell far short of the expectations raised by the Mont-Ford Reforms; and by the time even this charter was implemented it was outdated and had lost all political significance. The government was having second thoughts on the subject of allowing Indians to gain experience in governing. It had concurrent to the Montagu mission started the process of re-defining the 'Defence of India Act', a wartime emergency measure giving the government of India powers to deal with the revolutionary terrorism that had plagued the Raj since 1907. A committee known as 'The Indian Sedition Committee' presided over by Justice SAT Rowlatt had been formed on 10th December 1917 (by then the war had already taken a turn towards an Allies victory and Indians were no longer central to the British long term plans for ruling over the country) to study and make recommendations for ensuring continuation of the Empire.

Rowlatt Bill

The World War one came to an end in November 1918. India had made a massive contribution towards the victory of the Allies in the form of soldiers, money and resources. Out of a total of 5,79, 232 combatants, 29,010 died in the battlefields of distant lands, 61,916 were wounded and 10,610 were either missing in action or were taken as prisoners of war.[6] All this sacrifice had been encouraged by vague promises of administrative reforms and possibility of Indians being given some kind of freedom in governing their country. True to form, and now that the War had been won, the Government in London was in a hurry to renege from all the promises, clear and vague, made to the Indians when the Empire was under threat. Sir Sydney Rowlatt came to India to study the details and requirements of post war regime. The agenda of this Committee was:

- To investigate and report on the nature and extent of the criminal conspiracies connected with the revolutionary movement in India.

- To examine and consider the difficulties those have arisen in dealing with such conspiracies and to advise as to the legislation, if any, necessary to enable government to deal effectively with them.

The Committee assembled in Calcutta early in January 1918. It held all its meetings 'in camera' and examined a plethora of documents in possession of the Government of India in order to devise special legislations for dealing with revolutionary crimes after the Defence of India Act had ceased to operate at the end of war. Rowlatt and his committee, after reviewing the situation, and obviously under the influence of the hard-liners in the Chelmsford Council came to the conclusion that the ordinary Criminal laws were not adequate for dealing with the political situation in India. And in order to firmly deal with the situation the Committee reported, "The measures we shall recommend are of two kinds, viz. Punitive, by which term we mean measures that would facilitate conviction and punishment of the offender; and Preventive, i.e. measures to check the spread of conspiracy and the commission of crime." According to this assessment Rowlatt drafted two bills. The first one allowed the government of India to go on by-passing the normal processes of law in dealing with activities prejudicial to the security of the state—a phrase popular with dictatorial and totalitarian regimes. The bill also stipulated that for a period of three years, suspected terrorists could be arrested, interned, expelled, all without warrant, charge, trial or even assigning any cause for such an action against an individual. The second bill amended the Indian Penal Code to make these provisions permanent. So this was going to be the reward for all the sacrifices made by Indian soldiers on behalf of the Empire. People of Punjab were more hurt because out of the entire Indian contingent, about 3,60,000 soldiers were from that state.

Almost all the Indian leaders were lawyers, many of them had studied law at the famous and ancient London's Inns of Court: They were outraged and angry over this turn of events; from reforms to introduction of virtually a 'dictatorship' was not acceptable to them. When the bills were presented to the Imperial Legislative Council on 6th February 1919, and the Viceroy informed the House that the Government of India had decided to accept the recommendations and was going to introduce appropriate Bills to have these legislated, there was uproar. Sir William Vincent who actually introduced the Bill before the Council, said, "The Bill which I now seek to introduce is not aimed at patriots, it is aimed at criminals; it is not aimed at the suppression of politics at all; it is aimed rather at the purification of politics."[7]

Indian members of the Council were not impressed with the rationale of the government. They condemned these Bills without exception. Jinnah was the most vocal critic of the Rowlatt Bills when the Council was discussing these. "There was no precedent or parallel in the legal history of any civilised country to the enactment of such laws", he said.

And went on to highlight the folly of introducing them at a time when 'high hopes of reform had been raised.' He considered it his duty, he said, to warn, 'If these measures are passed, you will create in the country from one end to the other a discontent and agitation the likes of which you have not witnessed, and it will have, believe me, a most disastrous effect on the good relations that have existed between the Government and the people.'

Clearly, unlike Montagu, Jinnah and his understanding of the Indians cut no ice with Chelmsford, Rowlatt and the British members. They chose to ignore his prophetic statement. They also ignored the protests of Malaviya and others who with one voice declared that such a Bill was 'dangerously inexpedient, entirely inopportune and a negation of civilised law'. Although, seeing the agitated Indian leadership the second bill was dropped, the first was passed by the Council with all the 22 Indian members opposing and 34 British members supporting the motion. On 18, March 1919, what became to be known as the Rowlatt Act was passed into Law. Jinnah immediately walked out of the Legislative Council along with two other Indian members. Subsequently he resigned from the Council, so did Malaviya and some others.

In his resignation letter, Jinnah said," The fundamental principles of justice have been uprooted and the constitutional rights of the people have been violated at a time when there is no real danger to the state, by an over fretful and incompetent bureaucracy which is neither responsible to the people nor in touch with real public opinion.... In my opinion, a government that passes or sanctions such a law in times of peace forfeits its claim to be called a civilised government. I still hope that the Secretary of State for India, Mr. Montagu will advise His Majesty to signify his disallowance to this Black Act."(Chelmsford-Papers). Jinnah didn't rest on his laurels. He decided to sail to London to personally see the Secretary of State and apprise him of the serious reservations that the Indian leadership had over the Rowlatt Act.

Jinnah presented his case to the British prime minister in his usual forceful manner, couched with impressive legal terminologies and phrases. But Lloyd George remained unmoved with his rationale, Montagu also proved to be a 'spineless character', who having seen that the winds were blowing against his bold recommendations elected to remain dormant, offering no help, guidance, or encouragement to Jinnah. In any case, having resigned from the Council, Jinnah technically had no 'locus-standi' in so far as representing India or the Indians case before the British parliament was concerned. British convenience and so-called fair play and justice were just not available in the instant case.

While Jinnah was sailing to England, anti-Rowlatt demonstrations were erupting all over India. The demonstrators were led and inspired by Gandhi, who had by then caught the imagination of the Indian masses in a big way. He had already become some kind of a hero for his anti-apartheid and 'civil rights' work in South Africa. And within a year of his arrival in India he had become an undisputed leader of the Indian movement. Gandhi replaced the constitutional methods favoured by Jinnah, Motilal Nehru and their moderate associates, with his own anarchistic agenda, relying more on his intuition and appealing directly to the emotions of the masses, rather than taking a legalistic or intellectual approach to the whole issue. He decided to launch his Satyagraha movement with a vow communicated to the public in a letter to the press on 1st March 1919. The vow ran as follows:

'Being conscientiously of opinion that the Bills known as The Indian Criminal Law and The Criminal Law (Emergency Powers) of 1919 are unjust, subversive of the principle of liberty and justice and destructive of the elementary rights of individuals on which the safety of the community and the state itself is based, we solemnly affirm that in the event of these becoming law and until these are withdrawn, we shall refuse civilly to obey those laws and such other laws as a Committee to be hereafter appointed may think fit and we further affirm that in this struggle we will faithfully follow the truth and refrain from violence to life, person and property'. Satyagraha, to the British, meant sedition and, in the Punjab, from the chief secretary down, they held Gandhi responsible for the disturbances in the state.

Ignoring Gandhi's pleas and warnings the Bill was passed into law on 18th March 1919. Gandhi was in Madras at the time. On 23rd March he called upon the people to observe fast in protest, Hartal and offer prayers. The date for the start of the agitation was fixed for 30th March, but was subsequently changed to 5th April. Mrs. Besant was against any mass movements against the notorious Rowlatt laws, because she was aware of the dangers of exiting mob frenzy, which once aroused could not be brought under control unless the aim had been achieved. She met Gandhi and expressed her opposition to the idea of agitation on the issue. Her supporters were flummoxed. Earlier she had not hesitated to stir up discontent in India at a time when the British Empire was fighting for its very survival. General consensus was that in spite of her fine usage of the language and an apparent intensity for India's cause she was proving herself to be a foreigner and a white foreigner at that. She quickly lost her following that had been built over a long period. Gandhi gave her a patient hearing and told her that 'passive resistance' is the only weapon he had found to be effective against foreign rulers; that he had tested and tried it successfully in South Africa.

The Rowlatt Act was never actually implemented. Obviously, widespread resentment and unrest within the country and criticism abroad in some of the more liberal and democratic societies had given the Viceroy cold feet and the British government was forced to give a second thought to the whole thing. The Act remained in the statute book for the stipulated three years then allowed to lapse by default. But the situation created before; during, and after the Rowlatt drama gave a strong base to Gandhi to launch his kind of agitation and to take charge of the 'freedom movement'. Having had a first hand experience of Gandhi and his non-violent methods while he was in South Africa the British should have given a serious thought to the whole subject. Somehow they chose to ignore Gandhi and the sway he was building over the Indian masses.

Footnotes

1. William Archer India and the Empire, London (1917) p 295.
2. Annie Besant, *Builder of India* pp 75-76.
3. D G Tendulkar Mahatma Volume I page 234.
4. The Indian Annual Register 1919 pp 43-45.
5. Montagu Report pp 8-10
6. Gazette of India Part VI, March 8, 1919 p 267
7. Proceedings of the Indian Legislative Council 6th February 1919 The Gazette of India 15th February 1919 Part VI page 3.

6

Gandhi Arrives in India

On 11 January 1915, Gandhi stepped ashore in Bombay, fit again in body and mind, wearing a white cotton dhoti and turban, having foresworn western clothes forever. To the huge crowd assembled to welcome him he declared,' I propose to remain in India and serve the motherland for the rest of my life.' The failed barrister of the yesteryears, who had sailed away a long time back to South Africa, had now returned as the most well known face in India, virtually an international celebrity who now had the halo of a holy man. Wherever he went, crowds gathered round him eager for "Darshan" (a way of seeking blessings of a holy man), hoping that they will be able to absorb reflected holiness by seeing, or being close to a holy person. Both the Viceroy and Governor of Bombay sought private audience with Gandhi. A large number of receptions were organised by various societies and organisations in his honour. The Gujarat Sabha threw a. garden party at Jehangir Petit's palatial home where its chairman Jinnah made an extremely laudatory speech highlighting achievements of Gandhi. Most of the speakers, including Jinnah, spoke in English. Gandhi chose to respond in Gujarati, pointedly telling his audience that he preferred to speak to them in their own tongue. In the process he also took pain to observe that he was 'happy' to see a Muslim not only present but also chairing the meeting that basically was predominantly a Hindu get together. As the later day history of Indian Freedom movement tells us, a discordant note between the two was struck with this unwarranted remark.[1]

There, really, was no need for Gandhi to draw attention to Jinnah's minority religion. Gokhale had always said that Jinnah was 'totally free of all sectarian prejudices'. May be, Gandhi too had heard of Jinnah's impact over the people of India, and saw in him a potential rival for power, and thought it appropriate to announce at their very first meeting that India being predominantly a Hindu country, deserved Gandhi, a Hindu as its leader, and not a Muslim. Jinnah maintained a studied silence over this apparent, though minor, dig through out the proceedings of the meeting; but the incident did set the tone of their future relationship. This really was no way for one leader of national stature to draw attention to another, more so when Jinnah had been trying really hard for Hindu-Muslim unity.

Gandhi Enters Indian Politics

Gokhale wanted Gandhi to join his 'Servants of India Society'. Trouble was, a large number of members did not want him. They were critical of his "Hind Swaraj" and methods, modalities, and theories propagated therein. Gandhi's apparent hatred of scientifically advanced world with its modern amenities was an anathema to most of the people who wanted India to progress alongside rest of the world. Clearly, for them, Gandhi was out of tune with the times, and out of touch with the realities of life when he had set out to define the kind of society India should become. Before Gandhi could cause any further damage to his image, or the cause he represented, Gokhale advised Gandhi to spend one year in travelling through the country and meeting Indians of different hues before he started speaking in public or taking any active part in the country's political affairs. Gandhi also smelled some kind of hostility amongst a section of people he had come in contact with. He readily agreed to take Gokhale's advice in the matter and set out on a tour of the country.

When Gandhi went to Shantiniketan, set up as a center of arts and learning, by the poet Sir Rabindranath Tagore, the poet laureate welcomed him enthusiastically and the two quickly established a mutual admiration society. Tagore bestowed upon him the title 'Mahatma' (Great Soul), which was soon taken up throughout India. Gandhi made a tremendous impact on the residents of the institute, and was treated with great dignity and honour by the academic faculty. But, he had to cut down on his trip because Gokhale had died in the meanwhile. Both Kasturba and Gandhi went to Poona to offer their condolences and be seen as one with what Gokhale had stood for. He again tried for the membership of the Servants of India Society, but was not accepted. An Ashram, which Gokhale had promised to fund for Gandhi, also virtually died with him.

Trying to look elsewhere for land and funds, Gandhi settled for his native Gujarat. With local mill owners picking up the tab, he managed to establish his Satyagraha Ashram on 150-Acre site by the banks of river Sabarmati, on the outskirts of Ahmedabad in May 1915. Problems arose when he inducted an untouchable and his family into the Ashram as an equal. Most of the mill owners withdrew support and some of the Ashramites also deserted him. For once, even Kasturba also disagreed with his action as the people had not been prepared in advance for taking in untouchables as their equals, something that had never happened in a staunch Hindu society of Ahmedabad. Gandhi remained unmoved by this setback, and even prepared to move the Ashram to an area where only untouchables lived. An anonymous donor later identified as Amba Lal Sarabhai, gifted Rupees thirteen thousand, a big sum in those days, for continuation of the Ashram at its location.

With the Ashram now established, Gandhi set off to complete his tour of India he had earlier cut short due to various factors, including demise of Gokhale. Unlike his insistence on travelling first class and take up issue on the subject of discrimination with the racist regime of South Africa whenever there was any reluctance to find him a berth in that class because of the colour of his skin, he now decided to travel only in third class; for, it allowed him to interact with the poor of India. Gandhi was received with rapturous enthusiasm wherever he went. In Calcutta, a crowd of young men unhitched the horses from the carriage of his host and insisted on pulling the carriage themselves. Their leader was a 21 years old Marwari merchant who had already made a small fortune buying and selling textiles—he was Ghanshyamdas Birla. It was the first time that Birla had set eyes on Gandhi, he had been a staunch follower of firebrand Tilak, and he found Gandhi's message of non-violence somewhat disconcerting. But on seeing the disarming nature and feelings for the poor that Gandhi exuded, he had felt that Gandhi was genuinely a Mahatma—as Tagore had described him. In due course of time, Birla became the principal financier for all the tasks Gandhi undertook.

Even though the stipulated one year was up, Gandhi continued with his tour of the countryside, making speeches on social issues and religious matters, propagating use of Hindi, by both Hindus and Muslims, particularly in the north. He made no effort to join either the Home Rule League, or the Congress, in spite of the pleas and pressure from various nationalist leaders. Some critics say that he was looking for a suitable cause that could catapult him to the top of the leadership in the movement for freedom; there are others who ascribe no such motive to Gandhi. Nevertheless, the agitation by the indigo farmers of Champaran caught his attention, not because he was looking for a cause, but for the fact that a suffering farmer virtually pestered him to help the poor in that region.

The British entrepreneurs had brought indigo industry to Champaran, Bihar in the eighteenth century. Now, with much cheaper German version in the form of synthetic dyes becoming available there was no market for indigo. The White landowners were, therefore, demanding hard cash from the farmers instead of the farm produce, namely indigo, which the farmers were obliged to plant in 15 per cent of their land. Unable to meet this demand for cash in lieu of indigo, the farmers sought intervention of the courts, but got no redress. No prominent leader was willing to take up cudgels on their behalf, till one farmer managed to latch on to Gandhi, coaxing and cajoling the Mahatma to help poor farmers who were on the verge of starvation death due to unreasonableness of the planters. Finally, Gandhi agreed to go to Champaran.

The news of his impending trip sent a wave of relief and excitement among the hapless farmers. The local administration in this back of beyond region of India, seemingly, had not heard of Gandhi. On his arrival he was met by police and served with a notice ordering him out of the district. Gandhi refused to obey any such order. He was arrested and produced before the magistrate. Gandhi calmly informed the magistrate that he was deliberately disobeying the law in the interest of the poor farmers of Champaran and was ready to face the consequences of his action. After consulting with the higher authorities the magistrate decided to release him on a bail of one hundred rupees. Gandhi informed him that he had no money and would prefer to serve whatever jail sentence was imposed on him. The whole episode had already grabbed media attention all over India. The Viceroy was under pressure to ensure that the situation did not get out of hand so as to make Gandhi repeat his style of disobedience, which had caused a lot of problems in South Africa. The lieutenant governor of Bihar issued a sharp rebuke to the divisional commissioner, who in turn, asked the magistrate to undo the 'serious' mistake of taking Gandhi into custody. The Viceroy set up a commission of inquiry to go into the whole case, Gandhi was made a member of the commission. The commission vindicated the stand taken by the farmers and recommended a total overhaul of land tenancy system. The landowners were also required to refund the money they had squeezed out of the poor farmers. To everyone's surprise, and to the annoyance of the concerned farmers, Gandhi recommended that only twenty five per cent of the amount due be refunded; in so far as he was concerned, the principle of the whole thing was more important than the money involved.'

Gandhi's triumph in Champaran added another coat of halo to the already developing personality cult. He had single-handedly taken on the might of British Empire and had won. As a matter of fact no single event had so gripped the public mind after the mutiny of 1857 as did Gandhi's refusal to leave Champaran without achieving what he had come to obtain on behalf of the common people. British authorities were aware of what Gandhi could do once he captured popular appeal and imagination. According to some historians Champaran was Britain's imperial 'Waterloo'. It was seen as a beginning of an end: in one stroke Gandhi had displayed the power of Satyagrah to the Indian government, and at the same time conveyed to the masses that means other than violence could also produce results if the cause was right.

In November 1917, Montagu invited Gandhi to meet him while he was on a tour of India. Neither Gandhi's demeanour, nor his dress sense, or for that matter, his understanding of the situation as it prevailed at the time impressed Montagu. He described Gandhi as a mere social reformer, who does not understand details of schemes, and is a pure visionary 'out of his depth'. Obviously, like many others before him Montagu failed to realise that what he saw as Gandhi's weaknesses were actually his strengths, and that the reason Gandhi did not understand details was because he chose not to.

Back home in Ahmedabad, the mill-owners and the workers were locked into a major wage revision controversy. When informed by the workers and mill management of the precarious situation, Gandhi agreed to arbitrate. In the first instance he wanted workers to give up agitation, attend prayers with him and to generally behave themselves. Initially the workers agreed to abide by the conditions imposed by the Mahatma; but after three weeks their resolve began to weaken, and sporadic instances of violation of law started coming to light. Gandhi agreed with the workers that it was not possible to go hungry when there was no end to their problem in sight. He declared that he would go on a fast until the workers demand of a salary increase of thirty five per cent was met. Initially Ahmedabad police treated it as yet another stunt for drawing political mileage, but the mill-owners were terrified of the consequences should anything happen to Gandhi. Within three days of Gandhi having gone on fast they agreed to arbitration and the workers also returned to work.

In Champaran and Ahmedabad, Gandhi had tried two of his main weapons i.e. 'peaceful disobedience and fast unto death', these two were to form the basis of his armoury in the national independence struggle. He had succeeded in both the instances. He had not yet tried out the third in India—the mass Satyagraha. An opportunity arose when crops failed in 'Kheda', a rural district not far from Ahmedabad in 1917. The farmers (locally known as Patidars) were not able to pay any taxes.

The revenue code provided for total remission of land tax when the crop yield went below 25 per cent. The government refused on the premise that the farmers were fudging details of their crops. A rising young son of Gujarat, Vallabh Bhai Patel, himself a Patidar, was leading the agitation. Gandhi had the Patidar's claim personally verified, and finding it to be correct took up the issue with the governor of Bombay. The government refused to forego its revenue, and started confiscating cattle and household goods of the defaulters, and also started attaching the land of Patidars. By June 1918, the farmers were exhausted, and had hardly any energy left to continue with the agitation. Gandhi too was looking for a face-saving formula when he learnt that due to the on going war in Europe and the administration's need for his support and calm in the country secret orders had been given to the local revenue officers to stop harassing those who were really too poor to pay their taxes. No written orders were issued so as to prevent this being cited as a precedent in future, but Gandhi took the easing of pressure on the poor farmers as a victory and called off the Satyagraha.

All the three episodes added tremendously to Gandhi's reputation and his mass following kept on increasing. But in April 1918, when he was still leading Satyagraha in Kheda, he risked alienation of his followers when he accepted an invitation form the Viceroy to take part in a conference on India's contribution to the war effort. Gandhi offered to help in recruitment of more Indian soldiers (there already were over 800,000 Indians fighting on behalf of the Empire). In a communication to Gandhi, Tilak offered to get five thousand recruits from Maharashtra if Gandhi could secure a promise from the Government before hand that Indians would get 'Commissioned Ranks' in the army. Gandhi refused the offer saying that the help should not be in the nature of a bargain. Instead, Gandhi wrote to the Viceroy, "I recognise that in the hour of its danger we must give, as we have decided to give, ungrudging and unequivocal support to the Empire of which we aspire in the near future to be partners in the same sense as the dominions overseas." On 30th April, continuing he said, "But it is the simple truth that our response is due to the expectation that our goal will be reached all the more speedily."[2]

Gandhi's rationale behind supporting the British during the war in Europe was not clear, either to his supporters or his detractors. The followers found his decision against his credo of non-violence for a foreign ruler inconsistent with his professed inclinations, the detractors termed it as hypocritical. Undeterred, he elected to personally lead recruitment rallies in and around Kheda. He found hostility everywhere, and but for Sardar Patel and a few lesser lights all the rest of his helpers deserted him. So much so, he had to walk to all the six hundred villages of the district as no one would lend even a bullock cart to him. The mission wasn't particularly successful and eventually his health again broke down because the physical and emotional aspects of the past events had taken their toll. Stubborn by nature he insisted to carry on even when severe dysentery and high fever made him collapse during one such outing. Convinced that his end was near, Gandhi insisted on being taken to his Ashram. But he still continued to refuse taking of nourishing food and milk. On Kasturba's insistence and that of other followers, as a special concession, he agreed to take goat's milk. By the time he had recovered enough to return to public life, the war in Europe was over and the time of reckoning had arrived.

The atmosphere in the country at the time could only be described as uncertain, and hostile to the Raj, particularly in the north. Full of disenchanted, disturbed and demobilized soldiers, the region was squirming for some action, which was not late in coming their way. The soldiers had seen how some other European countries treated their subject races, had experienced exposure to a free world and were clearly unhappy with conditions prevailing in the country. Moreover, having fought alongside the white sahibs in the trenches of France the Indian had shaken off all awe and fear that he had so peevishly been carrying hithertofore. Indians, more particularly the Punjabis, had learnt the lessons of equality with the white sahibs during the war. Now they were getting restive because camaraderie that existed in the face of enemy had suddenly vanished. An average Punjabi thought this to be a clear case of breach of trust. And the word was spreading around the country how the British had let down those who had staked all they had for the sake of the Empire.

The end of war left India seething with discontent from many quarters and causes. The upheaval of changing from wartime to peacetime economy had brought rampant inflation, widespread shortages, and more importantly a slump in the textile trade. There were retrenchments in factories due to lowering of demands in their products. Looming unemployment and forthcoming series of new and uncomfortable laws, like the Rowlatt Bill, added to the general unrest. Home Rule Leaguers did try to hold protest meetings, but in the absence of a strong leader these remained localised affairs. Youth everywhere was becoming restive and they were in urgent need of a leader who had enough clout and charisma to bring their troubles to light in a big way so that some acceptable solution could be found. At that point of time India was woefully short of leaders of national stature. Tilak had left for England in the autumn of 1918 to pursue a personal libel case, and was likely to be away for most of 1919. Annie Besant, once she became Congress president had given up street level agitations; she wasn't even sure of what stand she should take on the issue of Montagu-Chelmsford reforms. Other leaders, like Motilal Nehru, did not have a mass following in their own right.

Under the circumstances Jinnah should have been a logical choice, he had already worked hard at raising voice against the bill pertaining to Rowlatt Act in various quarters. But his demeanour, his no nonsense approach to people and issues, and his inability to suffer fools was, reason enough to scare away the youth. His reputation was such that any body other than those who were close to him and those who knew him very well was not willing to suffer his sarcastic tongue. Another major factor ruling out Jinnah was the fact that, he being a Muslim, was not likely to be acceptable to a majority of Hindus. Technically it was virtually by default that the young men turned to Gandhi to show them the way as he had done in South Africa, and later in Champaran and other places. Many of the young men of the movement 'begged' Gandhi to provide leadership to agitation against the Rowlatt Bill. It was going to be Gandhi's first step to take on the Raj at national level. Never to shy away from a situation where he felt that injustice was being done to people, Gandhi immediately agreed.

B G Horniman, the British editor of the liberal *Bombay Chronicle* had already called for a Satyagraha in his capacity as the vice-president of the Home Rule League. Gandhi immediately formed a Satyagraha Sabha, with himself as the president and Horniman as his deputy. Despite his frail health, and recent serious illness, Gandhi set off on a whirlwind tour of India to whip up support, set up local committees, and make public speeches—though these usually had to be read for him, because often he was too exhausted and weak to speak. In spite of all the hard work Gandhi and his staunch followers were putting in, the perceived mass participation was, somehow, not forthcoming. Even some stalwarts of Congress and other senior Indian political figures, who saw him as a naïve Gujarati upstart, were putting up a stiff opposition to Gandhi's attempt to mobilise masses. Their apprehension was that Gandhi was playing with fire by trying to use Satyagraha against measures designed to control terrorism. The campaign seemed to be petering out even before it had taken off in a serious manner. On the night of 18th March 1919, Rowlatt Act became law.

Aftermath of The Rowlatt Act—Gathering of the Storm

Gandhi gave a call for a nationwide Hartal on 30th March 1919 to protest against the Act. He urged people to observe the day as one of fasting and prayer. When his deputies pointed out that eleven days was too short a time-frame to organise any sort of national event, which could have any serious impact on the ongoing events. Gandhi agreed to put it off by one more week. As to how the Hartal was to be observed was left to the local leaders.

There was, inevitably, more than a little confusion. Two major strongholds of the movement, Delhi and Amritsar observed Hartal on the originally decided date, i.e. 30th March. It passed off without any untoward incident in Amritsar; but in Delhi, due to some confusion and rumours to the effect that two of the local leaders had been arrested, things went out of control. Some agitated men went to the railway station and asked the canteen vendor to close down and join the protesters. The contractor, a deaf old man refused, saying that he was under contract with the railway authorities, and had to keep his stall open for passengers up to a certain time. Infuriated with his refusal to obey the diktat, the agitators tried to forcibly close down the stall, when some customers/passengers objected a scuffle broke out. The railway police intervened, and arrested two of the ringleaders. This infuriated the crowd even further and it went berserk damaging the station building and other equipment. Railway police, finding the situation to be going out of their control called in the army. Brickbats were thrown on the police and the army men. Troops opened fire, killing two and wounding about a dozen. The crowd melted towards Chandni Chowk where army men were guarding the Municipal office. Again a confrontation took place between army and agitators, and some more agitators were wounded and killed. In the meanwhile, Swami Shradhanand, a disciple of Gandhi on hearing about the trouble arrived on the scene and exhorted the crowd to calm down and end violence as it was supposed to be a peaceful Satyagraha. He managed to restore peace, but now the people wanted to take out processions for disposal of the dead and to hold a public meeting to protest against what seems to have been an overreaction of the police and the army. Both the police and army authorities were against any procession, or a meeting being allowed, as the calm had still not been restored. Before the situation could further deteriorate the chief commissioner of Delhi showing signs of great maturity and understanding, not only allowed a public meeting in the afternoon to mourn the dead, he attended it himself with his main subordinates. On an assurance being given by the Swami, he agreed to allow people to join in the final rites of those killed.

On 31st March, funeral processions carrying biers of four Muslims and five Hindus killed the previous day were taken to the burial ground and cremation ground respectively with tens of thousands of silent mourners following. Army was present throughout to ensure that the situation remained under control. Next morning the local leaders went around various Bazars exhorting people to resume their normal business. The situation had been successfully defused and the shops began opening on 1st April. (PRO Report of Hunter Committee—CAB 27/91). There was, however, still a certain amount of uncertainty and restlessness among the shoppers and the shopkeepers alike, which was accentuated when the military again appeared in the Clock Tower area without any apparent provocation. Rumours ran afoot that there would be another round of firing, particularly when the infamous Colonel Beadon—who was known to shoot first and talk later—and his officers were seen hobnobbing with some known hirelings of the administration, who were apparently inciting the people for another round of agitation so that the military could again display the might of the Raj.[3]

On 4th April about thirty thousand Hindus and Muslims gathered in the famous Jumma Masjid to pray for the peace of the souls of those who had fallen to the bullets of soldiers on 30th March. Army was present throughout this prayer meeting displaying Might of the Raj, unmindful of the solemnity of the occasion. It was, perhaps, the first time that a Hindu-Swami Shradhanand-addressed a congregation to preach from the portals of the famous Masjid. The situation remained calm but tense during the following days.

Ignoring the warning signs from Delhi, Gandhi pressed on with his call for a general Hartal on 6th April. On his instructions, proscribed literature, which included Gandhi's own works—*Hind Swarajaya, The Sarvodya or the Universal Dawn, the Story of a Satyagraha* and 'The *Life and Addresses of Mustafa Kamal Pasha*' were put on sale in various places. The hawkers were all prominent Satyagrahis and included Gandhi himself, Sarojini Naidu and many others. All hawkers had instructions to put their name and address on every copy they sold so that, if required, the Administration could trace them. Potential buyers were also to be warned that possession of copies of these works could land them in trouble. All these warnings did not deter people and the entire stock was sold out in no time. In some cases the books were resold for as much as hundred times the published price. The proceeds of the sale were subsequently utilised for furthering the civil disobedience movement. This, perhaps, was Gandhi's way to generate a feeling of fearlessness in people, a strategy that had succeeded tremendously.

Though degree of success varied in different parts of the country, it did create a lot of goodwill between Hindus and Muslims, particularly in places like Amritsar and Lahore. The peaceful nature of the Satyagraha demonstrations failed to assuage the Anglo-Indian diehards, particularly in the Punjab. Sir Michael O'Dwyer was about to retire after six years as lieutenant Governor of Punjab, and seemed to relish the prospect of a final showdown with the natives, whom he had always despised, before he left. So much so, next day during his farewell speech to his legislative council in Lahore he issued a clear warning to those who were opposing the Rowlatt Act. Inter alia, he said, "The recent puerile demonstrations against the Rowlatt Act in both Amritsar and Lahore would be ludicrous if they did not indicate how easy it is to sway the ignorant and credulous people, not one in a thousand of whom knows anything of the measure, can be misled...Those who appeal to ignorance rather than to reason have a day of reckoning in store for them."

O'Dwyer ordered armed police on to the streets of Lahore and Amritsar. On 9 April 1919, in both cities, British residents, Anglo-Indians and other officials were alarmed to see Muslims joining in the Ram Naumi festival celebrating the birthday of Lord Rama, the semi-divine hero of Hindu mythology. The Deputy Commissioner, Miles Irving, who was observing the procession from the balcony of the Allahabad Bank, was unable to conceal his concern. The vast crowds were chanting 'Mahatma Gandhi ki jai', and Hindu-Mussalman ki jai. Similar slogans were shouted in support of local leaders, Kitchlew and Satyapal who acknowledged the cheers with silent approval. The religious occasion had been turned into a political show of Hindu-Muslim unity much to the discomfort of the lieutenant governor and his staff. Although the crowd in Lahore was truculent and aggressive, taunting the policemen and soldiers on patrolling duty, there was no violence. In Amritsar there was even a carnival-like atmosphere, with marchers pausing to cheer the uneasy Deputy Commissioner Miles Irving. Their bands were merrily playing 'God Save the King', apparently unaware of its connotations. There was nothing in the atmosphere to suggest that the country's destiny was soon going to take a violent and unexpected turn but the deputy commissioner was visibly agitated.

O'Dwyer had heard that the people of Delhi had invited Gandhi to mediate between the authorities and people. What worried him was the fact that Gandhi was also proposing to visit Lahore. Gandhi had been propagating his theory of non-violence; saying, 'There is a fundamental difference between their civilisation and ours. They believe in the doctrine of violence or brute force as the final arbiter. My reading of our civilisation is that we are expected to believe in soul-force or moral-force as the final arbiter and that is Satyagraha. O'Dwyer promptly issued an exclusion order banning Gandhi from entering the Punjab. Gandhi's 'soul-force', he said contemptuously, would be met with 'fist-force'.

To get to Delhi by train, Gandhi would have had to pass through parts of Punjab; where O'Dwyer planned to seize him and deport him to Burma. Wisely, the Viceroy countermanded this; and ordered that Gandhi simply be confined to the Bombay presidency. Early next morning, Gandhi was taken off the train at the first railway station in the Punjab, and put on the next train to Bombay under custody. Gandhi accepted it with that quiet resignation of his, which had exasperated Smuts in South Africa; and the British were in the process of getting a taste of his 'passive resistance'. In a historic message to his countrymen while exhorting them to refrain from any violence, Gandhi said, "It is galling for me to remain free while the Rowlatt Legislation disfigures the Statute Book. My arrest makes me free. It now remains for you to do your duty which is clearly stated in the Satyagrah pledge."

The Satyagrah pledge was, "I will never forsake truth in all matters in which I can promote Satyagrah. I will never support 'untruth' and will never injure any person or any property and shall never try either directly or indirectly to do such things. I also swear to make others believe and act upon those principles. I will also inform men all over the land that truth should be observed in everything and violence should not be shown towards brothers."

First mistake the cunning British made, where Gandhi was concerned, was to treat his appeal to the Indian masses as something that did not actually tell his followers about their next course of action. The second was to consider it as unworldly and politically naive. It was a disastrous miscalculation, as the events of next twenty-four hours conclusively proved. To compound the error of judgment, Irving decided to arrest Kitchlew and Satyapal, sensible and educated leaders who carried a lot of weight in Punjab and particularly in Amritsar, apparently on orders of O'Dwyer, who in any case was bent upon creating a situation in which he could teach the Indians a lesson that would ensure that the Raj would survive for a long time to come.

India has never been bereft of scumbags. To help O'Dwyer in his mission, one Hans Raj, a good looking young man of twenty-three who was busy ingratiating himself with the authorities came forward to do so on his own. Until the previous month he had been considered to be a parasite by just about everybody who mattered, and there were whispers that he lived off the immoral earnings of his mother who was a bazaar prostitute. He had already been sacked from two jobs where he had been caught, embezzling funds. He had sought employment with the police, and, although turned down, he had been placed on the waiting list. May be that was his motivation to prove his loyalty to the authorities. Now he sought lift with Kitchlew while he was on his way to meet Irving who had invited both Kitchlew and Satyapal. Hans Raj was a late convert to the movement; only forty-eight hours ago he had been appointed joint secretary of the Satyagrah Sabha and was responsible for keeping the register of those who had taken the vow of passive resistance. Now he was in the process of proving his utility to the leaders of national standing. Satyapal had not been won over by Hans Raj and his antics but Kitchlew was more forgiving and gullible. He had been impressed when Hans Raj carried a Home Rule banner during the Ram Naumi procession and had been to the forefront when the Hartal of 6 April was planned.

Irving had invited both Kitchlew and Satyapal, ostensibly to discuss the situation in Amritsar. Soon after arrival at the deputy commissioner's bungalow they realised that it was not a simple invitation for consultation. Without any formalities they were told that their presence in Amritsar was prejudicial to public safety and they were being deported to a secret destination. Before being taken to two waiting cars, which took them to Dharamsala with a military escort disguised as a hunting party the two doctors wrote two brief notes to their families and friends. These letters were quite innocuous, and were handed over to Hans Raj to deliver; he made copies of them before passing over to the addressees. When he called at the two houses he also spoke of verbal messages from the doctors wherein they had asked the people to take revenge, not withstanding the fact that there was no such exhortation in their written communication. Hans Raj sent telegrams to Gandhi and some important newspapers, and then hired a vehicle with a town-crier asking people to come out of their homes and protest against the deportation of the two prominent citizens of Amritsar. Hans Raj succeeded in his mission, soon a huge crowd built up; there were instances of stone-throwing, retaliatory firing by the police leading to killing of three or four people and several injured. The situation soon got out of hand, and Irving found himself at his wits end. With the crowd becoming more and more hostile and some panicky policemen trying to get out of a sticky situation by firing their weapons, Kitchlew and Satyapal were soon forgotten. The crowd was now targeting any and every European they could come across.

The news of Gandhi's 'arrest' reached Bombay long before he did. There were immediate protests and people took to streets shouting slogans. But the agitation soon petered out when Gandhi himself arrived on the scene, scolded people, threatening to undertake a personal Satyagraha against them if they did not behave properly. But in Ahmedabad things went out of control where thousands of restless and retrenched mill-workers were already roaming the streets, they were easy meat for troublemakers. Vallabhbhai Patel and Kasturba Gandhi did manage to restore calm, albeit temporarily. During the night the mischief-makers went around spreading rumours about arrests of some other prominent leaders. A full-scale riot was the outcome. The mob went on a looting spree, attacking any European they saw, burning down some 51 government and municipal buildings. Graffiti appeared on the wrecked police and railway stations, instigating people to kill Europeans, and to destroy anything and everything owned by them. At Nadiad a troops train was derailed by agitating masses as they had removed a portion of the rail leading to derailment. Before the calm could be restored 28 rioters had been shot dead and at least 123 wounded. A horrified Gandhi arrived next day, Sunday 13 April. The commissioner allowed him to hold a public meeting where Gandhi exhorted people to return to their homes, observe penitential fast for a day, he himself would fast for three days, he declared. How many actually fasted is not known, but certainly there was no more trouble in Ahmedabad.

Footnotes

1. MK Gandhi—Collected Works, Volume XIII page 9
2. MK Gandhi - The Complete Works Vol. XIV p 262
3. Punjab Unrest - Before and After p 67

7

Massacre at Jallianwala Bagh—Raj's Biggest Blunder

I met a charming lady in her nineties who recalled meeting, a frail and prematurely old man who told her, "If I had my life over again, I would do exactly the same." Soon afterwards he died. He was Brigadier General Dyer.

Alfred Draper in his book- "Amritsar"

Build Up to Massacre

Thanks to O'Dwyer's exclusion order, there was no Gandhi when things went out of control in Delhi and Punjab. Just like other parts of the country, Gandhi's arrest had caused spontaneous Hartal in Delhi, Lahore and Amritsar. The most worrying aspect of the whole thing was that in Delhi the Satyagraha leaders soon became non-effective and some local groups, with their own agendas, started generating their influence on the proceedings on the very first day itself, sidelining people like Swami Shradhanand. In Lahore, when a number of protesters started marching towards the Civil Lines, O'Dwyer saw red. Even though the crowd had not shown any inclination towards violence of any kind, he thought that the Europeans were under threat. He sent out troops and police with orders to drive them back behind the walls of the old city. When the students at the head of the procession tried to explain that they were only trying to express their sorrow over the arrest of Gandhi, the police opened fire, killing eight of the marchers. The rest did scatter away but there was uneasy peace. A worried O'Dwyer called a meeting of the local community leaders, asking them to assert their authority, but no one would listen to them. In order to express their resentment over this unprovoked firing, the people observed complete

Hartal. Not a shop opened in the town. But there was no violence. The people damaged not a flowerpot or a windowpane belonging to the state.[1]

After a very serious consideration and as the continued Hartal was also affecting the common citizen, the local leaders formulated proposals for the consideration of the Lt. Governor so that the people could resume their normal life. These proposals, *inter alia*, were:

- The troops and the police who had occupied the city on the 12th should be withdrawn.

- Those arrested for the criminal acts between the 10th and 12th April should be released on 'security/surety'.

- In future, the government should act only after consultation with a committee formed of prominent local leaders.

Sir Michael O'Dwyer refused to even consider these terms; he was not prepared to "abdicate to the rebels", he responded. Soon after, the Lahore Civil Area was separated from the rest of the district and put under command of Colonel Johnson. Europeans and Anglo Indians were encouraged to buy weapons, government started requisitioning motorcars for military use and petrol was rationed. All this, clearly was a prelude to the Martial Law, which was to follow soon after.

Kasur, a small town with a population of about 25,000 and close to Lahore and Amritsar, was also affected by happenings in the big neighbourhood towns. The news about disturbances in Lahore and Amritsar created a lot of restive and uncomfortable rumblings amongst the labour community of the leather industry, and of course, among the students. On 11th April, Kasur observed its first Hartal in protest against firings and killings in Lahore and Amritsar. On the 12th, others joined the students and a procession proceeded towards the railway station, carrying a "charpoy" on which was spread a black flag as a symbol of death of liberty. All of them were chanting anti-British slogans and pronouncing their resentment against the Rowlatt Act. A train, with mostly British passengers arrived at the station. There were army officers, some civilians and other whites that suddenly became target of the wrath of the crowd. Most of them managed to escape, but for two warrant officers, who armed with their service revolvers, were over-confident about their ability to safe-guard the Empire from the 'rebels'. Standing at the doors of their compartment they started firing at the crowd, but caused no damage because there was no body within the range of their pistols. On running out of ammunition, they tried to scamper away, but were chased by the angry protestors. Their bid to seek help from the railway staff and police was also of no avail because those on duty had already fled fearing for their lives. The warrant officers then tried to run out of the entrance to the station but were hemmed in by the railings and were soon overpowered by the crowd. The Lathi bearing and by now visibly angry crowd, because of the shooting these two had indulged in, soon overpowered them and beat them to death. Thereafter the protesters left the railway station, and on their way back to town cut off the telegraph wires, looted and gutted the 'Wheat Mandi' post office, which was located close to the police station where as many as six constables and two head constables with six rifles between them decided to remain mute spectators. (During the enquiry into the episode the deputy superintendent of police testified that it would have been foolhardy to use the limited force to control a mob that was on a rampage). The main post office was also burnt. The crowd then moved to the symbols of the British authority—the Munsif's court and the Tehsil headquarters. Here the police opened fire; one man was instantly killed and several wounded. The crowd, having already spent its fury and finally finding toughening of the official stand dispersed at once. The mob fury had clearly subsided by then.

On the 13th April shops reopened and the town seemed to have calmed down, may be because the news about the arrival of an army unit under Colonel McRae had already spread. The situation was brought under control with the arrest of the ringleaders of the disturbances. But the news of Hartal at Lahore, Amritsar and riots in Kasur had by then reached Gujranwala with the rustic villagers who brought the news taunting the town folks for not having expressed their grief and resentment over the arrest of Gandhi, and for not protesting over the passage of the Rowlatt Act. Gujranwala, another small town about 36 miles from Amritsar, was disturbed when the body of a dead calf was found hanging from a railway bridge. People were confused because no one was quite sure what it meant, except that it clearly meant trouble because soon some pork (taboo for the Muslims) was also found to have been thrown in a mosque. Crowds of Indians were soon astir; this clearly was seen as instigation by the authorities to cause trouble between the two communities, and this prognosis knit Hindus and Muslims, who now wanted to teach the administration a lesson for having tried to cause a divide between them. They stoned a train, set fire a couple of railway bridges, the railway station, the telegraph office, the district court and an Indian church. Superintendent of Police, Mr. Heron, was attacked when he ordered his men to fire at the crowd.

Appeals for help from Amritsar put O'Dwyer in a predicament. He could not pull forces either from Lahore or from Amritsar, fearing a strong reaction from the already agitated masses if news of depletion of his forces in these two politically sensitive towns leaked out. So, he turned to the Royal Air Force, who very promptly sent a flight of three BE2c aircraft, each armed with a Lewis machine gun and carrying ten 20-pound bombs. They were under the command of Captain D H M Carberry, who seems to have been of the same stuff as (infamous) Brigadier General Dyer, and was in complete agreement with the treatment that had been given to the Indians. He had flown the reconnaissance mission over Amritsar for General Dyer two days earlier. Arriving at Gujranwala at 3.10 p.m., he dropped his first three bombs on a party of 150 people in the nearby village of Dhulla, who looked as if they were heading for the town. One bomb failed to explode, and two fell near the crowd, killing a woman and a boy and slightly wounding two men. The rest of the crowd fled back to the village. Carberry hastened them on their way by firing from the Lewis machine gun. The other two pilots apparently had no appetite for innocent blood. One of them—fired 25 rounds at a group of 25-30 people who were later said to have been busy harvesting-without hitting anybody; the other pilots, according to the official report, 'took no action'. Carberry continued to enjoy himself, he dropped four more bombs in the town of Gujranwala itself—two of them failing to explode—and fired 100 to 150 rounds at crowds in the streets. Later when asked at the enquiry why he machine-gunned crowds even after they had been dispersed, he replied: "I was trying to do this in their own interest. If I killed a few people, they would not gather and come to Gujranwala to do damage." His idea was 'to produce a sort of moral effect on them.'[2] The government also tried to play down this wanton killing of the innocents by claiming that there was a planned conspiracy to damage state property and was hatched at a private meeting of local leaders, where it was decided to follow the example of Lahore and Amritsar).

Colonel O'Brien, who had arrived earlier to take charge of the administration, arrested some twenty odd respectable citizens on the 15th of April. The arrested included several local lawyers and other notables who in fact had rendered active help in restoring calm and peace earlier. The prisoners were handcuffed and paraded through the streets, some in their undergarments because they had not been allowed to even dress up before being taken prisoner. In order to spite the display of Hindu-Muslim unity the handcuffed pairs included one Hindu with a Muslim attached to him. So that their humiliation was complete the prisoners were made to stand in the sun near the railway station, then made to run a sort of three-legged race and again made to walk through the town. Eventually when O'Brien was seemingly tired of his pranks, the prisoners were dispatched to Lahore in an open coal-truck without any food or amenities.

Similar acts of crude display of power and authority were enacted in different parts of Punjab wherever people tried to show their anger over arrest of Gandhi and passage of the Rowlatt Act by taking out processions. Whether such processions had any potential for violence or not made no difference to the administration. Where O' Dwyer was concerned he had been given an opportunity by the Indians to show who was the ruler and to teach them a lesson not to be forgotten in a hurry. Seeing the governor in such a vengeful mood some of the more enthusiastic officers suggested that the whole town of Amritsar should be bombarded in such a way that at least one thousand Indians die for every European killed during the preceding riots. Chances of hitting the Golden Temple by default and consequent resentment amongst the Sikhs, particularly reaction of the Sikh troops, is what made such a horrendous suggestion getting nixed. O' Dwyer was now thinking of something more innovative and destructive to bring agitating masses under control.

Events in Amritsar

In Amritsar on the morning of 9th April, shortly before the 'Ram Naumi' procession was due to start, Deputy Commissioner Irving called a meeting at his bungalow to discuss the situation with his commander of the local garrison and others, including Lieutenant Colonel Henry Smith, the civil surgeon who always saw Bolshevik conspiracy in any thing and everything which was out of tune with his perceptions; in addition, he was rabidly anti-Indian. Not satisfied with the line of approach Irving was likely to take to control the situation he set off on the two hour road journey to Lahore, to see O'Dwyer. O'Dwyer agreed with him that unless force was immediately used, there were chances of red flags flying all over India. He sent Smith back to Amritsar, with an order for Irving to arrest the city's two Indian leaders: Dr Saifuddin Kitchlew, a Muslim lawyer who was a member of Lincoln's Inn, a Cambridge graduate and a PhD of Munster University; and Dr Satyapal, a Hindu doctor who had qualified at Lahore Medical College and served during the war in the Indian Medical Service. Since the two had already been debarred from addressing public meetings, this arrest order apparently was designed to provoke reaction so that O'Dwyer could justify use of force. He had his stage for a confrontation when news of the arrest of Kitchlew and Satyapal leaked out. The two had been whisked away under military escort to the hill town of Dharamsala. By 11.30 a.m. a great and obviously agitated crowd started advancing towards Irving's bungalow, demanding to know what had become of their local heroes.

Soon enough the crowd built up to over 40,000, their mood becoming more and more sullen and aggressive. Stones rained down on the police and troops sent to head them off, and the troops opened fire. Three or four people were killed and several wounded. The authorities did not allow the relatives to take charge of the wounded and the dead, this apathy of the administration created ill-will and resentment. In no time the demonstration, which so far had been noisy but peaceful turned into a full-scale riot. Rising fury of the mob led them to the city centre where they destroyed the telegraph exchange office, burned down the town hall, and looted those shops which were slow in closing down as per the direction of the ring leaders. A Christian church and school, and two of the three European banks also became targets of the mass anger. Managers of the banks were killed in the melee and their bodies burnt. In all, during the day, at least, five Europeans and twenty-five Indians were killed. Miss Marcia Sherwood, a missionary nurse, who had set off to ensure safety of the girl students in Mission School ran into a mob, which chased her into a bylane, knocked her from her bicycle and left her for dead. A local Hindu shopkeeper saved her life at the risk of his own, picking her up from the gutter and hiding her in his own house. By this time, the remaining European women and children were being moved either to the railway station or to the Gobind Garh fort, where they were provided security by a mixed force of British and Indian troops, strengthened by a detachment of Gurkhas whose train had fortuitously stopped at Amritsar.

Military reinforcement kept arriving during the night, but the fire had already gone out of the demonstrations, and there was no further trouble, an eerie calm having descended over the city. The deserted streets were littered with debris and several of the buildings were gutted shells; others were still smouldering. The shops and bazaars were closed and a sullen and subdued population was making preparations for the burial and burning of the dead. On 11th April a group of local Indian lawyers asked Irving for permission to bury or cremate their dead, he agreed, provided there were no large processions: no more than four friends or family could accompany the bodies to the cremation or burial grounds.

Kitchin, the commissioner of Lahore Division, meanwhile, had accumulated as much evidence as he could about the previous day's rioting and was of the firm opinion that a state of war existed. He decided to return to Lahore and report his views to O'Dwyer and suggest that martial law should be proclaimed. On 11th April 1919 Brigadier Dyer GOC 45th Brigade located in Jullundhur was ordered to proceed to Amritsar where some kind of trouble was brewing. He was to take over the local command from one Major MacDonald as the deputy commissioner Miles Irving had already been advised to hand over the city's administration to him on orders of the Commissioner of

Lahore. At 9.00 p.m. Brigadier-General Reginald 'Rex' Dyer, with his brigade major, Captain FC Briggs and a Captain Bostock, arrived by road from Dyer's brigade headquarters at Jullundhur. He went direct to the railway station. There he immediately called a conference, which was attended by Irving and the Superintendent of Police. Irving gave him a complete run down on the situation and expressed the view that the crowd was still impenitently hostile and that a second Mutiny was in the offing. As they talked things over, Dyer became convinced that Miles Irving was cracking under the strain; he looked a broken man, utterly worn out by the heavy burden of his responsibilities. His fears were confirmed when the Deputy Commissioner confessed that he could no longer cope with the situation which was now beyond the control of the civil authorities. By midnight, Dyer had persuaded a worried and out of his depth Irving to hand over the city of Amritsar to his control. At the conclusion of the conference a document was drawn up and handed over to a number of leading citizens for distribution throughout the city. The document stipulated; that " The troops have orders to use all force necessary to restore order in Amritsar. No gathering of person or processions of any sort will be allowed. All gatherings will be fired on. Any persons leaving the city in groups of more than four will be fired on. Respectable persons should keep indoors." Thereafter, Dyer went around with his staff officers and found the city tense; anxious Indians and Eurasians were clamouring to be taken to a place of safety. There were a few British civilians also looking for some train to take them away.

Brigadier General Dyer

Brigadier General Reginald Dyer, the butcher of Jallianwala Bagh, was born on 9 October 1864, at Muree to a wealthy brewer. After his initial schooling in Bishop Cotton School in Simla he was sent to Ireland where he and his brother were boarders at Middleton College. He later entered Dublin University to study medicine, but departed after the first year because he found the dissecting rooms too much for his stomach. He decided instead to apply for the army and was accepted into the Royal Military College, Sandhurst. He transferred from the British Army to the Indian Army in 1887. During the 1st World War he was instrumental in safeguarding the interests of the Raj in the tribal belts of Afghanistan. With only a handful of Indian troops, isolated in one of the world's most primitive areas, he succeeded by sheer audacity and force of personality in winning over to the British cause most of the local leaders and their tribesmen. He was made a Companion of the Most Honourable Order of the Bath (CMHOB). Early in 1917 he was given command of the 45th Infantry Brigade at Jullundhur. The brigade was more than Division strength with a mix of different religions and communities. Dyer showed great deal of tact and intelligence in handling the racial and religious conflicts within the Brigade. But he was a very sick man; in addition to injuries sustained during various campaigns he was also suffering from arteriosclerosis, a degenerative and incurable disease. But Dyer was a soldier first and foremost with a tendency towards over-simplification. Life to him was made up of clearly defined blacks and whites; there were no subtle shades. Politically he was even more intransigent than his civil boss, O'Dwyer. Where Indians were concerned, Dyer's approach to them could be summed up in the phrase 'Thou shalt not agitate.' He sincerely believed that Indians did not understand Self-Government neither did they want it. To them 'the Raj was the ultimate, just and strong; where the British officer is a Sahib who will do them right and protect them from all kinds of enemies. With his violent temperament aggravated by physical pain, he was likely to overreact in an emergency, hardly the ideal choice to command an area that was seething with discontent.

In the meantime, at Lahore, uncertainty reigned supreme. O'Dwyer was consulting with Kitchin and others. An effort was constantly being made to assess the fragmented rumours and counter-rumours of rebellion and murder trickling in from dozens of towns and cities throughout the Province of Punjab. Poor communications fed the pervading fear that the British were about to suffer the same fate as their forebears in Meerut, Delhi and Kanpur in 1857. O'Dwyer telegraphed his concern to the Central Indian Government at Delhi. In response, he was told that, if troops were obliged to open fire, then they should "make an example". There was utter confusion in Lahore. So much so that O'Dwyer was not even aware of Dyer's arrival in Amritsar. A Lieutenant Colonel Morgan was detailed to go to Amritsar with the orders: "The city is in the hands of rebels. It is your job to get it back." But on arrival Morgan found that Dyer was firmly in saddle and there were no signs of any rebellion. It is surprising that all the characters that had arrived in Amritsar ostensibly because of a crisis had travelled by road and without an armed escort. None of them had any trouble in reaching their destination safe and sound. Even Kitchin who had gone to Lahore to report an uprising said that his trip to and from Lahore had been uneventful and he had encountered no trouble.

The Massacre

At first light on 13 April, Baisakhi Day, the day that marks the beginning of the harvest season, long columns of country people could be seen making their way into the city of Amritsar. The villagers were coming to make their devotions at the Golden Temple and to attend the livestock fair, which would continue for several days as per normal norms. They were placidly following their age-old customs in ignorance of the fact that O'Dwyer and Kitchin believed them to be on the verge of a bloody rebellion. Most of the pilgrims drifted through the streets in the direction of the Jallianwala Bagh, traditionally a gathering place for religious assemblies and a resting place for poor families unable to pay accommodation expenses. With some sticks for a cooking fire, and a blanket to cover themselves at night, they planned to camp here until the time came for them to go home.

Reports of the gathering crowds convinced Dyer that he must act quickly to impose his 'will' upon the local population. He would enter the city in person, leading an impressive body of troops, and announce that no further acts of defiance would be tolerated. A proclamation to this effect was drafted and, at 1030 am he set off in a motorcar, escorted by troops on foot and by two armoured cars that happened to be available. With him he had Miles Irving, the two senior police officers, Plomer and Rehill, and his Brigade Major, Briggs.

During the next two hours, Dyer's column made its way slowly through the northern and western quarters of the city. It halted at nineteen different points at which, by drum-roll and shouts from the town crier, nervous passers-by were called together so that they could hear the proclamation read out in Urdu and Punjabi. Given the lack of any amplifying equipment, it is unlikely that many people heard the proclamation. For that matter given the festive mood of the people in general it is doubtful if many of them gave it the importance the proclamation deserved. In sum those who cared to listen were informed that, " It is hereby proclaimed to all that no person in this city is permitted or allowed to leave the city in his own private or hired conveyance, or on foot, without a pass from one of the following officers: the Deputy Commissioner, the Superintendent of Police, a Magistrate, or the police officer in charge of the Kotwali. No person residing in Amritsar City is permitted to leave his house after 8.00 pm. Any person found in the streets after 8.00 pm is liable to be shot. No procession of any kind is permitted to parade in the streets in the city or outside of it at any time. Any such processions or gatherings of four men will be looked upon and treated as an unlawful assembly and dispersed by force of arms if necessary. Almost concurrently, a boy with the beat of an empty tin was announcing that a meeting would be held at 4 PM at the Jallianwala Bagh. No effort was made to restrain the boy from making this contradictory announcement. Nor were the people warned against meeting in the Bagh.

The proclamation of Dyer was, obviously unsound, and had not catered for practical difficulties. No restriction was placed on people entering Amritsar, who were coming in hoards for their traditional Baisakhi visit to the Golden Temple and thereafter gathering in the Jallianwala Bagh. General Dyer simply did not have sufficient troops and police under his command to implement the orders, which he was now announcing. His few hundred men could not possibly sustain a curfew; guard key buildings supervise the movement of people and traffic in and out of the city, issue thousands of individual passes (which had yet to be designed and printed), and simultaneously protect the Europeans in the civil lines. Clearly, a large part of the proclamation was totally impracticable in the circumstances. In the context of Amritsar's seething narrow streets, what constituted a 'gathering of four men' was difficult to define with large groups of pilgrims strolling among the sites of their holy city. Passing and re-passing and stopping to wish old friends, every street-corner and every thoroughfare was bound to have a 'gathering' much larger than four.

One of the great mysteries of General Dyer's behaviour that morning was his omission to go anywhere near those places which were most likely to attract the largest crowds. At no stage did he go closer than half a mile to either the Golden Temple or the Jallianwala Bagh. Even the local police officers, who were accompanying him made no effort to ensure that the proclamation was read in those areas, as the largest concentration of people was likely to be available in and around these two places.

On his return to the Ram Bagh, Dyer studied the reports, which had come in during his absence. Almost all of them described that a mass protest meeting was being organised later that day in the Jallianwala Bagh, and large crowds had already started collecting. Nobody, and certainly not the local police officers, told him that on such a day assembly of large crowds in Jallianwala Bagh was an annual affair with religious and social connotations without any past history of trouble of any kind. There were family groups enjoying the holiday, priests giving readings from the holy book, peddlers selling sweetmeats and religious souvenirs. The atmosphere was typically 'Mela'; in itself it was no threat to the Raj. In general the quality of intelligence reports was poor, and had obviously been generated by police informers who were keen on justifying their pay rather than provide any serious intelligence that could be used for decision-making.

With inputs of such dubious merit Dyer concluded that the time had come " to punish the naughty boys...teach them a lesson...make a widespread impression". Without consulting the Lt Governor at Lahore or without discussing the situation with Kitchin he decided to strike. Orders were given for a 'strike force' to be formed. It consisted of twenty-five riflemen from 1/9 Gurkhas and twenty-five more drawn from other sundry units. Heavyweight support was to be provided by the two armoured cars with a few riflemen inside each. He did not inform anyone of his intentions, and the only Europeans in his party were his aide Captain Briggs, bodyguard Sergeant Anderson, a Gurkha Rifles officer Captain Crampton, and the policemen, Plomer and Rehill.

If it crossed the minds of any of the European officers present that it seemed a trifle odd that the General should have taken personal control of the operation, no one spelled out his thoughts. Neither did anyone comment on the General selecting raw Gurkhas for the mission he had in mind when he had well-trained British troops at his disposal. Even more remarkable was the absence of the senior-most civilian officer in Amritsar, Mr. Miles Irving, the Deputy Commissioner whom Dyer had promised to consult before taking any major action.

The Jallianwala Bagh was an open stretch of almost bare ground, about eight acres in size, the whole being surrounded by the high walls of neighbouring houses. At one end was a narrow stretch of ground slightly higher than the rest. The only features within the Bagh were a small stone-built Samadhi, a well, and two small clusters of scrawny trees. The Bagh had always been used for public gatherings of various kinds. The Raj had even organised arrangement for supply of drinking water whenever there had been a large gathering anticipated in the Jallianwala Bagh. Even on this eventful day a platform had been erected for the speakers and poets near the well and a squad of hired sweepers had scurried across the dusty surface trying to make it as clean as possible. Water carriers were moving among the crowd dispensing drinks.

Estimates vary widely, but it seems likely that there were about 10, 000 people in the Bagh on that fateful afternoon. There is no doubt that political activists were using the Bagh as a forum for their protests against the earlier arrests of their leaders, and against the shootings of 10 April. Clearly, they ran the risk of being fired upon, particularly, if they had not heard the proclamations being made through the 'town criers'. The crowd was not necessarily a captive audience. There were those who were more involved in playing dice and cards, or simply gossiping with some friends they had met after a long while and was usual during Baisakhi Mela in the Bagh. Some others were just keeping guard over piles of shoes and sandals and other personal belongings placed in their custody by friends who had gone to the Golden Temple. In sum total the atmosphere did not indicate anything that could be termed as unusual or out of place for the authorities to take recourse to a strong military action. Hans Raj had been active all this time interacting with known CID detectives. No one seemed to be paying too much attention to the fact that, despite his recent political activities Hans Raj was still on amiable terms with the authorities.

Dyer and his supporters later claimed that known militants and revolutionaries were standing on a platform, and that one of them was addressing the crowd with a view to incite them. As to how anybody could give a speech in an open space without facilities like public address system and get, much less sustain, attention of so many people milling around with hardly anybody paying any heed to anything or anybody not directly forming part of a particular group was never considered by Dyer. The crowd also had a large number of demobilised soldiers who had formed part of the Allies forces till recently. If they had so wished, these experienced fighting men could have armed themselves and offered appropriate resistance to Dyer and his improvised little army. They did not, because they had not come to confront the government. The only weapons present in the Bagh that day were the 'ceremonial Kirpan' worn by some of the orthodox Khalsa (pure) Sikhs.

5.15 PM: 13, April Jallianwala Bagh

The British party arrived in the Bazaar Jallianwala. An alleyway thirty yards wide separated it from the Bagh. Dyer dismounted from his car and gave his orders. He intended to send the armoured cars into the Bagh, but the entrance was too narrow for them to pass. They remained in the lane while the riflemen trotted forward through the alley. Dyer strode through the alley strutting with the urgency of someone with an urgent mission. This, after all, was his show and he was in personal command. "Gurkhas left, 59th right", he shouted. His troops fanned out along the raised bank of the hard-packed ground on the Bagh's western perimeter and adopted kneeling position for firing. "Open rapid, Fire", commanded Dyer. As the first volley struck the crowd, a wail went up: "Agaye, Agaye" (they have come). Hans Raj who had doubtful reputation, shouted: "Be not afraid. Sit down. The Government will never fire. They are only blanks". Then he vanished from the scene. That he was mistaken, either by design or default; quickly became clear as people started to fall, crimson stains flowering over the white of their clothing. Seconds later the horror of the situation struck home and people began running for the walls and clambering over while others rushed towards the entrance through which the troops had emerged. Anderson noticed that there was no attempt to rush the troops. Captain Briggs was seemingly in a state of shock over this vengeful slaughter and tried to pluck at Dyer's sleeve, but he was too dazed to speak and the General ignored him and did not divert his attention from his gory mission.

The crowd swirled and eddied away from awful noise of the rifle fire. Some struggled to take cover. Many died before they had a chance. In a total panic, over 10,000 men, women and children were trying to escape from a killing ground from which there was no escape. Dyer's soldiers were blocking the westerly exit from the Bagh, and the other two alleyways were barely wide enough to permit the passage of men walking three abreast. In any case within the first minute, the flailing bodies of hysterical and injured people blocked both. The firing went on for ten minutes. No matter where they ran, the crowd was continually being cut down. Like animals trapped in a cage, the people in the Bagh ran this way and that, screaming, praying, calling out to their children, and falling under the merciless torrent of bullets. Some of those who could still retain a semblance of sanity tried to organise themselves into human ladders so that they could push and pull each other up and over the high boundary walls. Wherever such groups gathered, Dyer saw them and directed the attention of his marksmen to the tempting targets. When he saw other groups trying to find shelter amongst the trees and behind the small shrine, he made sure that concentrated fire was poured in those areas. All this time Dyer stood erect and calm behind the line of riflemen. All those who had accompanied him were too stunned to react in any manner. On and on the shooting went. To vary the targets, some of the soldiers fired at individuals who were foolish enough to look out of their windows and down from the balconies of the surrounding houses. Some of these people were also killed. There could be no dispute about the effectiveness of the firing into the heart of the crowd in Jallianwala Bagh. The people were trapped and no matter which way they ran there was no escape from the firing. So concentrated was the fire that some of the victims received more than one wound, each of them would have been fatal. Dyer obviously was enjoying himself.

Eventually the roar of rifle fire died away to a spasmodic crackle as the troops fired off their last remaining rounds. No order was given to 'cease fire'. The attack came to an end simply because there was no more ammunition in the soldier's pouches. The soldiers were brought to their feet, fallen in, and marched out of the Bagh back to their quarters. Dyer left without even a backward glance at the scene of carnage he had engineered. He was glad that some had escaped for they would serve as messengers to warn others of the dire consequences of rebellion. He did not know, and it would have meant nothing to him if he had known, that one of those trapped under the pile of bodies in the centre of the Bagh was a young lad named Udham Singh.

Jallianwala Bagh now resembled a deserted battlefield. The dead were deepest by the walls and the exits where people had tried to get out. Among them were a great many peasants and their children who had come from their villages to celebrate Baisakhi in the city of their *Gurus*.

Those who knew that their near ones had gone to the Bagh during the day ran towards the garden on hearing of the firing, but they stopped as they neared the gates. They stood terror-stricken as the crack of rifles echoed in the evening air. It was not until the armoured vehicles and motorcars moved off, followed by the soldiers that they ventured into the Bagh. Desperately anxious for the safety of their loved ones they finally entered the Bagh. Men with blood streaming from gaping wounds were crawling like stricken animals. The relatives turned over the dead and rummaged among the wounded, pulling them aside to expose those buried underneath, all the time calling the name of the person they were looking for. But their voices were drowned by the cries of the injured. Those who were lucky enough to recover the dead or wounded bodies of their loved ones bundled them on to charpoys and hurried away. The searchers worked feverishly, fearful that the soldiers would return and open fire on them for breaking the curfew.

No such fears inhibited the jackals, pi-dogs and vultures attracted by the stench of blood and unexpected banquet of human flesh so thoughtfully organised by protectors of the Raj. The government made no effort to provide any dignity to the dead. Instead, in the night Dyer set out from the Ram Bagh with an armed force, visiting the pickets and city gates; he toured the streets to make sure that the curfew was observed. He found the streets deserted and the city absolutely quiet. Fortunately he did not deem it necessary to visit Jallianwala Bagh; what might have happened to the dying, to the families searching for their loved ones and to those who were offering water to the injured if he had done so is not too difficult to imagine.

O'Dwyer received information about the event at 3 a.m. the next morning when Mr. G A Wathen, the principal of Khalsa College and Mr. Jacob a member of the Indian Civil Service raced on a motorcycle from Amritsar to deliver a personal dispatch from Miles Irving wherein the worthy had washed his hands off the whole thing and informed the Lieutenant Governor "The military found a large meeting of some five thousand men and opened fire without warning, killing about 200. Firing went on for ten minutes. I much regret I was not present."

The Lieutenant Governor immediately sent off a wireless message to the Government of India containing barest of details:

"At Amritsar yesterday Brigadier General Dyer and Deputy Commissioner read proclamation in city forbidding all public meetings. In spite of this, meeting attended by six thousand was held at 4.30. Troops present under command of General Dyer fired, killing about two hundred. Deputy Commissioner not present. Military report not yet received."

When the reports of the magnitude of the military action started reaching him and when he thought of the likely repercussions O' Dwyer started changing his tune while reporting to the central government. He knew that a massive cover up action would be required. So now he sent a fresh communication on the fourteenth.

'State of open rebellion exists in parts of districts of Lahore and Amritsar, Lieutenant-Governor, with concurrence of General Officer Commanding 16th Division and Chief Justice High Court, requests Governor General in Council to suspend functions of ordinary Criminal Courts in Amritsar and Lahore districts to establish martial law therein.'

The message also went on to ask for special tribunals to be set up to try people accused of offences arising from disturbances.

The Viceroy approved, but owing to the breakdown in communications the answer was not received in Lahore until late in the night; martial law could, therefore, only be proclaimed on the fifteenth. Later, however, O'Dwyer virtually forced the Viceroy to backdate the whole correspondence on the subject when the issue of the Amritsar massacre caught international attention.

On the fourteenth Dyer sent the following 'Action Taken' report to General Beynon-Commander 16 Division:

"I entered the Jallianwala Bagh by a very narrow lane which necessitated leaving my armoured cars behind. On entering I saw a dense crowd, estimated at about 5,000 (those present put it at 15,000 to 20,000), a man on a raised platform addressing the audience and making gesticulations with his hands.

I realised that my force was small and to hesitate might induce attack. I immediately opened fire and dispersed the mob. I estimated that between 200 and 300 of the crowd were killed. My party fired 1650 rounds.

I returned to my headquarters at about 1800 hours. At 2200 hours, accompanied by a force, I visited all my pickets and marched through the city in order to make sure that my order as to the inhabitants not being out of their homes after 2200 hours had been obeyed. The city was absolutely quiet and not a soul was to be seen. I returned to the headquarters at midnight. The inhabitants have asked permission to bury the dead in accordance with my orders. This I am allowing".

(Signed) REH Dyer, Brigadier General Commanding 45th Brigade

That the dead and the wounded Indians had been left to rot did not seem to concern General Beynon. He sought and obtained approval of O'Dwyer and sent off a personal message to Dyer which simply said, 'Your action correct and Lieutenant Governor approves.'

Later when the things heated up, O'Dwyer tried to wriggle out of the situation by saying if he had known the full facts he wouldn't have accorded his approval; this, not withstanding the fact that no one spent more time, energy and effort in suppressing the sordid details of the massacre than O'Dwyer.

Imposition of Martial Law

Martial Law was imposed and there was total curfew. The city grieved, the shops and businesses remained closed and the people remained indoors. Dyer summoned the leading Europeans to a meeting, and they arrived wearing their pistols at their sides. The bellicose Lieutenant Colonel Smith, though a doctor by profession, was all in favour of a further dose of shooting and even gained support for a suggestion that the town should be bombarded from the air to bring the population to its senses.

The mantle of British wrath, which had fallen on the city of Amritsar deepened as the people waited for the next blow to fall. With Dyer still in command, it was not long in coming. Assisted by Miles Irving, Dyer issued a number of orders. The first step was to force the merchants and shopkeepers to re-open their businesses and bring some semblance of normality back to the deserted streets. Their representatives were called to the Ram Bagh where Dyer gave them a simple ultimatum, "If you wish for peace obey my orders and open shops. Otherwise I shall shoot you." With sunrise and the ending of the curfew, crowds of rescuers came to carry away the dead for immediate cremation. Their families took injured people to any doctor who could be found to treat them. By mid-morning of the 14th April most of the victims had been removed. At this stage the police arrived. Indiscriminate arrests and brutal interrogation began immediately.

Doctors in the local hospitals were instructed to submit lists of names of injured persons. They protested that they had been far too busy dealing with a flood of shocked and dying casualties to note names and addresses. Some doctors were arrested. Arrests were indiscriminate and caused a deep sense of resentment. During interrogation they were told that it did not really matter whether they could produce a list of casualties or not. They could be released just as soon as they agreed to implicate as ringleaders any individuals whom the police happened to have on their list of suspects. No doctor named any body as a potential troublemaker. Consequently, the police and, in turn Dyer, became increasingly desperate, as the days went by, to prove that there indeed had been a deep and well organised conspiracy which, in turn, 'justified' the massacre. No such proof ever surfaced, but it was not for want of a relentless effort by Dyer and the police. Under Dyer's influence, Plomer and the police resorted to a variety of crude tortures to extract the kind of information that could have supported the official claim. The British were showing a total disregard for justice, but they had the backing of the European community. Furthermore, O'Dwyer seemed to be in total agreement with any harsh measures that were introduced. But all this torture and cruelty failed to provide the Raj with any legitimate reason for what the British had done in Jallianwala Bagh.

The only way that O'Dwyer and Dyer were going to obtain evidence to support the butchery of Jallianwala Bagh was to find a member of the 'Satyagrah' movement prepared to turn on his colleagues and to denounce them in court. The chosen Judas was Hans Raj, the very man who, according to Dyer and Plomer, had been inciting the crowd to rebellion on the 13th April. By a combination of threats and bribery, Hans Raj was persuaded to denounce thirteen of his associates. They included Kitchlew and Satyapal, both of whom had been in police custody at the time of the disturbances. During the trial Hans Raj faithfully recited the facts and dates, which he had rehearsed with Superintendent Plomer.

Unfortunately for O'Dwyer, the two men, he was desperate to nail and try under the martial couldn't be so tried because they had been under arrest 100 miles away from Amritsar when martial law was imposed, and could therefore not have taken any part in the disturbances. Another obstacle in his path was that there would be very little chance of getting them convicted in a higher court, where all the prescribed safeguards of the law would apply. So bent upon teaching a lesson to Kitchlew and Satyapal was O'Dwyer that he virtually blackmailed Chelmsford into 'backdating' the declaration of 'martial law' from 13 April to March 30. This, in spite of the fact, that no act of violence was committed in Punjab between 30th March and 10th of April. (Note: As per the existing constitution, Martial Law, meaning no law or negation of law as Jinnah termed it, could only be imposed when no other mean of restoring order was available to the government, and there was some danger or imminent threat to the government. Immediately such a threat was removed it was expected to be lifted. In India, only the Governor General, or the Viceroy in the instant case, could impose such a law). The real aim was to try summarily those who were considered to have been potential threat to the government in Punjab, and those who were agitating against the Rowlatt Act. Regardless of the illegality of its imposition, Martial Law remained operative in Punjab till 20th June when it was lifted after some noted members of the legal fraternity in England highlighted the incongruity of its imposition in the first place. But in Amritsar nothing could silence the increasing anger and bitterness of the people over Dyer's action; there was hardly any family that had not been affected and there was no reluctance on their part to re-tell the story to anyone who was willing to listen.

In Amritsar, Dyer apparently had not yet had a fill of his appetite for teaching an everlasting lesson to the hapless Indians. His most cruel order was the 'Crawling Order'. Dyer continued with his bizarre course with vigour. Now he erected a whipping frame in Kucha Tawarian where Miss Sherwood had been attacked by a mob on the 10th April. The narrow lane was sealed on both ends and over a period of seven days every Indian passing through this lane was obliged to squirm its 150 yards length on his stomach. There was no exception to this directive. Even a blind man had to go through this torture. If a hapless victim of this crawling order as much as raised his knees or back to avoid filth on the street, police and military rifle butts were freely used to restore his crawling position. The residents of this unfortunate street were the real sufferers. Their houses remained filled with filth as no sweeper could go to clean up. A large number had to survive without necessary provisions, and the sick had to go without urgent medicines. Since it was the residents of that area who had saved Miss Sherwood from certain death, it was a bizarre way of rewarding them for their humanity and courage.

Dyer also ordered the population of Amritsar to 'salaam' before any European they encountered in the streets or elsewhere. There was no exception to this command. Travellers in motor vehicles or carts were obliged to stop and dismount for this purpose. Anyone failing to comply with the order, or who did not 'salaam' in a satisfactory manner was flogged, or beaten or thrown into jail. These impositions and punishments were a matter of whim. They had no legal basis, not even under Martial Law. None of these humiliating and degrading acts of the Raj were confined to Amritsar alone. Similar punitive measures were being applied against the populations of other towns and cities as well. Dyer later justified his order on crawling by explaining that as we look upon women as sacred, or ought to, he had searched his mind for a punishment to fit the crime of hitting Miss Sherwood: and as Indian devotees went on all fours to places they held sacred, he thought that procedure appropriate for driving home the lesson.[3]

Imposition of Martial Law allowed the government to appoint military officers as administrators who were assisted by the deputy commissioners and other functionaries of the civil administration. These officers had neither any experience nor any training in administration of civil population. The inexperience showed when the martial law administrator of Lahore, Lieutenant Colonel Frank Johnson, issued more than six hundred martial law orders and notices. One of his most stupid order was stoppage of all 'Langars', i.e. free distribution of food.[4] Clearly, nobody had advised him that this ritual was an important part of the Sikh religion where in Sikh Gurudwaras fed people regardless of their colour, caste or creed. On 15th April he issued an order that other than Europeans or those in possession of special military permits were prohibited to leave their houses between 8 PM and 5 AM next morning. This order caused great inconvenience to people, because those who violated this order for whatever reason were whipped publicly. All vehicles, other than those belonging to Europeans were commandeered. Even Tongas (horse-driven cart), the common man's means of mobility were not spared. When these harsh and apparently unreasonable measures along with many such whimsical orders were brought to the notice of O'Dwyer he ignored all such protestations. The informers had a roaring time in settling personal scores with people who were not even actively involved with any anti-government activity. Not surprisingly, a large number of jail terms extending to years awarded by these administrators did not last even that many weeks because there were too many loopholes in the whole exercise and the sentences so awarded had to be set aside on orders of higher courts. O'Dwyer was upset with these developments but there was nothing that he could do to influence the tide of the times. More importantly, by then the massacre had caught the world attention and there were admonitions and criticism of the British government in handling of the whole affair.

This Lt Col Johnson was quite a character. One fine day, he called over a hundred leading citizens of the city and warned them that if any fire-arm is discharged or bomb thrown at the military or police, the exact location of such an action will be taken as a centre of a circle having a diameter of hundred yards, and that he would give people living in that area a notice of one hour in which to remove everything living from that circle, at the end of that period every building, other than a temple or a mosque, will be demolished. During his disposition before the Hunter Committee he deposed, "I refrained from granting exemptions in the case of Indian residents in Lahore, as I thought it desirable to bring home to them all—loyal and disloyal alike—some of the inconveniences of martial law in the hope and belief that in future the weight of their influence will be whole-heartedly thrown against seditious movements likely to lead to the introduction of martial law." When questioned about some of his apparently unreasonable orders by the Hunter Commission, this military officer was totally unremorseful. "Yes, I would do it again. It was one of the brainwaves I had", he informed the Committee.[5]

In Kasur, Lt Col Macrae and his deputy Captain Doveton also showed their imagination and innovative skills in humiliating Indians. Respectable and elderly people were made to dance wearing 'joker' caps, rub their noses on the ground and to do hop, skip and jump just to amuse the Martial Law Authority. On 1st May, the entire male population of the town was summoned to the railway station for an identification parade. A flogging post was erected at the platform and forty odd men were flogged because they had the temerity to complain about scorching heat and lack of water. Even school children were not spared. When a teacher was overheard talking of indiscipline of some of his students the headmaster was asked to send the rowdies for improving their conduct by the Sub Divisional Officer, one Mr. Marsden. The boys were sent up, but the authorities found them to be too weak and underfed, and mercifully the martial law administrator felt that those boys might not be able to withstand punishment he had in mind for improving the character and conduct of the younger Indian population. The school was ordered to send the entire lot of its senior students so that suitable material for demonstrative punishment could be selected. This was done, six fit and big boys were selected and were canned in public for no reason what so ever. In answer to Lord Hunter's question as to what was the object of this apparent abuse of authority, Mr. Marsden replied that there was no particular reason for doing so.[6]

Sir Michael O 'Dwyer, in his enthusiasm to sort the Indians, particularly of Punjab also set up a number of Summary Courts. These consisted of either a single military officer or a civil magistrate. Not withstanding the illegality of these courts under the British laws then operative in India these courts set about to try as many as 1437 Indians; 1179 of them were convicted for a wide range of crimes, real or imaginary. The punishment ranged from a jail term of two years or a fine up to Rs one thousand, if either of these two were thought to be impractical for any reason then whipping of the offender was resorted to. The crime committed by an individual could be 'showing disrespect to a European', or 'failing to salute a British officer'. The object of these courts was not to administer any justice, but to overawe and humiliate those Indians who were either unfortunate enough to be found at a wrong place at a wrong time, or were seen as potential threat to the Raj. A large number of college students were thus punished for no apparent reason other than the fact that it was apprehended that these educated students could eventually cause problems to the administration in due course of time. In their case it was largely a preventive measure that punishments were administered to ensure that the scars remained long enough for them to refrain from any activity that could cause a threat to the Empire.

Interestingly, Punjab was the only province in India where Martial Law was enforced while other places like Bombay, Delhi and Ahmedabad etc. where due to influence of Gandhi there was a much greater chance of trouble recourse to such draconian measures was not even contemplated. Clearly, the Government of India had a lot of 'misplaced' faith in O'Dwyer and in his capabilities to control a state like Punjab, which had provided the a largest contingent of troops during the first World War. That this faith in his capabilities was misplaced is clear from the fact that in spite of the full British might behind him, and with the Anglo-Indians and certain other categories supporting the harsh measures instituted in Punjab the agitation was showing no sign of dying down. In fact, this barbarity and the atrocities of the British only helped awaken Indians to the harsh realities of their life as slaves.

The legal proceedings were moving concurrently against all those Indians who were allegedly behind the unrest and which had led to the massacre by Dyer of innocent and unarmed people of Punjab, on a day that should have been a day of traditional festivities for the farmers of the state. Coached and bendable witnesses like Hans Raj were being located to strengthen the cases against those who were seen as enemies of the Empire. The two (Kitchlew and Satyapal) were tried along with 13 others and sentenced to transportation to a penal colony for life. Their properties were also forfeited. Seven of the accused were sentenced to death or transportation. In a proclamation issued by him on 26th April at Lahore, O'Dwyer claimed that order has been restored everywhere by the prompt action of the troops—British and Indian—whom the mischief-makers attempted to malign and by the loyal cooperation of the quiet mass of rural population. Existing precautions must, however, be retained till all criminals are brought to justice. (Hunter Committee Report p 127). The trial lasted for 21 days, but it is evident from both Indian and British accounts that it was a cruel travesty of justice. The judge, Mr. Justice Broadway, declared that O'Dwyer had been right: the riots had indeed 'constituted a deliberate and most determined waging of war.' By the time this sham trial ended, O'Dwyer had retired to England in a glow of self-satisfaction over having saved the Empire. Hans Raj collected his cash reward and departed for a new life, under a new name, to Mesopotamia.

The Punjab Government made all sorts of efforts to justify use of brute force against unarmed civilians. It had to establish without fear of contradiction that a conspiracy to create widespread revolt did exist. Therefore, in its lengthy report to the Government of India page after page were devoted to extract from speeches and newspaper articles to support the contention that sedition was widespread. Graphic and often harrowing accounts were given of the rioting and looting that took place in Amritsar on 10th April; there were particularly vivid descriptions of the attack on Miss Sherwood, the sacking and burning of the banks and other gory details that could only confirm an impression that the authorities apprehended a second mutiny that would have dwarfed the one that took place in 1857. While admitting that there were a number of peasants and children also present in the Jallianwala Bagh who couldn't possibly be connected with the political lecture then going on in the Bagh the Government's report made no effort to explain the reasons for these innocents also getting killed due to indiscriminate firing by General Dyer. During the Hunter Committee investigations on the Jallianwala Bagh massacre all kinds of weird reasons, including impending war with Afghanistan (an unlikely event because the Amir of Afghanistan had not shown any such serious inclination except flexing his muscles as a periodic exercise), were offered as official reason for imposition of Martial Law in Punjab. This, not withstanding the fact, that people of Punjab had denounced the actions of the Amir of Afghanistan and in spite of their differences with the government had offered all kinds of help to the administration in meeting the likely threat if it ever arose. O'Dwyer contradicted himself before the Committee when he also stipulated that the Sikhs had offered to provide ten thousand soldiers in case of war with Afghanistan.[7]

Aftermath of the Massacre

News of the true extent of the massacre in Amritsar, and what was going on in rest of Punjab, leaked out only slowly. Censorship was highly effective, travel was restricted, and for the first four days after Jallianwala Bagh massacre no telegrams were allowed to be sent from the city. The story in the 'Civil and Military Gazette' on 16th April under a small headline, 'Meet dispersed at Amritsar', considerably underplayed the incident, besides being largely inaccurate. All it said was:

"An attempt to hold a proscribed meeting at Amritsar was frustrated, after the arrest of some ringleaders. The General, with only Indian troops and police, gave the orders to disperse. As the crowd refused to go the order to fire was given. There were heavy casualties amongst the mob, several hundred being killed and injured and there was no further trouble."

The Times, normally renowned for its Indian coverage, preferred to be in the dark. On the 19th April, a paragraph announced:

There is no news of any trouble at Amritsar since the troops dispersed the rioters on Sunday with very heavy casualties. This was followed by a 'Report from Punjab',

At Amritsar, on 13th April, the mob defied the proclamation forbidding public meetings. Firing ensued, and 200 casualties occurred.

The British press was busy underplaying the tragedy. None of the reports, official or otherwise, gave any true indication of the extent of the troubles and turbulences then raging through Punjab, more specifically through Amritsar and Lahore. Explanation given to the readers was that the telegraph wires had been cut.

It was largely thanks to BG Horniman that the truth emerged, when he defied the censors and published in the *Bombay Chronicle* an unofficial report that had been smuggled out of the Punjab. The government of India promptly had Horniman arrested and deported back to England. Now they couldn't even muzzle him. Back home in London, he immediately began a campaign attacking not only the military handling of the Amritsar disturbances but 'the whole conduct of the Punjab Government over a long period of time'. The man responsible for the chaos—Sir Michael O'Dwyer, Lieutenant Governor himself was totally unruffled by the situation. He answered criticism with his typical arrogance: "It is all very well for armchair politicians in Bombay and Allahabad, to cry out about harsh measures but martial law cannot be carried out without taking the kid gloves off." Justifying Dyer's action he wrote, "The Amritsar business cleared the air, and if there was to be a holocaust anywhere, and one regrets there should be, it was best at Amritsar."

Gandhi was aghast at the events in Punjab. "When a government takes up arms against its unarmed subjects", he wrote, "then it has forfeited its right to govern. It has admitted that it cannot rule in peace and justice...nothing less than the removal of the British and complete Self-Government could satisfy injured India." Plassey, he observed, "laid the foundation of the British Empire. Amritsar had shaken it." For the rest of his life, he observed a 24-hours fast on the anniversary of the massacre.

On 30th May 1919, Rabindranath Tagore wrote to Chelmsford formally relinquishing the knighthood he had received after winning the Noble Prize for Literature in 1913. His eloquent letter, which was widely circulated throughout India, complained of the "enormity of the harsh measures taken by the government in the Punjab for quelling some local disturbances," of the "insults and sufferings undergone by my brothers," and of the way the universal agony of indignation...has been ignored by our rulers, possibly congratulating themselves for what they imagine as salutary lessons." "The time has come," he concluded, "when badges of honour make our shame glaring in their incongruous context of humiliation, and I for my part wish to stand shorn of all special distinctions by the side of those of my countrymen who, for their so-called insignificance are liable to suffer a degradation not fit for human beings." The Viceroy, unable as usual to make a decision, passed on the letter to Montagu, who sensibly passed it back to him, saying that it was a matter between the government of India and an Indian citizen. Chelmsford, in turn, informed Tagore that he could not relieve him of his knighthood, nor could he approach the king-emperor on the issue. Whatever be the official protocol, fact of the matter was that an Indian had thrown an honour back in the face of the Raj, and it was enough for the common man to feel a bit of pride in this gesture of Tagore.

By now a political row was boiling up in the British Parliament over the issue of Jallianwala Bagh massacre and its aftermath. There was an outcry for a detailed enquiry into the whole sordid episode. Montagu was forced to act, but finding a suitable politician to head the commission of inquiry became difficult. No one could be persuaded to take hold of such an obviously hot potato. Eventually he settled on Lord Hunter, a senator of the College of Justice in Edinburgh. The Hunter Committee— officially 'The Committee to Investigate the Recent Disturbances in Bombay, Delhi and the Punjab' consisted of four Britons and three Indians, in addition to Hunter himself. The Viceroy, Lord Chelmsford announced the formation of the committee while giving his opening address to the Imperial Legislative Council on the 3rd September 1919. In the same breath he also laid down the dictum that whatever be the findings of the Commission an 'Act of Indemnity' was also going to be passed.[8] This was apparently contemplated to ensure that the military officers and others who had carried out the carnage of death and destruction in Punjab were not penalised when found guilty. The Bill was strongly opposed by members of the Council like Pandit Madan Mohan Malaviya and some others; but, and sadly, representatives of Punjab Sardar (later Sir) Sunder Singh Majithia and Major Malik Sir Umar Hayat Khan voted in favour of the notorious Bill.

The Hunter Commission began its sessions in Delhi on 29th October 1919. The All India Congress Committee appointed lawyer cross-examined various witnesses and nailed numerous lies propounded by the administration as to the reason for use of excessive force in Punjab. The Congress also called forward its own witnesses; Hunter couldn't shake them because these were not 'coached witnesses'. The official theory that the Punjab government was suppressing a rebellion akin to that of 1857 fell flat.

Hunter thereafter moved to Lahore on 11th November, where the Commission spent over two months examining witnesses and records. Nobody from the All India Congress Committee appeared during these hearings because the government had refused to release those principal leaders of Punjab who could have convincingly refuted the official theory that the whole exercise had been conducted to suppress a rebellion. Dyer appeared before the committee on 19th November, giving full, frank and totally unrepentant account of his actions. Famously, when asked as to why did he finally stop shooting at the gathering in the Bagh: his reply was that his troops had run out of ammunition. When asked if he would have used the machine guns mounted on the armoured cars provided these cars could get into the Bagh, he replied in affirmative. The theme of his statement was, 'It was no longer a question of merely dispersing the crowd but one of producing a sufficient moral effect from a military point of view, not only on those who were present, but more especially throughout the Punjab. There was no question of undue severity'. During cross-examination by the Committee about use of excessive force when the crowd was evidently trying to get out of the Bagh, he exclaimed, "I could disperse the crowd for some time if I had allowed people to escape, then they would have all come back and laugh at me, and I considered I would be making fool of myself." He went on to say that everything pointed to the existence of a widespread revolt, which was not confined to Amritsar. The crowds before him were rebels who were trying to isolate his forces. The situation was very serious and I had made up my mind that I would do all men to death if they were going to continue the meeting. "Therefore I considered it my duty to fire on them and fire well." His reason for not attending to the wounded was that it was not a military matter. He was equally remorseless about his orders about whipping, making even elderly crawl in the street.

(Note: Pandit Jawaharlal Nehru had personally experienced the arrogance and utter callousness of Dyer when he had gone to Amritsar to get first hand information because Congress had started conducting its own enquiry on the massacre. He writes in his Autobiography, " The compartment I entered was almost full and all the berths, except one upper one, were occupied by sleeping passengers. I took the vacant berth. In the morning I discovered that all my fellow passengers were military officers. They conversed with each other in loud voices which I could not help over-hearing. One of them was holding forth in an arrogant and aggressive tone, and I soon discovered that he was Dyer, the hero of Jallianwala Bagh, and he was describing his Amritsar experiences. He pointed out how he had the whole town at his mercy and had felt like reducing the rebellious city to a heap of ashes, but took pity on it and refrained. He was evidently coming back from Lahore after giving his evidence before the Hunter Committee of Inquiry. (Nehru, Autobiography pp 43-44). Significantly, these utterances of Dyer changed Nehru's mind about the 'goodness' of the British Empire. Harrow and Cambridge-educated lawyer who had been a great admirer of Britain became, almost overnight, their implacable enemy. O'Dwyer, equally remorseless, returned to India to give evidence on 15th and 16th January 1920, as the last witness before the committee retired to Agra to sift through the evidence it had heard.

The Congress Enquiry Committee

On 12th November Lord Hunter was informed by the President of Indian National Congress that as the Punjab Government had refused to release the imprisoned leaders even on the guarantees of adequate securities and sureties so that they could not give evidence, the Congress would not appear before the Inquiry to give evidence on behalf of the people.

Having decided to dissociate itself from the official Committee set up by the Viceroy because of its apparent bias towards the government, the Congress Party set up its own Committee to go into the details of what had actually happened in Punjab. The Committee consisted of Mr. M K Gandhi, and had Mr. Motilal Nehru, Mr. Chittranjan Das, Mr. Abbas Tyabji, Mr. Fazlul Huq, Mr. Madanmohan Malaviya was its chairman and Pundit K Santanna was its secretary. This Committee examined over 1700 witnesses, and some of them were leaders in their own districts or villages. The enquiry was, however, confined to only those areas where martial law had been proclaimed. The disclosures made by this enquiry were alarmingly critical of the handling of the whole situation by the government of Punjab. The Committee observed that, "The Jallianwala Bagh massacre was a calculated piece of inhumanity towards utterly innocent and unarmed men, women and children, and was unparalleled in the history of modern administration". Famous thinker and writer Aldous Huxley observed, 'The situation (in Punjab) provided a fair field to the English to do things which should be absolutely unthinkable at home, these were not only thinkable but were doable and actually done in India. The Amritsar Massacre, for example.'[9]

Till about the middle of December 1919, the information about the whole episode was still full of grey areas where the rest of the world and a majority of Englishmen were concerned. *The Daily Express* managed to get the full story of the Jallianwala Bagh shooting, and splashed it across its front page on 13th December under the headline: '2000 Indians

SHOT DOWN. General's Terrible Remedy to Curb Rebellion.' The other papers also picked up the story, and a great deal of heat was generated with awkward questions being hurled at Montagu. Situation was partially calmed down when on 23 December 1919 Kitchlew, Satyapal and the others convicted by the martial law commission were released under an amnesty for political prisoners announced by the king to mark the introduction of the Montagu-Chelmsford reforms as beginning of a 'new era'.

It took the Hunter Committee until 8th March to prepare its draft report for submission to the government of India. Hunter placed the total blame on the Indians for having created a situation that could not have been handled in any other way. It was a total 'Whitewash' and it did not make any specific recommendations, which could have restored the people's faith in the fairness of the regime. The Indian members of the Committee, in the meanwhile, had stopped speaking to Hunter after he had lost his temper and shouted at them, 'you people want to drive the British out of the country!' (Sir Chimanlal Setalvad, a member of the Committee retorted, "It is perfectly legitimate for the Indians to wish to be free of foreign rule and Indian independence can be accomplished by mutual understanding and goodwill. The driving out process will only become necessary if the British are represented in this country by people as short-sighted and intolerant as yourself". (Setalvad- *Recollections and Reflections* p 311, and also quoted in *"Six Minutes to Sunset"* by Arthur Swinson, pp 95-96). Thereafter, the Indian members stopped even exchanging greetings with Hunter. They went through the motions of being part of the Committee and did keep a watchful eye on the proceedings but had clearly lost faith in Lord Hunter and fairness of the enquiry. The Indian members agreed with the report's criticism of the Punjab government, and condemned the riots, they also insisted on including a minority report rejecting the idea that the riots had constituted a rebellion. The report was presented to the government of India on 23rd May 1920 with its conclusions and findings. It was, *inter alia*, stated that, "After carefully weighing all the factors leading to the firing in Jallianwala Bagh the government concluded that General Dyer acted beyond the necessity of the case, beyond what any reasonable man could have thought to be necessary, and that he did not act with as much humanity as the cause permitted."

Among the prominent British leaders Montagu was perhaps, the only one who did have reservations about this sordid saga of butchery of innocents. On 29th August 1919 he had written to the Viceroy, "I am certain that we must treat these occurrences with courage. Don't let us make the mistake of defending O'Dwyerism right or wrong. Nothing is so fatal to the British prestige in a developing country like India as a belief that there is no redress for mistakes and that whatever an official does will be backed, and, not only that he will be backed, but that his methods will be perpetuated."[10]

Even when the Hunter Committee Report came up for discussion in the House of Commons on 8th July 1920, Montagu was at his eloquent best while expressing his disgust over the conduct of those who were showing no sign of remorse over conduct of the British representatives in India. He said, "I will ask the House only one question: If an officer justified his conduct, no matter how gallant his record is, by saying that there was no question of undue severity, that if his means had been greater the casualties would have been greater, and that the motive was to teach a moral lesson to the Punjab, I say without hesitation...that it is the doctrine of terrorism. Once you are entitled to have regard neither to the intentions nor to the conduct of a particular gathering, and to shoot and to go on shooting with all the horrors that were here involved in order to teach somebody else a lesson you are embarking on terrorism, to which, there is no end."[11] Montagu went on to characterise the order to 'salaam' officers and the whipping of schoolboys as frightfulness. "Are you," Montagu asked the House, "going to keep hold of India by terrorism, racial humiliation and subordination and frightfulness, are you going to rest it upon the goodwill, and the growing goodwill of the people of your Indian Empire." There was, Montagu said, an alternative to terrorism. "It is to tell the Indians; we hold British lives sacred, but we hold Indian lives sacred too." His stoic defence of the Indians and their plight was not to the liking of the majority of the House.

The government in England accepted the Hunter Report in its totality, condemning the actions of Dyer as a concession to the Indian sentiment over the whole issue. He was relieved of his command and sent back to England where he was first put on a reduced pay and then on a pension. The Army Council did not attach any stigma to his profile. Where the higher echelons of the military was concerned he had only committed a 'grave error of judgment'. The House of Lords was equally accommodating when by a majority of vote it stipulated that, "the House deplored the conduct of the case of General Dyer as unjust to that officer, and as establishing a precedent dangerous to the preservation of order in face of a rebellion; his defenders even moved a motion of censure against government for conniving at subversion in India". When Churchill on behalf of the Cabinet, tried to force the Army Council to dismiss Dyer, he met with stiff opposition. Justifying Dyer's dismissal to the British House of Commons, Winston Churchill, Secretary for War, said: "Frightfulness is the inflicting of great slaughter or massacre upon a particular crowd of people, with intention of affecting not merely the rest of the crowd, but the whole district or the whole country. We cannot admit this doctrine in any form. The august and venerable structure of the British Empire, where lawful authority descends from hand to hand and generation after generation does not need such aid. Jallianwala Bagh had not saved India. Our reign in India or anywhere else has never rested on a basis of physical force alone, and it would be fatal to the British Empire to try to base ourselves upon it." Lord Birkenhead, the Lord Chancellor was even more scathing when he stated "Dyer had committed a tragic error of judgment, and it would be disastrous for the Empire if it was thought the act was approved. Dyer had gone to the Jallianwala Bagh with the deliberate intention of taking life on a large scale, and when the crowd dispersed and tried to escape he had directed his fire where there were the most people. On his own admission if he had been able to get the machine guns into the Bagh the casualties would have been much higher." He went on to say "I claim that anyone who stands here and defends the case of General Dyer should be prepared to defend similar conduct in Glasgow or Belfast or Winnipeg."

The condemnation of Dyer for his actions was not universal; many diehard imperialists, both in the cabinet and on the streets felt that Dyer had been right in teaching Indians a lesson, and where they were concerned had actually saved the Empire. Even within India and, more specifically in Punjab, there were people who hailed Dyer not only as the 'Saviour of the Punjab' but the Saviour of India, and in a very short span of time he readily accepted the legend that was being created and convinced himself that his action had saved India from an open revolution. He and his Brigade Major, Captain Briggs, were (allegedly) made honorary Sikhs at a ceremony in the Golden Temple. It was an astute political move, for it was seen as conclusive proof that the Sikhs of Amritsar had bestowed the rare honour as a token of their gratitude, and public recognition that the General had saved them from a blood bath. No body in the administration seemed to notice that the Mahant of the Temple—Arur Singh was an appointee of the Punjab Government. But colourful details of the ceremony where Arur Singh asked Dyer to become a Sikh like John Nicholson, a British hero of the 1857 Mutiny started circulating. Dyer seemingly refused the honour because as a British officer he could not grow long hair as the Religion demanded, nor could he give up smoking. The ceremony did take place but it did not delight the Sikh community; it enraged them. People pointed out that Arur Singh was only a puppet of the government. The whole episode led to an agitation for the ending of Government-appointed managers of the Shrine. Sikh community the world over resented usage of the Golden Temple for drawing political mileage when the martial law was still in operation and coercive methods to bend and break people were in use. (*Amritsar The Massacre That Ended the Raj* by Alfred Draper page 119-120)

But the story was given credence in Britain where a growing body of influential politicians was throwing its weight behind Sir Michael O'Dwyer and propagating the legend that was being built around General Dyer. Dyer and his supporters claimed that he had been a victim of political expediency of Edwin Montagu, Secretary of State for India, who was more concerned with appeasing extremist Indian opinion than heeding the warning voice of the men who knew and ruled the country on behalf of the Empire. Conservatives throughout Britain joined Anglo-Indians in vociferous support for their hero. O'Dwyer expended considerable time, energy and effort in trying to justify the monstrosity of Dyer. He had his reasons to do so; he was the Governor of Punjab, and his neck would have also been on the block for allowing such a thing to happen. 'The Morning Post' launched a fund to raise money for 'the man who saved India'. Contributions poured in from all quarters and a reasonably good amount (Twenty-six thousand pounds—equivalent of over six hundred thousand pounds in today's value) was thus raised. Dyer was also presented with a jewelled sword inscribed 'To The Saviour of the Punjab'. This apparent vindication of Dyer was the final straw for many Indians who had previously been favourably disposed towards Britain and the Empire. Inevitably, Indian opinion was embittered by treating the man responsible for the Amritsar massacre as a British national hero and the bitterness and the complete distrust of British intentions gave rise to the Non-cooperation movement, which put paid to the exercise of the '1919 Reforms.' Dyer had been rescued from penury and elevated to the status of a relatively rich man. He eventually retired to the village of Long Ashton on the outskirts of Bristol with the purse collected by those who agreed with his methods, carrying curses of the Indians, and wracked by a variety of diseases. In Britain, even today after more than fifty years of the winding up of the Raj, there are people who subscribe to the theory that a little more of O'Dwyerism and Dyerism would have ensured the continuance of the Empire for another hundred years or more.

O'Dwyer lived long enough to allow the child Udham Singh (an eye witness and survivor of the massacre) to grow up. Having survived the shooting, Udham Singh had gone to the Golden Temple: and after a holy dip in the 'pool of nectar' he swore a solemn oath to avenge the massacre with the blood of O'Dwyer.

The events, before, during and after the massacre burnt themselves deep into the soul of India and symbolised to the poor and simple people of this country that the British rule was cruel, unjust and, therefore unwarranted. In a way these unfortunate and perhaps, avoidable events did more than anything else to unite the country in its resolve to be rid of the British rule. 'The butchers of Punjab have to go' became a common refrain all over India. "I realised then more vividly than I had ever done before, how brutal and immoral imperialism was and how it had eaten into the souls of the British upperclasses," wrote Jawaharlal Nehru.

O'Dwyer Meets his Nemesis

Caxton Hall: London 13th March 1940 4 PM

Brigadier General Sir Percy M Sykes, KCIE, CB, CMG was scheduled to give a lecture on "Afghanistan: the Present Position". The 2nd World War was raging in Europe and elsewhere, and the allies were worried about the Afghan position where it faced a threat from Russia. A large audience was expected because Sir Percy was an international authority on the history of Afghanistan and its neighbours. One of the attendees was Sir Michael O' Dwyer, GCIE, KCSI, a former Lt Governor of Punjab, who had retired in 1919. The lecture was followed by an intense debate with O'Dwyer making a forceful contribution. After the vote of thanks when everybody was politely clapping to show appreciation for the event, a dark-skinned man, dressed in a blue lounge suit and wearing a brown trilby hat stood up and headed towards the platform. He was carrying a large revolver in his right hand. As O'Dwyer and some others stood around the platform the gunman walked up behind O'Dwyer and pointed the revolver at the Irishman's back. He fired twice, at a distance of six inches. The first bullet went through the right lung, veered left through the heart, ripped out the left side of the chest and lodged in his clothing. The second bullet, four inches lower, tore through the right kidney and lodged in the intestines. O'Dwyer spun to the ground and fell on his back between the platform and the Press table, not yet dead but mortally wounded. The gunman fired three more shots injuring some others and still clutching the revolver he started to run towards the door of the hall shouting "Make way, make way", he had succeeded in discharging six shots from that heavy revolver in the space of five seconds and had scored five out of six hits. It had been remarkably skilled shooting for a man with no known training in the use of firearms.

After an initial stunned silence the hall became a shambles of screams and shouts. Everybody thought that a bomb had gone off. "My God, it's IRA", shouted a woman. The confusion was total. The gunman, in the meanwhile was making rapid progress towards the exit. Several men tried to grapple with him, but he was thickset and strong. Like a muscular rugby player, he lowered his head and weaved his way through. Halfway to the door he came level with the seat occupied by Miss Bertha Herring, a lady in her sixties who was also a volunteer wartime ambulance driver. This courageous woman launched herself at the man's head, tackled him around the shoulders and brought him to the floor. In an instant he was buried under the bodies of several men who piled on top of the lady and her opponent. On hearing the shouts for help, the first to arrive were Geoffrey Vennell, an Air Raid Warden on duty in the Caxton Hall area and Robert Stevens, an Inspector of the Metropolitan Special Constabulary, on routine anti-IRA surveillance from the nearby police station. Detective Inspector Richard Deighton arrived thereafter and took charge of the situation.

"I did it because I had a grudge against him. He deserved this for what he had done to my people in India", the assassin kept saying. After repeated questioning he gave his name as Mohamed Singh Azad and was taken to Cannon Row Police Station. The police could not establish any clear motive for the killing. Fleet Street was first off the mark in pinpointing a motive for the shooting. A quick reference to 'Who's Who' showed Sir Michael O'Dwyer as having been Lieutenant Governor of Punjab between 1913 and 1919. It was during his time the massacre of Jallianwala Bagh in Amritsar had taken place. Sir Michael had come in for a particular hatred. He had upheld the action of General Dyer in shooting on the crowds on that Baisakhi day twenty-one years ago. He had even led a campaign for exoneration of Dyer, and for his reinstatement in the army. Udham Singh was sentenced to death and was hanged on 31st July. Under covers of darkness he was buried in an unmarked grave below the prison walls. A request from the Sikh Temple for return of his ashes in order that they could be taken to India for cremation according to the religious rites of the Sikhs was curtly refused.

(Thirty-four years were to pass after the hanging before the ashes of Udham Singh were returned to his homeland aboard an Air India plane. The wooden casket was received at the airport by a large number of dignitaries. Indian newspapers carried large memorial advertisements calling on the people to pay homage to the great hero on his last journey. After the official ceremony in the capital the remains were taken on an extensive and emotional tour of the country to be finally taken to the Jallianwala Bagh for a period of lying in state. The ashes were finally taken to Anandpur Sahib and scattered on the sacred waters of Ganges and Satluj.)

Amritsar Congress Session—1919

That the 1919 session would be held at Amritsar had been decided long before the massacre. The Congress party decided to go ahead as planned; such a gesture would help in restoring the morale of suppressed people of Punjab, the party leadership thought. The city was still reeking with the blood of innocent and helpless people, with an insensitive government trying to crush their spirit. The political atmosphere was clearly clouded with fear, anxiety and panic. Local leaders were, largely, all in jail, with some of them condemned to long terms of imprisonment, and a few awaiting final decision on their death sentences. The government was worried because the Hunter Committee hearings and inept handling of the situation by the administration was already making international news; to top it all the Privy Council was likely to set aside most of the harsh punishments awarded to various leaders in Punjab. The district administration was willing to give sanction for holding of the session provided no reference was made to the recent happenings in Punjab, their causes and effects. This was not acceptable to the party. Finally, after a lot of uncertainty the session got under way as planned. The 'Extreme Moderates', however, refused to be a party to any decision likely to be taken during the session and held their own conference in Calcutta, coinciding with the Amritsar Session.

The district administration's worries were not entirely unjustified. A large number of attendees at the Congress session visited Jallianwala Bagh, treating it as a place of pilgrimage. Many of them while paying homage to the innocent dead touched the bloodstained earth with their foreheads, and smeared it on their faces as a mark of respect for the dead. Some of them even carried away some of that earth to be preserved as a holy treasure that would remind them for all time to come of the sacrifice of innocent lives in the cause of the country's struggle for freedom.[12]

In this emotion-charged atmosphere, Motilal was elected president for the year. In his inaugural address he reminded the delegates about the British having reneged from their assurances about the country's freedom after the World War. He ended his speech by saying, "We want freedom of thought, freedom of action, freedom to fashion our own destiny and build up an India suited to the needs and the genius of her people... We must aim at India where all are free and have the fullest opportunity of development, where there are no privileged classes or communities, where education is free and open to all, where the capitalist and the landlord do not oppress the labourers and farmers, where labour is respected and well paid. The terrible misery that we see around us under the British Rule will become a bad dream which would fade away from our memory on our awakening to welcome the morning sun".

All this while the British government was not sitting idle. Newer and more refined ways were being thought out to somehow win back the goodwill of the Indians. To coincide with the beginning of the Congress session on 24th December 1919, the Royal Proclamation announcing the 'reforms' was made. The King-Emperor also appealed for cooperation and reconciliation. He directed the Viceroy to exercise full measure of clemency to political offenders. The proclamation also proceeded to announce the establishment of a 'Chamber of Princes' and the forthcoming visit of His Royal Highness the Prince of Wales to India.

The declaration of political amnesty had a profound and calming effect. The leaders along with a large number of common people who had been arrested and were given long terms in jail were released. Some of the released leaders were able to reach Amritsar while the Congress session was still on. All this time Gandhi was trying to have resolution condemning 'mob violence' in Punjab passed by the Party. He was also propagating that revenge was no answer. In his opinion Indians had now to demonstrate that they were morally superior to their masters, and thus could use liberty. Peaceful, non-violent protest alone was to be the weapon. If it got out of hand it was to be discontinued. He refused to prescribe any timetable for the line of action he was projecting; "moral regeneration was not a matter of overnight adjustments", he said. Gandhi was severely disappointed when the 'Subject Committee' rejected any such proposal out of hand. However, when he insisted and persisted with his agenda a watered down version of his resolution was taken on record.

The subject of Montagu-Chelmsford Reforms was a major issue under discussion because it was supposed to be a major step towards self-rule. C R Das and many others wanted to reject the package because it fell far short of the expectations. Gandhi, on the other hand, wanted to accept whatever was on offer in the light of the proclamation made by the King-Emperor. Finally, a formula was evolved and a modified resolution with a specific paragraph ' this Congress trusts that as far as possible, the people will work on the proposed reforms so as to secure an early establishment of a full Responsible Government.'

(Note: There is an interesting aside to this drama of 'reforms'. Four days before the Report was actually signed, the Viceroy told Mr. Montagu that the whole game plan was his and that the 'Reforms' would always be known as Montagu-Chelmsford Reforms; therefore, he must sign first. Mr. Montagu, not to be outdone by a mere Viceroy, pointed out that he being the Secretary of State held a more exalted position, and was therefore entitled to put his signatures before those of the Viceroy. Finally they both agreed to put their signatures alongside and in the same line.)

Unfortunately for India, Montagu-Chelmsford Constitution produced two main trends in all-India politics, a centrifugal trend and a communal trend. Provincial priorities started affecting the movement in a manner that was contrary to what the national level leaders perceived to be the requirement of the day. Most of them came to the conclusion that in order to remain in the mainstream of national politics they had to bow before these pressures. Continuation of the separate electorate set the two communities at each other's throat because just about every act of leaders of one community were viewed with suspicion by the other, as it happened in Punjab. Importance of provincial Muslim opinion and the reluctance of the Mahasabha to grant validity to these became a common feature. Resultantly, communal polarisation also gained momentum during the period 1923-1927.·

Motilal in his capacity as President of the party had the pleasure of steering through the acceptance of the Montagu-Chelmsford reforms. In keeping with the practice, Muslim League also held its session in Amritsar to coincide with that of Congress. The Khilafat and Jamait-ul-Ulema all held their sessions in Amritsar. Hakim Ajmal Khan was elected the president of the League. A large number of prominent Hindu leaders also attended deliberations of the League. Hakim Saheb made a strong plea for Hindu-Muslim unity. Jinnah who had a tremendous influence on the League worked hard to ensure that the appeal for unity does not remain a mere paper exercise. He agreed with Motilal on his approach to the issue of reforms. They both obtained the approval of their organisations where reforms were concerned. This was taken as a symbol of Hindu-Muslim unity, besides being a victory for the Moderates in the Congress. Even Gandhi joined in urging Congress to co-operate with the government in implementing the reforms. Without holding any official position Gandhi had by now taken control of the movement. In the next twelve months, he would change the political agenda out of all recognition, carrying not only Jawaharlal but also Motilal with him.

Jawaharlal Nehru

Until he was nearly thirty, Jawaharlal lived in the shadows of his dominating, larger than life father—Motilal Nehru. But by 1919, he was ready to cast off one father figure in exchange for another: Motilal was to be replaced by Gandhi. Jawaharlal was basically a well educated, thinking young Indian whose ideas of economy and industry were organised on scientific lines. It was astonishing that he should succumb, intellectually and politically, to a traditional Hindu god-man. "I was bowled over by Gandhi straight away," Nehru wrote later. It was only natural that when Gandhi announced the Satyagraha Sabha, Jawaharlal was one of the first to sign up and take the vow of civil disobedience. 1920, in fact, turned out to be a watershed year for both father and son. It was also the year which established Gandhi's supremacy. Anyone and everyone who counted in the Congress hierarchy had expressed opinion against non-cooperation. Tilak, Besant, Lajpatrai, B C Pal,

Malaviya, C R Das, all of them having national stature termed the idea as 'Gandhian anarchy'. Tagore and Aurobindo wanted to know as to what was to be achieved by boycotting schools and colleges, abstaining from courts and even the assemblies with elected Indian majorities. Tilak's call for 'Responsive Cooperation' cut no ice with Gandhi who had set his heart on taking on the Raj his own way.

Like most moderates, Motilal was appalled at the idea of Satyagraha. As a lawyer, he found the idea of deliberately disobeying law as something not done. What good would it do, he wanted to know, if hundreds of hitherto blameless Indian young boys were sent to jail, ruining whatever future they might have otherwise had? More to the point, he dreaded the thought of his only son winding up behind bars. There was uneasy quiet at Anand Bhawan—the Nehru House in Allahabad. Things could not go on like this for long; Motilal invited Gandhi to Allahabad to discuss his dangerous influence on his son. They had several long talks—from which Jawaharlal was banned—before Gandhi emerged to advise the young Nehru 'not to precipitate matters or do anything to upset his father'. He refused to take Jawaharlal with him to the Sabarmati Ashram, telling him that his relationship with Motilal was more important. Gandhi had no wish to alienate Motilal at this critical juncture in the country's struggle for freedom.

Circumstances forced Jawaharlal to take up the cause of rural peasants who were getting crushed under the heels of landlords and talukdars, who were bleeding them dry with excessive rent demands, impossible interest charges, and arbitrary evictions. It was actually by default that Jawaharlal had got involved in this affair. Some 500 peasants from rural Jaunpur and Pratapgarh districts had hoped to see Gandhi on his way from Benares, as he always stayed at Anand Bhawan, they thought it will be easier to get an audience at that place. Gandhi hadn't returned yet, but Jawaharlal was present. He was a lawyer, he was available and then he was a Nehru. The peasant leaders turned to him for redress and prevailed upon him to visit their villages and see things for himself. Nehru finally agreed to do so. This visit to the real, poor and rural India was what gave the young Nehru a cause of his own to fight for. Nehru took up their fight against oppression, corruption and injustice through the medium of Kisan Sabhas, which were coming up all over central India. These Sabhas were the first genuinely grass roots level political movements in the country.

Along with the peasants, the industrial workers throughout the country were also organising themselves into politicised labour unions. All India Trade Union Congress was established under the leadership of Lala Lajpatrai in 1920. In the first half of that year alone, there were some 200 strikes, involving more than a million workers. The Indian Communist

Party was formed the same year. Many young Indians found its doctrine of violent revolution more attractive than Gandhi's Ahimsa, but perhaps because of the Mahatma's unique charisma, or because Russian style communism was incompatible with India's religious nature it was never a threat to Congress. But the government was uncomfortable with these developments. The authorities were worried over, what they thought, to be emergence of Bolshevism in the country. Nehru was marked down as a potentially dangerous revolutionary, and his every movement was seriously followed and reported to the intelligence agencies. Nehru did not succeed in his mission of alleviating the conditions of the peasants, but one of the first things he did on becoming the prime minister of free India was to abolish the Taluqdar system.

Dyer's vindication and the orchestrated public support for him in Britain rubbed salt in the wounds that were still raw. But it was the oldest running sore, the future of the Islamic caliphate—known in India as the Khilafat—that provided Gandhi with an immediate excuse to launch a new campaign against the Raj.

Footnotes

1. Pandit Madan Mohan Malviya—Proceedings of the Indian Assembly, dated 18/9/1919, The Gazette of India Part VI p 1155
2. Report, Proceedings and Memoranda of Cabinet Committee on Indian Disorders –1920.
3. Ian Colvin Life of General Dyer p 197
4. The Congress Punjab Inquiry Vol. 1 P-80
5. Hunter Committee Report
6. Hunter Committee Report p 147
7. Disorders Inquiry Hunter Committee Report P 130
8. Proceedings of the Indian Legislative Council dated 3rd September 1919, Gazette of India Part IV 13th September 1919.
9. Aldous Huxley Ends and Means p 18
10. Edwin Montagu by SD Waley Asian Publishing House Bombay, 1964
11. Ref ibid.
12. Earth of Jallianwala Bagh packed in small packets was also sold at Rupee one a packet and thousands of such packets were sold at various public meetings. (Baba Gurdit Singh, Voyage of Kama Gatamaru, Part II page 133)

8

Khilafat Movement

The tragedy of Jallianwala Bagh probably did more than anything else to embitter racial relations between the British and Indians; but the Congress did not immediately abandon the policy of cooperation. May be, it was still in the process of recovering from the magnitude of the horror of the massacre. However, with the publication of the 'Treaty of Sevres', which liquidated the power of the Caliph, a surge of pan-Islamic feeling swept through the Muslims of India, and the Congress, led by Gandhi, determined to enter this Khilafat movement and further the case of Hindu-Muslim unity so as to become more powerful to challenge British power.

The basic issue was the status of the Sultan of Turkey as the Caliph, the religious leader of Islam and protector of holy places. After Turkey having joined hands with the 'axis powers' had lost the war, it appeared that the sultan would be losing on his relevance. Earlier, the British Prime Minister, Lloyd George had assured Indian Muslims that when Turkey was defeated Britain would respect the sultan's position as the spiritual leader of Islam and protector of their holy places. But that was during the war, when Britain needed the loyalty and support of Indian Muslims. Now that the war had been won Lloyd George felt no qualms over reneging to his Muslim subjects. He was willing to share the booty with France and was ready to dismantle the Ottoman Empire and divide the spoils in a manner that totally ignored the Muslim interests and sentiments. To the British government, the treaty was purely a political issue between the Allies and Turkey, and had nothing to do with religion, or with India. Indian Muslims saw it as a deliberate attempt by the Christian West to destroy the power of Islam. Anti-British feelings started stirring strongly in the Muslim hearts over this dismemberment of the strongest of the Muslim states in the world.

In 1918, the Khilafat Committee was formed to lead the protest against the imperialist designs to reduce the authority of the Caliph—the Sultan of Turkey, who was the ecclesiastical head of the Sunnite Muslims. Faced with the problem that was difficult to explain to the illiterate Muslim masses, the leaders formed a committee, in keeping with the usual Indian culture of the time (that the 'committee culture' still continues is not being discussed as is not relevant to this narrative). The Muslim League, dealing with much more serious issues, was totally disinterested; Jinnah, living up to his secular credentials was keeping himself aloof. He was of the opinion that the fate of distant Turkey and of its Caliph (or Khalifa) was none of India's business. The Nizam of Hyderabad, a consummate opportunist, banned the Khilafat agitation in his state. All this did not deter the average Muslim from feeling that a massive wrong had been done to his faith; and the leaders were doing nothing to ensure that their holy places were not desecrated or neglected in any manner. The anti-British sentiments among the Muslims gained in momentum in 1919 when the British-Afghan war started. A large number of Muslims serving in the army deserted and joined hands with the Afghans in order to safeguard the honour of Islam. By the summer of 1920 as many as 18 to 20 thousand Muslims had left India for Afghanistan. Not all were soldiers, and many could not survive harsh climate and rough conditions of the country. Those who survived the journey went jobless as Afghanistan hardly had any industry or other kinds of employment opportunities.

The Khilafat agitation gave an extremely dangerous turn to Muslim politics. At that point of time, for the harassed and confused Muslim population there really was no light at the end of the tunnel. There was no leader of consequence who could tell them what to do when their religious places were under threat. Jinnah, who was originally not particularly enthusiastic about the agitation, had gradually developed growing reservations about the fairness of the British; more so after the Jallianwala Bagh and the 'eye-wash' enquiry that followed that sordid chapter in the Indian history.

Luckily for the Muslims, Gandhi had elected to pick cudgels on their behalf. Anything that had a religious base, and could be turned into a weapon against the Raj, had a natural appeal for him. He believed that in appealing to religious feelings, the common man's fervent adherence to his customs would increase his love for national traditions and would inevitably bring him into the struggle against foreign domination. At the same time he used religion as a means of keeping the mass movement within the framework of non-violence. He shrewdly assessed the objective value to the national movement of this acutely felt Muslim grievance.

Reasoning that his support would place Muslims in his debt, strengthening Hindu-Muslim unity against the British, and could harness Muslim energies to his campaign for Swaraj, he threw himself wholeheartedly into this new cause. In his own words, he saw in the situation "an opportunity of uniting Hindus and Muslims as would not arise in hundred years." He was sure that in the conditions of the rapid growth of the national struggle, the Khilafat movement, not withstanding its religious tinge and non-violent form, played a positive role, since it promoted unity between Hindus and Muslims in their common struggle against the British Imperialism.

Predictably, for Gandhi, his involvement in the movement started on a wrong foot. It was a stand, which Gandhi could hardly explain to his Hindu followers when most of the Muslims themselves were not very clear about the issues involved. His call for a Hartal to observe a 'Khilafat Day' in October 1919 was a failure. But he persevered. In Delhi on 23 November he urged the first national Khilafat conference to adopt the tactic of 'non-cooperation' with the Raj. It was the first time that he had used the term and, as with many of his earlier pronouncements and initiatives, even he was not very clear exactly what he meant by it. But the delegates, who had been a confused lot thus far, were hooked. If Gandhi was sponsoring then there was mileage to be drawn from the agitation, seemed to be the general feeling. Expanding on the theme, it was resolved that no Indian will take part in the forthcoming victory in the war celebrations, and all Indians will boycott British goods.

The Khilafat Committee gained momentum when some of the leaders who had been interned or imprisoned during the war were released under the general amnesty for political prisoners and they returned to start where they had left. Notable among those who were released were the brothers Muhammad and Shaukat Ali and Abul Kalam Azad. All three were Maulanas, learned men, and thus automatically commanded respect among the believers. They were capable of arousing the masses with fiery rhetoric. Muhammad Ali led a deputation to London to inform the government that the Muslims were morally bound to ensure that the Arab land where Muslim holy places existed always remained in the hands of the faithful; this is what the prophet had commanded with his dying breath. The Holy Prophet himself, he emphasised, ordained this, therefore the control of the region, i.e. Iraq, Syria and Palestine should remain with the Caliph, not withstanding the fact that the Caliph had joined hands with the 'axis' during the war and had lost. Lloyd George was not impressed. Ali and party returned, bitter and empty handed. Soon enough they joined hands with Gandhi, who had already smelled a suitable cause to further embarrass the Raj, and promote the case of India as such. Ali brothers and the Maulana, like Gandhi, placed their trust in God and gave little thought to the consequences of their actions.

Gandhi continued to prod the Khilafat Committee to launch a national campaign of non-cooperation throughout 1920. That the Turks themselves had deposed the Sultan in the meanwhile and had expressed a desire for control on the oil-rich area of the region without any particular affiliation for the religious belt was not reason enough for Gandhi to let go this chance for what promised to be good fight. Where he was concerned, a tide had come in India's affairs, which he had to convert into a flood. On 9th June at a meeting in Allahabad they unanimously agreed, and as he was hoping, they asked Gandhi to lead it. Among the invited guests were Motilal Nehru, Sir Tej Bahadur Sapru and Annie Besant, the three pillars of Congress establishment. Gandhi knew that these stalwarts of Congress were not likely to approve and support his ideas on the subject. In South Africa he had been successful because there was just about nobody else who could be considered as intelligent enough, or educated enough to take on the government on issues that were dear to the Indian population: out there he could have his way. Back home in India, he had already found that the level of intellect in the leaders of the movement was high enough to plunge headlong just because the Mahatma had so willed. By side-stepping the Congress leadership and launching his campaign through the Khilafat Committee, he was throwing down a challenge, which the Congress leaders could not ignore. Predictably, they decided to examine all facets of the issues involved and to consider the idea of non-cooperation; the leaders were conscious of the fact that launching of such an agitation where the majority population was not directly affected by the actions of the British government had massive, unpredictable and potentially uncontrollable consequences. They wanted to call for a special session of the Party before any concrete step was taken on the issue. Gandhi kept up with the pressure on Congress by going ahead without waiting for the outcome of the 'special session'.

Gandhi was not deterred by these reservations expressed by the Party stalwarts. On 22nd June, he wrote to the Viceroy, warning him that unless the injustices heaped on Turkey, and consequently to the Muslim sentiment in India were not removed by 1st August, he would mount a national campaign of non-cooperation, asserting the right recognised 'from time immemorial of the subject to refuse to assist a ruler who misrules.' Ninety odd Muslim leaders signed and sent a similar letter to the Viceroy. Chelmsford was already full of everything going wrong in India and was determined not to get involved. Montagu was helpless in the face of Lloyd George's hostility to Turkey. So, the campaign was officially launched on the prescribed date. Gandhi, seemingly, had forgotten his having rued the fact that Jallianwala Bagh massacre probably wouldn't had taken place if the masses had been suitably and appropriately educated about the do's and don'ts of the agitation then going on. He had called it as his 'Himalayan mis-calculation'. Just eighteen months down the line, amid scenes of wild enthusiasm, he was promising Swaraj within one year if his programme was followed. Doubters like Besant, Pal, Das or Jinnah were being dismissed contemptuously when they tried to voice their fears about launching non-cooperation before the masses had been educated about its principles and the methodology to be followed. Gandhi marked the beginning of the campaign with a suitably dramatic gesture of publicly returning his Kaiser-I-Hind gold medal and other medals he had won in the Boer and Zulu wars. Thereafter he set off an all India tour to drum up support for the Khilafat movement, and to win over as many Congressmen as he possibly could before the all-important special session of Congress to be held in September. He had already taken over the presidency of the Home Rule League at the invitation of Motilal Nehru.

On Gandhi's insistence, a special session of the Congress was held in September 1920. At the stormy plenary session held in Calcutta, Motilal, Jinnah, C R Das, Annie Besant etc, and the prominent Hindu Mahasabha leader Madan Mohan Malviya, were of the opinion that to take up a purely Muslim cause in a predominantly Hindu country was fraught with danger, particularly when the issue involved related to another country— Turkey. They, however, agreed to accept the idea of non-cooperation. When the motion was put to vote all the Muslim members, except Jinnah, desired Congress to be a party to the Khilafat movement. Feelings ran high: at one point Shaukat Ali had to be physically restrained from striking Jinnah, who had been most vociferous in expressing his disagreement with the Khilafat movement while giving his presidential address to the League. Gandhi refused to compromise in any way. It had to be Khilafat based non-cooperation. If the Congress leadership did not approve his line of action then he would continue with the agitation without it. To the surprise and dismay of the Congress leaders, Motilal suddenly changed his tune. He along with some of his followers voted in favour of Khilafat movement, and the motion was carried by 144 votes to 132. Motilal's change of heart was attributed to his fears that his only son Jawaharlal, who had become a staunch follower of Gandhi, could be alienated from him if he did not support Gandhi.

The motion was to be voted upon by all the party members present in the open Congress. Special Khilafat trains had brought thousands of Muslim workers from Bombay and Madras, to vote for whatever Gandhi proposed. Anyone who paid the price of admission to the Congress tent was immediately registered as a member, and was allowed to vote. One of Gandhi's opponents later told Dr. B R Ambedkar, leader of the untouchables, that a large majority of the delegates were no other than the taxi-drivers of Calcutta who were paid to vote for the non-cooperation movement. (M K Gandhi, *Autobiography*, p291). Any reservations that the Party leadership had on the issues involved had no meaning when the tidal wave of overwhelming response to Gandhi's call was there for every body to see. Congress was now in the process of being transformed from an elite middle-class debating society into a popular mass movement. Sensing that Gandhi's call for Khilafat linked non-cooperation was likely to sway common Indian towards his movement, rest of the Party leaders gave in. It was now proclaimed that the policy of progressive non-cooperation would continue until the Khilafat and Punjab wrongs were righted, and Swaraj established.

Jinnah had also called for a simultaneous session of the Muslim League at Calcutta; by now he could also feel that, in addition to having a lot of political mileage, the agitation could shift Muslim loyalty towards Gandhi, thus making his case for the community leadership weak. He was ready to shed his reservations about a purely communal agitation; his political future hinged on a pro-Khilafat stand.

At the special session of the Muslim League held at Calcutta on 7th September 1920, Jinnah, as the party President, made a bitter attack on the authorities. He referred to the Rowlatt Act, the Punjab atrocities, and the break up of the Ottoman Empire and the Khilafat. He asserted that the Indians could not rely either on the Government of India or His Majesty's Government to govern the country with justice and humanity, or to represent India's voice in matters international. "One thing there is which is indisputable," he said; and that is that this government must go and give place to a responsible government. One degrading measure upon another; he went on, "disappointment upon disappointment and injury upon injury, can lead a people to only one end; It led Russia to Bolshevism. It has led Ireland to Sinn Fein-ism. May it lead India to freedom." Though he did not wholly approve of Gandhi's programme, Jinnah agreed that there was no other course left open to the people except to inaugurate the policy of non-cooperation![1] Gandhi was pleasantly surprised when in December 1920, the Congress adopted non-cooperation as the next stage in the struggle for freedom. The League also now voted for Gandhi's programme, the shrewd Mahatma had been right, he had won the confidence of Muslims; to whom the united appeal of pan-Islamism and nationalism was now irresistible. Nationalism and Khilafatism were now organically related as "the avowed twin objectives of the entire country."

Wily politician that Gandhi was he was also not averse to make concessions, if his grip on the country and the movement could be strengthened in the process. On 19th March 1921, he wrote; "Muslims have special Quoranic obligations...(and) reserve to themselves the right in the event of the failure of non-cooperation-cum-non-violence... to resort to all such methods as may be enjoined by the Islamic scriptures.[2] This was a calculated risk not in tune with his basic principles but he took the gamble. May be his involvement in a purely Muslim cause would bring Hindus and Muslims closer, would be another reason for him to associate with the issue. (Writing in *'Young India'* on 11 May 1921), Gandhi declared that the Khilafat question gave the Hindus and Muslims an opportunity of a lifetime to unite. "If the Hindus", he wrote, "wish to cultivate eternal friendship with the Muslims they must perish with them in the attempt to vindicate the honour of Islam." Gandhi really had no other option else his career as a leader of the movement would have been at stake.

In one of those quirks of fate, that somehow had always helped Gandhi, Tilak died in the early hours of 1st August. As an orthodox Brahmin, Tilak had been strongly opposed to any Congress involvement with a purely Muslim campaign. He was the only one who could have been a 'Hindu' rival to Gandhi as a popular national leader, and probably the only man who could have turned Congress against Gandhi on the issue, his death fortuitously (for Gandhi) removed him from the scene. It, in fact, helped him because the nationwide mourning and hartals merged inextricably with Gandhi's call for non-cooperation. In the absence of an event of this magnitude and the countrywide reaction, his call on behalf of the Muslims might have turned into a damp squib.

Gandhi's programme of 'progressive, non-violent, non-cooperation' had all the ingredients the Swadeshi campaign of 1905 had. It called upon Indians to boycott all foreign goods, surrender all titles, honours and nominated positions in various government sponsored committees and councils, a boycott of official functions, withdrawal of children from government schools and colleges, which were to be replaced by national schools, boycott of British courts by both lawyers and litigants, no Indian was to offer himself for recruitment in the military, clerical or any other government service. Forthcoming elections to the 'reformed councils' were to be boycotted by both candidates and voters. The resolution was passed by 1886 votes to 884. There were 3, 188 delegates who expressed their disquiet by abstaining. Annie Besant described Gandhi's movement as "a channel of hatred". Sir Dinshaw E Wacha, the Parsi leader of the National Liberal Federation spoke for many when he complained of "the wrongs this mad man is now inflicting on the poor country in his mad and arrogant career". "The vast unthinking multitudes," he said, seemed willing to follow "like a flock of sheep, this unsafe shepherd who is bringing the country on the very brink of chaos and anarchy." (Cabinet

Committee Report, Proceedings and Memoranda of Cabinet Committee on Indian Disorders-1920). Even Tagore was unhappy with this call for giving up on British education because he felt that such gestures were counter productive and 'an abstraction which is ready to ignore living reality.' In a letter to Roman Rolland he said, "If people cannot think scientifically, our first battle should be against that state of mind. Such incapacity is the original sin out of which all other ills flow."

From Calcutta, Gandhi and Jinnah went on to a Home Rule League meeting that had been called at a short notice. Only 61 out of 6000 members were present, but that completed the quorum and the meeting was called to order. Gandhi took the chair and immediately proposed changing both the name and the constitution of the League. Henceforth, he announced, 'the League will be known as Swaraj Sabha': continuing with his statement he further announced that the mission of the League stands changed from 'Attainment of self-government within the British Commonwealth…by constitutional methods' to 'secure complete Swaraj, or 'Purna Swaraj' for India according to the wishes of the Indian people.' When Jinnah demurred arguing that taking of a negative attitude of non-cooperation in Indian politics could be counter-productive, Gandhi told him anyone who could not accept the majority's decision was free to resign. Two-thirds of those present voted for the motion, Jinnah, with his 18 supporters left the meeting and the Home Rule League which he had spent so much effort to groom, and once had led. To his credit his efforts for creating Hindu-Muslim unity had borne fruit; in that, along with him a large number of prominent Hindu leaders of the Home League, men like M R Jaykar, Jamanadas Dwarka Das, Kanji Dwarkadas, K M Munshi and many other Hindus also resigned from the organisation.

By 1920 Jinnah saw the real basis of Hindu-Muslim cooperation dissolve when Gandhi took over the leadership of Congress. He was certain that Gandhi's spirituality would charge the Congress Party with a religious enthusiasm, Hindu in content, which would arouse Muslim distrust. Disillusioned, in 1920 he resigned from the Congress Party and the Imperial Legislative Council. In his letter of resignation, Jinnah made no bones about his feelings for Gandhi: "Your methods have already caused split and division in almost every institution that you have approached hitherto…not only amongst Hindus and Muslims but between Hindus and Hindus and Muslims and Muslims and even between fathers and sons…your extreme programme has for the moment struck the imagination of the inexperienced youth and the ignorant and the illiterate. All this means disorganisation and chaos. I do not wish my countrymen to be dragged to the brink of a precipice in order to be shattered." Gandhi lost no sleep over exit of one of the stalwarts of the movement.

Instead, he spent time and energy in preparing a new constitution for the Congress.

We Divide Ourselves and You Rule

So far as can be ascertained from the available records, Jinnah was willing in principle to work with the Congress so long as the Congress allowed the Muslim community separate electorates and more seats in the legislatures than their strict numbers would justify. The Congress leaders took the disastrously simple view that the Muslim fuss was really the offshoot of British 'Divide and Rule' approach to their continuation in India. The Muslims reacted violently to what they regarded as cavalier overriding of their rights. The younger and more imaginative among them came up with the idea of having a state of their own—to be formed out of India where Muslims would rule supreme. Cunning British felt that at this stage some kind of political concessions and consideration for the Hindu sentiment was essential for the continuation of the Raj, nothing could add to the already existing mutual distrust than one community gaining an upper hand over the other for reasons other than the merits of the situation as perceived by either community. This was sound tactics. Montagu-Chelmsford Reforms had created enough vested interests in the provinces for the two communities to be vary of each other; more importantly regional (and communal) leaders were now more involved in establishing their supremacy in states like Punjab rather than supporting their national level leaders to work out a solution that could help consolidate position of the nationalists where freedom of the country was concerned. Local leaders from both the communities were proving to be stumbling blocks; and with such a communal polarisation taking place in states which provided most of the soldiers and had the most productive granaries, like UP and Punjab, there was no way the British could ignore such inviting signals to further their cause for continuation in the country. There was a clear connection between political ambitions at the provincial levels and growth of communal antagonism between Hindus and Muslims. Community first and the Country later became the immediate concern of leaders and workers in different states and at different levels.

One cannot really exonerate Indian leaders (at national level) for germinating and even consolidating an idea in the British mind that Indians could be subjugated for long if Hindus and Muslims continued to distrust each other; because in spite of making noise about the 'Divide and Rule' policy of the British, as they saw, the leaders did nothing to allay the reservations of the minorities. They never bothered to introspect that their attacks on the ramshackle conventions and tenets of the western civilisation could be equally applied to those local customs and traditions that had kept India backward and subservient for centuries. They frequently complained against the British policy of creating cleavage between various communities and religions but made no real effort at countering it in their programmes and policies. Mainly the problem was that (and still is) the democratic practices and traditions of pre-independence India were affected by ingress of religion in politics. Extremists of different hues, terrorists and revivalists used religion as their take-off point. Even Gandhi used the religious appeal to gain political advantage all through his leadership of the country's freedom movement. Many of those who imagined themselves above sectarian prejudices failed to see that key issue was not the question of music before a mosque or cow slaughter or even political representation that would satisfy all sections of the society.

Nehru perhaps, was the only one of that stature who felt that industrial and economic growth could neutralise the divisive forces. He wrote in his Autobiography: "The Congress has largely kept out of this communal darkness, but its outlook is pretty bourgeois and the remedy it seeks for this and other problems is in terms of the petty bourgeoisie. It is not likely to succeed that way." He resented dogmatic and little-minded nature of communalism: writing to a friend he said, "I have no patience left with the legitimate and illegitimate offspring of religion." (*Builder of Modern India*, edited by M Chalapathi Rau pp 35-38). But did nothing to check Swami Shradhanand, the hero of Delhi in 1919 when he addressed a congregation at the Jumma Masjid exhorting people to be united, and now in 1923-24 leading a re-conversion campaign. For that matter Saifud-Din Kitchlew, the hero of Amritsar, who responded by launching a counter- campaign, also went unchecked. Patriotism and total devotion to the cause of India's freedom of these two respected leaders, adored both by Hindus and Muslims, is beyond any question, but the fact that their actions were leading to polarisation of the communities as Hindus and Muslims was never brought home to them. The Swami was eventually assassinated by a fanatic in 1926.

The Party Constitution-Congress

As per the decision taken during the last session, activity associated with the writing of new constitution for the party started in right earnest. But there were hiccups. More experienced lawyers like Motilal, Das and others who could have contributed to the exercise were busy with their respective legal practices in addition to their work for the country, and had no time to devote to this exercise. Gandhi had a free hand to do what he liked. The party constitution that he drafted was entirely to his own whims and fancies. During the December session of Congress held at Kanpur, he presented it to the 14,500 delegates to great acclaim.

Seeing Gandhi catching the imagination of the youth of the country, Das, Lajpatrai and Motilal had by now swung into line behind him. Indeed, Lajpatrai seconded his motion on the new constitution, which began by changing Congress's main objective to 'the attainment of Swaraj by the people of India by all legitimate and peaceful means'. Das was persuaded to propose the main resolution on non-cooperation.

Most of the Congress stalwarts, some of them former presidents, who could not stomach the Mahatma's radical policies stayed away, among them were Pandit Madan Mohan Malviya, Surendranath Nath Bannerjee, Bipin Chandra Pal, Tej Bahadur Sapru and C Sankaran Nair were the more prominent absentees. Once again, only Jinnah had the nerve to question Gandhi's wisdom. It must have taken great deal of courage and bravery to take on the Mahatma that day. When he tried to introduce a reasoned and logical argument, calling for careful study of the situation before taking any decision that could have serious ramifications for the country, he was shouted down with cries of 'shame, shame' and 'political impostor'. Resentment against Jinnah grew when he refused to address Gandhi as 'Mahatma'; instead he called him plain Mr. Gandhi. The partisan crowd wouldn't let Jinnah speak, and he was driven from the platform and from the tent. Gandhi seemed to have made no effort to check his followers who now were becoming more and more insulting in their behaviour. Jinnah left Nagpur by the next train, his political career in ruins. He did not even bother to attend the Muslim League session, knowing full well that it, too, was in the hands of his opponents.

As soon as the Congress session at Nagpur was over, Gandhi set off on the campaign train through the towns and villages. He had promised Swaraj within one year and was clearly in a hurry to meet the self-defined deadline. Hindus and Muslims everywhere took up his call, fired by the two key words, 'Swaraj' and 'Khilafat'. Swaraj everybody understood clearly, but in the hinterland Khilafat caused confusion as hardly anyone could relate to the issue involved. Nevertheless, for the illiterate it sounded like 'Khilafat', which in Urdu meant 'against', ergo they were required to oppose the government, not a very difficult thing to do when the Mahatma was wanting them to do so.

The movement gathered momentum as the months went by. The boycott of schools and colleges was more successful in areas other than the south, where traditionally education had always been given priority by the people. The law courts couldn't be totally avoided as people did have important cases going on, but certain nationally prominent lawyers did withdraw from the courts. Prominent among them were C R Das, Saifuddin Kitchlew, Vallabhbhai Patel, C Rajagopalachari, and, of course,

Motilal Nehru. Nehru, in fact, followed the Mahatma's directive in totality; he had never been one for half measures. He withdrew his daughter Krishna from the school, resigned from the United Provinces Council, and closed down his law firm. He sold his horses, carriages, and cars, cut down on his army of servants to just one, and replaced his Seville Row suits with a Kurta Pyjama and a Gandhi cap. Jawaharlal took quite easily to this sudden change.

Not many title-holders returned their honours, not many gave up their government jobs, and boycott of British education was also patchy because of the reservations of the middle classes about alternate arrangements: but one area where the campaign was a huge success was the boycott of foreign cloth. Gandhi started it off by personally supervising a great ceremonial bonfire of imported finery. It is said that the import of cloth from Lancashire was reduced by fifty per cent in 1921 itself. Shops selling foreign cloth were picketed till they promised to sell Khadi, which became the uniform of the nationalist movement. Gandhi went around the country exhorting people to adopt Khadi. When students in Madurai complained that it was too expensive, Gandhi advised them to wear less. He promptly discarded his own dhoti and kurta in favour of a loincloth, with a cotton shawl for winter. It became his trademark dress for the rest of his life.

Despite all the agitation openly aimed at over-throwing the Raj, the government of India steadfastly refused to intervene. Chelmsford wanted no repetition of the tragedies of 1919, not withstanding constant coaxing by some of his principal staff officers and complaints from various governors that the day-to-day work in different parts of the country had virtually come to a stand still, most upset over this lack of stiff governmental response were the Anglo-Indians.

In 1921, Lord Reading, a distinguished lawyer who had been the solicitor-general, lord chief justice and special envoy to the USA, replaced Chelmsford. Immediately on taking charge he had as many as six private conversations with Gandhi, conducted on both sides with exquisite courtesy. At one encounter Gandhi observed that as 'every action of the Government which appeared to be good, and indeed was good, was actuated by the sinister motive of trying to fasten British dominion on India.' "India had no cause to be grateful," he said. Reading also elected to let Gandhi carry on with his agitation, but the Ali brothers, who were becoming more and more belligerent with each passing day, soon tested his resolve. The brothers went on to propagate that it was religiously unlawful for a Muslim to continue in the British Army or to induce others to join the same. Lord Rawlinson, the commander-in-chief, declared that the time had come for action. Reading and his council were forced to agree; especially since there was evidence that Shaukat Ali had been interfering with the army. As soon as Ali brothers were arrested, Gandhi led Congress and Khilafat leaders across the country in publicly repeating their words, and then publishing them in a printed manifesto, clearly with a view to incite a reaction for him to draw political mileage. But the government had been expecting this, and refused to take the bait. Reading was content to bide his time and wait for Gandhi to make a more serious mistake, or for the movement to run out of steam, as he believed that it surely would.

The movement soon turned into a platform for sorting out local, personal and property disputes between people. The discontentment was fanned further when some of the Maulanas and mullahs, taking recourse to Qur'an started talking of a Jihad and to killing of the infidels. Malviya and some other prominent leaders were quick to point out that if the British were non-believers then so were the Hindus. In August 1921, the cracks widened further when on the Malabar coast down south, a fanatical Muslim group known as Moplahs rose against their Hindu landlords and the British, killing both indiscriminately. The Moplahs were descendants of Arab traders and sailors from the ancient period when Malabar was a trading center for pepper. They married low caste Hindus and openly received converts. They belonged to a fanatical religious sect, the Sunni, which revered the Sultan of Turkey. Homicidal riots usually started when a convert to the sect decided to return to Hinduism. Now they believed that the British were against Islam and that was the genesis of the Khilafat movement. Agitated Moplahs went on a burning and looting spree. When a rumour was floated that a mosque had been defiled, the Moplahs let loose a virtual reign of terror. A British regiment was sent to restore order and there were pitched battles, Moplahs burnt down courts, police stations, Hindu homes, destroyed temples and raped women. Before order could be restored an estimated 4,000 Moplahs and 100 British troops had been killed. Gandhi came in for a lot of criticism when he defined the rebels as "brave God-fearing Moplahs".

The Congress Working Committee, while condemning Moplah excesses, asserted that the Moplahs had been provoked by the circumstances for acting in the way they did, the Committee also felt that the official reports of violence by them were exaggerated. During the agitation, the Moplahs had forcibly converted thousands of Hindus to Islam. Hindus on the Congress subjects committee were shocked when a Maulana who was a member of the committee refused to condemn this, arguing that the conversion was voluntary and not forced by the Muslim leadership. Malviya's Hindu Mahasabha joined hands with the Arya Samaj in mounting a campaign to 'reconvert' and 'purify' those low-caste Hindus who had become Muslims. Inevitably, tensions between the communities increased and communal rioting broke out.

The dependence of the Khilafat movement on circumstances and events outside India necessarily limited its long-term importance. But it was not without significance for political developments inside India. This was a prelude to a decade of unprecedented inter-communal hatred and violence. In the next five years alone there were no fewer than 112 major communal riots, mostly in the northern parts of the country. This movement was the most significant mass movement among the Muslims before the 1940s, and many of the politicians involved in it were later to figure on the Muslim League platform when demand for Pakistan picked up momentum. The communal tension generated by giving undeserved importance to the Ali brothers by Gandhi, and by the government in allowing them to carry on with their Khilafat movement to the discomfort of the Hindus, finally culminated in the partition of the country twenty-five years later. Why Gandhi was so enamoured with the duo is shrouded in mystery. But then there is not much of a mystery in this if one goes by the letter that Gandhi wrote to Mohammad Ali when he was still in custody. ('My interest in your release', he wrote 'is quite selfish. We have a common goal and I want to utilise your services to the uttermost in order to reach that goal. In the proper solution of the Mohammedan question lies the realisation of Swaraj,' (*Collected Works of Mahatma Gandhi*, vol. Xv pp 63-64). Maybe the Ali brothers saw themselves to be used by Gandhi in pursuit of his own agenda, and they did react in a manner that was not particularly friendly to the Mahatma, or the Congress. Even during their honeymoon with the Congress, the Ali Brothers were not slow to shout from the housetops that the Muslims were a 'master race'. Mohammad Ali while throwing venom on Gandhi declared, "Yes, according to my religion and creed, I do hold an adulterous and a fallen Muslim to be better than Mr. Gandhi." Clearly, and in spite of all the latitude given to the Ali brothers by Gandhi even having annoyed some Party stalwarts in the process, to them a control over their own community was more important than their standing with the Congress.

With 1921 coming close to its end, and no freedom in sight, which Gandhi had promised, there were signs of disillusionment among his supporters, people were becoming progressively restive and worried over the fissure that had emerged between the Hindus and Muslims. The movement was showing clear signs of winding down. Something had to be done before it disintegrated altogether. Gandhi decided to move to the next stage in his plan: active civil disobedience. To the All India Congress Committee in Delhi, he informed that he wanted to start a trial campaign in one district on 23rd November. And depending on its success the agitation will be extended to the rest of India. The district he chose was Bardoli, near Surat in his native Gujarat. He had timed it to coincide with the goodwill visit of the Prince of Wales, who was due to arrive in Bombay on 17th November for a 246-day familiarization trip to India. Congress boycotted the visit and called a highly successful Hartal on the day the prince arrived, not only in Bombay but also in a number of other northern cities. Almost all Bombay's Hindus and Muslims stayed away from the ceremonies connected with the welcoming of the prince. But the city's Parsi and Eurasian communities were eager to welcome the royal visitor.

As the prince stepped ashore, Gandhi was addressing a crowd of some 60,000 only a few hundred yards away, before going to supervise a great bonfire of British goods. As always, his message to his followers was to be peaceful in their protest. But when his meeting was over, and the primed up crowd came across the loyalists returning after welcoming the prince, an exchange of taunts and jibes was inevitable. Soon all ideas of non-violence were forgotten, Hindus and Muslims fell upon the loyalists with an unbridled ferocity. The rioting and looting that followed continued for the next five days, the situation was made worse by the roaming bands of agitated textile workers who had declared a strike to coincide with Gandhi's call for Hartal. By the time the disturbances had burnt themselves out 60 people had been killed and countless injured. Gandhi was hurt over this violence; he went on a five days fast to expiate the sins of his followers. His hopes of a peaceful civil disobedience had been shattered yet again—he called off the agitation. The doubters were proved right once again; the Indian masses were not yet ready for a peaceful Satyagraha.

Reading also was finally awakening to the realities of the situation; he was now convinced that action would have to be taken against the non-cooperators. The prince was to visit Calcutta on 24th December, any more violence as was seen in Bombay would not have reflected well on the Viceroy's performance report. Orders went out for preventive custody of the prominent leaders. Among the first to be pulled in were, C R Das in Bengal, Lajpatrai in Punjab and of course the two Nehrus in the United Provinces. During the next two months over 30,000 people were arrested in India as a whole, and of the top leadership only Gandhi remained free—the government judged that arresting him was too dangerous, and in any case, Reading needed someone to negotiate with.

Sensing the danger of the Liberals and the Moderates getting back in the Gandhi camp the Viceroy threw the carrot of a round-table conference, promising to release all political prisoners, and even grant 'full provincial autonomy' if Gandhi would call off the non-cooperation movement, and in particular the Hartal in Calcutta on 24th December. At first, Gandhi agreed. But he quickly changed his mind, stipulating that the non-cooperation movement can only be called off as a consequence of the conference becoming a success.

Preventive measures taken by the government and Gandhi's reluctance to do anything that could lead to a repeat of Bombay ensured that the royal visit to Calcutta went off peacefully. Four days later at the stormy annual session of Congress in Ahmedabad, Gandhi came under attack both from those who wanted to seek accommodation with the government and those who wanted militancy to accentuate so that the government could be forced to react. But in the end, as always, Gandhi carried the day. He announced that the postponed campaign of 'offensive civil disobedience' in Bardoli would go ahead. Some of the Moderates were still hoping that a way out could be found if Gandhi agreed to a meeting with Reading. Jinnah and Malviya called an all-parties conference in Bombay for mid-January 1922. Some 300 leaders from all of India's major political parties attended. Gandhi attended 'informally.' The motion calling for a round table conference was passed unanimously. But then Gandhi threw another spanner in the works by refusing to take part. He was, obviously, obsessed with putting full-scale Satyagraha to the test, he declared that a conference 'for devising a scheme of full Swaraj is premature. India has not yet incontestably proved its strength, let us not go into waters whose depth we do not know', he observed.

Gandhi, by his stubbornness, had handed back the moral and strategic advantages back to the Viceroy, who could now sit back and watch Gandhi's support base crumbling, where he was concerned Gandhi was now programmed to "self-destruct". All that Reading needed now was for Gandhi to provide the right excuse to arrest him. When Reading ignored all of Gandhi's letters threatening action if his demands were not met, the Mahatma had no choice but to activate his Bardoli campaign. Gandhi had called for the rest of the country to stay calm, but on 5th February, what began as a minor disturbance in the remote village of Chauri-Chaura in the United Provinces, blew into a major incident and changed everything. An altercation between the tail end of the procession of the Congress and Khilafat and the local police suddenly turned violent. 22 policemen and government officials, who were inside the local police station, were burnt alive. The place was so remote that it took two days for the news to reach the outside world. On hearing of the calamity, a shattered Gandhi called off the agitation, and in keeping with his tradition went on a 'fast' for atonement of the sins committed by the people of Chauri-Chaura. "I know," he wrote, "that the reversal of practically the whole of the aggressive programme may be politically unsound and unwise, but there is no doubt that it is religiously sound."[3] Those followers like the Nehrus, Sir Tej Bahadur Sapru and C R Das who were intellectuals in their own right were shattered by this latest about-face. They had been preparing for this battle with the Raj for 18 months and now their general had deserted them. "If one incident was enough to stop the Mahatma from giving a political fight to the opposition, then all that Britain had to do next time was to provoke such an incident and all threats of Satyagraha would vanish," the thinking Indian community concluded.

Seeing Gandhi's popularity waning, London started pressing Reading to muzzle Gandhi and to arrest him, but Reading, on the advice of Sapru, kept his nerve for another month, and was rewarded by seeing most of the non-cooperation movement crumble into total collapse. When Gandhi was eventually arrested on 10th March 1922 it was greeted with deep satisfaction by most of the British in India; there was not a single Indian protest or Hartal in the whole country. A week later, he pleaded guilty to "bringing into hatred or contempt...the Government established by law into British India". He was sentenced to six years simple imprisonment. The non-cooperation movement was finished, and the Raj had survived three years of its most dangerous crisis since the great revolt of 1857. (*The Proudest Day*, pp196). The movement, which had started with a great deal of enthusiasm, had floundered for a whole lot of reasons: the deep-rooted antipathies of Hindu and Muslim, non-cooperation among various segments of the country's population in non-cooperation movement, and the wish among self-rule supporters to accept elections to the new councils and so make constitutional progress by cooperation with the British.

All this time, Reading was also pursuing his agenda of reforms, and in 1923, he fulfilled three of the most cherished dreams of the early Congressmen: ICS entrance examinations were held in New Delhi as well as London, with the avowed objective of equalising the numbers of British and Indian members; the first batch of Indians began training as commissioned officers for the army, and above all, India was to have its own Budget—at long last fiscal freedom was given to the government of India. As additional bonuses, the costs of the India Office were to be borne by the British Government, the Indian army was to be used solely for the defence of India except in dire emergency, and even then only with the consent of the government of India. Costs of such a usage, if and when made, were to be borne by Britain. Newly established Tariff Board abolished the excise duty on Indian cotton, and to make up the revenue loss on this account reintroduced tax on salt, soon this levy was doubled. Since this levy directly affected poorer of the poor, unwittingly, another situation had been thus created for Gandhi to exploit in due course of time.

While Gandhi was serving his jail term, the Congress had virtually come close to extinction in the absence of his charismatic presence. Difference of opinion between Das and Motilal Nehru on one side, and with Rajendra Prasad, C Rajagopalachari and Vallabhbhai Patel on the other on how to revive the party arose. The two wanted to have nationalists seeking elections instead of boycotting the councils, on the premise that by sitting out the Congressmen were doing no good either to the party or the country; Rajendra Prasad and other most faithful disciples of Gandhi wanted no such thing. Motilal and Das promptly formed their own 'Congress-Khilafat Swaraj Party, splitting Congress into 'pro-changers' and 'no-changers'. The split threatened to destroy Congress, but eventually a compromise was reached, and a special session in September gave its consent to Congressmen for taking part in the November elections. The party nominees did well in the elections, taking effective control of Bengal, the Bombay presidency, and the United Provinces, but lost out in Madras and Punjab, where communal elements held sway. In the Central Legislative Assembly, there were now 40 Swarajists, 23 Independents and Liberals and 36 official nominees. Das, Motilal and Jinnah were among those who had been elected to the Central Assembly.

Jinnah immediately set about the task of generating an atmosphere of friendship and cooperation. He had no desire to rejoin a Congress dominated by Gandhi, but his successes in the Assembly elections enabled him to recapture Muslim League. Even though, he was not the president of the League, he presided over its session in May, calling for a renewal of Hindu-Muslim unity; particularly, when both the non-cooperation and the Khilafat movements had brought nothing but misery and hatred, he described the unity between the two communities as a pre-requisite condition to achieve Swaraj. Pirzada- (*Foundations of Pakistan* Vol. 1 pp 576-7) Alongside, Jinnah also managed to persuade the independents to bury their many differences and work together on his programme of basic reforms. He then went to Motilal and Das, seeking their blessings in bringing the 42 Swarajists into a solid Nationalist bloc, which could always outvote the 36 official members. Similar deals soon followed in provincial and municipal councils. That this wasn't a particularly effective means of wresting power from the British, they all learnt the hard way: the governors, lieutenant governors, and of course, the Viceroy could always overrule any decision of the council without assigning any reason, the majority in the councils, both at centre and different states gave no real power to the elected representatives. To make matters worse both, Swarajists and the League were separated by political ideology. Nehru's party was recruited chiefly outside the Presidencies; Jinnah's party, on the other hand, was recruited almost entirely from the Presidencies. This led to a situation where political interest groups supported by the Raj gained an upper hand. The Raj needed them to work the Reforms and in most cases it was in their interest that Raj remained intact. In all provinces, therefore, parties with a vested interest in the continuation of the existing political dispensation came into being. Consequently, the exercise of power in the provinces transformed the nature of all-India confrontation with the Raj. The magnetic attraction of provincial office drew political energies away from the issue of freedom; the British were more than pleased with these developments.

Jinnah realised that in order to neutralise the pro-government lobby that was building up with more and more provincial level leaders joining the bandwagon there was a need for the Congress and the League to show some kind of solidarity where national interests were concerned. He at once set on a mission to generate a platform that expounded the theme of Hindu-Muslim unity in national interest. Swayed by Jinnah, the League passed a resolution to work for Swaraj, which it defined as a federal union of virtually autonomous provinces, with central government responsible for only the minimum number of areas 'of general and common concern.' It also agreed to continuation of separate electorate as the common electorate had been found to be creating friction among the communities. Religious freedom was to be granted to all. The alliances so generated, and statements by prominent leaders calling for Hindu-Muslim brotherhood dismayed Reading no end. He termed it as a Jinnah coup, specially when various committees created to work for the aforesaid resolutions were all chaired by Jinnah; not only that, League appointed Jinnah its 'permanent' president for the next three years.

The Nationalist coalition demanded a round table conference, 'with due regard to the protection of the rights and interests of important minorities,' to 'take steps to have the government of India Act revised with a view to establish fully responsible government in India.' Reading had no option but to appoint a Reforms Inquiry Committee—which, though chaired by the Home member, Sir Alexander Muddiman, was always referred to as 'the Jinnah Committee.' Initially, both Motilal and Jinnah had been invited to sit as non-official members on the Committee. Nehru was keen to accept this invitation but opposition from the Swarajist Executive obliged him to turn down this invitation. Jinnah, being less subject to any such pressures, accepted with alacrity. It gave him an ideal platform to pursue his ambitions for Reforms, to explore views of

others, and where necessary to convert them to his point of view. He
had a three point agenda; firstly, to establish that the constitution needed
overhauling; secondly, he wanted to counter the argument that
communal tension was not an obstacle to advance politically; and thirdly,
to ascertain the terms on which the Lucknow Pact could be modified.
Besides the chairman, Sir Mohammad Shafi, the Law Member, who had
been put on the committee to represent the communal point of view,
gave him strong resistance. But Jinnah got tremendous support from the
Muslim leaders of Punjab and some leaders from the United Provinces.
There, however, was a general disagreement between the Hindu and
Muslim representatives over the issue of percentage of Muslim
representation. The main opposition to a renegotiated settlement with
the Congress came from the Bengali Muslims who were disheartened
because majority of their coreligionists were supporting a Hindu leader
(Das) in Bengal. Their main grouse was an appropriate revision of the
Lucknow Pact, which would allow for a greater representation to the
Muslims than what was originally contemplated. Not withstanding these
internal differences, when it came to signing the Reforms Enquiry
Committee Report, Jinnah, Sapru and other prominent leaders demanded
that their requirement of 'provincial autonomy to the states and
responsibility in the centre' be made central theme of the Report. They
refused to sign the Majority Report and produced a Minority Report
condemning Dyarchy unequivocally, demanding provincial autonomy
and responsibility in the central government.

Unfortunately, at about the same time, Gandhi who had since been
released from jail after doing only two of his six years term, started
asserting his own authority on Congress. He took off by publicly
condemning entry of Congressmen in the Council. He wanted them to
resign. Motilal argued with him that asking so many people to leave
councils in the centre and states without any serious provocation could
be termed as invidious and even dishonourable to do so. Motilal also
brought out that some of the elected members could even leave Congress,
finding this to be an unpalatable demand on their loyalties. This pragmatic
analysis of the situation would definitely have figured in Gandhi's own
reading of the prevailing political climate in the country. He allowed
himself to be persuaded by Motilal provided all Swarajists were directed
to start a blanket obstruction of government legislation. Motilal had no
other option but to agree to this 'obviously unreasonable' demand.
Gandhi was too shrewd a politician not to have foreseen the consequences
of Swarajists throwing spanner in anything and everything, just because
they had been asked to do so. Coalition, built by Jinnah with such care
and pragmatism, started crumbling because the Independents were not
obliged to follow Motilal; they wanted to judge every issue on its merit.

Swaraj Party also started disintegrating because of the unreasonableness of the whole thing.

Clearly, feeling that he needed to do still more to bring Congress to its heel, Gandhi decided that he would be president of the Party that year, for the one and only time. With no other immediate issue at hand to further embarrass the government, Gandhi was in an urgent need to consolidate his political base: unlike South Africa, where hardly any Indian was even literate. Back home he had found too many intellectuals, and to his discomfort some of them were capable of independent thinking. In a fascinating example of his political wiles, he wrote to Motilal, who was now the only senior leader who could have stood in his way, as Das was mortally ill, offering his influence to have Motilal elected as president. As though it was an afterthought, he casually mentioned that several prominent Congressmen were 'insistent' that he should become president, though he was, of course, most reluctant. "The only condition that would make me reconsider my position on the issue, 'he wrote,' would be your desire that I should accept." Motilal took this heavy hint. Gandhi was duly elected. He, obviously, hadn't finished with his personal agenda of putting Jinnah in his, what he thought to be, and the right place.

When Jinnah learnt that Gandhi was to be president of the Congress, he immediately moved the Muslim League's annual session from Belgaum, where Congress was due to meet in December, ending the practice of simultaneous sessions which he personally had started in the cooperation and 'Hindu-Muslim' unity filled heady days of 1915. The clash of personalities and ideologies between these two leaders, who sought the same end but by different means was achieving what the British had failed to do; driving a wedge between the two main communities and political parties in India. Clearly, we did not need any outsider to divide this country, our own leaders were capable and willing enough to do so on their own. Their monumental egos refused to consider any friendly and constructive alternative even when the freedom of the country was too far away. Gandhi and Jinnah were obviously enjoying this sparring regardless of what damage their antics were doing to the freedom movement. Question is, why did Rajagopalachari, both the Nehrus, Rajendra Prasad, Vallabhbhai Patel and many more who had a vast following of their own, had respect of the majority of the party-men did nothing to reverse the trend? Jinnah, in any case, was the only Muslim leader of any note at the time and he was now trying to consolidate his base among the Muslims.

The final collapse of both the Khilafat campaign and non-cooperation left the young men of India frustrated and angry. Emergence of Soviet

Russia, and how the youth there had taken to arms for overthrowing the Czar inspired these restless Indians to do something on those lines. The Russians even set up a training camp for Indians in Tashkent. In Kanpur, a group formed the Hindustan Republican Army (HRA) based on the IRA, with the avowed aim.of getting rid of the colonial rule through armed revolution. Lack of expertise, funds, and proper guidance plus harsh measures of the government, like hanging and deportation, hastened the demise of HRA. Botched attempts for train robberies, and lootings added to the speed of closure of the HRA. Five years later, the would-be revolutionaries set up yet another organisation in the Punjab, known as the Hindustan Socialist Republic Army, it did not meet with any notable success either. Revolutionaries were equally active in Bengal, but similarly inefficient in their pursuit of the 'self' designated goals. When a young terrorist, Gopinath Saha, bungled the assignment of shooting the hated police commissioner of Calcutta, Charles Tegart, killing a businessman Ernest Day instead, the police had enough reason to swoop down. All the suspects were arrested under a newly promulgated ordinance. Among those caught in the net were a large number of Congressmen as well, including the authorities, pet hate—Subhas Chandra Bose.

Subhas Chandra Bose

The British accused Bose of conspiring to plan terrorist attacks. It was alleged that he and an another man had planned to throw a bomb in the Calcutta council chamber—a most weird and unlikely charge, considering that Bose himself was the council's chief executive. To, somehow, put him out of action, it was also alleged that he had planned the assassination of Tegart. Bose protested, but the British government was in no mood to allow yet another leader, who was not necessarily non-violent to come up in India. Bose was sent to Mandalay after a sham trial lasting about seven weeks, the rationale was that Mandalay had cured Tilak of his violent leanings and it could do the same to Bose. In Mandalay Bose kept up writing to various authorities on the unfairness of the whole situation, but nobody cared. On 18th February 1926, Bose launched a mass hunger strike in Mandalay prison; the agitation spread and prisoners in other places also took up the call for hunger strike. The authorities started force-feeding the prisoners with all the attendant consequences such an action implied. Shaukat Ali was sent to persuade Bose to give up his agitation, as it was an avoidable risk to his life. By then Burmese government had also become restless about the likely consequences if anything happened to Bose while he was in their custody; to make matters worse Bose was diagnosed to be suffering from TB. Immediate problem for the British government was what to do with him. Bengal government wanted Bose to be as far away from the state as was possible. As a sop, the government in Delhi, worried if the disease proved fatal and thus lead to serious problems for the Raj, offered Bose a passport to go to Switzerland for a cure. He declined the allurement, and refused to move unless all the charges against him were withdrawn. In the end, he returned home to Calcutta with his demands met. Subhas Bose represented the transition to a "modern" political style, encompassing modern militarism as well. Historically, traditional militaristic beliefs were not strong in Bengal, although Nirad Chaudhuri traces "vicarious militarism" to the nineteenth century Hindu Renaissance. (Nirad C Chaudhuri, *The Continent of Circe*).

In his teens, Bose had come under the influence of the teachings of Swami Vivekanand, who sought to combine 'muscular Hinduism' with western scientific ideas. Bose had a brilliant mind, and had come fourth in the ICS examinations in London in July 1920. This guaranteed him a place as one of the heavens born, and lifelong prestige, power and security at the very heart of the Raj. But to his father's fury, he resigned and turned down the chance of a glittering career in the ICS. After Jallianwala Bagh he felt no Indian should serve the British. So he returned to Calcutta and became principal of one of the National Colleges there, one of the 800 schools and colleges set up throughout the country to replace boycotted government institutions. Although younger by six years soon he was sharing the Kisan Sabha leadership with Jawaharlal Nehru. The two men were to be political rivals for the next twenty years. Bose's career was the prototypical of the development of a militaristic approach to political activity. As a Bengali he resented the British ridicule of the Bengalis for their alleged non-martial, unmanly traits. This ridicule was expressed in many ways, but particularly by the lack of opportunities for Bengali youth to receive military training or participate in the defence of India.

Two experiences forced Bose to "develop politically and to strike out an independent line for himself." The first was a series of unpleasant encounters in public places between Indians and the British—in tramcars, railways, and public streets. Bose records that since the law did not protect the Indians in inter-racial disputes, Indians began literally to hit back. "The effect was instantaneous. Everywhere the Indians began to be treated with consideration. Then the word went round that the Englishman understands and respects physical force and nothing else. This phenomenon was the psychological basis of the terrorist—revolutionary movement—at least in Bengal", he wrote.

The second experience that shook Bose's political consciousness also concerned the use of force. He considered his moral philosophy, just before the World War one, and the war provided the final catalyst. He had earlier accepted the notion that the Defence of India might be left to the British while internal politics could increasingly come under the control of Indians: this assumption was now challenged. (Was it possible to divide a nation's life into two compartments and hand over one of them to the foreigners, reserving the other to ourselves? The answer that I gave myself was a perfectly clear one—if India was to be a modern civilised nation, it would have to pay the price and would not by any means shirk the physical, the military problem. Political freedom was indivisible and meant complete independence of foreign control and tutelage. The war had shown that a nation that did not posses military strength could not hope to preserve its independence. (Subhas Chandra Bose "*An Indian Pilgrim*" (reprinted Ed: p23)

Bose's interest in military like organisations and dress reflected his deep political differences with other Congress leaders, especially Gandhi and Nehru. He differed fundamentally with Congress on the nature of British opposition to Indian independence. Gandhi and Nehru were imbued with British liberalism and understood it thoroughly. They sought to direct their appeal for independence to this liberalism. Bose stressed the obverse side of the British Raj. For Bose "the revolutionary movement was born out of a conviction that to a Western people physical force alone makes an appeal." (*The Indian Struggle*).

Bose made no secret of the fact that he rejected Gandhi's non-violence: 'Give me blood.' He once said,' and I promise you freedom.' He was about the only one, except for Jinnah, who was immune to Gandhi's charm, never calling him' Bapu' (father) like Jawaharlal Nehru and most Congressmen of his age group. He chose to address him as more formal 'Gandhiji' or 'Mahatmaji', much to the discomfort of Gandhi who was used to winning people over through warmth and humanity, ensnaring political associates in a web of affection as well as respect. Bose was also scornful of Gandhi's political tactics. Gandhi, he wrote later, 'did not have a clear idea of the successive stages of the campaign (to bring about Indian Independence)'.

Gandhi's political success was in a large part due to his ability to offer a promising option that was different from the futile violence and extremism of Tilak, and the ineffective constitutionalism of the so-called moderates. This philosophy of non-violent resistance to evil promised action and occasionally brought success; very few of Gandhi's colleagues actually shared his philosophical convictions, but many were willing to suspend criticism and follow his political leadership. ('*The Indian Army*' Stephen P Cohen, The Oxford University Press 1990. pp 102).

At the time of Bose's release from prison in Mandalay, Congress was in total disarray. Accord with Muslim League had gone defunct, Das was dead, and several other leading figures, most notably Lajpatrai and

Malaviya, had jumped ship to follow their communal consciences through the Hindu Mahasabha. The Ali brothers and many of their Muslim supporters had also departed to stir the bubbling cauldron of communal strife. In the growth of communalism in the country, the part played by religious leaders of both the communities was marginal. Arya Samaj campaign had been sparked off by effective and efficient mobilisation of the Muslims by Mullahs and Maulvis; but the main reason for the widening chasm between the two communities was the political rivalry of the Swarajists and Liberals. The lurid picture of an all-devouring Muslim domination conjured by such intelligent men, as Malaviya and Chintamani bore almost no relation to the Muslim status as a minority community with only thirty per cent of the elected representation in the Councils. Between 26th November and 17 December 1924, Lajpatrai published thirteen articles in *The Tribune* criticising Muslim leadership, including Jinnah. He told his readers that communal electorates, once established, would not be abolished without a civil war; that to accept them was to divide the country into Hindu India and Muslim India; and that as the Punjabi Muslims were unwilling to grant weightage to minorities it would be better to partition Punjab, and if necessary Bengal, and to establish a federation of autonomous Hindu and Muslim states. At the same time, in a circular to prominent Hindus of all provinces, he condemned the Congress for its part in the Lucknow Pact and urged these Hindus to make Hindu Mahasabha their political mouthpiece. All these utterances of prominent Hindu leaders bore a great deal of relation, however, to the reality of power within the Hindu community itself. Primarily the effort was directed towards out-manoeuvring each other in order to take control of the Hindu masses. None of these leaders realised that once the communal bandwagon had been set to roll, it was virtually impossible to arrest its progress downhill. Gandhi's criticism of Arya Samaj did not help the situation improve as the urban Hindus took it as a sign of the Congress trying to win over Muslims at their expense. The government also saw the growth of communalism in political terms, but it chose to cast itself, officially at least, in the role of spectator. In Bombay, Gandhi told reporters that he intended to put the Hindu-Muslim problem on one side. It was an insoluble riddle and he had no alternative but to wait on God for its solution.

The division between Motilal Nehru and Jinnah started widening. Nehru, in order to counter machinations of the Mahasabha, became more of an obstructionist in the Assembly. Jinnah, though disappointed, with the whole thing refused to lend support to what he considered to be wrecking tactics. By the spring of 1925 the two men began to disagree publicly on regular basis. This led to the collapse of the united front against the government. However, according to certain historians, though the two men disagreed publicly privately they appear to have seen each other as complementary elements in the same endeavour. Nehru was the stick; Jinnah the carrot. "Please do not allow yourself to be disturbed," Nehru wrote to Purshotamdas Thakurdas, "Do not for a moment think that we are creating an impassable gulf between ourselves. We can afford to fight like Kilkenny cats and still be friends." Unfortunately for India, as later day history of the country tells us, Nehru's derisive utterances in public were given more weightage by the masses and leaders alike than his private hopes.

For an all-India confrontation with the Raj to be successful it was necessary to out-manoeuvre the vested interests created in the provinces by the Montagu-Chelmsford Reforms. Except perhaps for Jinnah no other national leader had seen through the Imperial game in its true light; but Jinnah hardly had a serious mass following at the time to make himself heard at national level. Gandhi had withdrawn from active politics on the premise that his premature release on health grounds from jail after doing two years out of the six given to him meant that he was morally bound to refrain from political activity for four years. He, instead, started concentrating on spiritual matters and other social problems of India, particularly "untouchability". While untouchability remained, he declared, there could be no true Swaraj; to render India free; it must be freed from itself. Where he was concerned, India must repudiate Western norms, and return to the simplicity of Indian village, where the seasons provided the cycle of work and necessities of life, and prayer was the link with God. Not many either agreed with this philosophy or, for that matter, understood its impact on the common man. It should have been possible for the intellectual class to decipher Gandhian thoughts where these concerned the country, harmonise those with the modern thoughts where necessary and educate the nation. No such effort was made. The nationalist movement, to sum up, was disheartened and in total disarray. The only thing that could revive it was a new issue that would re-ignite the passion for freedom and re-unite various factions pertaining to different political streams. With typical ineptitude, the British government provided just such an issue, they set up yet another Commission.

Simon Commission

Under section 84-A of the Government of India Act of 1919, a statutory commission was to be appointed within ten years to examine how the Montagu-Chelmsford reforms were working in practice. At various times Indian leaders had tried to speed up the process, but without success. In Britain, however, the political situation was becoming more and more unsettled. The prime minister decided to prepone this detailment because if he were to be defeated in the 1929 elections—

a very certain possibility, his likely successor— Ramsay MacDonald, who was already promising India a dominion status may appoint someone who could actually make good the promise of 'dominion status' to Indians which he felt was 'frankly inconceivable'. He was of the opinion that India will never be fit for Dominion self-government.

Edwin Montagu, disenchanted by Lloyd George's cynical dismemberment of the former Turkish Empire, foolishly allowed publication of confidential telegrams urging the British government to avoid losing the support of moderate Islam in India. He had to go and was replaced by F E Smith, now Lord Birkenhead, who had always distrusted Montagu's reforms and doubted that India would ever be ready for self-government. Immediately on taking charge and without making any realistic assessment of the political situation in India now started looking for someone who had appropriate credentials for heading such a commission, and was also pliable enough to toe the official line, which wasn't expected to be conducive to India's ambitions. Looking around for someone of sufficient weight who had no major commitments, his choice finally fell on Sir John Simon, a personal friend and one of the most successful lawyers of the day. Simon was ostensibly a Liberal, which was calculated to impress the Indian politicians who might have been unaware that he had come to India earlier on a major legal case; and was firmly of the opinion that Indian reforms should 'proceed very slowly indeed.' Where the prime minister was concerned, Simon was the right man for the job; he wrote to Irwin,' the man possesses the qualities of acuteness, industry, tact and is quick at decision-making.' What he did not add was the fact that Simon was famous for his use of 'judicious indecision'. The government chose to make it a Parliamentary commission, thereby making it exclusive only for peers or MPs. In spite of the fact that Lord Sinha and Shapurji Saklatvala, both MPs were available, no Indian was included in the commission. The official reason for this non-inclusion was that there being no Muslim or a Sikh who fulfilled the basic requirement inclusion of only Hindu members could cause resentment. Birkenhead filled the commission with people of doubtful integrity; where cause of the Indians was concerned, none of them could boast of any great knowledge of India. Clement Attlee, a Labour MP, was considered harmless enough to be a member. Attlee, however, was convinced as he later observed that the ills from which India suffered "will require a giant's hand to remove (them), and I am certain that that hand cannot be an alien hand. It can only be done by the people of India themselves." (Speech in the House of Commons 2nd December 1931)

The Simon Commission showed the British administration at its most inept. The Commission did not bring an offer of immediate dominion status, so both Hindu and Muslim leaders boycotted it. All Indians, moderate and extremists alike, were infuriated because it had no Indian member. Indians thought it to be an ultimate insult that the future of their country should be decided entirely by foreigners. The Simon Commission muddle was a most graphic illustration of the difficulties that can arise when a power with democracy at home attempts to run the affairs of distant Colonies allowing the natives to have no stakes in running of the administration. Indian reaction to this all white commission surprised everyone by its sheer ferocity. This 'imperial insolence' threw the country into an avoidable chaos. There were widespread Hartals, and protest meetings. Even the ultra-loyal Sir Tej Bahadur Sapru, leader of the extreme right, to whom Viceroy looked for support, termed the constitution of the Commission as an insult to Mother India. Scheduled Caste Federation, the Indian Christians, Parsis and other minorities were not particularly upset, but the larger groups and organisations like the National Liberal Federation, the Hindu Mahasabha and Congress were united in their determination to boycott Simon Commission. There was difference of opinion within the League on the issue, and a group (mostly Punjabi) split from the parent body, which was firmly under Jinnah, who had called for a boycott of the Simon Commission. During his presidential address to the League he declared a 'constitutional war' on Britain. 'Jallianwala Bagh was a physical butchery, he thundered, the Simon Commission is a butchery of our souls. 'By appointing a pure whites commission Lord Birkenhead has declared us unfit for self-government', he continued. Jinnah had been called the ambassador "of Hindu-Muslim Unity" by Gokhale and Sarojini Naidu when he had emerged on the national scene. He was clearly living up to the epithet. By invitation Sarojini Naidu, Annie Besant and Madan Mohan Malviya were also present on the occasion. Referring to them, Jinnah announced that by default the prime minister had given a new lease to the theme of Hindu-Muslim unity. (Pirzada *Foundations of Pakistan,* Vol. 2 pp 127)

Anger and resentment over the issue dominated the annual session of Congress at Madras in December 1927. Riding on the tide of discontent, Jawaharlal Nehru managed to get a last-minute resolution passed calling not for dominion status but for complete independence—a major and important step for Congress. Nehru had just returned from a long drawn tour of Europe where he had taken his wife for treatment. In the process he managed to take part in the "Comintern" sponsored International Congress against Colonial Oppression and Imperialism. Nehru was a natural charmer. This was his first exposure at international level, and he quickly became one of the stars of the conference. This success was crowned with his appointment as honorary president of the League against Imperialism and for National Independence. Nehru definitely was in an elite company—other members of the executive committee were Albert Einstein, Roman Rolland, the French author and biographer of Gandhi, the former British Labour leader George Lansbury, and China's Madame Sun Yat-sen. Nehru was greatly impressed by another young leader from Vietnam—Nguyen Ai Quoc, later became world famous as Ho Chi Minh (he who enlightens).

Both Motilal and Jawaharlal were invited by Russia to attend the tenth anniversary of the revolution with the Soviet president Kalinin personally receiving them. Jawaharlal was greatly impressed by the progress made by the country under the communists and this influence seemingly guided his policies in his later life. By now Jawaharlal was an internationally recognised leader in his own right, not withstanding the reservations of senior Congress leaders about his apparent leanings towards Comintern.

Birkenhead, in the meanwhile, continued to stubbornly refuse to listen to the voices of protest. He wrote to Irwin, offering him what he clearly thought was a masterly game plan: I should advise Simon to see at all stages important people who are not boycotting the Commission, particularly Muslims and the depressed classes. I should widely advertise all his interviews with representatives Muslims. The whole policy is now obvious. It is to terrify the immense Hindu population by the apprehension that the Commission having got hold of by the Muslims, may present a report altogether destructive of the Hindu position, thereby securing a solid Muslim support and leaving Jinnah high and dry. (Birkinhead to Irwin, 19th January 1928, Birkenhead pp255). The policy of Divide and Rule had never been put more baldly. However, although it may have worked in the past, this time it was doomed to failure. Indians had been getting wiser to the British manipulations.

The Simon Commission landed at Bombay to begin the first of its two planned visits to India on 3rd February 1928. Despite torrential rains, demonstrations turned out in their thousands, carrying black flags and banners inscribed 'SIMON GO BACK'. A few of the minority groups were also there, but they could hardly make their presence felt. The city of Bombay was totally closed down. Gandhi sent his congratulatory note to the organisers, noting that he was happy to see the Liberals, Independents and Congressmen coming together for the cause. For whatever reason he had, obviously, overlooked the contribution of Jinnah and the League.

Concurrent Hartals and black flag processions in the rest of the country led to confrontations with the police, in which many people were killed. Wherever Simon went there was no respite for him from the public resentment. In Lucknow, the local Muslim League leader, Choudhary Khaliquzzaman, conceived the brilliant and innovative idea of painting "Go Back Simon" on kites and balloons and floating them over the official reception organised by the Taluqdars in the Kaiserbagh gardens. Simon was on the verge of despair, Clement Attlee, a member of his delegation and a future prime minister of England found the situation to be too complex for a speedy Westminster inspired solution. Attlee felt that the main stumbling block to a political solution was not the communal question but the princely states. How could hundreds of princedoms, ranging in size from mere dots on the map to the size of France, be fitted into a parliamentary democracy? How could the princes, most of them medieval autocrats, be brought within a parliamentary institution? After all, the princes had propitiated the Raj only to keep their ancestral gods, palaces and retainers, not withstanding the fact that they got little recognition for it. They had always been kept waiting by British officials, snubbed socially, lectured on their general conduct and subjected to insolent inquisitions into their domestic affairs, and they had accepted these insults just so they could continue to enjoy their pleasures and perks. Attlee felt, and rightly so, that most of the princes were too despotic to be left on their own. Reputation of the princes was such that the 'future' prime minister was of the opinion that invocation of democratic processes in their case would only make things more difficult for the British government.

At that stage Attlee favoured some form of federation for India. But the terms of reference of the commission did not provide any kind of latitude that could deviate from the Westminster model. To both Congress and the Muslim League the future of the princes was a peripheral issue, to be settled at independence, when they expected to inherit all the powers and prerogatives of the crown, which included relations with the princes. To the very end of the Raj and even when the partition of the country had become a virtual reality, the princes resolutely held that their treaties were with the British crown, not with the governments of India or Pakistan. In practical terms, paramountcy could not be transferred; it could only lapse. All powers surrendered in treaties with the crown reverted to the 565 or so independent states who had, therefore, to negotiate a new relationship with the successor states of British India. With Britain's departure there was no way she could protect any princely state from one of the two dominions except by infringement of its sovereignty. To the credit of Lord Mountbatten, who had finally arrived as the Viceroy for dismantling of the Empire, it was his persuasive skill that primarily made the princes realise that in new dispensation they had no future, other that to be part of one or the other independent nation. He managed to convince them that if they wanted to retain their titles, palaces and privy purses then they had to sign away their powers, gun salutes and other fringe benefits they had enjoyed hither to fore under the Raj.

To add to the confusion then prevailing, the Indians themselves were divided over the form of the future government. Whereas, most of the leaders were happy with the dominion status, those like Jawaharlal Nehru wanted nothing less than complete freedom. The exercise of draft constitution itself was stuck on the issue of 'safeguards' for the Muslims. The Hindu Mahasabha wanted to do away with separate electorates entirely, without substituting any other form of protection. Jinnah had been propagating one-third seats for the Muslims in the Central Legislation regardless of their political affiliations—the elected members could be Congressmen, Khilafatists, and just members of Muslim League. Congress had endorsed these proposals in 1927, but now under pressure from the Mahasabha backed off. An opportunity for an acceptable compromise was thus lost even before the British had given any sign of allowing Indians any kind of freedom, however limited, from their rule. Jinnah had not given up hope, he met the Viceroy with his own suggestions to resolve the deadlock—one, convert the Simon Commission into a mixed commission; alternatively nominate a parallel Indian Commission with commensurate authority. Birkenhead turned down the suggestions on the premise that there was no need to take these quarrelling Indian politicians seriously.

Jinnah was totally shattered over this rejection of his proposals, both by his peers in the other parties and by the British government. His attempts to build an alliance for reforms at the national level had floundered. Throughout the 1920s, Jinnah's political ambition remained at the all-India level, where for some years he and his liberal allies cooperated with the Congress Swaraj Party in demanding introduction of political responsibility. Regrettably, his efforts to forge another Hindu-Muslim pact to pressurise the British fell foul of the escalating demands of Muslim political interests in the provinces and their increasingly vociferous Hindu nationalist opponents. To make his misery total, his wife Ruttie moved out of their home to Taj Mahal Hotel in Bombay and thereafter left for Paris. Jinnah himself left for London to be with his old friends.

All Parties Conference again met on 18th May to arrive at a solution that would be acceptable to all shades of opinion. A committee, under the chairmanship of Motilal Nehru, was appointed but no compromise formula on the reservation issue could be arrived at. To further compound the committee's problems, the young Turks of Congress under Jawaharlal Nehru and Subhas Bose, refused to accept anything short of total independence. Obviously, these two were not very clear about the term 'dominion status'. "A climb down from Independence to Dominion Status will bring the Congress into ridicule", was their refrain. The 1926 Imperial Conference had officially defined the constitutional relationship between Britain and its dominions, the definition, *inter alia,* stipulated:

"They are autonomous communities within the British Empire, equal in status, in no way subordinate one to another in any aspect of their domestic or external affairs, though united by a common allegiance to the Crown, and freely associated as members of the British Commonwealth of Nations." The definition included Britain itself. And the phrase 'freely associated' implied that any member state was free to dissociate as and when it chose. Commonwealth carried the implication of partnership rather than subordination to Britain but was otherwise a word of ornament. The word "Empire" itself is derived from the Latin 'imperium' meaning supreme command. The English had originally used it in such expressions as the 'Imperial Parliament' and 'Imperial State Crown'. Older Congress leaders like Gandhi and Motilal understood the semantics and had thus no serious reservation over the issue, but the younger men (Jawaharlal and Bose) feared that their integrity would be compromised by the semantics of colonialism, and refused to accept the 'dominion status'.

The committee did produce a draft report, which was generally accepted with a few cosmetic changes proposed by Sapru. M C Chagla, a noted lawyer in his own right, accorded accent on behalf of the League as Jinnah was still away. Jinnah was furious when he returned, but there was little he could do as he found himself outvoted and increasingly isolated. He could only watch helplessly as his League quarrelled, fragmented and finally disintegrated over the issue of percentage of reservations and where all were to have the reservation based on the 'minority factor.'

The Simon Commission returned to India in October 1928 for a second visit. This time a seven-man Indian Provincial Committee and a nine-man Central Committee assisted it. The protests and Congress-led boycott, however, continued with full vigour. 'SIMON GO BACK' had become virtually a national chant. In Lahore, on 30th October, Lala Lajpatrai, Malaviya and local Sikh and Muslim leaders headed a march of several thousand protesters carrying placards and black flags towards the railway station where the Commission's special train was due to arrive. They were stopped about 200 yards from the station by barbed wire and wooden barricades. The police, led by the young Superintendent Scott, began to wade into the crowd, beating the leaders with their metal-tipped 'lathis'. Many collapsed, among them Dr Satyapal, one of the heroes of Amritsar in 1919. Scott, wielding his own heavy knobbed stick, struck Lajpatrai twice on the chest. A constable joined in hitting Lala Lajpatrai, who now fell on the ground. The aged 'Lion of Punjab' was more shocked than physically injured; a long time heart patient, he succumbed to his injuries after eighteen days. Lajpatrai's death provoked a wave of anger throughout India. In Lahore, the revolutionary terrorists of the Hindustan Socialist Republican Army avenged the death of Lalaji by gunning down Sanders—a police officer. India declared a day of mourning on 29th November, which happened to be the day when the Commission was due in Lucknow. For days, Jawaharlal had been preparing Congress supporters in the city for a demonstration on a truly grand scale. While leading the procession denouncing Simon Commission, Jawaharlal was singled out by the mounted police and beaten along with another leader Govind Ballabh Pant. University students who shielded them with their own bodies saved them from more serious injury. It was a first and painful experience for Jawaharlal, but he played it down. It immediately raised his status all over India. Gandhi sent his blessings and love, adding portentously: "it was a brave thing to stand up to police brutality; you have to do much more for the country's freedom. May God make you His chosen instrument for freeing India from the foreign yoke." Pant carried for more than thirty years and till the end of his life, visible effects of that assault on his body.

On Gandhi's advice Jawaharlal had already been touring the country and making his presence felt. All the old stars were already fading from the 'freedom struggle' scene. Rising new stars like Jawaharlal and Subhas Chandra Bose were making their presence felt by having given the call for total freedom. Congress was on the verge of splitting over the issue when Gandhi came out with his compromise formula of Britain giving India dominion status within one year; in case it did not happen Congress will then bid for 'Purana Swaraj': To achieve it they would launch a nation wide campaign of non-violent, non-cooperation, including a general refusal to pay taxes. Everybody was not happy with this resolution, but Gandhi set out on a nation wide tour to educate people about the basic tenets of non-violence. This whole thing brought Gandhi back on the centre stage of national political scene.

Jinnah, on the other hand had been feeling left out of all the action. He was also convinced that the safeguards promised to the Muslims at Lucknow in 1916 were no longer tenable as more and more hardcore Hindu leaders were emerging on the scene. Motilal, Ansari, Azad and Chagla though still treated him as a real leader of the Muslims and were coaxing him to discuss the issue of reservations. They were willing to retain separate electorates, to reserve seats for the Muslims in the Central Assembly, and to vest residuary powers in the provinces, rather than the central government. But all this was dismissed out of hand by staunch Hindu Mahasabha leaders, as in their opinion Jinnah no longer represented the majority Muslim opinion. Jinnah left the meeting after making what was to be his farewell speech to Indian nationalism. He reminded his audience that: "we are sons of this land. We have to live together. We have to work together..." He went on, "If we cannot agree, let us at any rate part as friends." On the last day of 1928, he left Calcutta for Delhi, to attend a meeting of the anti-nationalists All-Parties Muslim Conference presided over by the Aga Khan—its members were those very 'Mullahs' and 'Maulanas', whom he had fought and reviled for the past thirty years.

Jinnah was obliged to change his political objectives; Congress was not willing to accept him as a 'mass' Muslim leader, and within the community there were enough upstarts and leaders with local influence who refused to see beyond their nose. More importantly, by now the Punjabi Muslims were in the 'driver's seat' and others were more or less camp followers of this landed gentry. Here was the heart of Jinnah's dilemma. For him, it had ceased to be possible to occupy a central position in Indian politics; to his discomfort he found that in order to be a national leader one had to be either in the Congress camp or the Muslim camp. Jinnah's main difficulty was that he had no solid political base. He was more of a 'consultative' politician. Consequently, however sincere his 'nationalism', he could only survive by acting as a broker between Muslim politicians in the provinces and his Congress colleagues at the Centre. Since he was not engaged in provincial politics his task of carrying his community along had become all the more difficult. He had his compulsions; he was not prepared to accede to the Congress; and then he wanted to take as large a body of Muslims with him as possible. In 1927, he put forward four proposals, in 1928, they became six; and in 1929, fourteen.

Jinnah had formulated a resolution to sustain the Hindu-Muslim unity, its key features were:

1. The form of the future constitution should be federal with the residuary powers vested in the Provinces.

2. A uniform measure of autonomy shall be granted to all Provinces.

3. All legislatures in the country and other elected bodies shall be constituted on the definite principle of adequate and effective representation of minorities in every province without reducing the majority in any Province to a minority or even equality.

4. In the Central Legislature, Muslim representation shall not be less than one-third.

5. Representation of communal groups shall continue to be by means of separate electorates as at present; provided it shall be open to any community at any time, to abandon its separate electorate in favour of a joint electorate.

6. Any territorial redistribution that might at any time be necessary shall not in any way affect the Muslim majority in the Punjab, Bengal and the North-West Frontier Province (NWFP).

7. Full religious liberty, i.e. liberty of belief, worship and observance, propaganda, association and education, shall be guaranteed to all communities.

8. No Bill or resolution or any part thereof shall be passed in any assembly or other elected body if three-fourths of the members of any community in that particular body oppose such a bill.

9. Sind should be separated from the Bombay Presidency.

10. Reforms should be introduced in the NWFP and Baluchistan on the same footing as in other provinces.

11. Provision should be made in the Constitution giving Muslims an adequate share, along with other Indians, in all the Services of the State and in local self-governing bodies having due regard for the requirements of efficiency.

12. The Constitution should embody adequate safeguards for the protection of Muslim culture and for the protection and promotion of Muslim education, religion, personal laws and Muslim charitable institutions and for their due share in the grants-in-aid given by the State and by local self-governing bodies.

13. No Cabinet, either central or Provincial should be formed without there being a proportion of at least one-third Muslim Ministers.

14. No change shall be made in the Constitution by the Central Legislature except with the concurrence of the States constituting the Indian Federation.

(Hanif Qureshi pp 321 324)

Throughout the twenties, the Muslims in India remained predominantly preoccupied with the problem of how best to safeguard their interests in any future political set up in the country. By placing this charter of demands before the Hindus, Jinnah was hoping; firstly, to ensure that the Muslims did not feel insecure in any future dispensations; and secondly, to establish that he was the well-identified leader of the community with whom anybody and everybody will have to negotiate. The Indian body politic was being divided, government and Muslims on one side, Hindus on the other. This made the Muslims cease taking any marked interest in the question whether or not India was to remain in the British Commonwealth. It became for them very much a subsidiary question. Jealousy of the Hindus was stronger than antipathy to the

British. It was elementary on their part not to be carried away by revolutionary zeal and annoy the British Government by talking of going out of the Empire, for they knew full well that if they fall foul of the government they would be thrown at the mercy of the majority community to be treated at best as second class citizens. Nor was the League as yet a mass organisation. Its leadership was in the hands of territorial magnates and upper middle class men—loyal and liberal by temperament, conservative and compromising in politics.

There was hardly any chance of his entire charter being accepted by the die-hard Hindus; Gandhi said that he would give Jinnah a 'blank cheque' and a 'Swadeshi pen' with which to sign it.... an offer that infuriated the later who said he wanted not a blank Cheque but the 'fourteen points', which neither Gandhi nor the Congress was willing to concede. Nehru was far more derisive than others. He wrote to Gandhi: "If I had to listen to my dear friend Mohammad Ali Jinnah talking the most mitigated nonsense about his fourteen points for any length of time, I would have to consider the desirability of retiring to the South Sea Islands, where there would be some hope of meeting some people who were intelligent or ignorant enough not to talk of the fourteen points". (RJ Moore, *The Crisis of Indian Unity*, 1917-1940). This clearly was a situation where a bit of pragmatism and understanding of the other's point of view would have helped. But Nehru and his colleagues were in no mood to give any elbow-room to Jinnah. In the initial stages of the Conference, Muslim delegation under Aga Khan stuck rigidly to the Muslim Conference demands. The Hindus were seemingly prepared to concede substance of Jinnah's 14 points, but they wanted concrete response from the Muslim leadership about the centre-state relationship. Muslims were either not in a position to make a commitment or didn't want to show their hand at that stage. This led to a split between the Hindu leaders over the issue, with Sapru trying to negotiate with the Muslim leadership and the Mahasabhites negating all that unless the Muslim leadership made its stand known over the powers of the Central government. There was, thus, a deadlock.

Congress leaders should have known the magnitude of the sway Jinnah held on the Muslims; they made the mistake of imagining that such demands came from people who were "more famous than representative" This was a dig at Jinnah because he was allergic to mass movements and his links with his people were hardly visible. Jinnah was upset over this negation of, what he thought to be, reasonable demands. On hindsight, it appears that Congress leaders should have shown some pragmatism and accommodation over the issue. A little bit of give and take on both sides could have resolved the issue of separate electorate, and other contentious aspects of these fourteen points, which were, by no means malevolent or intolerably aggressive. If the Aga Khan is to be believed, Gandhi showed a peculiar insensitivity to the needs of the times. The Aga Khan has put it on record that he had asked Gandhi to show himself "as a real father to the Indian Muslims," whereupon Gandhi, usually responsive to such well-meant hyperbole, threw a "cold douche" on the gesture by rejoining: "I cannot in truth say I have any feeling of parental love for Muslims"—an unlike Gandhi remark which had, the Aga Khan wrote, a "chilly effect" on the ensuing conversation (Citations from *Aga Khan and The Partition of India*).[4] 'This is the parting of the ways,' Jinnah is said to have told a friend. He forwarded his charter of demands to the Viceroy and the prime minister for acceptance. They both promised to have them considered sympathetically at an appropriate level, rubbing their hands in glee over this definite polarisation of the two communities over the kind of government India should have in future. Yes, the Raj was safe because Hindus and Muslims were not likely to ever agree on the issue of the country's constitution, and in the absence of a unified stand how could the British be expected to leave. British Government, posing as virtuous and unwilling arbitrators, pressed home the advantage by decreeing, after some time, the Communal Award, which the Congress could neither accept nor reject. An uncomfortable stalemate followed. Maulana Azad rightly observed, 'The Muslims were fools to ask for safeguards and the Hindus were greater fools to refuse them.'

The Viceroy was also in a fix over the political stalemate between the two leading communities of the country. The Government could not rule India on the backs of the Muslims, and as Congress influence increased, so did the government's need to be conciliatory. Nehru and Bose and other hardliners were difficult to be won over, but the bulk of educated Hindus could be prevailed upon to toe the official line where the Reforms process was concerned. Congress, in the meanwhile, was having its own political pot boiling with Gandhi pitching for Jawaharlal to take over the presidency of the party, overlooking the claims of Vallabhbhai Patel. Provincial Congress committees unanimously wanted Gandhi to take up the reigns himself, but the shrewd Mahatma knew that he had no need for any official position in the Congress; he already was some kind of a super-president whose opinion on various issues, including leadership of the party carried weight. He wanted Jawaharlal because he could manipulate him whichever way he wanted. Another reason was that Vallabhbhai would have meant another Gujrati at the top, a situation that might not have found favour in the north, and Subhas Chandra Bose wasn't exactly a puppet, which would sing to Gandhi's tunes. And then he wasn't the son of a long time friend of Gandhi—Motilal Nehru.

On 8th April 1929, Bhagat Singh and Batukeswar Dutt of the Hindustan Socialist Republican Army, the men who had gunned down Sanders in Lahore to avenge the death of Lala Lajpatrai, threw two bombs from the public gallery of the Central Legislative Assembly. No one was seriously hurt: the bombs were intended as leaflets thrown at the same time declared, 'to make the deaf hear'. (The leaflets were published in the name of 'The Hindustan Socialist Republican Army' and read—"In order that the deaf might listen, the noise must be strong.") Both of them were arrested, as they desired, along with dozens of their supporters without offering any resistance and shouting slogans like "Inquilab Zindabad", "Down with Imperialism". Jawaharlal took on himself to organise their defence. Then a number of those arrested went on a hunger strike to protest against their treatment as political prisoners. One of them, a delicate young man named Jatindranath Das, died after 61 days of fasting, creating a national sensation and more public exposure for Jawaharlal, because this sacrifice of Das for principles that he lived on acted as a profound inspiration for the youth of India, there was massive and mass awakening of the Indian youth. Since Nehru was seen as organising defence for the 'under trials' he naturally got associated with their cause, it was almost unavoidable for the press not to mention his name while highlighting the case. Bose was disappointed that "*Young India*" published by Gandhi carried no demonstrative grief over this unfortunate death of a young man who had been fasting for certain principles. A follower of the Mahatma who was also a close friend of the deceased, wrote to Gandhi enquiring about silence on the subject. The Mahatma replied to the effect that he had purposely refrained form doing so because he did not agree with the rationale of the revolutionaries and their actions, therefore he could not have commented favourably on the episode.

During the trial in the Court of the Delhi Session Judge on 6th June 1929, Bhagat Singh declared, "The revolutionaries believe that the deliverance of their country will come through revolution—the revolution they are constantly working on and hope will not express itself in the form of armed conflict between the foreign government and its supporters and the people of India. This will also usher in a new order. The revolution will ring the death knell of Capitalism, class distinction and privileges...We take this opportunity to appeal to our countrymen, to youths and peasants, to the revolutionary intelligentsia, to come forward and join us in carrying aloft the banner of freedom...Let cowards fall back and cringe for compromise and peace. We ask not for mercy and we give no quarters. Ours is a war to the end: To victory or death...long live revolution." (India's Struggle for Freedom-Department of Information and Cultural Affairs, Government of West Bengal 1987 p30)

Gandhi, around this time, was buzzing around the country like a wasp in a jam factory, preparing ground for the civil disobedience movement, which was to be launched once the 'year's grace and polite ultimatum' to the government expired at the end of December. This notwithstanding the fact that there were indications that 'dominion status' was virtually on the cards. Lord Irwin, on his return from England on 25 September 1929, made an announcement to this effect, carried as a banner headline by all the major newspapers. Most of the leaders, including Jinnah, were willing to accept the invitation of the Viceroy for a round table conference for this purpose. But Gandhi refused to relent unless certain conditions laid down by the Congress were accepted. The conditions were twofold; one, there should be a preponderance of Congressmen at the conference, and a general amnesty for all political prisoners. Secondly, and more importantly, it was stipulated that the Conference is to meet not to discuss when Dominion Status is to be established, but to frame a scheme of Dominion Constitution for India. Irwin's promise of dominion status at some future and unspecified date or period was not acceptable to Congress. Congress policy remained unaltered-dominion status by the end of 1929 or total independence. Not getting any positive signal, the Congress in its December 1929 session voted for 'complete independence of India', directed its members to resign their seats in various assemblies. The All India Congress Committee was authorised to launch a programme of civil disobedience. In his capacity of Congress president Jawaharlal was initially reluctant to sign the document, which came to be known as 'the leaders manifesto' because to him it meant giving up the demand for independence. Gandhi managed to persuade him to toe the line, but he cut no ice with Subhas Chandra Bose who firmly declined to have anything short of complete independence from the British.

Even in England, the call for a dominion status to India raised a storm of protests against the Labour Government, which had come into power in the interim. Birkenhead, who earlier, as secretary of state, had engineered the hoax of Simon Commission and his deputy, Winston Churchill were the most vocal. But he chose to express himself not in the House of Commons, but in the 'Daily Mirror'. Out came the well-defined Imperial prejudices, "The rescue of India from ages of barbarism, tyranny and internecine war," Churchill thundered, "and its slow but ceaseless forward march to civilisation, constitute upon the whole the finest achievement of our history. Dominion status can certainly not be attained by a community which brands sixty millions of its members, fellow human beings, toiling at their side, as 'Untouchables', whose approach is an affront and whose presence is pollution...while India is a prey to fierce racial and religious dissentions and when the withdrawal of British protection would mean immediate resumption of mediaeval wars...while the political classes in India represent only an insignificant fraction of the three hundred and fifty millions for whose welfare we are responsible." Any lingering trust which Indian nationalists may have had in British good faith and fair play was destroyed when Birkenhead stood up in the House of Lords and abandoned all pretence by declaiming: "What man in this house can say that he can see in a generation, in two generations, in a hundred years, any prospect that the people of India will be in a position to assume control of the Army, the Navy, the Civil Service, and to have a Governor General who will be responsible to the Indian Government, and not to any authority in this country." (Brilsford pp 21)

Irwin was astonished at the 'violent political explosion' at Westminster, but he continued with his efforts for a round table conference with the Indian leaders. He, along with Jinnah, had been working for over two months to bring leaders of different hues to a conference table. Eventually their effort did succeed, but to break-up almost at once. Gandhi and Motilal flatly declined to discuss any conference that was not guaranteed to result in immediate dominion status. Irwin refused to accept any preconditions. He wanted free and frank discussion of problems besetting the country before arriving at any constructive decision. He could not prejudge findings of the conference, nor could he commit the British to anything in advance. This, of course, was not acceptable to Congress, and the meeting broke up. The participants went their separate ways— symbolically, Gandhi and Motilal travelled in one car, Jinnah, Sapru and Patel in another. The parting of ways, which Jinnah had spoken of exactly a year ago, was now complete. Bitter, angry and disillusioned, he turned his back on his former colleagues in Congress, abandoning all hopes of a rapprochement.

The Congress session held at Lahore, under the presidency of Jawaharlal Nehru, declared that the year of grace was over, the polite ultimatum had expired; and the British have done nothing concrete towards granting India any independence. On the night of 31st December, Jawaharlal led a procession to the banks of river Ravi, raising the tri-colour flag of Indian nationalism. Amidst the shouts of "Inquilab Zindabad", he declared 26th January as the Independence Day. On that day, huge crowds gathered in towns and villages throughout India and took the pledge of Independence. There was no violence, no untoward incident. This led Gandhi to believe that all his work of educating and preparing the people for Satyagraha was bearing fruit. The time, he felt, was ripe for some concrete action, with little fear of another Jallianwala Bagh or Chauri Chaura. All that he needed now was a suitable cause that could ignite the people's imagination leading to the downfall of the Raj.

The Salt March

Gandhi is universally accepted as the greatest exponent of what might be described as symbolic politics. He had an extraordinary flair for dramatising political issues through easily comprehensible yet potent images, which even the simplest peasant could relate to and understand. So the common 'Salt' it was. The item had been taxed heavily since the times of the East India Company along with tobacco and betel nuts. Even those living next to the sea couldn't pick a lump of salt from the seaside without the fear of heavy fine when caught. 'Salt suddenly became a mysterious word,' Jawaharlal Nehru recalled later, 'a word of power. The Salt Tax was to be attacked; the salt laws were to be broken. We were bewildered and could not quite fit in a national struggle with common salt.' But the common people had by now seen the virtue in breaking laws, particularly when the Mahatma so ordained.

On 2nd March, Gandhi wrote to the Viceroy conveying him his intentions. On 11th day of this month, Gandhi wrote, 'I shall proceed with such workers of the Ashram as I can, to disregard the provisions of the salt laws...It is, I know, open to frustrate my design by arresting me. I hope that there will be tens of thousands ready, in a disciplined manner, to take up the work after me, and, in the act of disobeying the Salt Act to lay themselves open to the penalties of a law that should never have disfigured the Statute-book.' Typical of the British, the Viceroy elected to take Gandhi's communication lightly. In a brief reply he expressed his regret that the course of action the Mahatma was contemplating there was bound to be violation of law and therefore danger of public peace being disturbed.

Gandhi's estimate of tens of thousands of followers joining in was amply justified when hoards of people fetched up at the starting point at the Sabarmati Ashram. Gandhi wanted to lead a march of 240 miles to Dandi on the Gujarat coast. There he proposed to make salt by boiling up deposits left by the tide on the mud flats. The march began at 6-30 A.M on 12th March 1930, with Gandhi staff in hand, leading a band of 79 men belonging to almost all the regions and religions of India. The crowd following him kept building up as he went along. Enroute, thousands of people came out of their homes to pay their respects to Bapu. It turned out something, akin to a vast religious procession, like Peter the Hermit leading the Children's Crusade.

At first, the British authorities ridiculed 'Mr. Gandhi's fantastic project,' the more arrogant among them concluding that India was still in 'the kindergarten stage of political revolution'. To them, the idea that the Raj could be brought down by a half-naked native 'boiling sea-water in a kettle' was clearly absurd. But the march caught imagination of the nation, leaving the British, as Gandhi had predicted, 'puzzled and perplexed'. It took him 24 days to reach Dandi, and news of his progress and enthusiastic crowds welcoming the marchers on their way started making international headlines. Reports of his speeches became the 'leading' news in every radio bulletin. The very symbolism of this defiance epitomized Gandhi's genius as a showman and artist par excellence, and was more potent than its effect. Salt tax had now become an icon for oppression, and rebellion against oppression a virtuous action. The two Nehrus, father and son, and other important leaders kept the kettle of agitation boiling all over India. Soon, the whole of India, and indeed the whole world was waiting expectantly for the final act of this drama.

With immaculate timing, Gandhi arrived in Dandi on 5th April, ready to make the decisive move the next day, the anniversary of the first national Satyagrah and the first day of National Week, which was celebrated every year to commemorate the events of that week in 1919 which culminated in the Jallianwala Bagh massacre. At 5.30 AM Gandhi led a crowd of supporters into the sea for a ritual cleansing. Police and officials had deliberately stayed away, having thwarted Gandhi's original plan by stirring the salt deposits into the mud. Undaunted, Gandhi simply bent down and picked up a lump of salt from the beach, to a jubilant cry of "Hail, law-breaker" from Sarojini Naidu. It was the signal for the start of civil disobedience. The government put a ban on political activity and the Congress Working Committee was also made redundant with almost all the leaders put behind bars.

Across India, hundreds of thousands of supporters began making their own salt. That most of it was not usable was not the point of issue with any one of them. The fact that a draconian law was being broken was enough to raise their spirits. Satyagrahis also organised raids on salt works. Many were injured when police tried to break up anti-salt law agitations. An American journalist, Webb Miller, watched with growing sense of outrage police reacting brutally to the peaceful agitation. 'The spectacle of unresisting men being methodically bashed into a bloody pulp sickened me so much I had to turn away,' he reported. Not withstanding the police brutality the salt marches continued to be staged in various parts of the country. The resistance rapidly spread to include other items as well. Boycott of foreign cloth was virtually total, and shops selling it were picketed; British schools, colleges, law courts and other institutions were boycotted; anti-tax campaign flared up in Bengal, Bihar, Gujarat and the UP. Local officials resigned their posts, including three hundred in Gujarat alone.

Gandhi now targeted his female following by asking them to lead agitation against liquor shops. His wife Kasturba was first in the line at Ahmedabad. In Allahabad, entire women folk of the Nehru clan, including Jawaharlal's wife Kamala who had been sick for a long time, joined the protest marches with a lot of gusto. Throughout India, women emerging from the seclusion of centuries took on the agitation playing prominent and public role in the struggle. Gandhi was finally arrested just after midnight on 5th May, in a village three miles from Dandi, sparking off a tidal wave of protest, with strikes, hartals, and burning of public buildings throughout India. He was taken to Yervada Central Jail. The salt agitation and Gandhi's arrest gave a new lease of life to the revolutionary terrorist activity in Punjab, UP and Bihar, but Bengal again became the most active centre, with large scale killings of officials, police informers and some British magistrates who were known to be rather harsh while passing judgment on the Indians.

Though civil disobedience had united people across the country, be it rural countryside or urban areas the Muslim leaders saw it to be a largely Hindu effort. Most Muslim leaders, following Jinnah's lead took no part in the Salt agitation. But one notable exception was Khan Abdul Gaffar Khan, 'the Frontier Gandhi', a Pathan nationalist and unlike most of his clan, a staunch believer in the doctrine of non-violence. The Khan cut a highly impressive figure, tall, gaunt and with the air of an Old Testament prophet, he dreamed of uniting the Pushtu-speaking people of the NWFP into an independent state stretching from Baluchistan to the Hindu Kush—a dream that was political anathema to the British. The Khan's followers, known as 'Khudai Khidmatgars', (Servants of God), popularly known as the Red Shirts couldn't absorb the insult of their leader being arrested by the British. Unlike other freedom fighters, the Khidmatgars straightaway pulled out their guns, took control of Peshawar for over a week and generally made life difficult for the government. The proud Pathans could only be cowed down when the fight became unequal with the British sending armoured cars and aircrafts to chase them, killing hundreds of tribes men. At one point the authorities called in two platoons of the 18th Royal Garhwal Rifles, a Hindu regiment, but the troops refused to fire on the Muslim demonstrators and even handed over their weapons to the crowd.

The Round Table Conference

Simon Commission had come to the conclusion that there was no possibility of a unitary government of a democratic kind in India. A democracy of 250 million people, it said was, 'unprecedented'. If self-government is to be a reality, it must be applied to political units of suitable size. Publication of the report, naturally, did not bring any solace to the Indians, nor did his conclusion that 'future political advancement in India should be a gradual evolution, a series of slow stages leading to some as yet unspecified goal' lead to any slowing down of the agitation. As far as the Indians were concerned, the British had reneged yet again on the promise of Self-Government, which they had been making for the last twelve years or so. Muslims were hurt over the Report for entirely different reasons; the Report had suggested that, "It would be unfair to let the Mohammedans retain the very considerable weightage they now enjoy in six provinces, and that there should at the same time be imposed, in the face of Hindu and Sikh opposition, a definite Muslim majority in the Punjab and Bengal." Organisers of the Muslim Conference alleged that the report 'had practically established Hindu Raj, under British protection, in all provinces throughout India, including the two provinces of Bengal and Punjab where the Muslims were in a majority.' In England, the Conservatives found the report to be reassuring and constructive, but the Viceroy, bewailed the 'amazing lack of imagination' revealed by Simon. Someone in England observed that the report assumed that 'the British are born rulers and the Indians born to be ruled.' Indian nationalists totally agreed with this observation. There were those who termed the Report as 'a prehistoric monster moving in the wrong geological age'.

Irwin continued to hope that the round-table conference would break the deadlock. With Gandhi and other leaders in jail the Viceroy had nobody to talk to and work out an agenda. The Congress also toughened its stand. It demanded a total acceptance of its manifesto; in fact, added new one stipulating that India will 'have the right to secede at will from the Empire, and full-self government including defence and finance. There were serious objections to holding the conference even in England. Churchill, who had assumed charge of the Conservatives with Birkenhead having died on 30th September, kept up with his tirade against giving any concessions to the Indians. He fulminated about handing power to a party bent on the humiliation of Muslims, and which was also resolved to walk out of the British Empire. He criticised those who were trying to bring in 'Gandhi Raj' in place of benevolent British Raj. In spite of all the objections, King George V opened the conference in London on 12th November 1930. The prime Minister chaired it but kept Simon away so as to convey to the Indians that he was not in agreement with his recommendations. Leaders from various political organisations, princely states and religious organisations from India were present, but the Congress refused to have any truck with it.

In the absence of Congress, Jinnah assumed centre stage. With his inimitable sense of theatre, he ended his speech by looking around at the assembled guests and telling them: "I must express my pleasure at the presence of the Dominion Prime Ministers and representatives. I am glad they are here to witness the birth of a new dominion of India, which would be ready to march with them within the British Commonwealth of Nations". (*The Times*, 13th November 1930, page 14). During negotiations and discussions, the Punjab clearly emerged as the main stumbling block to any agreement. The Punjabi Muslim representatives demanded a majority by separate electorates. The Sikhs and Hindus felt that such concessions negated democratic norms. Ramsay MacDonald, for his part, inclined to favour the minorities. He told the Muslim leaders that it would be impossible to talk of democracy 'if all the seats were fixed and reserved,' and he suggested a scheme of his own 'reserving in a mixed electorate 80 per cent of the seats and leaving twenty per cent to go to anyone. (Mohammad Ali Papers). Mohammad Ali was willing to discuss a solution on the basis of 'mixed electorate' but he was adamant that the Muslim majority in the Punjab should be recognised. The Hindus were not willing to make this concession and the talks broke up. During his closing speech, the prime minister announced that the government was prepared to accept devolution of power at the Centre if a legislature could be constituted on a Federal basis. But India representatives had failed to come to any agreement among them on the type of future government, so a dead-end had been arrived at. In any case, with the Congress having abstained nothing was expected to be achieved from the conference. But there was a general agreement among all the Indians present; the idea of All-India federation caught just about everyone's fancy, but safeguards for the minorities remained to baffle the constitution-makers for a long time to come; in fact, in due course of time the partition of the country was seen to be the only solution to this problem.

Jinnah was totally frustrated by the attitude of both the Hindu and Muslim leaders present at the Conference. In his opinion the former showed rabid communal mind, and the later were toadies and flunkeys lacking in understanding of the major issues involved. Except for the closing speech he generally kept himself aloof from the proceedings. Clearly, all the intrigues and machinations of different participants were not in consonance with his temperament.

By nature Irwin was a conciliatory man. Also, he was capable of learning from experience. He believed that the Congress, Gandhi and the Nehrus were real and not illusory forces with whom it was essential to come to terms; he saw that they had captured the Hindu majority of India. He had fought unsuccessfully with Birkenhead to get Indian members appointed to the Simon Commission. After two years in India he realised that only two workable alternatives existed for British policy. Either dominion status should be promised or the British should be prepared to carry out a programme of repression of unprecedented severity, holding India by naked force. He regarded the latter idea as both impracticable and undesirable, and so he came down on 'dominion status'. Unfortunately for him, and for India, almost the entire British officialdom in India, his own Conservative Party at home, and even the King-Emperor disagreed with him. They all thought that the old ways could continue indefinitely.

Gandhi-Irwin Pact and After

On 25th January 1931 Gandhi and others were released from jail so that they could reconsider their position with regard to the progress made in London, particularly in the light of the offer made by Ramsay MacDonald. There then were hectic consultations and negotiations between Congress and the Liberals. Irwin called Gandhi for talks before he demitted office as his tenure was coming to an end. Gandhi responded that he did want to meet, not the Viceroy, but the man inside the Viceroy. On 17th February 1931, Gandhi in his scanty dress and clasping his bamboo staff appeared at the new Viceregal Palace. He had come to talk on equal terms with the representative of the Raj. Churchill was angry over this announcement of Gandhi-Irwin talks. 'It is alarming and nauseating,' he told the Conservatives of West Essex, 'to see Mr. Gandhi, a seditious Middle Temple lawyer, now posing as a 'fakir' of a type well known in the East, striding half-naked up the steps of the Viceregal Palace, while he is still organising and conducting a defiant campaign of civil disobedience, to parley on equal terms with the representatives of the King-Emperor.' Churchill's ranting and raving was not without reason; this single event when a nationalist leader went straight from jail to the conference with the Viceroy epitomized the beginning of the end of British Empire.

The talks between Irwin and Gandhi began on the afternoon of 17th February 1931 and dragged on until 7th March. Irwin described Gandhi as a 'relentless bargainer', but gave very little away in the form of concessions to the Indians. He made Gandhi agree to call off the civil disobedience campaign, which was running out of steam in any case. In what came to be known as the Delhi Pact of 5 March 1931, the Government agreed to suspend rule by ordinance and to release all political prisoners, and the Congress agreed to accept Dominion Status as its objective, and to attend the second round-table conference. Gandhi agreed to himself attend the next conference in London. All Gandhi got in return was for the villagers on the coast to make salt for their own use. Naturally the pact was not popular with Indians, and Gandhi faced criticism from many of his followers, including Jawaharlal and Patel. Many others thought that before signing the pact, Gandhi should have demanded a reprieve for Bhagat Singh and two others who were under sentence of death for conspiracy and throwing the bombs in the assembly. While people understood Gandhi's refusal to condone violence, they could not understand why he did not extend this to the violence committed by the state in taking lives. The three (Bhagat Singh, Rajguru and Sukhdev) were hanged on 23rd March, six days before the annual session of the Congress, and became martyrs. Bose, hurt over the terms of Gandhi Irwin pact, as well as the execution of Bhagat Singh trio addressed the Navjawan Bharat Sabha on 27th March 1931. He said," Bhagat Singh was a symbol of the spirit of revolt, which has taken possession of the country from one end to the other. That spirit is unconquerable, and the flames, which that spirit has lit up, will not die. India may have to lose many more sons before she can hope to be free. India is the keystone to the world edifice and a free India spells the destruction of imperialism throughout the world. Let us, therefore, rise to the occasion and make India free so that humanity may be saved. (Selected speeches of Subhas Chandra Bose, Govt. of India Publications Division, 1961, p. 59). For once, it was Gandhi who faced black flag demonstrations all along his route to Karachi.

Gandhi's real victory lay in the fact that he had negotiated with the Viceroy as an equal. Wording of the agreement itself was such that it read like a treaty between equal sovereign powers rather than an arrangement between the Viceroy and a private citizen. The 'prestige' to which the British had attached so much importance could never be the same again. Before the Pact was signed, the government had virtually brought civil disobedience to an end by the use of extraordinary powers. But with the suspension of these powers and relaxation of administrative control, the way was clear for the reassertion of Congress influence. The government had accepted the Congress as the principal voice of India. It was an opportunity, which many leading Congressmen seized with both hands. In a circular to local Congress committees written on 10th March, Jawaharlal Nehru indicated that he saw the Pact as 'a truce only and no final peace'. 'That peace can only come', he wrote, 'when we have gained our objective in its entirety'.

The government's apparent capitulation to the Congress inevitably raised questions about its capacity to protect its friends. It was not lost on other Indian leaders, including Jinnah that while they had played the game according to British rules, had gone to London and returned virtually empty-handed, Gandhi had emerged from prison to negotiate face to face with the Viceroy himself and on the wishes of the Viceroy. Reassertion

of its authority on the Indian politics led most Congressmen to feel that
their rule was close at hand; this created a feeling of insecurity among the
Muslims in Punjab, Bengal and UP leading to massive communal riots.
The atmosphere was so charged that in Benares when some Congressmen
tried to enforce a Hartal on Muslim shopkeepers as a sign of mourning
at the execution of Bhagat Singh scuffles ensued leading to riots and killing
of innocent people belonging to both the communities. It is to the credit
of both Hindus and Muslims that they also tried to save members of the
other community from the outrages of the mob; but even the death of
so prominent a Congressman as Ganesh Shanker Vidyarthi, who was
killed by a Hindu mob while protecting his Muslim neighbours, did little
to assuage the feelings of insecurity the 'revitalisation' of Congress had
generated among the Muslims of North India. The Muslims were quick to
reach to the conclusion that they were experiencing the first fruits of the
Congress victory. In this, vested interests from both the communities
continued to foment trouble by carrying out relentless propaganda against
each other. The Muslim Conference held a special session on 5th April at
Delhi where it passed the following resolution: "This Conference warns
the Government in England and in this country that their spineless handling
of the situation due to their continued pandering to the Congress will
create a condition of things in India which will spell the complete ruin of
this unfortunate country."

Another fallout of the riots was that the call for maximising provincial
autonomy gained momentum. In part, this was due to a feeling of
insecurity among the minority-province Muslims. They felt that their
future was more insecure in any dispensation where Hindus were in
majority. Many of the Muslim leaders from these provinces thought that
a strong and Muslim majority Punjab was their best guarantee of even-
handed treatment within their own provinces. The Punjabi Muslims
were also apprehensive because all this time they had been striving for
provincial autonomy knowing that the Hindus and Sikhs had strong
reservations about their safety and security in a Muslim dominated
Punjab. Muslim leaders from Punjab had also been demanding that the
provinces should enter a Federation as sovereign units on virtually the
same terms as the states. They had also been demanding that there
should be no change in the Federal constitution unless all the constituent
units agreed on the subject.

In the wake of Gandhi-Irwin pact, the government called for a
'second round-table conference' in London later in the same year.
Calling for a conference at that level so soon after the first one was seen
as a ploy to ensure that Congress did keep its commitment. Another
reason was, having seen criticism of Gandhi, even by his staunchest of

followers, the Government was hoping to create a rift in Congress—may be it could cut Gandhi to size. The government was obviously not skilled enough to match Gandhi's wits, because he nominated himself to be the sole Congress representative of the Party, not even Nehru who was keen to attend was included in Gandhi's contingent for London talks. The fond hope of the government that the differences between the Congress leaders would be exposed for all to see, thus diminishing Gandhi's stature as a national leader was dashed to the ground in one stroke. By going alone Gandhi demolished any such hopes and enhanced his stature immeasurably. He could demonstrate that his 'writ' would run regardless of all kinds of opposition.

Second Round Table Conference

Gandhi sailed from Bombay on 29th August 1931 for the conference accompanied only by his personal staff. The party arrived in London on 15th September, having finished the journey by train from Marseilles, where they had been besieged by crowds of French students hailing Gandhi as 'the spiritual ambassador of India.' Such was the reach of Gandhi and his style of living that at Paris station someone actually fetched up a white goat to supply the Mahatma with fresh milk, but the French police would not allow it on to the platform. To avoid the embarrassment of similar welcome at Victoria station, the British authorities sent an official car to meet Gandhi at Dover. In London, Gandhi insisted on staying at Kingsley Hall, a mission for the poor in Bow, among the slums of the East End. There was a further complication when British summertime came to an end: all clocks and watches were put back one hour-except Gandhi's. He decided it was bad for watches to keep changing them, so he got up in the morning an hour earlier than he need have done, which meant that anyone staying with him at Kingsley Hall had to do the same. But for much of the time and except for meetings with intellectuals Gandhi appeared to be revelling in playing the role of the half-naked fakir.

On the opening day of the conference, when Prime Minister MacDonald began by welcoming "My Hindu and Muslim friends", Gandhi interrupted, telling him "There are only Indians here." MacDonald a seasoned politician, and used to interruptions from those who were not in tune with him, was not thrown. He began again: "My Hindu friends...and others." In his reply Gandhi repeated the call for independence, and ended by declaring that he still aspired to be a citizen, "not in the Empire, but in a Commonwealth". Unfortunately for him, his having come alone and with so many divergent views among the Indians who had been invited to attended; his claim to be the sole representative of the aspirations of the Indian people carried no weight during the round table conference. There were too many views, which were not in agreement with those of the Mahatma's dictates. Before long Gandhi realised that his mission had failed. Knowing of his importance in Indian politics and in order to give him some kind of leverage to be used back home the prime minister allowed him to address the House of Commons. When Gandhi addressed the House of Commons on 28th September, he told the members that what India wanted was an equal, not a subordinate relationship. But nobody, seemingly, took him seriously because the word was already out that the Mahatma had been clearly outwitted—he apparently had too much, and perhaps, misplaced faith, in his own negotiation skills.

When the delegates were invited to Buckingham Palace, the Secretary of State—Sir Samuel Hoare (later Lord Templewood—had already told, and some what bluntly, to Gandhi that there was no question of an immediate or early independence for India or Dominion status) approached the King to ask if Gandhi might have an audience. The king objected to the little man with no proper clothes on and bare knees. 'What! Have this rebel fakir in the Palace after he has been behind all these attacks on my loyal officers.' Finally the King relented because his advisers told him that such a gesture would go well with the Indians. Finally when Gandhi was invited to Buckingham Palace to take tea with the king, reporters asked him if he intended to go in his usual dress. "I shall go in minus-four," he responded. And he did go in his usual dress. Towards the end of this meeting the King couldn't resist telling Gandhi that civil disobedience was a hopeless and stupid policy. To which he politely replied that he must on no account be drawn into an argument with his Majesty. After the event when there was some criticism about his dress for the royal audience, he silenced his critics by telling them "The King was wearing enough for both of us".

If Gandhi could have taken with him an agreed Hindu-Muslim brief, Self-Government might have come earlier. As on previous occasion, the issue of Muslim majority Punjab as demanded by the Muslim Conference became the main stumbling block. Neither the Hindu Mahasabhites nor the Sikhs were willing to accept any such dispensation. Try as he would, Gandhi could not even get the agreement of his own party to the concessions that the Muslims demanded; unfortunately for the country he was bound by the Congress Party's claim that it alone represented the voice of India, and its refusal to concede separate communal electorates. The nature of the Congress position as the representative of the people of India precluded it from being party to any agreement that allowed disproportionate concessions to the Muslims. Trouble was that Gandhi was willing to be only a mediator in any dispute between communities because he never wanted to be seen as taking sides, certainly not where the issue was Hindu-Muslim.

Gandhi knew the power of communal appeal, and he knew what it would mean for Congress if he committed himself publicly to stand against communal Hindu stand on the issues involved. He was aware of the fact that within the existing electoral system, until such time as it became clear what concessions were forthcoming, it could only mean a communal backlash and loss of mass support for the Congress. Gandhi concluded that it would be far better to let government make the decisions and bear the unpopularity that they would bring. And so, he put the ball firmly back into the government's court. During the second session of the round table conference he said, "The Congress would accept any agreement accepted by all parties. But in the meanwhile it was incumbent on the government not to hold up constitutional progress. For there would no progress at all if unanimity was demanded, whereas iceberg of communal differences will melt under the warmth of the sun of freedom." (Proceedings of the Federal Structure Committee and Minorities Committee—London 1931 p 530)

(Criticising Gandhi personally for his poor performance, Subhas Bose wrote, "There is no doubt that the Mahatma's visit to England was badly planned—if there was any plan at all—and his personal entourage did not consist of any adviser worth the name. His indecision till the eleventh hour, about attending the London Conference was largely responsible for his lack of plan for his late arrival in London, which considerably handicapped him. During his stay in London, he had to play two roles in one person, the role of a political leader and that of a world-teacher. Sometimes, he conducted himself not as a political leader who had come to negotiate with the enemy, but as a master who had come to preach a new faith—that of non-violence and world-peace. Because of his second role he had to spend much of his time with people who were quite useless in promoting his political mission." The Indian Struggle, p- 322)

Not long after the round table conference ended, the Congress resumed civil disobedience movement. To sustain its hold on the masses it was a logical thing for the party to do so. Despite the outward show of conciliation, the polarisation of political forces at provincial level, which by 1928 had divided Indian politics into communal camps, had remained essentially unchanged even during the immediate aftermath of Gandhi-Irwin Pact when the Congress had gained considerable political advantage. It was now necessary for the party to reassert itself, lest it became a common refrain that the Congress was not necessarily the sole representative of the Indians. For the government allies, and particularly for the Muslims, it was a disturbing period. It was difficult for the leaders of the Muslim Conference, let alone rank and file, to distinguish between appearances and reality, and as government conciliated Congress, and Congress prestige rose among the masses, even Muslim masses; there seemed real possibility that the government would sacrifice Conference interests. In the absence of a communal settlement between the main protagonists and the government having taken on the responsibility to do the needful to live up to its promise of political reforms it became essential for the Muslim Conference to talk tough and show its independence from the government's stand. As the Communal Award approached, the Conference leaders became increasingly belligerent; they were apprehensive that central responsibility would be conceded on terms favouring the Congress. At the initiative of the Aga Khan a 'minorities Pact' between the Muslims, the Anglo-Indians, the Indian Christians, the Europeans and the Depressed Classes had already been formed. This pact united the Muslim majorities in Bengal and Punjab with the Muslim minorities in other provinces, and with the Depressed Classes also joining hands this cartel could not be ignored by the government under any circumstance, and with Congress having resumed civil disobedience the government had no wish to ignore this substantial body of support.

As for Jinnah himself, conditions were far from right for his own political ambitions. There was hardly anybody listening to him, in or out of the government, or for that matter his political peers, within his community and outside. Disillusioned and dismayed, he decided to give up his practice in Bombay and to settle down in London. He acquired chambers in King's Bench Walk in the Inner Temple—whose treasurer was Sir John Simon, who expressed himself to be happy to have such a distinguished lawyer within 'our boundaries'. Jinnah settled down to devote himself entirely to appeals before Privy Council, the highest court in the empire.

Footnotes

1. The Englishman dated 8th September 1908.
2. DG Tendulkar Mahatma, Volume I p 346.
3. H Mukerjee, Gandhiji—A Study (Calcutta, 1928 p 67).
4. The Partition of India pp381-82, and citations from the Aga Khan.

9

Call for Pakistan

Consequent to all the apprehensions and reservations the community had vis-à-vis the Government and the Congress, the cause of Muslim separation was taking a significant step forward. Dr Muhammad Iqbal (originally a Kashmiri Brahmin), a noted poet and philosopher from the Punjab, presided over the annual meeting of the Muslim League in Allahabad, while Jinnah was away in England. Iqbal, who had his own vision of the future of Indian Muslims, unveiled the same during this meeting. "I would like to see,"' he told the gathering, "The Punjab, the NWFP, Sind and Baluchistan amalgamated into a single State. Self-Government within the British Empire, or without the British Empire, the formation of a consolidated North-West Indian Muslim State appears to me to be the destiny of Muslims, at least of North-West India. He encouraged members of the audience to put their religion and culture before their citizenship of India. The British government, he said, could no longer be relied on to hold the balance impartially between the communities; Hindus and Muslims were being driven into a 'kind of civil war'. The situation was one in which every community would have to look to its own strength. The Muslims must not be found wanting. (Pirzada, *Foundations of Pakistan*). Dr Iqbal's definition of the proposed Muslim State greatly disturbed the Sikhs; for, acceptance of this demand would lead to the division of the Sikh population. Hindus were equally worried about Muslim dominance in Punjab and a large number rushed into the folds of Arya Samaj and Hindu Mahasabha. (Note: The demand for a separate Sikh State was revived in 1943 when the Pakistan scheme was being feverishly discussed at the national level. Master Tara Singh emphasised that the scheme was conceived to protect the Sikhs from the communal domination of the Muslims. He argued that Hindu and Muslim minorities could always look upon the provinces where their co-religionists were in majority; the Sikhs had no such leverage anywhere in India. He, therefore, insisted upon this form of protection—Azad

Punjab until a better and more practical form of protection could be identified. The Akali party also expressed its willingness to barter away some areas provided places held Holy by the Sikhs even though they were in minority in these districts were given to the Sikh State. Akalis were willing to an exchange of population and property with other communities towards this end.)

Various Muslim leaders in India and abroad soon picked up the poet's thoughts. A small group of Muslims in Cambridge, calling themselves students though they were all in their thirties, brought out a four page pamphlet in January 1933 titled 'Now or Never'. Choudhary Rahmat Ali and three of his friends defined the 'fatherland' they sought and gave it a name Pakistan. Rahmat Ali claimed to have received a divine guidance wherein he was advised that the name of the 'fatherland' should be chosen to represent all the Muslim dominated areas. So P stands for Punjab, A for Afghanistan (the NWFP), K for Kashmir, S for Sind and Tan for the last part Baluchistan. Rahmat Ali had added Kashmir, which Iqbal had thought it expedient to omit, but neither had included Bengal in their proposed fatherland. Rahmat Ali also showed a map of India showing three independent Muslim nations joined in a triple alliance. They were Pakistan in the northwest, Bang-I-Islam consisting of Bengal and Assam in the northeast, and Usmanistan in the south-Usman was the family name of the Nizams of Hyderabad. There was one other significant difference between what Iqbal had propagated and what Rahmat Ali and his friends were asking for. Iqbal foresaw his northwest state remaining in an all-India federation. Rahmat Ali and his group wanted a separate federation of their own on the premise that there can be no peace and tranquillity in the land if the Muslims are 'duped' into a Hindu-dominated Federation where we cannot be the masters of our own destiny and captains of our own souls. (Rahmat Ali Papers quoted by Wolpert in 'Jinnah of Pakistan').

At that time few people took much notice of the idea for a separate Muslim state. Jinnah still vigorously pursued his aim of autonomous provinces within a loose Indian federation. Most Muslims also dismissed any other suggestion. But the Hindu leaders in Muslim majority provinces were alarmed at what they saw as a new pan-Islamic movement posing a military threat to India. They began a nationwide campaign against it, calling the British to crush any such movement before it began. It was the best publicity the Pakistan idea could possibly have hoped for. Most Muslims still dismissed it as speculative and impractical, but the seeds for a separate Muslim nation had been planted. The Tories, having smelled the rising tide of Muslim aspiration spared no effort to create further rift among Hindus and Muslims. Jinnah, who was by now bored with his practice and yearned to be back in active policies, was not happy over this separatist twist the struggle for India's freedom was taking. Durga

Das, a noted journalist, when contacted Jinnah to use his good offices to salvage the situation found the great man despondent over the whole thing. He complained to Das: 'I seem to have reached a dead end. The Congress will not come to terms with me because my following is very small. The Muslims do not accept my views, for they take orders from a plethora of local leaders.' He did not expect the Muslim Conference to achieve anything tangible. 'The British will only make an exhibition of our differences', he prophesised: adding, 'the Muslims were led by either the flunkeys of the British Government or the camp-followers of the Congress'. And Jinnah was proved absolutely right. The British hardly needed to stir themselves to reveal the differences between the various participants from India—the Indians managed to display them perfectly well on their own. The Muslims and the various other minorities –the Sikhs, Indian Christians, Eurasians, the British business interests and the Depressed Classes—were all agreed on one thing, that they should all have separate electorate.

After the Round Table Conference in 1931 Gandhi was less interested in the constitutional discussion with the British Government than the reconciliation of communities within India itself. He was particularly hurt with the 'Depressed Classes' clamouring for separate electorate. To him, India's 50 million untouchables were an indivisible part of Hinduism, even though he had described the concept of untouchability as its greatest blot. He had started calling the untouchables as Harijans, children of God, as a way of encouraging a fresh and more humanitarian approach to them. Always known to lead by personal example, he included Harijans in various community related affairs as his equals, despite deep-rooted objections even from his 'deeply' religious wife. The untouchables had only recently emerged as a force on the political scene, due to the efforts of one remarkable member of their community—Dr Bhimrao Ambedkar, who was representing them at the conference. This forty years old lawyer had somehow managed to escape the curse of a ghetto, obtained a degree in law in London, then went on to achieve a doctorate at Columbia University, New York. Now, he demanded justice for his people, whom he knew the Hindus, would never grant voluntarily. 'Just like Muslims, their voice also needed to be heard; they were as much a minority as the Muslims were', was his opinion. With all his good intentions Gandhi was not acceptable to Ambedkar as a spokesman for the untouchables. Communalism and separatism, which had scuttled all earlier attempts at constitutional progress, had struck again. The conference failed. Gandhi returned empty handed to India on 28th December 1931. In the meanwhile, the new Viceroy, Lord Willingdon had taken over from Irwin. He was an old India hand. In 1913, he had been appointed as governor of Bombay, where his high-handedness and undisguised contempt for

Congress and all it stood for had brought him into bitter conflict with local Indian politicians, and in particular with Jinnah. On a personal level, he had earned Jinnah's undying enmity when he insulted Ruttie Jinnah at a dinner party by calling for a wrap to cover her dazzling but revealing Paris gown. Jinnah swept his wife out of the house, and bore a grudge against Willingdon for the rest of his life.

On his return as a deck passenger on SS Pilsana on 28th December 1931, the Mahatma found the country in turmoil once again. The government had clearly decided that the Gandhi-Irwin truce was over and it was time to assert its authority once again. Nehru was arrested two days before Gandhi arrived for having gone out of Allahabad when he was on his way to receive the Mahatma. Nehru was leading a no-tax campaign for the peasants and tenant farmers of UP because the great depression had destroyed the market for their produce. Subhas Bose was arrested at Kalyan railway station when he was on his way to meet Gandhi. Bose fell sick and a hoard of old maladies, including tuberculosis caught up with him. He was finally allowed to go to Europe for treatment, and on 11th March 1933 he was admitted to Dr Furth's sanatorium in Vienna. By pure chance, Vitthalbhai Patel, a veteran Congress leader was also convalescing in Vienna. The two met, and their mutual disenchantment with the Gandhian way of trying to achieve independence brought them closer. In Vienna, and to their utter disappointment, did they learn about Gandhi again calling off his 'Civil Disobedience Movement.' In the Bose-Patel Manifesto issued on 9th May 1933, the two stated that, "It is futile to expect that we can ever bring about a change of heart in our rulers merely through our own suffering or by trying to love them...We are clearly of the opinion that as a political leader Mahatma Gandhi has failed. The time has therefore come for a radical reorganisation of the Congress on a new principle and with a new method. For bringing about this reorganisation, a change of leadership is necessary". (*Subhas Chandra Bose*, Dr Girija K Mookerjee, Government of India Publications Division, November 1992 reprint, p 107). Both of them were in for a bloody revolution to throw out the British. But they were too far away from India to make any serious impact on the events back home.

In the NWFP, Gaffar Khan's Red Shirts were on the warpath and had already restarted civil disobedience. In Bengal, the terrorists were active again; two girl students assassinated a British magistrate, and a Muslim police inspector was shot dead in Chittagaon, provoking massive Hindu-Muslim rioting. Everywhere, a series of far-reaching government ordinances had banned virtually all political or public activity. Willingdon refused to meet Gandhi on the subject of problems in the troubled states. Instead, Gandhi and Vallabhbhai Patel, that year's Congress president, were arrested and jailed without trial. Nehru was sentenced to two years of imprisonment and a fine of 500 rupees was imposed on him. Congress was not banned, but it had over 36,000 members behind bars. Gandhi was soon back in Yervada jail and, though civil disobedience continued, it was headless. The Mahatma continued to hold court within the jail premises, where he enjoyed all the privileges and comforts consistent with the demands of his austere life-style, civil disobedience was dying on its feet and working the political system was becoming more attractive to many Congressmen. Clearly, the strategy formulated during the period of relative calm was to isolate Gandhi and Congress, and to press ahead with constitutional reforms so as to give the impression that the future of Indians was an issue dear to the British government. Too clever by half, the government had encouraged provincialism to offset challenges to its authority at the Centre: but had also become dependent on the Provincial leaders in the process and these leaders had now started demanding their pound of flesh. Muslim leaders were more vociferous in expressing their concern about the clout of majority community, particularly in UP and Bengal. A worried Willingdon approached the Government in London as he apprehended that in the absence of adequate guarantees the Muslim leadership during its forthcoming session at Lahore could reach decisions, which would have far-reaching impact on the political situation in the country. A cleverly worded communiqué was received in time for the Lahore session of the Muslim Conference but it did not have the desired effect. In his presidential address, Mohammad Iqbal exhorted members of the audience to put their religion and culture before their citizenship of India. The British government, he said, could no longer be relied on to hold the balance impartially between the communities, Hindus and Muslims were being driven indirectly 'into a kind of civil war'. The Muslims must not be found wanting. It was also decided to dissociate from the ongoing Reform process unless the British government came out with clear-cut guidelines that protected Muslim interests. The government was given three months to announce its decision so that the community could know where it stood. The Working Committee was tasked to come up with a plan for 'Direct Action', and to set up branches in all parts of the country, enrol volunteers who were willing to sacrifice everything for safeguarding Islam. Now the Raj was forced to tackle the problem urgently. The dilemma was—should the Muslim provincialism be encouraged further? Apparent tactics seemingly were to label Congress as Hindu and 'loyalist' Muslims opposition to it as 'Muslim' opposition to a Hindu Congress. Loyalist Hindu opposition to the Congress was to be ignored because none of its leaders had sufficient clout to neutralise Gandhi and his hold on the majority community. Sikhs, Christians, Anglo-Indians and other minorities did not merit any consideration in the British scheme of things.

10

Divisive Winds Gain Momentum

On 16th August 1932, Ramsay MacDonald announced his decision on electorate representation for the minorities. He confirmed separate electorates and reserved seats in provincial legislators for Muslims, Sikhs, Europeans, Indian Christians, and Anglo-Indians. There were also reserved seats for women (divided communally), for labour, commerce and industry, mining and landholders. The publication of Award was a crucial event in the history of Muslim separatism. For it gave to the Muslims of Punjab and Bengal the possibility of dominance in their own provinces. The award was also significant for the future of the government of India. It was a gambit to ensure continuation of the Imperial power at the centre because the Muslims wanted a 'British Centre'. In fact, the Aga Khan had already been telling the Secretary of State that his community's survival depended not only on the substance of Jinnah's fourteen points but also on 'the permanence of the real authority of the Imperial crown throughout India'. The Communal Award had fortified the Punjabi and Bengali Muslims against any other kind of centre. In terms of the structure of the system of Imperial control, this was a crucial milestone on the road to Pakistan.

Instead of seeing through the manipulations of the Imperial power in dividing the communities virtually as Hindus verses the Rest, the Congress continued to be guided by its own vision of political dominance. No effort was made to seek rapprochement with the Muslims. Guided by Gandhi's concern over the untouchables' identification as a separate entity the Party devoted itself to rectify only this segment of the political situation; obviously they were still taking the Muslims for granted. For the first time, the untouchables were given separate seats and a separate electorate. Gandhi immediately announced a fast unto death if the government did not reconsider its decision with regard to the Harijans. There was certain exasperation among some prominent Congressmen at what they saw as a distraction from the basic political issues but this announcement produced an immediate emotional response bringing Gandhi back into the national spotlight. Rabindranath Tagore sent him a telegram of support: 'It is worth sacrificing precious life for the sake of India's unity and social integrity ... Our sorrowing hearts will follow your sublime penance with reverence and love.' But Tagore never offered to join the fast himself.

The British looked on with cool interest on the goings on. When Gandhi's condition started worsening, Malaviya and other Hindu leaders prevailed upon Ambedkar to relent on his stand regarding separate electorate for the untouchables. After four days of hard bargaining a deal was struck. The text of the same was cabled to MacDonald, he readily accepted the recommendations as the terms of Communal Award had already provided for its amendment if the parties concerned agreed among themselves. But Ambedkar had driven a hard bargain. In return for combined electorate, he demanded and was given double the number of seats originally decided on for the untouchables, and these seats were to come from the Hindu's quota. Gandhi broke his fast once he was certain that the untouchables would remain within the Hindu fold.

On Gandhi's advice and in order to bring awakening among the caste Hindus an 'Untouchability Abolition Week' was celebrated throughout India. The Hindu Leaders Conference passed a resolution: 'That henceforth, amongst Hindus, no one shall be regarded as an untouchable by reason of his birth, and those who have been so regarded hitherto, will have the same rights as other Hindus in regard to the use of public wells, public schools, public roads and other public institutions.' Temples that had always been closed to untouchables were opened to them. But this egalitarian atmosphere was too good to last. These religious taboos were too old and strong to be broken that simply. Caste Hindus largely resented the directive issued by the Mahatma. Before long, caste Hindus were abandoning the temples opened to untouchables, and taking their children out of the schools where there were children of the untouchables as new entrants.

The government was delighted. Irwin reported to the prime minister that giving Gandhi opportunity to get immersed in Harijan affairs might take heat out of the civil disobedience campaign. Gandhi was given full facility he needed to run his campaign against untouchability from the jail. He was even encouraged to start a newspaper, *Harijan*, editing it from his cell, provided he refrained from making any reference to the civil disobedience, or any political subject apart from untouchability. It was a masterly stroke from the government. It effectively removed Gandhi from the head of civil disobedience movement, and at the same time gave him something closer to his heart to remain occupied. He was not encouraged by the authorities to do any politicking, when he asked for permission to take part in some Hindu-Muslim negotiations; he received a very frosty response. The civil disobedience movement was also petering out in the absence of any leader of credible credentials. The government had succeeded in its mission without losing any sleep over Gandhi and his high-profile agitation.

A third round-table conference in London in November 1932 was a bigger washout than the first two. There was no Gandhi, no Nehru, or Jinnah—he had not even been invited. None of the rulers of major princely states bothered to attend, by now they had realised that any kind of democracy in their neighbourhood was not healthy for their autocratic rule. The conference turned out to be a failure as it was destined to be. The government announced that Muslims would be guaranteed one-third of total seats, though they made up only a quarter of the population; and Sind would be made into a separate predominantly Muslim state. To contain any Hindu resentment over these two issues, shortly afterwards, as a counterbalance, it was decided to divide Orissa and Bihar into two separate, Hindu-majority provinces.

As a part of 'Reforms process' the government was contemplating provincial elections. The White Paper on the new Indian constitution was published in March 1933, and a month later a joint select committee of both the houses of Parliament was set up 'to consider the future government of India'. The White Paper made no mention of dominion status, but Atlee, who was a member of the committee made a speech in the Commons clearly reaffirming the party's policy: self-government and self-determination, leading to an equal partnership in the British Commonwealth, if that was what the Indians themselves wanted. He, however, made no mention of any timeframe for achieving the proclaimed reforms.

Smelling power in the provinces, a large number of Congressmen were feeling uncomfortable at the possibility of being left out of the new constitution if they did not participate in the elections and get into a position of power. With the civil disobedience agitation also fizzling out, Gandhi also seemed to be losing his relevance where the freedom movement was concerned. In order to regain his standing he announced another 21 days fast for self-purification on the issue of untouchability. 'The fast will have nothing to do with the civil disobedience movement,' he declared. He was immediately released from jail so as to fast at peace for a non-political cause.

Caught on a wrong foot, and definitely confused over this turn of events, Gandhi announced that he was suspending civil disobedience for six weeks, but would start it again if the government failed to release the remaining political prisoners. The government totally ignored him. Gandhi extended the suspension of the civil disobedience by another six weeks, hoping against hope that something will happen in the interim for him to save face. Eventually, he announced that, as a mass movement, the civil disobedience was at an end, though he would continue with it as an individual. This line of action made no sense to the common man, much less to those Congressmen who had suffered during the movement.

Many Congress members were, logically, furious with Gandhi for what they saw as his abject surrender. The left wing, led by Subhas Bose, called for Gandhi's suspension, insisting that he had failed as a political leader and that Congress needed 'radical reorganisation.' Other left-wingers formed a Congress Socialist Party, with a strongly Marxist line, within Congress. A group, headed by Ansari, Asaf Ali, Satyamurti and Bhulabhai Desai started a new Swarajist Party to contest the forthcoming elections. Malaviya started his own Hindu organisation calling it 'Congress Nationalists' repudiating MacDonald's Communal Award in its entirety. In sum total Congress seemed to be on the verge of extinction at that point of time. The British government, naturally, watched these developments with glee. Gandhi, depressed, dejected and defeated, considered leaving Congress and politics altogether, something, which many of his critics in the movement would have welcomed. Instead, he undertook a countrywide tour to educate people against untouchability. His critics, particularly Subhas Bose, decried this tour as a diversion from nationalist issues. Staunch Hindus were even more riled, and were vociferous in their criticism, wherever Gandhi went black flags greeted him, inflammatory leaflets were distributed, even an attempt to kill him was made at Poona; the bomb thrown at car they believed to be carrying Gandhi injured seven people. Even Ambedkar distrusted him. He disagreed violently with Gandhi's defence of the caste system, believing that only the destruction of caste itself could bring about the emancipation of the untouchables.

In October 1934, Gandhi resigned from the Congress because of his disagreement with both the socialists and the right-wingers. On 6th June 1935, the government withdrew all restrictions placed earlier on Congress so as to enable its party men to contest forthcoming elections. After initial reservations, Congress contested the elections, and won enough seats to form governments without coalition in five states. Over all, Congress did well winning 44 seats, Malaviya's Congress Nationalists won 11, but it failed to overcome Muslim suspicion of a Hindu Raj. The government and its supporters—Europeans, officials and nominated members—also mustered strength of 55. The balance was held by 22 Independents; all but three of them were Muslims. The Muslim League did not put up any candidate. The Viceroy was unhappy over this turn of events, but could do little except hope for another spat within the

Congress party. The surprise leader of the Muslim independents in the new Central Assembly was Jinnah.

It appears that while Jinnah was getting bored with his legal practice and itching to be back in mainstream Indian politics, Liaquat Ali Khan, a minor nobleman of UP—and an ardent supporter of Jinnah, while honeymooning in London with his wife went to pay complements to him. During the course of the meeting, the extremely pretty Mrs. Liaquat and an adoring fan of Jinnah, pleaded with him to come back and put new life into the League. Always vulnerable to flattery, Jinnah's defences were breached by her hero-worship and Liaquat Ali's pleadings. The League was hopelessly split into two main groups, who would have nothing to do with each other. But their two leaders were willing to stand down and bring their factions together if Jinnah would become president again. Finally, he agreed, and was still in London when he was elected unopposed for his old Bombay Muslim seat. There is a story that Jinnah had been induced to return as a retort to an alleged remark by Jawaharlal Nehru that he, that is, Jinnah had been "finished"—"not the last of Nehru's casual utterances", as a British writer observed.[1]

Jinnah had always been pleading for a Hindu-Muslim unity to take on the Raj. Now, almost the first thing he did on arriving in New Delhi was to meet that year's Congress president, the Bihari lawyer, Rajendra Prasad for a heart-to-heart talk in an effort to resolve the communal deadlock. It was of no use. Prasad might have been inclined to listen to him, but Malaviya and his Congress Nationalists refused even to consider Jinnah's case for Muslim safeguards, and the talks were fruitless. Jinnah, however, was still hopeful of some kind of understanding with the Congress leadership which would assure the Muslims that 'it is not going to be Hindu Government, but an Indian Government in which the Muslims will not only have a fair and just representation but also that they will be treated as equals of Hindus.

Government of India Act-1935

On 2nd August 1935, eight years after the appointment of the Simon Commission, the British Parliament passed the new Government of India Act. There was a widespread disappointment in the country because all it contained were some provisions for 'limited' self-government at provincial level; there was absolutely no suggestion of the country ever achieving dominion status, leave alone independence. Nehru described it as a 'machine with strong brakes but no engine', and 'a charter of slavery'. Jinnah dismissed it as 'thoroughly rotten, fundamentally bad, and totally unacceptable'. It is not as if everybody in the British Parliament was in agreement with the provisions of the Act. Its most virulent critics were the imperialists of the Conservative Party led by Winston Churchill. He declared that the choice was between "a good government and self-government," calling it a sham built by pigmies. As a good socialist, Clement Attlee felt that the bill gave too much power to the princes and not enough to the "living forces of India." In essence, the Act was a series of compromises between demands of the minorities and the majority, between British and Indian economic interests, between the Tory and Labour parties, neither of which was disposed to grant India full independence.

The new Act proposed an all–India federation with a two-chamber assembly at the centre, including for the first time not only the provinces of British India but also the princely states. The Viceroy, as governor-general, would retain control over the usual sensitive areas-defence, ecclesiastical affairs, foreign affairs and the tribal areas—and would have special powers to safeguard the country's financial stability, the services, commerce, the minorities, and the maintenance of 'peace and tranquillity'. The accession of the princely states was to be voluntary, and the federation would only come into existence when enough states had joined to fill half the number of seats allotted for them in the 'upper chamber'. Princely states and the Muslims had been given weightage in such a manner that Congress could never dominate the assembly. The princes had no interest in giving up their freedom, and not one of them joined the federation.

The second major part of the Act, giving full autonomy to the eleven British provinces, went ahead as planned. This allowed elected governments in the provinces to come about. Governors were no longer absolute rulers, but they could overrule legislations without assigning reasons. An obvious 'hidden agenda' was to undermine Congress as a national organisation by creating powerful provincial leaders. In fact, Linlithgow and his colleagues hoped that the Act would split Congress so severely between right and left that it would destroy itself as an effective political force. This analysis was based on certain ground realities— Nehru was in prison, and Bose was in Europe for TB treatment; most Congressmen who were free were far too eager to grab their first real chance of power refusing to see any catch that was to the Indians' disadvantage: they would resist any attempt to deprive them of it. Not to everyone's surprise, Gandhi was not averse to accepting the Bill, largely on the advice of the industrialist Ghanshyamdas Birla, who had been actively acting as intermediary on behalf of the Congress in England.

Perhaps the only positive fall out of the Act was that for the first time the concept of 'federal structure' created a political entity spanning the entire subcontinent. India is an ancient civilisation but it has never been a political unity except for brief periods. The empire that the Mauryas had built from 321-185 BC did not last for more than one and a half century. Even the Mughals faded out after about two hundred years. What held on were the smaller entities, principalities or kingdoms, extending over small areas. Nine-tenths of the Indians lived in villages, which had not changed much since the dawn of human history. Caste, village and family formed the natural environment of life of an individual. Things had started changing with reformists, and later with nationalists, who had embarked on a mission to seek freedom from the foreign ruler, bringing in awareness and awakening among the masses. By 1935, sufficiently large number of people had got into the act. Their universe was becoming more open to the outside world, thanks largely to the ongoing freedom movement and Gandhi's exhortations for the leaders to involve lowest of the low in this mission. People were now becoming aware of the subtle nuances of elections and politics.

Jinnah, who had once again been elected as 'permanent president' of the 'now severely dilapidated League,' decided that the League should contest the elections so that it is not cut off from the mainstream politics of the country. To his credit, he once again called upon his followers to 'stand shoulder to shoulder' with Congress and other Hindu majority parties; he still felt that such a display of unity would make the British quit India faster. He also invited these parties to join hands with the League in finding that common ground which would guarantee unity of the country. At that stage Pakistan was still just a dream of few extremists; Jinnah's aim was not to set up a separate state but to provide a vigorous Muslim party to contest against the Congress the elections in 1935 for the legislatures under the new constitution. In his opinion, 'Constitutional agitation' was the only sound way for the Indians to force the British to grant their demands, since 'armed revolution' was impossible because the country's environment did not offer any hope for its success and 'non-cooperation' had been tried and failed. To the discomfort of Gandhi and Nehru, Jinnah had been able to rally the Muslim masses to his side as effectively as they had been able to influence the Hindus.

Provincial Elections-Route to Final Divide

During the build-up to the elections, Jinnah and Nehru had indulged in a slanging match that had increasingly become personal. While asserting for cooperation, Jinnah would also warn Hindus and the Congress to leave the Muslims alone. "We are not going to be the camp followers of any party or organisation," he would proclaim. In Nehru's opinion there were only two forces in the country, the Congress and the government: an assessment that was not acceptable to Jinnah. He was quick to retort, "I refuse to line up with the Congress. There is a third party in the country and that is the Muslims. We are not going to be dictated to by anybody". (*The Statesman*, Calcutta 7th January 1937)

Nehru's response was insulting to the hilt. It revealed his disdain for the political and long-term role a communal organisation such as the League could play on the Indian political scene. He described Jinnah's views as 'medieval and out of date' and communalism to the nth power'. He ridiculed the 'new test of orthodoxy' being enunciated by Jinnah— that Muslims were 'only those who follow Mr. Jinnah and the Muslim League. He derided the League as representing only the 'higher reaches of the upper middle classes' and added cuttingly: "May I suggest to Mr. Jinnah that I come into greater touch with the Muslim masses than most of the members of the Muslim League? I know more about their hunger and poverty and misery than those who talk in terms of percentages and seats in the councils and places in the state service." (*Selected Works of Jawaharlal Nehru*, Vol. viii page 121). Clearly, Nehru forgot that Jinnah had been the rising crown prince of the pre-Gandhian Congress politics; that, Jinnah had done enough spadework for laying the foundations of the nationalist era in the company of Tilak, Motilal Nehru and Anne Besant leading to the Lucknow Pact of 1916.

Jinnah chafed under Nehru's derisive view of the League even as he attacked what he regarded as Nehru's claim to be the 'sole custodian of the masses.' With a sarcasm that matched that of Nehru, he challenged the Congress claim that it was a national organisation and defended the communal character of the League. 'The League does not believe in assuming a non-communal label with a few adventurers or credulous persons belonging to other communities thrown in and who have no backing of their people, and thus pass off as the only party entitled to speak and act on behalf of the whole of India.' (*Leader, 23 January 1937*).

Jinnah was also critical of the Congress ways. He would tell his supporters: "...to obtain leadership, to sit like a goat under the police 'lathi' charge, then go to jail, then to complain of loss of weight and then to manage release. I don't believe in that sort of struggle." Such direct assaults were not expected from leaders of that high a stature. With the passage of time Nehru's remarks about Jinnah and the League became more and more personal and rude. Jinnah could, and had, absorbed a lot, but taunts and insults were definitely unacceptable to him; he was now seething with anger, looking for revenge. He had to bide his time. For the moment he was more concerned with the survival and revival of the League following electoral reverses.

The elections revealed the strength of the Congress as an all India force. It contested 1161 seats in the general constituencies and won 716, securing a clear majority in six out of the eleven provinces of British India. In its euphoria of such a landslide victory an aspect, which Congress failed to register, was the fact that it had hardly attracted Muslim voters.

It contested only 56 out of 482 Muslim seats in British India, and won 11. It did not secure a single seat in the UP, Bengal and Punjab—NWFP was the only exception where it won 15 seats. Only consolation for Congress was that where the Muslim voters were concerned the Muslim League had fared equally badly even in the Muslim majority provinces. Of the 117 seats allotted to Muslims in Bengal it won 38. In the Punjab it contested 7 and obtained only two out of 84 Muslim seats, and in Sind it won only three out of 33 Muslim seats. The League had not been able to find even enough candidates for the seats reserved for the Muslims clearly vindicating the Congress stand that the League lacked a popular base even in the Muslim majority provinces. The League was virtually routed in the elections; and in order to survive Jinnah had to find some way to remain in the limelight. He did make conciliatory gestures towards the Congress; but Congress, under Nehru was adamant, 'power will not be shared with anybody' was his and the Congress Parliamentary committee's stand. Under the new constitution governors had been instructed to ensure that prominent minorities, in effect Muslims, were suitably represented in provincial governments. Nowhere it was said that they have to be from the League, and the Congress was determined to find Muslim ministers from its own ranks—there were enough, and obviously competent, Muslims within Congress.

In UP, where League and Congress had virtually formed a joint platform because of personal equations between leaders of both the parties, it should have been possible to come together. But it was not all that easy. In a government where there were six ministerial portfolios, two were for the Muslims, and based on an informal pre-election alliance the nominees had already been identified, the third by default was for Rafi Ahmad Kidwai, a Nehru protégé. But that would have meant three or fifty per cent Muslims forming government in a state, which had only sixteen per cent Muslim population, a situation not acceptable to Congress Hindus. Now efforts to engineer defections from the League started in right earnest so that its bargaining power could be neutralised. Nehru termed this effort as the 'winding up' of the League group in UP, and its absorption in Congress. Trouble was, the Muslim leaders directly involved were, Khaliquzzaman and Ismail Khan, both scions of respected and old families. They refused overtures of Pant and Azad to defect from the League. That the Congress should have even considered it possible for them to betray Muslim interests for the sake of ministerial berths was an insult they wouldn't forget.

Some Congress Chief Minister designates did ask Jinnah to offer nominees to join the government. But Patel and Nehru refused to entertain any such candidate unless he joined Congress and was willing to accept its discipline before being considered for a ministerial berth in any provincial government. It was obvious that no self-respecting individual, who also happened to be a disciplined member of a political party, would agree to such conditions, which could lower him in the esteem of his peers. Thus, the likely candidates would lose their chance by default (or more appropriately Congress scheming would succeed by design). In desperation, Jinnah turned to Gandhi to use his influence in making Congressmen refrain from making such demands, which were conterminous to his idea of Hindu-Muslim unity. Gandhi expressed his helplessness because he was sure that most of the senior Congress leaders no longer were under his influence. All that Jinnah's letter elicited in reply was that on Hindu-Muslim unity the Mahatma relied solely on Azad, and Jinnah should contact him, Gandhi knew fully well that there was no love lost between Jinnah and Azad. Nehru could have played a positive role in this situation, but he elected to refrain from saying or doing anything that could have helped the cause of Hindu-Muslim unity. It has been said on his behalf that he had to reckon with colleagues like Govind Ballabh Pant, Purshotamdas Tandon and Rafi Ahmad Kidwai, apart from others who were entirely allergic towards the League; and that, the newly emerging 'Left' forces in the Congress considered the League to be a body dominated by feudal landlords whom the masses hated, and thus in their opinion the League had no real popular base. This assessment of the League's popularity (or lack of it) with the Muslim masses was confirmed with the election results. Congress leaders failed to see that the Hindu Mahasabha had also been routed in the general constituencies, thereby establishing that for the masses the communal question was not necessarily important.

'It is the duty of every true nationalist', Jinnah wrote on 17th March 1938 'to whichever party or community he may belong to help achieve a united front'. But Nehru was hell-bent on putting Jinnah in, what he thought was, his right place. On 6th April 1938 Nehru wrote a letter to Jinnah wherein he said: "...Obviously, the Muslim League is an important communal organisation and we deal with it as such. But we have to deal with all organisations and individuals that come within our ken. ...Inevitably, the more important the organisation, the more the attention paid to it, but this importance does not come from outside recognition but from inherent strength..."

Jinnah replied: "... Your tone and language display the same arrogance and militant spirit, as if the Congress is the sovereign power...I may add that, in my opinion, as I have publicly stated so often, that unless the Congress recognises the Muslim League on a footing of complete equality and is prepared as such to negotiate for a Hindu-Muslim settlement, we shall have to wait and depend upon our 'inherent strength' which will 'determine the measure of importance or distinction' it possesses".

Nehru, inherently, disliked communal organisations and was against having any truck with anyone with whom he did not share economic or political philosophy. Clearly, Nehru, whether or not he saw the motives behind Jinnah's cautious overtures to the Congress, turned them down. He rejected the suggestion of a coalition on the theoretical ground that a cabinet must be homogenous and that no Muslim should be admitted into the Cabinet unless he joined the Congress Party. It is now universally recognised that this preference for theoretical, as opposed to practical considerations, led to the partition of India. Maulana Azad says in *"India Wins Freedom"* 1f the U.P. League's offer of cooperation had been had been accepted, The Muslim League would for all practical purposes have merged in Congress. Jawaharlal's action gave the Muslim League in U.P a new lease of life. Mr. Jinnah took full advantage of the situation and started an offensive which ultimately led to formation of Pakistan." Now the League launched vigorous counter propaganda to highlight the negative Congress stand with regard to Muslims, which was so effective that in a number of bye-elections in Muslim constituencies the Congress candidates were defeated. These defeats had no impact on the Congress leaders who failed to realise that they had made a tactical error by not carrying along Jinnah and his League.

Frank Moraes in his biography of Nehru expresses similar sentiments when he writes, "Had the Congress handled the League more tactfully after the elections, Pakistan might never have come into being.... Jinnah certainly created Pakistan. But Congress by its sins of omissions and commissions also helped to make it possible. Misreading the poor showing of the Muslim League at the polls.... the Congress spurned Muslim League's overture for a coalition. The result was not to drive the League into political wilderness but to strengthen Jinnah's hands as the foremost champion of Muslim claims and rights." It was not difficult for the Muslim leaders to convey to their community at large that unless the Muslims displayed a unity of purpose and as a separate entity there was no political future for them in any future dispensation.

In 1937, the Congress leaders were clear about total supremacy of the Party in the country. The Muslims were uneasy over this situation but they had not seriously thought of creating a country of their own. To bring the Muslims back into its fold the Congress leaders only had to be a little conciliatory in their dealings with the Muslims. There was nothing to differentiate between the League and the Congress where their policies and politics were concerned. A coalition would have been a most natural thing to have, and it would have worked. But the Congress spurned all such overtures of the League, thereby fanning the impression that the Congress was essentially a Hindu party. That the impasse between the League and the Congress had the inherent danger of a political divide on communal lines did not seem to worry Congressmen. Congress leaders, particularly Gandhi and Nehru, yet again, failed to read the situation correctly while dealing with Jinnah, or Muslim sentiments. Another opportunity—perhaps the last—to heal the deep-rooted wounds of Hindu-Muslim differences and make a fresh start had been lost.

Jinnah's position in March 1937 was an unenviable one, Not only had the Muslim League failed to capture a majority of Muslim votes; there were few signs of Muslim unity which Jinnah had tried to build up since 1934 as provincial Muslim leaders of the League were showing no sign of any interest in a united Muslim front, and some prominent Leaguers were even suggesting that it would be better if the Congress and the League could reach some sort of understanding. Jinnah skilfully veiled his apprehension about the future of the League as he persisted in upholding its separate identity. He exhorted Muslims to rally round the Muslim League banner. "It was not possible for Muslims and Hindus to merge their identities", he would say, "but it was feasible for them to march together towards the goal of freedom." He did not want the Muslims to be camp followers but to be in the vanguard. Nehru saw all these exhortations of Jinnah to Muslim leaders as an unrepresentative union of Muslim landlords and aristocrats, having little contact with or understanding of the Muslim masses and even of the Muslim lower-middle class. Clearly, Nehru, whether or not he saw the motives behind Jinnah's cautious overtures to the Congress, he turned him down. Instead, his reaction was to mount a 'Muslim mass contact' programme designed to attract lower-class Muslims to join Congress by stressing its economic and social aims. It was, of course, an effort to isolate the League by reiterating Congress claim to be representative of the 'poor' regardless of their colour, caste or creed. The implications of the Congress Muslim Mass Contact programme being quite clear, Jinnah's sharp reaction to its inauguration was not surprising. He regretted that Nehru should have found a solution, which would produce more bitterness and frustrate the object that every nationalist had at heart. To Jinnah, the Congress attempt 'under the guise of establishing mass contact with the Mussalmans, is calculated to divide and weaken and break the Mussalmans, and is an effort to detach them from their accredited leaders'. (Pirzada Documents p 270) One thing, however, is clear. The Congress Party did recognise that it lacked a base among Muslims and considered it politically sensible to win them over. And yet, the Party allowed the programme to fizzle out by the summer of 1939. No reasons for doing so were ever given; but the failure of this campaign was, perhaps, an important factor in limiting the chances of the Congress securing an 'undivided' India in due course of time.

Jinnah was too astute a politician not to see through this charade. He was also aware of the 'theatrics' required for identification with the illiterate Muslim masses. If Congress could be a broadly based umbrella organisation, then so could be the League, particularly when it had a charismatic leader like him. He was also concerned with some of the League leaders in UP trying to seek a chance to share power with Congress. Discussions between G B Pant and Khaliquzzaman had already started for an amicable adjustment for inducting Muslim representatives in the government, which was now to be formed in the state. Nehru was not pleased with these developments. He was not inclined to 'support moves for pacts with communal organisations which had no common political and economic policy, were dominated by reactionaries, and looked to the British for favours'. He thus rebuffed the overtures of the League for a Congress-League ministry chiding those Congressmen who talked in terms of pacts and compromises with Muslims or other religious groups. Nehru ruled that all those who wanted to be part of the governments in the states where Congress had a clear majority must join Congress shedding all other affiliations. Jinnah was more than happy with this dogmatic approach of Nehru; he knew that the 'blue-blooded' Muslim leaders of UP would not accept any such condition imposed unilaterally by the Congress leader, and would be seen as insulting and hurtful by them.

Jinnah was right in his assessment of the likely reaction of prominent Muslim leaders of the province. Muslims like Khaliquzzaman who had previously been sympathetic to Congress and more than willing to work alongside it were permanently alienated, they were too self-respecting and classy to be treated in a manner that could show them to be lacking 'in ethics'. Moreover, the Congress programme of mass contact with the Muslim masses was creating some consternation and alarm in the UP Muslim League. Khaliquzzaman was also finding himself marginalized due to Jinnah's rhetorics against any Muslim joining a Congress led government in the provinces on the restrictive terms, which the Congress had manifested. Feeling that Jinnah could have them marginalized all those Muslim leaders who were working towards a relationship with the Congress quickly distanced themselves from the 'Hindu Majority' Party. Hereafter Jinnah could count on their support in building a new, powerful League to protect Muslims from the arrogance and insults of Congress and threats of a Hindu Raj. And if that protection meant the creation of their own Muslim state, then so be it. He had been extending a hand of friendship all through, but for reasons known only to the Congress leaders of the time these overtures were always treated with disdain; a treatment someone

like Jinnah did not deserve. (In his essay, '*The Good of the People*'
written in 1914 Rabindranath Tagore says, "The partition of Bengal did
not hurt us materially; it wounded our feelings. And the hurt was indivisible
just in so far as our heart is indivisible. The reason, however, why the
Bengali Mussalman did not feel one with us in our grief is that we have
never linked our heart with his".) With so much of wisdom available and
with the basic problem having been identified so far back in time by the
great poet and thinker; and with him having a direct and open link with
Gandhi and other prominent Hindu leaders it is surprising that this rationale
on the partition of Bengal and the present issue of Muslim hostility to the
Congress was never critically analysed and corrective action taken to take
them along at national level.

There were by-elections in some predominantly Muslim constituencies
in UP and Bihar; in spite of putting up Muslims as candidates the
Congress lost primarily because of extensive and intensive propaganda
by the League which managed to convey to the Muslim masses that
their interests could only be served by the League. The animosity displayed
by the Muslim League towards the Congress on the occasion of
Bundelkhand by-election symbolised 'the alarm that has been caused
among the Muslims generally by the Congress attempts to capture the
Muslim masses', the strong feeling among them 'that if the community
is to retain its individuality, no efforts must be spared in resisting the
attempts of the Congress to absorb them', became the theme of Jinnah
led League stalwarts. Congress leaders, obviously, refused to be any
wiser after their electoral debacles in different by-elections.

In Congress-ruled states, the party song "Bande Matram" (considered
to be idolatrous and anti-Muslim) was imposed as a national anthem.
In schools, the children were made to sing it as Morning Prayer; they
were also required to salute the Congress tri-colour with Gandhi's charkha
at its centre. In some states, the schools themselves were renamed as
"vidya mandirs" (temples of learning), whose very names were seen as
deliberate affront to Muslims since the term mandir had an idolatry
connotation, something not acceptable in Islam; what was more, no
effort was made to either create Muslim centric schools or even to
include teaching of Urdu in the curriculum. These were little things
perhaps, but they indicated an undercurrent of discontent among the
minority community. The result was that Jinnah started equating Congress
governments with 'Hindu' Raj. He alleged that the Congress was 'pursuing
a policy which is exclusively Hindu.' By identifying the Congress with the
majority community, Jinnah sought to create Muslim apprehensions
against the Congress. As if to help him in this mission, and to further
widen the gulf, Congress governments attempted to ban the traditional

rights of Muslims to sacrifice cows or to eat beef. At the same time, turning a blind eye to playing of Music in front of mosques, or to condone activities that hurt Muslim sensitivities were viewed as normal for Hindus who had been enslaved by Muslims for centuries and had suffered all kinds of indignities, particularly under Mughals. No senior leader of the Congress found it necessary to reign in those who were, by their actions, widening the rift between Hindus and Muslims. Instead, Congress leaders like Nehru, Patel and Bose kept on insisting that Congress alone represented all Indians regardless of their religion or political affiliations. They continued to treat Jinnah and the League as one of the many Muslim 'communal organisations'. Clearly, Gandhi with all his sagacity and political wisdom had failed to carry the Muslims of the country with him; and, Nehru was too much in awe of the Mahatma to think differently.

With all his awareness and apparent dislike for communalism Nehru took no particular action to stem the rot. He was too much under Gandhi's spell; who, though not a communalist, did tend to give reason to the Muslims to feel neglected. Where Jinnah was concerned, he realised that power and strength could not be built up until he gained a foothold in the Muslim majority provinces. His ability to do so depended on the position of provincial Muslim leaders and their loyalty to him rather than on any communal sentiment. By early thirties, Jinnah had come to the conclusion that political differences between the League and the Congress were far too deep for any reconciliation or commonality of a stand on issues that involved the country's future. "All the talk of hunger and poverty is intended to lead people towards socialistic and communistic ideas, for which India is far form prepared", was his usual refrain while countering Nehru. He was right in concluding that the British would never leave India in the hands of the Congress unless the Muslims subscribed to the idea. A seasoned lawyer that he was, he altered his strategy to be reactive to Congress opinions on matters of national importance; this allowed him to be more meaningful and realistic at any given point of time. Indifference of the Congress to the League and to himself infuriated him no end; and the Congress leaders taking their direction from Nehru about what he thought of the League and Jinnah gave him ample opportunity to project himself as a leader of a community the Hindus 'wanted to subjugate after the British left'.

Fact of the matter is that the people of India and its leaders failed to realise that a country like India with an extraordinary legacy of a variegated (and often violent) past could not have found any easy solution to the issues involved. A great deal of platitudes was uttered now and then by the leaders of both the communities on the subject of Hindu-

Muslim unity; but nothing tangible was ever done. Way back in February 1912, Mohammad Ali had written in his weekly '*Comrade*': "The 'nationalists of the Congress school would swear by 'nationality' and patriotism and point, with a mild deprecating gesture, to 'Muslim Leaguers' and their cries for 'separate electorate'. The Muslims would hold forth on the woes of 'minorities', the imperative duty of self-preservation, and the aggressive spirit and character of Hindu 'nationalism'. These self-righteous attitudes prove that the 'patriotism' in vogue in this country is exclusively Hindu or Muslim.[2]

There definitely was a trend towards communalism among some important Muslim leaders of the time, but Hindu leaders had even less justification for doing the same, there were far too many Hindus in the country for any power to make them feel inferior to any community. Heterogeneous character of India with its different cultures, religions, castes and even nationalities allowed the imperialists to exploit this weakness; and the Indians let themselves down by taking away the sheen from the freedom won later when the destructive communal conflicts, gained an upper hand in what could have been a glorious end to a struggle for freedom.

Trouble was that the Congress refused to accept Jinnah's demand that the League was the only representative body of Muslims in India because it was felt that the Congress could not give up its national character. Jinnah's talks with Gandhi failed on this score. Subhas Bose, who had become the president of the Congress in February 1938 for once agreed with Gandhi that the Congress had a 'national character' encompassing all communities, races and ethnic groups in India: he rejected Jinnah's stand on the League being sole representative of the Muslims saying that it would 'not only be impossible, but improper' for the Congress to agree to that suggestion. On 16th December 1938, the Congress Working Committee emphatically closed the door on all likely compromises with the League by declaring both the League and the Hindu Mahasabha as communal organisations and forbidding any Congress member to belong to either. Prior to this decision being taken, Nehru had met Jinnah as a Congress spokesman. True to form, Jinnah reiterated his 'fourteen points' demand. Nehru wanted this 'charter' to be forwarded to him for examination by the Congress Working Committee. Jinnah took it as an affront. He was never the man to humble himself, or, as he put it later, 'to bow our head before Anand Bhawan'. In any case, by now his hold on the Muslim community was getting strengthened by the day. He wrote to Nehru, "If you desire that I should collect all the (League's) suggestions and submit to you as a petitioner for you and your colleagues to consider, I am afraid I cannot do it.[3]

In the meanwhile, communal tension between Hindus and Muslims was intensifying all over the country. The League had realised that it could not challenge the Congress on political issues having been made to face defeat in the provincial elections. Instead, the League sought to embarrass Congress governments by alleging that these governments were either incapable or unwilling to safeguard the religious interests and cultural rights of Muslims. Real or imaginary issues and instances were floated among the Community to justify accusations of communal bias against the provincial governments. The League set up a committee known as the Pirpur Committee to examine all the grievances of the Muslims against the government in Congress-ruled states. The Committee contended in its report that with the acceptance of office by the Congress, Muslims were being discriminated against not only by Congress officials and workers, but also that 'People of a particular community were encouraged to believe that the government was not theirs. Congress governments were in fact accused of deliberately engaging in actions, or formulating policies that offended the religious sentiments of Muslims. Singing of *Bande Matram*, which the League saw as anti-Islamic and idolatrous, hoisting the Congress flag in public places, attacks on the religious right of the Muslims to slaughter cows, and the suppression of the Urdu language by the Congress government were quoted among instances of the government's apathy towards the minority community. There was a definite merit in some of these findings; some Congress governments were not opening Urdu schools where there was a demand for them, or were abolishing Urdu classes in schools. Departmental examinations were held in Hindi in Bihar but not in Urdu; municipal committees in the Central Provinces did not entertain applications in Urdu. The Pirpur Report cited instances where by sheer weight of majority the Hindus had obstructed Muslim religious processions and the government had done nothing to ensure that Muslims were allowed to observe religious rites. Gandhi's emphasis on cow protection was seen as a direct affront to the Muslim's religious sentiment. At a later date Jinnah in fact said that Hindus and Muslims couldn't coexist, Hindus worship cows and we eat them. These controversies and the consequent communal tension was more than welcome to the British Government. British officials supported the Congress view that the Muslim League was often responsible for communal violence. 'Finding themselves unable to effect much by parliamentary methods, they are inevitably tempted to create unrest and disturbance; and there is no doubt that the Muslim League have set themselves quite deliberately to this policy', wrote the Governor of Bihar to the Viceroy. This tacit support of the British to the Hindu-majority Congress added to the discomfort of Jinnah and his colleagues. Jinnah had still to find a political vantage point, he did not as yet have a solid mass base of followers; with Huq and Sikandar Hyat

Khan often showing their independence he was in an urgent need of a handle that could bring total obedience of his followers, his only weapon against the Congress was negative and rather unconstructive. So he had to awaken the Muslim Community and give a jolt to the likes of Huq and Hayat.

Many observers of the Indian scene at the time, and research scholars are of the opinion that the methodology adopted by Congress to isolate League is what sowed the seeds of Partition of India. (In this context, V P Menon wrote to Evan Jenkins on 7th July 1945, that: "Up to 1935, Muslims, generally speaking, were under the impression that their interests would be safeguarded if they could get adequate representation in the legislatures. Thanks to the Congress policy of excluding all the other parties from the Provincial Executive, the minorities learnt that the majority party in the legislature set at naught the wishes of the minorities and that representation in the legislature would not alone be a sufficient safeguard. This was the real motive power behind Jinnah's cry for Pakistan. Exclusion from a share in power was the real foundation on which the present position of the Muslim League was built up. It is therefore not surprising that the cry for Pakistan is more vociferous in the Provinces in which the Muslims are in a minority than in the majority Muslim Provinces. *Transfer of Power*, Vol. XII, Appendix I at p 790)

Populism had never been Jinnah's style—he had consciously avoided anything that smacked of demagoguery. He realised that in order to counter Congress, he would have to become a good Muslim, something that was alien to his essentially a secular mind. But now the actor-manqué was prepared to play a new role, a combination of Gandhi and Nehru for India's Muslim masses. At that year's League session in Lucknow, which opened on 15th October, he discarded his Seville Row suits for the first time for a more traditional Muslim dress—a shervani—the long Punjabi coat, he topped it with the regulation black 'Persian cap' which contrasted most elegantly with his white sideburns. The symbol became as well recognised as the 'Gandhi cap' worn by the Congressmen. His supporters responded enthusiastically by giving him a title to match Gandhi's 'Mahatma'. They began speaking of him as their "Quaid-i-Azam"; their 'Great Leader'. Jinnah's effort to identify himself with the Muslim interests in totality started bearing fruit. All Muslim leaders knew very well that none of them had the status to match that of Jinnah at an all India level. Very quickly they started aligning with the League. The two most important, and most widely differing, provincial leaders—the radical Fazlul Huq, now premier of Bengal, and the reactionary Sir Sikandar Hayat Khan, premier of the Punjab—both agreed to enter the League fold, bringing their parties with them. The premier of Assam, Sir Muhammad Saadullah followed suit.

Jinnah's presidential address at the Lucknow session of the League was a resounding success in bringing the Muslims towards his redefined goal, viz—a Muslim homeland. He forcefully denounced Congress for pursuing a policy, which he described as 'exclusively Hindu', and demanding 'unconditional surrender' as a price for cooperation. He called on the Muslims to organise and equip themselves 'as trained and disciplined soldiers' to fight against the 'forces which may bully you, tyrannise over you and intimidate you'. It was only, he declared, 'by going through this crucible of the fire of persecution...that a nation will emerge, worthy of its past glory and history, and will live to make its future history more glorious not only in India, but in the annals of the world. Eighty million Muslims of India have nothing to fear. They have their destiny in their hands...There is a magic power in your own hands." (Pirzada, Foundations of Pakistan Vol. II, pp 265-73). That Jinnah was a top class orator needed no testimonial, that he could stir emotions of people was also a well-established credential. In the instant case the wild cheer that greeted his call for Muslim unity to fight for an independent homeland, and to be ready to make sacrifices for it electrified 5000 members present in the great tent in Lucknow.

The results of this clarion call were immediately evident. Within three months, the League had established over 170 new branches nationwide. In UP alone there were now ninety new branches with over 100,000 newly enrolled members. This explosion of League strength was marked by overwhelming successes in the by-elections held immediately in the aftermath of Lucknow session, Congress candidates were all but wiped out: Nehru's mass contact campaign had failed utterly. This remarkable turn-around in the League's fortunes had been achieved largely through blatantly communal appeals from the leaders. That old Khilafat campaigner, Shaukat Ali, led the way by perpetually raising famous war cry 'Islam is in danger'. Such theatrics, particularly in the light of provincial Congress government' pro-Hindu stance, would always ensure that more and more Muslims now started shying away from the Congress.

Seeing this hardening of stand by Jinnah, and more and more Muslims coming under his sway Congress realised that there was a need to be more accommodating where Jinnah's and Muslim aspirations were concerned. The Party appointed a committee to edit out portions of Bande Matram to which the Muslims were sensitive; the committee was also to re-examine the 'colours' of the national flag, in order to accommodate the Muslim reservations on the subject. They had apparently left these overtures to the Muslims to be too late to mean any change of heart on the part of Jinnah and his colleagues who were by now seeing a country of their own. Gandhi was monotonously talking of his 'blank cheque' to Jinnah, knowing fully well that it had lost all it's meaning where Jinnah's and Muslim aspirations were concerned.

Obviously the Congress leadership learned no lessons from their debacles in the by-elections. A dynamic movement at this stage to remedy communal aberrations and reservations could have helped restore Jinnah's confidence in the unity of effort and that of the country. While the high command continued to proclaim its high-minded non-communal ideals, the lower ranks were overwhelmingly filled with Hindus who were determined to favour their own kind. The lower rung leaders—having got into position of power for the first time, indulged in all kinds of corrupt acts; finding jobs for the wife's useless brother, or to reward friends with contracts and lucrative positions became routine. Nehru did observe that by doing all this, "we are sinking to the level of ordinary politicians who have no principles to stand by and whose work is governed by a day-to-day opportunism." Nehru was also depressed with the widening rift between the 'left' and 'right' of the Congress party, with both ideologies trying to consolidate their respective hold over the masses. In this 'power game' the country and its freedom had definitely taken a back seat.

Branding the League as 'Communal', which in any case it was, left no room for the Congress for any further negotiations for a common platform. Jinnah was by now fully convinced that parliamentary democracy could not work where there was a permanent majority and a permanent minority as in that set up parliamentary government would mean Congress hegemony in India. Equality of power between Hindus and Muslims or a separate Muslim State were the only two options he was willing to consider. For him, the only solution for India 'lay in partition.' The dye for division of India was cast with all other options virtually closed for good. The situation now was that just about anything that could brand Congress as a Hindu party and the congressmen as diehard Hindus or Hindu centric and any action of theirs which could even vaguely be termed as pro-Hindu was taken as an affront to Muslim sentiments. So much so, the introduction of Basic education methods—virtually a contribution of eminent Muslims, like Zakir Hussain, M Mujeeb and Abdul Husaain, was frowned upon as un-Islamic just because they belonged to the Congress Party and were thus suspect in the eyes of Jinnah and his followers. Apparently, the problem was that in the absence of any genuine popular movement, which could transcend these trivial communal emotions, the propaganda about the arrogance of Congress, and more particularly that of Nehru and Gandhi, had started having far too great an appeal for the Muslims of the country. Refusal of the Congress Party to contemplate parity between the two communities and its implementation of 'what came to be termed as a Hindu agenda' while in power in UP was already being seen as a threat to the Muslim Culture, property and future prospects when the British eventually were to leave India. Immediately, the All India League gave its approval for Jinnah to start 'exploring a suitable alternative to the Government of India Act, 1935, which would safeguard the interests of Muslims and other minorities'. In March 1939 it set up a committee to examine various schemes 'for dividing the country into Muslim and Hindu India.' Earlier, in October 1938, the conference Sind Muslim League held in Karachi, had already recommended to the All India Muslim League to devise a scheme of Constitution under which Muslims may attain full independence.

Gandhi, in the meanwhile, had been propagating that the Congress Party should be dissolved after independence had been achieved because that was the ultimate aim of the whole exercise. He was out of his depth. Congressmen had by now been in power in some states and had relished the fruits of that power. They were not going to let go such a golden goose just because the Mahatma felt so. It is not surprising that when he was elected president of the Congress Party in 1938, Nehru was vehemently opposed to the idea of dissolving the party once the freedom was won because he was convinced that the party that wins freedom for India was the only one that could take appropriate measures to give right kind of lead to the masses in achieving their mission in life. Not surprisingly, he declared, "India could not escape an Industrial revolution, and this would not be a gradual process as in Great Britain, but must be a forced march as in Russia. The party will have to take over power, assume responsibility for administration, and put through a programme of reconstruction. Otherwise there would be chaos. The British Empire stands at one of the crossroads of history. It will either go the way of other empires or it must transform itself into a federation of free nations. Either course is open to it". Since he was far too familiar with the undercurrent of hostility between the Hindus and Muslims; he added for good measure, "every Empire is based on the policy of divide and rule, but I doubt it if any empire has done it so skilfully, systematically and ruthlessly as Great Britain." Gandhi and his flock did not agree with what the president of the party thought of the whole thing. The party president, apparently, had not had any time to examine the crucial issue of Hindu-Muslim unity when he knew that Jinnah had already taken a stand that if the Muslim demands were not met he would like to press for a separate homeland.

That the Viceroy and the secretary of state for India, Zetland, were 'quietly' encouraging the Muslims to pitch for a 'homeland' was not a particularly well-guarded secret. And yet, but for Azad, Zakir Hussain and a few other Muslim leaders who were trying hard to keep the country united, no Hindu leader of substance tried to alley Muslim fears of being a 'permanent minority' in a 'permanent majority' Hindu India. For followers of Islam anywhere in the world to feel special bond among themselves was natural; but there was nothing, in Azad's view, to think that Muslims could not co-exist with others in a free India. But for Subhas Bose, who in any case had been sidelined by Gandhi, no Congress leader was even willing to consider various demands made by the Muslims over the years. The idea of a Muslim State carved out of India was not a 'live' issue in the twenties and thirties. The issues raised by the Muslims during those years were not insoluble. It was only the apathy of Congress leaders and staunch Hindus like Lala Lajpatrai who even wrote to C R Das in 1925 that the 'Muslim history, Muslim law and the loyalty of the finest and most patriotic Indian Muslims to their scriptural injunctions seemed to make Hindu-Muslim unity a fairly impractical proposition.' Later day Hindu leaders dwelt on the same theme. Hindu Mahasabha's permanent president, V D Savarkar, spoke aggressively of Hindus as a nation, of India as "the abode of the Hindu nation". "Hindustan being 'the land of Hindus', where Muslims were only territorially Indians, would have the rights of citizenship but must agree to live as a minority in the position of subordinate cooperation with the Hindu nation, he exclaimed. (H Mukerjee, *India's Struggle for Freedom*) "[4]

No Congress leader questioned this assertion of Savarkar. Clearly, Congress was bankrupt of top class leadership and bereft of ideas where the burning issue of communal unity was concerned. This inadequacy allowed Jinnah to take the centrestage on behalf of the Muslims, now that he had given up all hope of unity. After a long spell of wilderness he had also realised that to sustain leadership of the Muslims his USP now had to be his support for the movement gaining momentum; that is, for Pakistan. The natural outcome was the adoption of the Pakistan resolution at its Lahore session in March 1940. All that the Congress leadership did to counter these divisive talks of the staunch Hindu and Muslim leaders was to seek an understanding with the British that a 'national government' will be formed at the centre. No effort was made to seek such an understanding with the League. At the Allahabad session of All India Congress Committee (April 1942), Rajagopalachari made a pragmatic effort that the Congress might "acknowledge the Muslim League's claim for separation, should the same be persisted with, when the time came for framing the constitution of India." He wanted to take up negotiations with the League for a "national government". He also pleaded that Congress accept Pakistan as a necessary evil, for someone would have to swallow this bitter pill and the Congress alone had the strength to do so. He was overruled by the AICC, which compounded the problem by pledging to retain the 'unity of India' at any cost. First response of the Muslim leadership to this gesture of Rajagopalachari was positive and constructive, it was seen as a wise and statesman like approach to the whole issue. But subsequent and vehement rejection by the Congress Working Committee of this proposal only added fuel to the already simmering fire of mutual distrust and animosity. The tragedy was that most of the Indian leaders (both Congress and the League) would travel all the way to London to score a debating point against each other, but they were not willing to sit across the table within the country and discuss their mutual problems.

Footnotes

1. Hugh Tinker, South Asia: A Short History, (London 1966 p. 219).
2. Sukhbir Choudhary, Growth of Nationalism in India, Vol. I p 373.
3. J L Nehru, A Bunch of Old Letters pp 270-272.
4. H Mukerjee, India Struggles for Freedom, 2nd edition pp 175-76.

11

Congress—A House Divided

The Congress, in the meanwhile during 1939-40, was going through an internal turmoil, Bose was clearly building up a loyal support base which concurred with his ideas on the subject of Indian independence, but Gandhi-Nehru combine had too vast a following to let him get away with his revolutionary theories. Subhas Bose, who was the president of the party decided that he would stand for a second term as president—Nehru had two terms, so why shouldn't he? The responsibility of office had not mellowed his radical views, and for this reason he was not acceptable to Gandhi, Patel and some other senior leaders of the party. The Congress High Command, which clearly meant Gandhi, was not prepared to let him be at the helm of the country's, and the party's affairs any longer. Not withstanding Gandhi's animosity, Bose was as much confident as adamant to contest for a second term, he knew that his decision was unusual but not improper or unconstitutional.

When it became obvious that there will be a contest, the leadership started looking for a candidate who could give fight to Bose. Gandhi's choice was Azad, but he declined, not withstanding the fact that a Muslim Congress president at the time could have given a boost to the party's image, which had been taking a severe beating because of acts of commission and omission of various functionaries while handling Hindu-Muslim affairs. Ultimately, Pattabhi Sitaramayya, the Congress historian was put up against Bose. What surprised everybody was the fact that in spite of Gandhi's blessings and the party machine doing its best to ensure his success, he lost.

The 1939 session of Congress at Tripuri reminded the congressmen of the clashes between Tilak and Gokhale more than thirty years before at a similar session. Bose thought that the time had come for the Congress to issue an immediate ultimatum to the British, giving them six months

to clear out or face total civil disobedience. Gandhi and other leaders
balked at this hardening of approach as they felt that neither the Indian
people nor the Congress were ready as yet for such a make or break
stand on the issue of freedom. Bose taunted them, calling them cowards
and even implying that they were collaborators of the Raj. Majority of
the Working Committee members resigned when Bose refused to dilute
his stand on the issue. Nehru tried to mediate between him and other
leaders but it was hopeless as the rift became more and more personal.
Gandhi, who never wanted Bose in the first place, advised him to resign
if the party was not in tune with his policies and plans.

Jawaharlal often made the same criticism of Gandhi and his methods
as Bose did. Only difference was that unlike Bose who was frank and
honest and never shied away from expressing his opinion, Nehru was
more circumspect. He stayed loyal to Gandhi. As the late Frank Moraes
put it, 'he was susceptible to Gandhi's blandishments and blarney.' "I
had realised at that stage that Gandhi was India. Anything that weakened
Gandhi weakened India. So, I subordinated myself to Gandhi although
I was in agreement with what Bose was trying to do." (Jawaharlal Nehru
A Beacon Across Asia, p 89).

So Nehru remained the 'preferred one' of the Mahatma; while he,
the Mahatma, that is, went about destroying Bose within Congress. He
was vindictive to the point where he was not satisfied with humbling
Bose at the Congress gathering in Tripuri.   Aware of Gandhi's hold on
the Congress, Bose went out of his way to win the confidence of the
Mahatma because he knew that without Gandhi's approval nothing
could really be achieved by him. But Gandhi was made of a sterner
stuff, and he had been a politician for far too long to smell a potential
rival to him and to his protégé (Nehru). Bose was a charismatic leader
in his own right, and the Mahatma found himself to be in an
uncomfortable situation for such a person to be heading Congress when
he had already conveyed that he did not want Bose. Gandhi was clear
in his mind that with people like Bose who were willing to express an
opinion that was contrary to his, the Congress and the country may
soon start listening to these voices of dissent, and this the 'Mahatma'
could never accept.

Gandhi sulked and the Congress leadership, brought up on the
theory that the 'Bapu' had to be kept in good humour, else he might
start a 'fast unto death' with or without any serious provocation, started
shying away from Bose. Recognising defeat, Bose resigned. The
reconstituted Working Committee appointed Rajendra Prasad in his place.
Bose had been under the impression that in such a situation, at least the
Bengali politicians would support him. But when it came to a straight

choice between him and the Mahatma there was no contest. (To Hugh Toye, one of the most exhaustive biographers of Bose it was "the grievous injustice—the injustice of his own people and his own comrades. His popular mandate had been denied by intrigue, intrigue not against himself, but against the democracy which had elected him." Another historian, Gerard Carr puts it this way, "the manner in which Gandhi set out to destroy Bose was totally out of character. He was vindictive to the point where he was not satisfied with humbling Bose at the Congress gathering, but wanted him out of the presidential chair altogether.") Bose wasn't the one to give up a good fight when he thought that he was right; he continued with his tirade against those who had unseated him. For a while this was tolerated, but when he gave a public call for an all-India protest against various decisions of the AICC, the Working Committee barred him from holding any party office for three years. Defiant to the end, Bose and his brother Sarat set up their own party, the Forward Bloc, dedicated to militant action against the British. In emulation of Mussolini's 'Duce', Hitler's 'Fuhrer', Bose invested himself with the same title in Bengali: 'Netaji'.

While Congress was carrying on with its latest bout of self-destruction, the Muslim League was consolidating its newfound strength. Earlier, Nehru had made a highly successful visit to Europe and made a large number of new friends while reviving old ones in Britain. Jinnah felt that there was a need for him to counter that by sending his own emissaries to put across the Muslim point of view. His representatives, Khaliquzzaman (still smarting from the treatment given by Congress) and Siddiqi called on Colonel Muirhead, who had replaced RA Butler as under-secretary of state for India. They found him to be most helpful to the Muslim cause. 'We have got a great sympathy for you but we do not know how to help,' he told them. By way of reply, Khaliquzzaman walked over to a map of India hanging on the wall and pointed to the provinces in the northwest and east. The colonel took their point. 'Yes', he agreed, that is an alternative, but he wanted the subject to be discussed at a higher level. They met his boss, Lord Zetland. Khaliquzzaman, in his own account of the meeting says he suggested partitioning 'the Muslim areas from the rest of India and proceeding with your scheme of federation of the Indian provinces without including the Muslim areas, which should be independent from the rest'. He further told Zetland that the Muslim League intended to announce its demand for partition at its next annual session, to be held in Lahore in March 1940. He was sufficiently encouraged by the British response to his proposals that on return while giving 'feed back' to Jinnah, he prophesised that the British would ultimately concede partition.

The Viceroy, Lord Linlithgow, was worried over the growing conviction of Muslims that they would be able to ensure partition of India on their terms. 'He did not see', he said, 'how could the Muslims possibly torpedo the Federation scheme, unless they could discover means to prevent a sufficient number of (princes) from acceding'. The princes, on the other hand, seeing a widening rift between the Congress and League had been emboldened to take a stand that the terms of the federal offer were no longer acceptable to them.

India and the Second Great War

The overall situation took a sudden turn for the worse when on 3rd September 1939 the Viceroy, after issuing a somewhat bald Gazette of India notification to the effect that the war had broken out between His Majesty and Germany; followed it up with a broadcast to the nation where he announced that he expected Indians to postpone all kinds of agitation for the duration of war. This was the first that the country had heard of being involved in a war that did not concern them in any way. What hurt more was the fact that all the 'white dominions' had been given an option to participate or not to take part, Indians had been given no such choice, they had been taken for granted because of their status as 'slaves' of the Empire. The declaration of war by Britain in 1939 was sufficient to involve all its colonies, and no option had been given to the natives to express any opinion on the subject of their participation. There was no consultation with the colonial people and, indeed, no machinery existed through which they could have been consulted. As in 1914, the proclamation made in London was sufficient to involve the remotest tribesman who had never heard of Hitler or Warsaw. India had a vigorous political life, with recognised national leaders, and an elected central legislature; therefore, there was a moral case for consulting public opinion before making any declaration on war. What hurt the Indian sentiment was the fact that Linlithgow just announced that 'war has broken out between His Majesty and Germany'; and therefore, India being a British colony was at war.

In strictly constitutional terms, India did not have a choice—but it was singularly insulting and in poor taste for Linlithgow not to have made even an attempt to consult the Indian leaders until after the event. He was fully aware of the feelings of men like Gandhi and Nehru on the subject, particularly that of Gandhi on the issue of use of violence under any circumstances. The leading Indian nationalist, Jawaharlal Nehru, too was bitterly resentful on not having been taken into confidence about the events affecting the Indians, as were all his Congress associates. The prevailing Congress view, though, was that German Nazism was even worse than British imperialism and should be resisted by force.

What Congress found difficulty in stomaching was a war fought, according to British propaganda, for 'democracy' being conducted in India on autocratic lines. Only three days earlier, the Congress executive after having condemned fascism, had also observed that the British did not stand for freedom and democracy where it concerned Indians. Nehru was of the opinion that 'in a conflict between democracy and freedom on one side and fascism and aggression on the other our sympathies must inevitably lie on the side of democracy'. 'But we are not going to throw' our resources in defence of Empire'; instead, we would gladly offer those very resources for the defence of democracy, the democracy of a free India lined up with other free countries,' he declared. Congress provincial governments were instructed to refrain from offering any assistance in preparations for war. But to utter dismay of Congressmen, the youth—largely unemployed, flocked recruitment centres, eager to swell the ranks of the army. No immediate intake was made, but it gave the Viceroy enough confidence in his government's capability to help Britain in its war effort; but he also knew that once this initial support of the unemployed waned there would be a greater need to take the national leaders along if the War turned into a long drawn affair, as it was expected to be.

The Viceroy was intelligent enough to realise that he needed total cooperation of the political parties for the war effort if he was to expand the numbers and to preserve the loyalty of the army, the ultimate bulwark of the Empire. Sensing that the people, particularly the national leaders did have a say in the running of the country the Viceroy undertook a damage control exercise. He tried to apply salve on the hurt feelings of the Indian leaders by inviting Gandhi, Jinnah and the chancellor of Princes to come and see him. He met them separately. Gandhi was the first, he expressed an opinion wherein he favoured total and unconditional support to Britain, though he also said that it was his personal opinion and he could not forecast the Congress stand on the issue. In return, he hoped that the Viceroy would use all his efforts to encourage the Muslims to co-operate with Congress. In the Congress Working Committee, Gandhi was alone in suggesting unconditional support for the British on a non-violent basis (*Harijan*-23rd September 1939). As to, how any non-violent support would have helped the British was clear neither to the Mahatma nor to his cronies.

Jinnah, on the other hand, was prepared to promise Muslim support, but in return he wanted the Viceroy's assurance that something would be done to clip Congress's wings. ('If ...Britain wants to prosecute this war successfully, it must take Muslim India into its confidence through its accredited organisation—the All India Muslim League...Muslims want justice and fair play'- *The Times of India*, 9th September 1939). But Sir Sikandar Hyat Khan, the premier of Punjab had already beaten him to the draw. Jinnah was furious to learn from the Viceroy that Sir Sikandar had volunteered full support of Punjab for the British without demanding anything in return, 'whatever Jinnah and his friends might say.' Apparently, in return for this service Sir Sikandar wanted the Viceroy not to give too much of importance to Jinnah, or make him more difficult to deal with. Linlithgow needed to keep Sir Sikandar in good humour because Punjab provided fifty-two per cent of soldiers for the army; but he also had to keep Jinnah happy because in overall dispensation, Punjab was only one province, and he needed Jinnah's support for recruitment elsewhere, and for the general cooperation of Muslims in the war effort. Viceroy played on Jinnah's hatred for the Congress and made him to relent in favour of the British. A visibly harried Viceroy did heave a sigh of relief when the chancellor of the Chamber of Princes, not only promised unconditional support but even offered financial contributions to the war effort.

Subhas Bose, who had been invited to the special Working Committee meeting at Wardha from 10 to 14 September 1940, to help decide Congress policy on the war, was quite clear in his mind, as to what India's stand should be. He spoke with considerable passion, declaring that this was India's golden opportunity. There could be no question of supporting either side in the European war, since both were imperialists fighting for colonial possessions. A Britain at war meant a weak Britain— "now was the time to launch the final struggle for independence with a great new non-cooperation movement," he thundered. The argument of Bose and his socialist allies was a powerful one. Congressmen representing provincial governments had strong reservations about this line of approach. They were enjoying power in the provinces for the first time in their lives, and they were not eager to give it up just because someone like Bose was taking the War as an opportunity to be rid of the British.

The whole thing was utterly confusing. With such a divergent and conflicting range of opinions and interests, Congress was not able to make up its collective mind. In the end, Gandhi threw his lot with Nehru, who was in China at the invitation of Chiang Kai-shek when the war broke out but rushed back home to India at once on hearing the news. On 14th September the Working Committee came up with the statement drafted by Nehru. It was a long and rambling statement, wordy, worthy, and full of righteous indignation. While condemning fascism and Nazism, it declared that 'the issue of war and peace for India must be decided by the Indian people'—they could not fight for freedom for others while they were not free. This principle, the statement added, also applied within India itself—the offer of the princes to support the cause of democracy in Europe would be more fitting if they introduced democracy in their own autocratic states. Indians were eager to help in every way, but they wanted a quid pro quo. The statement, *inter alia*, stipulated : '...The British Government to declare in unequivocal terms what their war aims are in regard to democracy and imperialism and the new order that is envisaged, in particular how these aims are going to apply to India and be given effect to it in the present. Do they include the elimination of imperialism and the treatment of India as a free nation whose policy will be guided in accordance with the wishes of her people.'

The League's Working Committee met immediately after the Congress statement was issued, and formulated its own demands, which were simple enough, but were likely to further muddy the political climate in the country. The Muslim League Resolution of 18th September stated that: firstly, the British must recognise that the League was the sole voice of Muslims in India; secondly, the 1935 constitution must be revised in the light of the experience of provincial autonomy; thirdly, the present scheme of federation, 'which must necessarily result in a majority community rule, under the garb of democracy', must be dropped; and lastly, no declaration on constitutional change should be made without the consent and approval of the League. In consequence, and much to the relief of diehard imperialists, the prime minister announced that 'Britain would not transfer power to any system of government where authority is directly denied to large and powerful elements in India's national life'. The Muslim League had demanded a virtual veto on constitutional advance. The Viceroy war relieved to hear all this, now he had a handle with which to resist Congress demands because the League was demanding a veto on the terms laid down by the Congress. Zetland gleefully announced that the British could not meet Congress demands, and in the present situation the Viceroy should avoid offering Congress any concessions, which might antagonise the League. (The resolution of the Muslim League at Lahore on 24th March 1940 referred to "independent states" in which the constituent units shall be autonomous and sovereign. For the present the League was willing to accept a unified state whose constitution provided for these.)

Britain could not sustain its war effort for long unless manpower rich India lent a willing hand. Congress, the largest political party, wanted a large number of assurances concerning India's future before committing itself; the Viceroy couldn't make any promise unless the League also agreed on the issue. Faced with this political deadlock with no end to bickering among the Indian leaders in sight, the Viceroy embarked on a frenetic round of talks with the more important of them. Over the next month he invited no fewer than 57 of them to meet him individually in Simla. The invitees ranged from Gandhi and Nehru to Ambedkar and Jinnah, plus the Sikhs and some of more important princes. These parleys did not yield anything tangible. There were too many disagreements over interpretations of the 1935 scheme of giving India a federal structure. But the consensus was that the Indians did not want that scheme to be implemented. The Congress disagreed with the proposal because the scheme did not give it enough power; all the others felt that it gave Congress too much power. The Liberals, the Hindu Mahasabha, the untouchables and the Parsis joined together to remind the Viceroy that neither the Congress nor the League represents everyone in India, and that to accept Congress's claim to be the only national party would be 'a death blow to democracy'.

After these prolonged confabulations with Indian leaders of different hues, the Viceroy finally made his long-promised 'policy statement'. The statement was a major disappointment to just about every section of Indian opinion. All it offered was a reiteration of the old pledge of dominion status at some unspecified time in the future, and a vague promise that at the end of war the government would be "very willing to enter into consultation" on possible amendments to the 1935 Act. This statement had been forced on him by London, and he was very sure that it wouldn't satisfy the Indians, and it didn't. Congress condemned it out of hand as nothing but a repetition of the old imperialist policy. Working Committee ordered all Congress governments to resign by the end of the month.

Caught in the crossfire of British intentions and the effects of Hindu nationalism, friends and enemies were now indistinguishable for Jinnah. Sensible solutions to the issues involved were proving to be tenuous. That it was largely a doing of the British seemingly missed his notice—the British government, by its constitutional reforms of 1917 and thereafter, did not provide enough of a basis for political growth, no culture of cooperation between the two communities was ever encouraged by them. Linlithgow later agreed that the policy of the League could be criticised as 'the sole' or 'most important' obstacle to the achievement of Indian independence, while Jinnah himself admitted that his attitude was exposing him to a very formidable indictment—that he was a supporter of imperialism. This conclusion of Jinnah was based on Linlithgow's observation that the safeguards for Muslims which were demanded by the League were 'quite incomparable' with any relaxation of British control over India. Congressmen were also dismayed over the speech of Samuel Hoare in the House of Commons on 28 October wherein he had observed that 'the absence of unity amongst Indians themselves was the main obstacle to Dominion Status'. Jinnah's refusal to support the Congress demand for independence had indeed weakened his position. Jinnah could not openly support the British, for he would not have been able to carry the League with him. The Congress decision to withdraw from office deprived Jinnah and the League of their chief weapon of attack against it—the Muslim grievances against Congress ministries. So Jinnah would have to wait for political developments in order to reassert himself as the sole spokesman for the Muslims against the Congress. Nevertheless, and in order to reiterate separate identity of the Muslims and to keep anti-Congress feelings high, he called for a national 'Day of Deliverance and Thanks-giving' on Friday, 22nd December 1940, 'as a mark of relief that the Congress regime has at last ceased to function'.

Wizened with these developments, Congress leaders made an attempt to draw the League into a united nationalist front. Jinnah refused to accept this olive branch from the Congress, which had in any case come rather late in the day. Instead, he catalogued Muslim grievances against the Congress governments, which 'have done their best to flout the Muslim sentiment, to destroy Muslim culture, and have interfered with their religion and social life, and trampled upon their economic and political rights.' Congress naturally denied the charges, and offered to have them investigated by a federal judge, Jinnah refused. An impartial inquiry perhaps would have deprived the allegations of their propaganda value for the League. Instead he asked for a Royal Commission to investigate the charges, knowing that the Congress would not agree, as it would have implied acquiescence to British intervention in Indian affairs (*Bombay Chronicle*, 16th December 1939).

Fortunately for him, other minorities supported Jinnah. Dravidians in the South, the All-India Depressed Classes Association, various Anglo-Indian groups, Ambedkar and his Independent Labour Party; all joined in celebrating Jinnah's Day of Deliverance. Congress leaders were naturally infuriated over these overtures of Jinnah directed at the 'Depressed Classes' and others. 'There is a limit even to political falsehood and indecency but all limits have been passed', wrote Nehru. 'I do not know how I can even meet Jinnah now.' Evidently Jinnah did not want a settlement with Congress. When Linlithgow asked him if he would be able to settle with Congress if the British assured him that no constitutional departure would be made without the approval of the League, he replied, "But what have you to lose if no agreement is reached?" (Linlithgow to Zetland, 16th January 1940).

All this high level bickering between the two main claimants to India's freedom was music to the ears of the Viceroy and the Government in London. So long as the Congress and the League remained divided, the British could mark time and wait out the War. Evidently, Jinnah did not want any settlement with the Congress unless there was some sort of guarantee that the Muslim interests would be safeguarded in any future dispensation. Also, this was Jinnah's ploy to secure a vantage point at the centre, for himself and his League. By now Jinnah was also for an independent Pakistan because the majority of Muslims were not likely to settle for anything less; he rightly calculated that real or imaginary problems in predominantly Hindu governments in the provinces would bring the Muslims closer to him and the League. 'He might get more popular support for an idea which promised Muslims salvation from imagined Hindu domination'; he seemed to have calculated.

Congress felt that there was an immediate need to arrest Jinnah's growing influence on the minorities, and to woo back Muslims to its fold. Gandhi finally managed to persuade Azad to be the next president of Congress during its 1940 session, held at Ramgarh in Bihar. And to further the cause of reassuring the Muslims, Azad inducted three other Muslims in his team more important among them was the 'Frontier Gandhi', Abdul Gaffar Khan. He also brought Nehru back on the Working Committee.

There was only one resolution at Ramgarh, and it consisted of just three paragraphs. The first called for civil disobedience, with a proviso that the agitation be undertaken only after the masses had been sufficiently indoctrinated. The second declared that Congress would accept nothing short of full independence. The third was more dramatic; it stipulated that 'India's constitution must be based on independence, democracy and national unity'. It repudiated any attempt to divide India in any manner. Jinnah's reaction to Congress proclamation made at Ramgarh was far too resentful in its approach. He let out his venom against the Congress and what he called its total Hindu identity that was being imposed wherever Congress was in power may have had some merit. Exploiting this amateurishness of the provincial Congress leaders who were busy unleashing their kind of fundamentalism with neither Gandhi nor Nehru restraining them Jinnah had found the perfect handle to browbeat Congress and the British government during the League's session held in Lahore only a few days later. In a more than two hours long address, he stressed upon the fact that the Muslims are not a minority, they are a nation by any definition. He called upon the British government to 'allow the major nations separate homelands by dividing India into 'autonomous States'. 'Then only peace and happiness can be ensured,' he continued. In the end he challenged Gandhi to come to him 'as a Hindu leader proudly representing your people and let me meet you proudly representing the Muslims'. (VP Menon has given the full text of Jinnah's speech in the annexure to his book 'The Transfer of Power in India' pp 443-458).

Nehru and the Congress made the fatal error of continuing to regard the Muslim League as a temporary aberration caused by the British. They refused to share power and set up purely Congress administrations after the 1935 elections. That Jinnah envisaged a sovereign Pakistan was clear from his assertion at Lahore, 'The problem in India is not of an inter-communal character, but manifestly of an international one and must be treated as such', he observed. To him this was the basic and fundamental truth; he wanted any future dispensation in India to realise this while taking decisions that affected Muslims. In 1940, the Muslim League finally adopted 'Pakistan' as its objective. On behalf of the Empire, Linlithgow was more than satisfied with the Congress League rift.

The Lahore Resolution

The political stalemate was also worrying Jinnah. His platform of negativism was wearing out. Even Linlithgow was tiring of Jinnah's tactics and had advised him to formulate constructive suggestions for a political settlement between the Congress and the League. Jinnah sulked at the British refusal to sideline Gandhi. He was a worried man; in Bengal, Huq was engaged in one of his yet another flirtations with the Congress; and in the NWFP, the possibility of an inter-communal ministry appeared to be imminent. Muslim Leaguers themselves were urging Jinnah to define the party's goals, some even suggesting a Congress-League pact. (*National Herald*, 20th February 1940). Jinnah, furiously resentful, became steadily more extreme. Where he was concerned, if the Muslims were not to be allowed to share power with Congress then they must aim at establishing their own 'homeland'. It was against this background that the Lahore session of the League was held.

That Jinnah envisaged a sovereign Pakistan was clear from his assertion at Lahore: that 'The problem in India is not of an inter-communal character, but manifestly of an international one and must be treated as such. In 1940, the Muslim League finally adopted 'Pakistan' as its objective. Throughout his long speech Jinnah did not utter the word 'Pakistan' even once. Nor was it mentioned in the resolution that was passed by acclamation the next day. It was the Hindu newspapers, which labelled it the 'Pakistan Resolution', and they raised an outcry against what they saw as the first step towards the vivisection of Mother India. They were right in their thinking because the cleverly worded resolution clearly contained: "...no constitutional plan would be workable in this country or acceptable to the Muslims unless it is designed on the following basic principles, viz., that geographically contiguous units are demarcated into regions which should be so constituted, with such territorial readjustments as may be necessary, that areas in which Muslims are numerically in a majority. As in the Northwestern and Eastern zones of India, should be grouped to constitute 'independent States' in which the constituent units shall be autonomous and sovereign. The minorities in these regions were to be assured of the protection of their religious, their cultural, political, administrative and economic rights and interests in consultation with them. The resolution also stipulated that similar assurances be given to the Muslims of those areas where they would be in minority. "(Pirzada *Foundations of Pakistan*, p 340) The contents had been kept deliberately vague because the Muslim leader from the East, Fazlul Huq wanted two independent Muslim states with his Bengal to be one of them; the Muslim leaders in the North, on the other hand— particularly Sir Sikandar Hyat Khan, wanted a loose federation for a whole of India, united by a minimal of Central interference.

By maintaining existence of two nations in India, to a certain extent Jinnah escaped the dilemma of whether to aim for power at the Centre or to retain power in the Muslim majority provinces. Effectively, he had called for India's division into autonomous but non-independent states within an entity, which would still remain India. He very cleverly skirted the question if there would be two Muslim states, one in the Northwest and another in Northeast, and would these nations be part of a federal or co-federal structure? The resolution was thus open to any number of interpretations and Jinnah made no effort to clear any doubt and reservations on the subject. He wanted to keep all his options open till the stage for a final struggle for independence was reached, particularly when he was not very sure of the stand of other splinter Muslim groups, who had come together under an umbrella organisation known as the 'Azad Muslim Conference'. This group announced its support for Congress in its struggle for complete independence, and disputed the League's claim to speak for all Indian Muslims. But by this masterpiece of ambiguity, that is the Lahore Resolution, Jinnah had captured the imagination of the Muslim masses; it became the symbol of their renaissance, and the average Muslim started seeing in Jinnah a hero who would get him a country he could call his own where his Islamic brothers would decide the destiny of the country. More importantly, it gave the Muslims of Hindu-majority provinces a hope of escaping from their minority status. To them it meant equality with the Hindus even when the latter were in majority in a particular region. This growing influence of Jinnah and his League negated the Congress claim that it spoke for the whole of India.

But Jinnah's influence was largely restricted to those provinces where the Muslims were in minority and were feeling insecure due to provincial Congress governments' endeavour to establish predominantly Hindu culture by doing all kinds of things noted hithertofore. Because Punjab was a Muslim majority state and had its own Muslim leaders who were not in awe of Jinnah the things were not as smooth for the League as

Jinnah would have liked them to be. These leaders felt that if they had to retain their power bases they had to have their presence registered with the average Muslim. Sir Sikandar Hyat Khan, the premier of Punjab and not a great fan of Jinnah, now saw a chance to assert his authority in the North. In a speech on 11th March 1941 when asked for his interpretation of the resolution, *inter alia*, stated, "The facts are that in seven provinces Hindus are in majority. In those provinces let the Muslims accept that majority and cooperate with them. In four provinces the Muslims are in a majority. In these provinces, Hindus and Sikhs should accept that position and cooperate as honourable partners. We have to live together as we have been living together for the last thousand years or more and no one can convert a majority into a minority or vice-versa by squabbling among ourselves. We do not ask for freedom, that there may be a Muslim Raj here and a Hindu Raj elsewhere. If that is what Pakistan means, I will have nothing to do with it. If Pakistan means unalloyed Muslim Raj in Punjab, I will have nothing to do with it. If you want real freedom for the Punjab, that is to say a Punjab in which each community will have its due share in the economic and administrative fields as partners in a common concern, then that Punjab will not be Pakistan but just Punjab, land of five rivers...This then briefly is the political future which I visualise for my province and for my country under new constitution." His ministry announced plans to promote communal harmony by organising lectures on the subject, subsidising newspapers sympathetic to the idea, and organising common birthday celebrations for the founders of different religions. Sikandar was making it clear that the Punjab had no use for Pakistan or any separatist scheme.

The sharp (and expected) reactions of Congress, Hindu Mahasabha and Sikh leaders to the Pakistan resolution, along with the calculated silence of the British on the subject who were more than happy with the two communities at each other's throat giving a longer reign to them, gave more substance to the demand for Pakistan than perhaps it deserved. It gave Jinnah a foothold in Punjab, and stirred a different kind of emotions in the Sikhs, who were a minority in every district of the province that was their homeland. They had reasons to be worried, some Muslim leaders did suggest during the Lahore session of the League that Pakistan should be an Islamic state based on Sharia (Quoranic laws). And if, the Muslims could not trust Hindu majority then the Sikhs had even lesser reason to have any faith in a Muslim majority Pakistan. Rajagopalachari described the two-nation theory as 'a mischievous concept...that threatens to lead India into destruction' Nehru declared that the Congress would not have anything to do with the 'mad scheme' of the Muslim League and ruled out the possibility of any settlement or negotiations. (*The Tribune*, 14th April 1940). Gandhi, true to form, was more philosophical about the whole thing. Writing in the *Harijan* of 13th April 1940 he said: "Partition means a patent untruth. My whole soul rebels against the idea that Hinduism and Islam represent two antagonistic cultures and doctrines...I must rebel against the idea that millions who were Hindus the other day changed their nationality on adopting Islam as their religion."

Impact of the War on India's Affairs

By now the events had overtaken all the participants in this saga. The British Empire was thick into a World War, and there was now neither a breathing space in which to simmer down, nor the setbacks suffered by Britain conducive to any rational solution to the issues involved. The war in Europe had gained in momentum. Hitler had invaded Denmark and Norway on 9th April 1940, and British withdrawal from Dunkirk on 27th May exposed Britain to a possible German attack. Chamberlain was accused of pussyfooting and allowing Hitler to crush Europe. He resigned: and was replaced by Winston Churchill, who was not a great admirer of Gandhi, Jinnah or even any British leader who spoke of freedom for India. He started with removal of 'pro-Indian freedom' sympathisers from the scene. Cripps, who was still vigorously pressing for a firm promise of freedom for India was dispatched as a special envoy to Russia, Zetland was removed from India Office—he, in any case, was still recovering from the gunshot wounds he had received at the hands of Udham Singh when caught in a cross-fire at the Caxton Hall where O' Dwyer paid for his sins in Jallianwala Bagh.

Churchill's views on India and Indians were further hardening due to the attitude of Indian leaders with regard to India's support for war. Gandhi's somewhat philosophical appeal to Britain to 'accept the method of non-violence instead of that of war' annoyed him no end. Gandhi sent a message to the British government, asking them to let Hitler take away whatever he wanted, because 'you will not give either your soul or your mind, and if the Nazis wanted to occupy your homes, you vacate them'. Gandhi offered his services to go to Germany or anywhere else to plead for peace. Even the Congress Working Committee dissociated itself from Gandhi's views, having found them to be too impractical. 'The Indian National Congress is a political organisation pledged to win the political independence of the country. It is not an institution for organising world peace,' the party leadership announced. However, in keeping with the Gandhian philosophy and wanting to keep Bapu in good humour, the leadership resolved not to take advantage of an opponent's misfortunes. Even left-wingers like Nehru were reluctant to embarrass Britain at such a critical moment.

Emery, recognising this as India's sympathy to the British position and wanting to ensure greater help in the war effort in terms of manpower and financial resources, encouraged Linlithgow to make a firm promise of freedom immediately after war, and directed him to appoint Indian political leaders to his Executive Council. Emery really had no other option. With the West European nations defeated in one month, the French Army brought under the 'jackboot' in six weeks, the only obstacle before Hitler was Britain, largely dependent on the Empire. The Americans felt that British immobility on the constitutional position was making India an uncertain ally. In their opinion it was important that India stood fast to help Britain out of trouble. Largely it was their cajoling that forced the British Government to make some kind of offer of freedom that met aspirations of Indians. The actual offer was vague; all it said was that 'no system of government refused by large and powerful elements in India's national life would be forced upon Indians'. (This clause, apparently, took into account the Lahore resolution and gave Jinnah, what Indian historians have called, not necessarily for a valid reason, a veto on the future constitution.) Churchill flew into a rage when he learnt of all this. He charged Emery of encouraging revolution in India and with misleading the cabinet. He re-wrote the draft resolution on India prepared by Emery; in this he changed all those clauses that promised India freedom after the war: instead, with typical Churchillian prose he negated all that the Viceroy and Emery had promised. There was a dubious kind of promise that Indians should draw up their own constitution after the war, but there was no indication of when or how. Linlithgow fell in line with the latest thinking of the government on the subject. He was now ready to drop his carefully nursed policy of not taking sides, that is, if the League wanted to enter the Executive Council while Congress refused, he would go ahead with those who were willing to work with him and with each other. Jinnah's price for full cooperation was that the League should be recognised as the sole representative of Indian Muslims and have total parity with Congress in all councils and discussions on any subject related to India's future. The Viceroy did not want to further antagonise Congress. Jinnah's terms for co-operation were not acceptable to him, nor were the terms of Hindu Mahasabha, which demanded three times as many seats as the League. There was a total political stalemate while a war raged in Europe.

To revive its fortunes, Congress contemplated with the idea of starting its 'civil disobedience movement', but Gandhi was still against it; primarily, because he was aware that in the absence of adequate preparation the movement could get out of hand, and then he still did not like to embarrass the British when they were going through difficult times. Alternative to the agitation, Gandhi proposed 'individual Satyagraha'. His plan was for hand-picked Congressmen to court arrest, one at a time, by making anti-war speeches after first informing the authorities. The British were stumped. They had resources to deal with violent agitations; they could remove leaders from the scene and force people to do their bidding. But they had no answer where their leaders were ready to accept every punishment and the agitationist would automatically plead guilty to whatever charge was levied. Soon the prisons were choked to the brim, and the British had still not been able to come up with any tangible counter-move to this form of agitation. (Atlee once remarked about Gandhi: I neither approve of the tyranny of dictators or saints—E Eriksson, *'Gandhi's Truth'*, 1970 p 108). The agitation took off in October 1940.

Jinnah found the stalemate worrying, perhaps because there was nothing for him to reject and so keep himself in the limelight; and to make matters worse for him the League was not making any headway in provinces like Punjab, Bengal and Sind. Where Sikandar Hyat was concerned he had already said that Punjab had no use for Pakistan or any separatist scheme. He made full use of the press and other mediums available to him to promote communal harmony. He and other Muslim Unionists stayed away from Jinnah's meetings in Lahore on 1st and 2nd March 1941. These rising differences between Jinnah and Hyat worried the Viceroy no end. Punjab was in the forefront where supply of troops for the ongoing world war was concerned. Hyat was also seen as more inclined towards providing safety to the Sikhs who were providing bulk of the soldiers, and he did not want to antagonize central government. Linlithgow prevailed upon Hyat to resolve his differences with Jinnah whom he described as having 'unified the Muslims over the last forty years' and whose control over them appeared at the moment to be effective. Muslim leaders of Punjab and Bengal were concerned that such a certificate from the Viceroy could undermine their position in their respective provinces. For Viceroy this obviously was a ploy to keep Congressmen on their toes; he wanted them to realise that by agitating and sending their leaders to jail they were allowing Jinnah to gain control of the Muslim population and thus weakening their own position. Where the Viceroy was concerned, the League was the only counter-poise to the Congress at the all India level: and to keep them at each other's throat was essential for prolonging the British hold on this country; it was also necessary to encourage this domestic feud amongst the Indians so that the supply of men and material remained uninterrupted for the war.

True to form, the Congress refused to learn any tangible lesson from their misadventure of 'individual Satyagrah'. Soon enough most of the leaders, including Nehru were in jail, and the campaign failed to gather momentum because there was no Congress leader of national stature to tell the common man as to what was expected of him. The movement could not ignite the public imagination, partly because of the prevalent censorship which, kept people ignorant of happenings; more realistically, the common man was happy with the jobs created by the booming war-time industries and the demand for greater food production. In its initial stages the war was good business. War production revived the economy to full capacity. Many new industries were set up in order to provide for the Army's needs and feed the expanding domestic market. The British government had by now concluded that the Congress was not going in for anything that could seriously jeopardize its war with Hitler. The bureaucrats and the politicians, in fact, had become quite complacent about the whole thing. They all knew about Subhas Bose and his hatred for the foreign ruler but they decided to ignore him as nothing more than a mere pinprick. After all, he had earned the wrath of Gandhi and his favourites, and was almost a loner by now so why worry when the Indian masses were enjoying some kind of prosperity and Gandhi with his followers was more than keen to ensure that Britain did not succumb before Hitler.

By the middle of 1941, Britain was on the 'back foot' in its war with Hitler. Rommel had already reversed early British victories over the Italians; his Afrika Corps was now fast threatening to take over the Suez Canal, thus cutting the umbilical cord between Britain and India. The war was now expanding in the East and Middle East. Hitler had overrun Yugoslavia and Greece, and successfully invaded the Soviet Union. Worried over this development, and in order to keep Indians under some kind of check, the Viceroy unilaterally inducted five more ministers in his Executive Council on 21st July 1941. He also created a new consultative body, the National Defence Council (NDC), with 30 members drawn from as many parts of Indian national life as possible, including representatives from the princely states. Premiers of Punjab, Bengal and Assam, Sir Sikandar, Fazlul Huq and Sir Muhammad Saadullah respectively were also included in this body. At no point did he consult either the League or the Congress while going through this exercise.

Indian reaction to these new moves were mixed. Gandhi issued a statement saying that nothing had changed in so far as Congress was concerned. The Hindu Mahasabha welcomed this 'as a step in the right direction', but suggested that a Sikh should also be included in the Executive Council. Jinnah was furious that the Viceroy while nominating the Muslim leaders had not consulted him. He drew the attention of the League Prime Ministers to his circular of June 1940, which barred Muslim Leaguers from joining war committees. At first, the premiers stood up to him. The Prime Minister of Assam made it clear to Jinnah that he was already on provincial war committee. He threatened Jinnah that if he had to resign from NDC or from the League, it would be the end of his ministry and a setback to the League in Assam. Sikandar wavered; but felt that his position would·remain secure in the Punjab even if he fell out with Jinnah. But by then the demand for Pakistan had gained sufficient momentum and the Muslims all over India were now seeing Jinnah as the only one who could save them from a Hindu majority India. The provincial level leaders were obviously losing out to Jinnah.

Backed by his Working Committee, Jinnah insisted that the provincial leaders resign from the NDC. With great reluctance, and after a lot of pressure they did so. But Huq also quit the Working Committee of the League at the same time, as a protest against the party president's 'arrogant and dictatorial conduct'. On being expelled from the party, he split along with his provincial colleagues, forming a fresh government in Bengal with the support of Bose's Forward Block and the Mahasabha. The others also made their protest against Jinnah's orders known, but by then he had been able to increase his authority over the League in such a manner that just about nobody could dare disagree with him on any issue. He confirmed his firm hold on the League by the end of October by pulling out all League members from the Central Legislative Assembly for the entire session.

The gulf between Congress and the League kept on widening. Gandhi described it as a domestic quarrel, which could disappear in a fortnight once the British left the country. The Muslims took it as an indirect threat, and Jinnah fully exploited this sentiment. He called upon the government to stop its policy of appeasement towards those who are bent upon frustrating your war efforts' and doing their best to oppose the prosecution of the war and the defence of India at this critical moment (clearly meaning Congress and its civil disobedience movement).

Churchill, by now in a corner and under extreme pressure due to German advances on all fronts, met President Roosevelt of USA aboard the American cruiser Augusta in Placentia Bay seeking American help in the war effort. Roosevelt was non-committal because America was still officially neutral. Nevertheless, they agreed to issue an eight-point declaration of peace aims that became known as the 'Atlantic Charter'. An operative clause of this charter-article III, which Churchill, uncharacteristically missed, affirmed that the two countries 'respect the right of all peoples to choose the form of government under which they live and they wish to see sovereign rights and self-government restored to those who have been forcibly deprived of them.' The Indians and other colonial peoples, however, spotted it at once, and greeted it with great enthusiasm.

Leo Amery, the Secretary of State, was quick to realise the implications of the 'article', and he prepared a lengthy statement for Churchill to make, explaining that the Atlantic Charter had nothing to do with India or the rest of the British Empire. Churchill ignored it, preferring to make his own. He made it on 9th September, declaring that the Charter was intended to apply only to Europe, and did nothing to change British policy towards India, or its 'responsibilities to its many creeds, races and interests'. This abrupt denial naturally caused great resentment in India. The Viceroy made no bones about his desire for the Home Government to take some kind of initiative that could bring the Congress back to cooperating with the government. He wrote to Amery, " India and Burma have no association with the Empire from which they are alien by race, history and religion, and for which as such neither of them have any natural affection, and both are in the Empire because they are conquered countries which had been brought there by force, kept there by our controls, and which hitherto have suited to remain under our protection." In order to make some kind of conciliatory gesture to Indians in general, and to Congress in particular, the Viceroy decided to free those Indian leaders who were still in jail for having made 'anti-war statements'. Churchill wanted all the Congressmen kept locked up indefinitely, but his own War Cabinet overruled him. He finally relented, saying, "I give in. When you lose India, don't blame me." Nehru, Azad and the others were released on 4th December 1941. Three days later, the Japanese attacked Pearl Harbour. The day after that, they bombed the Philippines, Guam, Midway, Wake, Hong Kong and Singapore; occupied the International Settlement in Shanghai and landed troops in Malaya and Thailand. Indian borders were now under direct threat. Till then the war had been something abstract and distant for the Indians. Taking advantage of British reverses and egged on by the Japanese, Burma declared its independence. There was no preparation for such a situation, the British could easily restore status quo ante and arrested the Burmese premier U Saw for hobnobbing with the Japanese.

That the Japanese were no lovers of democracy, and certainly had no special concern for the Indian leadership, was a well-known fact. Congressmen were naturally worried over these developments. Azad and Rajagopalachari were so concerned that they managed to persuade the Congress Working Committee to offer full co-operation against the Japanese. All they wanted in return was a 'national government' at once and a firm promise of freedom immediately after the war. Gandhi, who refused to contemplate any involvement in any war, promptly resigned his leadership.

12

Bose and His Indian National Army

The Azad Hind Fauz

During the earlier stages of the war a very large number of Indian soldiers were taken as prisoners during the campaigns in North Africa and elsewhere. Most of them were eventually transferred to Annaburg 'prisoners of war' camp in Germany. German officers manning the camp were surprised to observe that most of them disliked their British masters, but they had no idea about drawing propaganda mileage out of this animosity of soldiers who had fought under the British flag. Subhas learnt of their existence on German soil when he found that a few Indian soldiers had been brought from Annaburg to Berlin to translate Hindi news bulletins broadcast on the BBC and certain other radio stations. He went to the German authorities with a proposal of setting up an autonomous military outfit with willing Indian POWs. Anything that could help the German war effort, even indirectly while causing discomfort to the British at the same time, was welcome to the authorities and sanction to form what came to be known as Azad Hind Fauz was accorded. Formal sanction of the Fuehrer to set up the India Legion with Subhas as its Chief was accorded on 19th December 1941. The force eventually built up to a strength of over three thousand soldiers by the end of 1942. Though the 'Legion' did not contribute much to the German war effort and was virtually decimated when the Allies started gaining an upper hand with the liberation of France, it did become the forerunner of the later day Indian National Army of Subhas Bose.

Bose Escapes from India

The war had started turning the Allies way by the winter of 1942 when America also joined directly. The Indian National Congress was not very clear about it's future course of action, and Jinnah was busy consolidating his hold on the Muslim masses. Churchill could now concentrate on the war leaving India and her problems on the back burner. In August 1942 the All India Congress Committee approved a 'Quit India' movement; the Party also promised that India would join the allies, if the British actually quitted. Congress was once again declared a prohibited association and its leaders arrested. Britain ruled over a sullen, uncooperative but, despite Gandhi's assertion that they were in 'open rebellion', largely a quiet India. Only fly in the ointment was Subhas Bose, who had been becoming more and more belligerent by the day, Throughout the spring of 1939 and early summer of 1940, he revelled in Britain's difficulties, hailing each setback in the war and continued to call for action, violent if need be. With the fall of France his conviction that the end of British Empire was near, gained momentum. Bose was arrested, but could not be held captive for long because when he went on a hunger strike on 29th November 1940, his health deteriorated immediately. The British authorities, not wanting to be in any further trouble with the Indians should anything happened to him, released Bose from Jail and put him under house arrest instead. By then Bose had been able to contact the Russians, Germans and the Italians through their ambassadors. His financial backer, a Lala Shanker Lal, who had been to Tokyo on such a mission, had done this. On 16th January 1941 Bose, disguised as a Muslim in wide pyjamas, a long coat and a black fez cap, slipped quietly out of the house and away from the watching police: he had become Mohammad Ziauddin, a travelling inspector for the Empire of India Assurance Company.

Bose had planned to go to Germany via Afghanistan and Russia. Accompanied by one Bhagat Ram, he finally arrived in Kabul on 27th January 1941. There was no reception committee for him; in fact, the Russians were extremely suspicious of Bose. He then turned to the German ambassador, Dr Hans Pilger, whom he had known earlier. Even Pilger was not sure of Bose's intentions, worrying that he might be a British agent, contacted Berlin for instructions. Berlin was not particularly interested in Bose, until Pietro Quaroni, the Italian ambassador in Kabul, sent a report to his government: 'According to Bose, India is morally ripe for revolution; what is lacking is the courage to take the first step. Bose says that if 50,000 men—Italian, German or Japanese—could reach the frontiers of India, the Indian army would desert, the masses would up rise and the end of English domination could be achieved in a very short time.' He concluded that Bose was intelligent, able, and full of passion; and without doubt the most realistic, may be the only realist, among India national leaders. (Mihir Bose-p 161)

Hearing of this analysis by the Italian ambassador, the Germans suddenly got interested in Bose. He was issued with an Italian passport in the name of 'Orlando Mazzotta', travelling via Bokhara and Samarkand Bose reached Moscow, from there he was flown to Berlin. One week after his arrival in Berlin, Bose submitted the first of his many memoranda to the German Foreign Ministry. Entitled 'Plan for Co-operation Between the Axis Powers and India'. It included a 'Declaration of an Independent India', with proposals for setting up Free India Government in Berlin along the lines of the Free French and Polish governments in exile in London.

Bose was accommodated in a luxurious villa, he was given a generous allowance for personal expenses and money was also provided for carrying out propaganda against the Raj, but there was no assurance about India being granted freedom. On 29th April, Bose met the Nazi foreign minister Ribbentrop, who was his usual bombastic self while talking of future division of the world where Germany would rule Europe and Britain could retain its colonies. Bose pressed him on the possibility of recruiting Indian prisoners of war to fight the British, but Ribbentrop was non-committal. 'Only the Fuhrer could take such a decision,' he said. But Fuhrer was in no hurry to meet Bose, there were more important things occupying his mind and time. Hitler did not seem to be overenthusiastic in helping Bose; for, he was convinced that the British destiny was to rule black men, the Germans, white. ("England will lose India only if it allows its administrative machinery to be dominated by the Indians or when it will be forced to give up India as a result of attack on India by a more powerful enemy of England. The Indian rebels will never be able to realise this...I, as a German, prefer to see India, in spite of everything, under British domination than of any other country"). Adolf Hitler –Mein Kemph (*A Beacon Across Asia*, p50)

Bose was also getting restless with this lack of activity and apparent disinclination of Hitler to take him seriously enough where India's freedom was concerned. Towards the end of May 1941 he went on a visit to Vienna and Rome where he learnt about the German invasion of Russia on 22nd June 1941. This upset him no end, and on 17th July 1941 Bose met Dr Emst Woermann, a Secretary of State of the Reich, to apprise him of his reservations; he felt that German invasion of Russia would adversely affect his mission of liberating by alienating the sympathy of pro-Russian Indian masses against Germany. He now wanted an early and unambiguous declaration of Indian independence by Germany. No such declaration was made, but anything that caused problems to the British was welcome to the Germans, so Bose was given funds to organise and maintain the proposed diplomatic mission in Berlin—Free India Centre— for good measure a propaganda unit known as Azad Hind Radio was also allowed to be established as part of the Centre. During the formal inauguration of the Centre on 2nd November 1941, Rabindranath Tagore's famous poem, which was later adopted as Indian national anthem, was sung for the first time as the anthem of Free India Centre.

Gandhi was among those who were influenced by the Japanese broadcasts, and by those of Subhas Bose from Berlin. Deep inside he was, perhaps, convinced that England would lose war; and if it was so what was the point in discussing 'independence' with someone who was not likely to prevent its coming after peace came. He began a series of articles in *Harijan* demanding the withdrawal of foreign troops from Indian soil—not only British but also the Americans who were just beginning to arrive. Soon he progressed to demanding the immediate withdrawal of all the British. 'The presence of the British in India is an invitation to Japan to invade India,' he wrote. On April 26, 1942, he wrote, "If the English abandon India to her fate as they did with Singapore, non-violent India has nothing to lose. The Japanese would probably leave her in peace." Then again on 24 May he wrote, "Leave India in the hands of God, that is what in the modern jargon is called anarchy. This anarchy will for a time result in civil wars and looting. From it will emerge a true India in place of this false one which we see today."[1] He announced that he was not asking them to hand over the administration to Congress or any other person or party. He wanted India to be left to its own fate, and not be destroyed just because the foreign ruler was fighting with Japan. The message he had for them was simple: 'Leave India to God—or to anarchy.' Churchill was not impressed by this development. Indian soldiers were, in any case, fighting on behalf of the Empire on different fronts, owing allegiance to the King-Emperor. Worried over likely revolt by the local population in Bengal, Orissa and Assam in case of a Japanese invasion, the Viceroy also advised the government to ignore this appeal of the Congress.

The Japanese had calculated that it would take them 100 days to overrun Malaya and capture Singapore. They actually took only 70 when Singapore fell on 18th February 1942. British defeat and its shockwaves reverberated throughout the Empire. Nowhere were they felt more strongly than in India—among the 130,000 men taken prisoner during the Malayan campaign were no fewer than 60,000 Indians.

Many Indian nationalists rejoiced at Britain's misfortunes. But none was more pleased than Subhas Chandra Bose, who was now allowed by the Germans to break cover and start broadcasting under his own name on Azad Hind (Free India) Radio. "The fall of Singapore means the collapse of the British Empire", he told his listeners. He denounced those Indians who had collaborated with the British and declared, "vast majority of the Indians were with him in the struggle for freedom." His followers, particularly in Bengal, were stirred to action by the sound of his voice. A fresh wave of terrorism swept the province, it continued spasmodically until the end of the war. Threat of a Japanese invasion also mounted with the Japanese Radio network beaming anti-British propaganda into India.

Since August 1942, secret parleys had been going on between the Germans and the Japanese about taking on the Allies in the East. The likely role of Bose and his Azad Hind Fauz was also analysed in the light of inputs provided by those Indian revolutionaries who were now gaining prominence in Japan and in the Japanese scheme of things. Hitler, in a one to one meeting, had already conveyed to Bose that Germany was too far away from India to be of any practical help in its freedom struggle: he opined that Bose should move to join hands with his Axis partner, i.e. Japan. Taking a complicated route and as diverse a range of transportation mode that included submarines, aircrafts and land vehicles Bose finally arrived in Tokyo on 16th May 1943. From here he moved to Singapore where some of the Indian POWs resentful of abandonment by their British officers had already formed a sort of Indian National Army with encouragement and assistance of the Japanese.

Two days after landing in Singapore, Bose formally assumed the office of the President of India Independence League; and, in due course of time took control of the Indian National Army or the Azad Hind Fauz. On 21st October 1943 he declared formation of 'Provisional Government of Free India (PGFI)' with himself as head of state, prime minister, war minister and foreign minister, in addition to his position as supreme commander. Japan, Germany and other Axis members extended an immediate recognition to this government. Two days later Bose declared war on Britain and America. On 28th October he flew to Tokyo to attend a coordinating conference. At the conference on 6th November Tojo (Japanese Premier) announced that Japan had decided to hand over recently liberated islands of Andaman and Nicobar to the PGFI. "By the acquisition of this territory the Provisional Government has become a national entity in fact as well in name," Bose announced when he visited the island for the first time on 29th December 1943. He renamed the islands 'Shahid' (Martyr), raised the flag of Azad Hind and appointed the first Indian chief commissioner, Lieutenant Colonel Loganadhan of the INA. Nicobar was renamed 'Swaraj'. His appointees soon found out that the Japanese had no practical use for their advice of any kind where military control on these islands was concerned. One major gain of his association with the Japanese was that when he got the wind of a proposed air raid on Calcutta, Bose managed to convince them that the political consequences of bombing the city would far outweigh any temporary military advantage that might accrue. His persuasive skills came in handy and the Japanese abandoned that plan.

Initially, the Japanese commanders were reluctant to employ INA men in combat role because Field Marshal Count Terauchi, Commander of the Japanese forces in Burma, had felt that not more than 12,000 of 25,000 INA men were trained for the kind of combat he had in mind. Under pressure from higher authorities, no doubt on persuasion of Bose, Terauchi finally relented to have 3,000 men. A Subhas Brigade was formed in a hurry from the INA 1st Division. Fighting alongside the Japanese, the soldiers of Azad Hind Fauz entered India on 18th March 1944 after a successful campaign in Arakan province of Burma. To be close to the impending action, Bose immediately moved his headquarters to Rangoon, where the entire Burmese Cabinet welcomed him as a Head of State.

The INA soldiers were not the best-equipped troops fighting for India's freedom; they were short of just about everything and that included arms, ammunition, rations and clothing. What they had in an ample measure was commitment for a cause and an unflinching determination to do or die for India; and of course, a total faith in the leadership of Subhas Bose. That alone could have kept them going for a very long time. Unfortunately, and for unspecified reasons to compound their woes the Japanese commanders on the ground did not have much faith in their fighting abilities and qualities; may be because they were originally from a defeated British Army, and as per the Japanese culture a soldier who gives up is not trained and motivated enough to give up his life for the cause and the King.

Therefore, the Japanese, largely, employed these soldiers for road building, repairing bridges, extinguishing jungle fires, and performing all the 'duties of a labour battalion'. Finally they got a chance to show their courage and fighting skills when Lieutenant Colonel Shah Nawaz Khan was told that his brigade would be seeing action at long last, and to join up with the 31st Division in the Kohima sector. After a long and arduous march through the Kabaw valley, Khan and his men arrived just in time to meet the 31st Division in full retreat. The Gandhi and Azad brigades also suffered very heavy casualties when the Japanese attack on Imphal failed. Some 6,000 INA men surrendered during the campaign, including those who had taken the first opportunity to cross the lines in the hope of rejoining the advancing British Indian army.

Yet nothing deterred Netaji. He continued broadcasting to the Indian people, beginning each speech with his stirring war cry 'Dilli Chalo', 'On to Delhi'. 'Whatever happens', he would declare, 'the INA must continue advancing into India. As soon as all our preparations are complete we shall launch a mighty offensive against our enemies once again'. He was in the words of a famous Japanese commander 'inclined to be unrealistic'.

To quote Hugh Toye (The Springing Tiger), "As a revolutionary army the INA's morale was very high and it was quite well organised, but the standards of its tactics, training and leadership was low...it lacked in particular, offensive strength and tenacity". And one might add, any suitable equipment worth the name. All that they had was courage and the spirit to fight for the freedom of India. But that alone wasn't enough when you are at war. Consequently, the force could not hold on to the territory it had wrested from the British. Japan itself was suffering reverses and withdrawing from Burma. The INA eventually withered away with most of the soldiers and commanders getting captured by the advancing Allies forces, and Japan surrendering after atomic bombs were dropped on Hiroshima and Nagasaki—two important cities of Japan. Characteristically, Bose took all these happenings as only temporary setbacks to his mission of liberating India from British rule. Bose, then moved to Singapore, and apprehending capture at the hands of the British decided to seek sanctuary elsewhere. In fact, he was persuaded by his followers to leave because if he was captured and tried for war crimes against the British, consequences could be very grave for millions of Indians across the globe who had identified in him a symbol of their hope for freedom. With both, the Japanese and Hitler out of the picture, Netaji now turned to another of his heroes—Marshal Stalin. In his broadcast of 25th May 1945, he declared that the struggle for Indian independence now lay in association with Soviet Russia. Three days after the Japanese surrender on 17th August, he and seven of his staff flew out of Saigon, heading for Russia, via Manchuria. Their transport was an overloaded, decrepit Japanese bomber with a crew so inexperienced that the captain was not even a qualified pilot. As they took off again after a night's halt at Taipei in Formosa, there was a loud explosion and the port engine fell off. The plane caught fire and nose-dived into the ground. Bose survived the crash, and managed to climb out of the wreckage with his clothes ablaze. Badly burnt and with serious head injuries, he was rushed to a Japanese military hospital, but died shortly afterwards. On 20th August, his body was cremated and the ashes taken to Tokyo, where they were left in the keeping of Buddhist monks of the fiercely nationalistic Nichiren sect. (Note: This is the official version and not many Indians believe that Bose perished in this manner. His disappearance from Singapore, and news of his death in an air crash continue to be surrounded in mystery till date.)

That Bose was a nationalist; a revolutionary and true patriot is never disputed. What continues to be disputed to this day is the manner of his disappearance. For almost fifty years after his disappearance some Indians, mostly Bengalis, continued to believe that he never died in any aircrash. There was a widely held belief that he was in Russia, or had been living as a hermit in the Himalayas. There have been a large number of investigations, searches and even political parleys with governments of different countries, but no firm proof of the exact nature of Netaji's end has emerged to date.

American Initiative

All through America had been pressurising Britain to offer some kind of a promise to the Indians about their freedom after the war. Churchill didn't want to submit to the American diktat because he hated the very idea of a 'free India'. But some of his own ministers were also getting restive over the issue of India's freedom. Ernest Bevin (Minister of Labour and National Service in the War Cabinet) wrote to Amery: "I must confess that leaving the settlement of the Indian problem until after the war fills me with alarm...We made certain definite promises in the last war and practically a quarter of a century has gone, and, though there has been an extension of self-government, we have not in my view delivered the goods. It is quite understandable that neither Muslims nor Hindus place much confidence in our 'after war promises.' It seems to me that the time to take action to establish Dominion status is now." With pressure from Roosevelt and the Americans mounting on the subject of independence and democracy; and with an important member like Bevin insisting on immediate and positive action Churchill decided to be seen as relenting on the issue. India Committee, constituted earlier to study the Indian independence case, now came up with a statement to the effect on 7th March 1942 with the approval of the prime minister, who only wanted to have some kind of a window dressing, a display of good intent for the benefit of the Americans, which could not possibly succeed-or be allowed to succeed. The statement, *inter alia*, stipulated:

"His Majesty's Government...have decided to lay down in precise and clear terms the steps which they propose shall be taken for the earliest possible realisation of self-government in India. The object is the creation of a new Indian Union which shall constitute a Dominion, associated with the United Kingdom and the other dominions by a common allegiance to the Crown, but equal to them in every respect, in no way subordinate in any aspect of its domestic or external affairs." All the proposed changes were to be brought about only after the war was won. There was no immediate sign of that happening. Rangoon had already been run over by the Japanese, and the local population was treating it as a deliverance from the British. Worrying over the impact of these reversals so close to India, the British government decided to send a Mission under Cripps. That too much should not be expected too soon was also made clear to the Americans. The British kept Americans in good humour by showing them that the Indians were so immersed in their own Hindu-Muslim squabbles that the cry for freedom was merely that—a cry with no serious intent behind.

Cripps arrived on 22nd March 1942 carrying with him a draft Declaration. The Declaration said:

- Immediately on the cessation of hostilities steps are to be taken to set up an elected body charged with the task of framing a constitution for a fully self-governing Indian Union within the Commonwealth. The composition of the elected body was also stated.

- Any province or provinces or States can stay out of the proposed Indian Union and form a separate Union of their own and would have the same status as the Indian Union.

- Interim Government would be formed immediately but control over defence would rest with the C-in-C who was to be the War Member. However, an Indian representative would be allowed to look after the ancillary department of the Defence Ministry.

- Provincial elections were to be held immediately after the war, following which the entire membership of all the lower houses would elect a Constituent Assembly based on a system of proportional representation to draw up a new constitution of India. British interests and obligations, including those to minorities and the princely states, were to be covered by a treaty between the British government and the Indian constituent assembly.

- The British obligations and interests to India were to be settled by a Treaty freely negotiated between HMG and the constitution making body.

Cripps brought this document from Churchill to India for discussion with the Indian leaders. How Cripps was expected to win over the Congress and the League with promises, which were both contradictory and vague in terms of real transfer of power and responsibility to the Indians, is not very clear. The Plan placed the entire responsibility for finding a workable solution towards unity on the Indians themselves with very subtle hints that the break up of the country would also be acceptable to the British. Cripps tried to justify the terms of the Plan by saying that the Congress would have to realise that the way to freedom lay in their accommodating Muslim aspirations and settling with the princes. Gandhi at once termed it as a plan for Balkanisation of the sub-continent. The Indian leadership saw Cripps Mission to be merely a propaganda exercise devised to show the Indians in poor light and convince the Americans that the Indians themselves did not know exactly what they wanted. The fact of the matter was that there was no real intention ever to transfer real power to India and Cripps had been sent to appease President Roosevelt who understood the implications of Indian unrest and sympathised with India's aspirations. Churchill was never in favour of any such gesture to the Indians, but the American president demanded some concrete display of (non-existent) noble intentions on the part of the British Government.

It appears that Churchill seems to have thought of Indian political leaders to be illiterate and not wise enough to see through a ruse, an indecent one at that. How could he really hope to sell his plan to those who were as well versed as his own self in world affairs and had almost as good a British education as the prime minister of England? Linlithgow and Wavell – the Commander-in-Chief, and other provincial governors were also not happy with the proposals, which effectively allowed the provinces and princely states to make their own choice in the matter. They believed that such a scenario would lead to communal trouble; particularly, when the implication was that the Sikhs, by default, could be put under a Muslim majority ruled Punjab. Wavell feared that such a possibility could seriously affect the armed forces, where Sikhs contributed the largest number of soldiers. Sentiments of the Muslim soldiers, particularly Punjabi Muslims, were also to be taken care of.

Churchill explained to the Viceroy and others that he actually expected the Indians to disagree among themselves on various issues listed in the draft document. He could then inform Roosevelt that in spite of all his efforts and sincerity, if the Indians were not willing to come to any agreement among themselves about the future of their country he could not help but allow them to remain where they were. Seeing the trend of perennial fights between Congress, The League and various other groups he was not very far from the reality of situation in India.

Cripps Mission

Cripps, nursing prime ministerial ambitions himself, came to India with high hopes of seeing Indians of different inclinations, agreeing with the proposals. In this, he was also inspired by his recently cultivated friendship with Nehru and certain other Indian leaders who had met him while in England. Success of this mission could help him dislodge Churchill whose popularity was waning by the day with each reversal in war. Churchill was convinced that Cripps would fail, but the wily politician that he was, he was certainly not going to prevent a man who could prove dangerous to him from becoming embroiled in what appeared to him an impossible mission. Besides sorting out a potential rival he would have also conveyed to the Americans that he had all the intentions to

give freedom to India, only if her politicians could agree on the basics.
He was proved absolutely right in his assessment of the situation.

Liaquat Ali told Cripps that unless a constitution could be devised
which would make it impossible for one community to rule by itself, it
would never bring peace to the country. According to Liaquat Ali, the
Muslims had three thoughts. These were: (a) Partition, but not on the
lines of the Muslim empire, (b) Free and independent states, with a
federation of the Hindu and Muslim provinces and a Confederation of
the two, (3) Dominion Status for each of the provinces with a federation
at the centre to which should be given only such powers as the Provinces
agree to give, and giving the Provinces the right to opt out. Jinnah
rejected the proposals made by Cripps, but for exactly the reasons that
were contrary to the reservations expressed by the Congress. Where he
was concerned, the right of non-accession by the provinces did not
amount to a demand for Pakistan, which the League had not yet
formulated in its entirety. He pointed out to Cripps that in a Constituent
Assembly elected by proportionate representation Muslims would have
only twenty-five per cent of the votes, and would not be able to vote
against joining the Union. Cripps assured him that if less than sixty per
cent of the provincial legislature voted in favour of accession, the minority
would have the right to call for a plebiscite of the adult male population
of the province and the British government would implement the verdict.
The provision for provinces to opt out of the federation was also worrying
Jinnah because leaders like Sikandar Hyat Khan in Punjab and Huq in
Bengal were already propagating for a Congress-League rapprochement,
this way these leaders were hoping to retain their independence if the
country eventually decided to have a federal structure. This did not suit
Jinnah at all. In fact, throughout the war years Jinnah's difficulties with
the provincial leaders kept mounting as the Muslim leaders in NWFP
and Sind also started finding merit in what Hyat and Huq were saying.
Jinnah was now compelled to harp on Islamic ideology as the main
platform for an Islamic State.

Congress remained cool to the overtures of Cripps to communal
and political representatives of different hues for a quick settlement of
all the controversies and divergent views of various leaders of the political
parties. Here, the Congress leaders failed to see through the game plan
of Jinnah. They knew about the sentiments of the leaders of Punjab and
Bengal who were banking upon a support base consisting of inter-
communal interests within their provinces, thus making a case for a con-
federal structure—something not to the liking of Jinnah because in such
a situation unless he could get a prominent place in the central government
he would have been marginalised. Congress leaders also failed to realise

that the Cripps formula made provisions for partition before the transfer of power took place.

Through this draft declaration the British Government also made it clear that it envisaged the Congress and the League to be the main parties involved in the transfer of power. The principle of partition had in fact been incorporated into the Cripps proposals in recognition of the League's demand for Pakistan. These fears of the Congress were confirmed by the clarification given by Cripps to Sikh leaders, that the position of the Sikhs in the new constitution would be decided by agreement between the Congress and the League. He went on to allay their worries over the community's future in a Muslim dominated Punjab by saying that the Congress, in order to enlarge its majority in the Constituent Assembly, would try to win over the Sikhs by making the most ample provisions for them in the new constitution, which might even entail the sub-division of the Punjab into two provinces or the setting up within the province, of a semi-autonomous district for the Sikhs. For good measure, Cripps also pontificated that the League might woo them in order to enhance its majority. (He was not very wrong in his assessment of the Muslim response to Akali reservations on the issue). In what came to be known as Sikandar-Baldev pact of June 1942, the Muslims bent over backward to appease Sikhs. The terms of the pact included the extension of facilities for the provision of appropriate (and as sanctified by the Sikh religion) meat to all government institutions where separate kitchens could be provided, the introduction, as soon as possible, of Gurmukhi as a second language in schools where an adequate number of students desired it, and the establishment of a convention that in matters which exclusively concerned a particular community the members of that community alone would exercise voting rights in the Assembly. The Sikh representation in the provincial services was to be maintained at twenty per cent. Though most sections of Sikhs were satisfied with the contents of this pact, their political status in such a dispensation had not been clarified. Trouble was that so far the Sikhs had not received any assurance about their future from either the British, Congress or League—all three seemed to treat them as if they were of little or no political consequence. In Sikh eyes, the demand for Pakistan would remain 'a demand for civil war,' as Master Tara Singh put it. (In an interview he gave to the representative of the *New York Times*, he said, " I do not see how we can avoid civil war. There can be no settlement if the Muslims want to rule the Punjab. We cannot trust the Muslims under any circumstances....The Sikhs have started to organise their own private volunteer army in response to the Muslim League threats...I have sounded the bugle. Finish the Muslim League in Punjab.") As the future events proved this 'so called private army' or the Akal fauj existed only in the Master's imagination.

With all the manipulations, concessions, promises and even veiled threats, to his dismay, just about nobody agreed with Cripps. There were partial and subjective agreements, but neither the Congress, nor the League found proposals satisfactory. Hoping to win, at least the approval of Gandhi, he persuaded the Mahatma to meet him in Delhi. The moment Gandhi arrived, Cripps was hospitality personified, rushing to open the door of the car that brought the great man from the railway station, he greeted him warmly drawing attention to an earlier meeting that he had with Gandhi. Cripps was a little put out when Gandhi claimed not to remember anything of their earlier meeting other than conversation about vegetarianism.

After studying the proposals briefly, Gandhi told Cripps that Congress would reject them on three grounds: the inclusion of the Indian states in the proposed constituent assembly, the opt-out provisions, and defence being retained by the British government. Cripps failed to realise that without Gandhi's support his mission had no hope of success. But he carried on regardless, and found Jinnah to be much more responsive to the proposals, Rajagopalachari too, was encouraging, suggesting ways of redrafting the defence clause to make it more palatable to his Congress colleagues. But Azad was much more adamant, unwilling to accept that British troops could not be put under an Indian C-in-C, or why could an Indian not be given the Defence portfolio.

By now Cripps had shown the document to so many people that it could no longer remain a secret. On 29th March, he held a press conference where he released the full text and answered journalists' questions. During the question-answer session, Cripps announced that the constituent assembly would be free to decide for itself whether or not to remain in the Commonwealth. 'It could even start with its own declaration of independence,' he announced. On the vexed question of defence, he elaborated that an Indian Defence Minister would be responsible for the defence of India. He elaborated his ideas on the subject of India's independence, and these were not in entire conformity with those of either the Viceroy or the British government. Gandhi, when asked to comment on what all Cripps had said, termed it as a 'post-dated cheque', everything was to happen at a future date, which was yet to be specified. He rightly surmised that the proposals were full of contradictions and clauses that were not in the country's best interest. Earlier, Cripps had met the Mahatma at Wardha where Gandhi had told him, "The Government must make up its mind whether it trusted Congress, and if it did, must rely on Congress and the Constituent Assembly to safeguard the minorities, as, of course, they must." In other words, the Mahatma wanted Indians alone to deal with their future destiny. So, during their meeting in Delhi, Gandhi had summed up their discussion. "Accept it (Gandhi's theory, that is) or leave it," he declared, "but not one problem facing the country would be resolved by the plan that you have been propagating".

Cripps did not give up trying. He met Nehru, and then went to see Gandhi at Birla House, but gained little success. Cripps was in a hurry to arrive at an understanding with the Indian leaders because a wholehearted support of the Indian people; its industry and infrastructure were vital to the British war effort, a war that was going badly for Britain at that point of time. Gandhi and his close disciples were against any involvement in the war under any circumstances. Rajagopalachari, Azad and their supporters were eager to co-operate in the war effort, provided they had real responsibility and power. Vallabhbhai Patel and his group saw the war as an opportunity to gain their long-term objectives. Nehru remained undecided, he wanted to join the fight against Fascism, but he did not want to antagonize either Gandhi or other senior members of the party. On 22nd March 1942, he wrote to an English friend, "This war is our war. But you don't understand, in this war Great Britain is on the other side."

While Linlithgow and Wavell continued to have reservations on handing over defence to an Indian minister, Cripps managed to persuade them to agree to split the defence portfolio into two departments. They saw 'no serious risks in handing over to an Indian member of Councjl the charge of Defence Co-ordination, with limited powers. To lay it thick, and in order to make the proposal more attractive to Congress, they even agreed to give him the title 'defence minister' and make commander-in-chief 'war minister'. The new minister would be responsible for press relations, demobilization and post-war reconstruction, amenities and welfare of troops and their dependents, canteens, certain non-technical educational institutions, stationery, printing of forms for the army; also reception, accommodation and social arrangements for all foreign missions. He would also take over some areas with indirect bearing on defence, such as scorched earth policy, evacuation from threatened areas, signals co-ordination and economic warfare. In sum total, the Indian defence minister was to deal with just about everything other than actual conduct of war. Most of the 'tail' complement was his, but he had no control or say where 'teeth' element was concerned. Congress rejected the proposal out of hand, terming it as 'insulting and ludicrous'.

On 3rd April, Colonel Louis Johnson, a former US assistant secretary of war, arrived with a five-member team of technical advisers with a view to ascertain, as to, how America could help in developing India's production of war materials for the Allied armies in the Far and Middle

East. He had been given the rank of a 'minister at large,' which effectively meant that, where America was concerned, India was at par with Canada, Australia, New Zealand and South Africa. To the utter annoyance of the Viceroy and his staff, Johnson threw himself with blind enthusiasm into his (largely) self-chosen role of intermediary between Cripps and Congress. Seeing that the situation was getting out of hand with Cripps and Johnson making fresh (and obviously which nobody had told them to) proposals to Congress, the Viceroy complained to Amery and Churchill that their emissary, meaning Cripps, was in the process of making promises to the Indians which were beyond his brief. On hearing of the goings on in India, Churchill blew his top. He conveyed to the Viceroy that Johnson was not the presidential representative for mediation and interference in Indian affairs. His was only to survey Indian munitions and allied subjects. At the same time Churchill succeeded in obtaining from Hopkins-Roosevelt's special adviser in London a declaration according to which Colonel Johnson's mission did not give him the right to involve the American President in the ongoing debate vis-à-vis India's freedom. But the American President was keen on Britain making its stand clear on the issue: he ordered Hopkins to intervene with Churchill in favour of the Cripps mission, but it was already too late. Churchill no longer, had any reason to placate the president because he needed the American equipment and men to fight Hitler and the Japanese; America was by now in the thick of war on its own accord because the Japanese had hit Pearl Harbour in the interim.

On 10th April 1942, The Indian National Congress formally rejected the package on offer on the grounds that the proposed Viceroy's council would not immediately have the full powers of a dominion cabinet. The talks with Azad and Nehru—heir-apparent designated by Gandhi— failed on the following grounds:

- The non-accession clause by which each province had the option not to join the union,

- The nature of the interim government to be constituted for the duration of the War and before the adoption of a new constitution.

On the first point, Cripps reasoned that if you wanted to persuade a certain number of people to enter a room, it would be unfair to tell them that once they had entered, they would be unable to leave. Congress took this explanation as a ratification of demand for Pakistan.

Cripps was hurt, but he was now clear in his mind that all that was required of him was to sell the original proposals to Indians and nothing else: all his concessions, cajoling of Indian leaders to make his mission a success were now things of the past. As usual, wily Churchill had out-manoeuvred another potential rival of his while still retaining his original stand on the issue of India's freedom. The Congress negotiators were bemused next day when, instead of discussing the concessions he had offered, Cripps was now back to square one. Congress naturally, and as per their original response, rejected the proposals since there was no mention of an immediate national government in the document. Jinnah, who had been watching the goings on from the sidelines, immediately followed suit on behalf of the Muslim League; he could not afford to risk alienating mass opinion by openly expressing any support to the British proposals, which did not promise all that he had sought on behalf of the Muslims.

Despite failure of the mission, Cripps was relieved when Nehru expressed his opinion that there ought to be a total war against the Japanese, Jinnah also pledged unwavering support of the Muslims in the war effort, The Sikhs and other minorities were, in any case content with the war providing them with jobs, and had thus no reason not to support the Empire in this war. Churchill was now happy with the final outcome of the Cripps mission: there was no harm if Cripps returned without selling the original plan on self-government to the Indians. When Roosevelt urged him to let Cripps remain in India until a 'national government' could be set up, saying that the American public opinion was blaming Britain for the breakdown of talks by unreasonably withholding self-government from the Indians, Churchill just ignored the communication.

Before leaving for London, Cripps did meet the Viceroy in Calcutta and offered his over-simplistic solution to the problem of India's future. The Muslims, he said, should be made to put down in writing exactly what their demands were: Congress should then be made to put down in writing exactly how far they were prepared to go to meet them. It should then be up to the Viceroy to 'bridge the difference by negotiation'. As simple as that; the politician with prime ministerial ambitions had become an expert on Indian affairs in less than three weeks of stay in the country.

Cripps sudden departure from the scene caused serious disillusionment among Indian leaders. They were convinced that all this was just a sham to gain time and commitment from the Indians for the war effort. Every day, conviction was gaining ground that there was no way Britain could win: the Japanese had already bombarded Colombo, the capital and chief port of Ceylon (now Sri Lanka). Besides sinking a large number of British ships, they had also carried out raids on some of the Indian ports between Calcutta and Madras. There was a lot of panic when first bombs fell on Indian soil, but there was also a good deal of expectation of more humiliation for the British. The Japanese Prime Minister, Hideki Tojo, broadcast a warning that the Indians would suffer heavy losses if they remained under British military control. This threat was followed by a broadcast by Rash Behari Basu, now leader of the Indian Independence League formed in Japan. He assured his fellow countrymen that the Japanese would not invade India if the Indians drove out the British themselves. The Congress had also calculated that if the British left India, the Japanese would have no reason to invade the country. It was a calculation that appealed neither to Washington, nor to London. In any case it was far too naive and apparently did not have any logical reason behind it.

The pledge, given in near panic conditions of August 1940, to allow the Indians to elect their own constituent assembly can be seen in retrospect to have marked the watershed of British policy. For the first time, the British had explicitly renounced their claim to determine the future of India. Both the Congress and the Muslim League had, however, rejected the offer. The Congress had hoped that by holding out it might acquire immediate self-government. The Muslim League—committed since March 1940 to the aim of a separate Muslim state, namely Pakistan—had made the unacceptable stipulation of equal Hindu and Muslim representation in any central government. Consequent to the failure of Cripps Mission and with no sign of Britain relenting on the issue of India's freedom even Gandhi seems to have had second thoughts on his principle of 'non-violence'. The following speech to a group of volunteers on 28th May 1942 is very clear in this regard: "But today we have to go a step further. We have to take the risk of violence to shake off the great calamity of slavery. But even for resorting to violence one requires the unflinching faith of a non-violent man."[2] Linlithgow showed signs of discomfiture at the 'indecently outspoken' tone of Gandhi's writings in *Harijan*. There is no room...for withdrawal, for negotiations,' explained Gandhi, 'either they recognise India's independence or they don't... There is no question of one more chance, After all it is an open rebellion."

Jinnah's reaction was predictable. He accused the Congress of aiming to establish Hindu Raj 'under the aegis of the British bayonet, thereby placing the Muslims and other minorities at the mercy of Congress Raj.' (*Statesman* 15 July 1942). Jinnah's perennial fear was that the British would be pressurised by the Congress into accepting its terms leaving the League out in the cold. With all his ambitions now focused on a Country of his own: during the League's meeting in Delhi, Jinnah had said, "Can't we say, unite, unite and unite, and get the British out?" The war acted as a catalyst in Indian politics. The Congress leaders were encouraged by Britain's difficulties to set their aims high. The situation also allowed them to take an extreme position. The League also joined the bandwagon and raised its bid correspondingly. The Viceroy, Lord Linlithgow did nothing to stem the communal tide. May be, he didn't want to; or, perhaps, was incapable of mastering the communal and separatist forces that were shaping India's destiny.

The Congress Working Committee demanded a declaration of Britain's 'war aims with regard to democracy and imperialism', and how these aims would apply to India. The British cabinet reacted to the Congress resolution with indignation. 'What I feel', wrote Amery, 'is that Congress has definitely shown its hand as claiming to be an authority parallel to the Government of India and entitled to tell the public to defy the authority of the latter.' 'The challenge must be taken up', he wrote to Linlithgow on 13th July 1942. 'They, (the Congressmen that is) will not be able to stand up to the two of us together...This is a time when a fire brigade cannot wait to ring up headquarters, but must turn the hose on the flames at once'. But there were very few signs of preparation for any serious agitation by the Congress. 'Lack of any real eagerness' for this latest assault on the British Raj by Congress was very noticeable throughout the country, noted intelligence officers. This, coupled with 'the apparent lack of preparation', cast 'an air of unreality' over the whole movement, and raised doubts as to whether it was not all 'a piece of bluff on the part of Gandhi', was the conclusion of the intelligence summary put up to the Viceroy on 31st July 1942. But Linlithgow was a worried man. He wrote to Churchill, ' Here I am engaged in meeting by far the most serious rebellion since that of 1857, the gravity and extent of which we have so far concealed from the world for reasons of military security.'

At the CWC meeting in Wardha (July 6-14), 'Quit India' became the slogan of the whole party. It was a call for open rebellion, using all available means and methods of popular civil disobedience. The Government allowed the process to go on until the AICC meeting on 7th August at Bombay. As soon as the Central Committee ratified the decisions taken at Wardha, the administrative machinery swung into action as per a pre-prepared plan of action to be implemented if Congress tried to stir up any trouble for the government. A carefully planned raid on 9th August 1942 at dawn led to the arrest of all the members of the Congress Working Committee; and all those militants who were considered to be dangerous were also apprehended.

Footnotes

1. Stanley Wolpert Transfer of Power Vol. I pp 789-790.
2. In Complete Works of Mahatma Gandhi Vol. 76 p160.

13

The Quit India Movement

Once Gandhi gave his call for 'Quit India', and the news about the arrest of all the leaders who mattered spread, trouble broke out at many places. Very quickly workers in a large number of places, including Jamshedpur where TATA Steels was contributing to the war effort, and Ahmedabad Textile mills making uniforms and other items for the troops, struck work. After mid-August, the unrest spread to the rural areas, especially in Eastern UP, Bengal, Bihar and Orissa: even short-lived 'national governments' were formed in some of these places. Government assets, like the railways, police stations, telegraph and telephone exchanges came under attack by the people who were now determined to take the final stand against their foreign rulers. The Viceroy took immediate and brutal reprisal measures to suppress the situation; deploying almost fifty odd battalions of troops destined for the battlefields of Europe the situation was brought under control. But the 'violent' movement went on for a while in the form of terrorist attacks, especially in the bigger cities, and the rural guerrillas of Bihar led by Jayaprakash Narain kept up with the tempo.

Jinnah described the movement as a 'most dangerous mass movement' intended to force Congress demands "at the point of a bayonet," which, if conceded, would mean the sacrifice of all other interests, particularly those of the Muslims in India. He appealed to Muslims 'to keep completely aloof' from the movement, and to the Hindu public 'to stop this internecine civil war before it is too late." (*Statesman*, 10th August 1942). He called on the British to give half the seats in the Executive Council; 'if the Muslims are to be roused to intensify the war effort it is only possible provided they are assured that it will lead to the realisation of Pakistan', he added for good measure. This notwithstanding the fact that the most remarkable feature of the Quit India movement was the absence of any communal disorder or incidence.

The political responsibility of the Congress was evident for the events of 1942, even though it had not organised this violent revolt. The movement was mostly an improvised affair, grass-root militants had taken the Mahatma's call as a mandate for them to hasten departure of the British as they saw fit. The events were also influenced by British defeats in the East where the Japanese had given them a bloody nose and the defenders of the Raj had abandoned the Colonies in order to save themselves from the marauding attackers. It was, clearly, the biggest challenge to the Empire after the revolt of 1857, but once again the Indians in uniform, be it Police or Military came to their rescue. Too many sons of the soil were fighting in far-off lands for the common man to actively associate himself with the agitation for any length of time. A factor that worked for the British was the fact that the Punjab Sikhs and Muslims had too many of their sons fighting the war on the side of the British, and for these two communities anything that could weaken the Empire at that point of time did not augur well. Worried over their future dispensation the Sikhs could not alienate the Congress. The Akali reaction to the Quit India movement was to allow a limited number of followers to offer token civil disobedience while Tara Singh exhorted his followers to support the British. Another thing that worked in favour of the British were the recent reverses suffered by Rommel in Africa, and the failure of the Japanese offensive in the 'Coral Sea' battle in the Pacific. Unfortunately, for the Indians this decisive turning point in the Second World War coincided with the Quit India Movement. Montgomery had been able to regain some ground in North Africa. During a celebratory speech, Churchill made his memorable remarks where he declared, "I have not become the King's First Minister in order to preside over the liquidation of the British Empire."

The Bengal Famine

Both in Bengal and Punjab, the local leaders were losing their hold on the masses. Where Bengal was concerned, a massive famine had gripped the state. It is easy to prove that the crafty British engineered the famine that killed more than two to three million people. With the production of foodgrain not having declined in the country during the war years, and there being no serious breakdown in the transportation systems, the government could have easily overcome any shortfall in the production of food grain in Bengal but it did not elect to do so; instead breakdown of communication with Burma due to its occupation by the Japanese and consequent disruption of movement of rice to Bengal was given as the official reason for lack of concern and action which could help overcome the situation.

That the administration was complacent over this tragedy is clear from the fact Linlithgow, who otherwise prided himself where compassion was concerned, refused to visit Bengal for a first hand account of the calamity. Even his wife's pleadings for him to go to Bengal did not stir him. Instead, he stayed aloof in Delhi and Simla, blaming everything and everybody but himself or his government. He was aware of the fact that the famine had been caused by greed of the hoarders, and indifference of the administration. Stern and timely action could have, at least, alleviated the sufferings of the people of Bengal; but it was in the British interest to keep Bengal occupied in this shameful manner. The reason was simple, with Bose and his INA knocking at the door from the East and the Japanese having taken control of Burma and the Quit India movement gathering momentum there was no way the government could keep the Bengalis quiet unless there was no food and the people of Bengal kept busy in fending off the hunger of belly rather than think of their ambition to be free.

In Punjab, Jinnah and his call for partition had created its own set of problems for Sir Sikandar Hyat Khan. He tried to explain to his followers that the call for self-determination for the Muslims would only lead to the breaking up of the province. His death in December 1942 came to Jinnah as a relief; but the successor of Sikandar Hyat— Khizar Hayat Tiwana, was equally unbendable. In addition to the avoidable pinpricks from Jinnah, Tiwana's difficulties were further accentuated with ever increasing demands of the central government for providing more and more soldiers for the war and to concurrently increase availability of foodgrain. Jat Sikhs formed the backbone of the agriculture in Punjab and Tiwana could not see a way out for himself unless he formed some kind of an understanding with the Sikh leaders so as to keep Jinnah at bay. He went into a pact with Sardar Baldev Singh, a moderate Sikh leader; this alliance changed the political equation in the state and instead of easing the situation led to further tensions between the communities because the Leaguers felt threatened with this coming together of Sikhs and Unionist Muslims. The League tried to stir the pot to generate some kind of conflict between the two communities; but to the credit of the leaders of the two communities it must be recorded that there was not even one communal incident or disorder. In report after report, notes Hutchins, the entry under 'Communal' was the single phrase "nothing to report"[1]. The League had been successful in keeping the Muslims away from the movement except in NWFP; it had even succeeded in persuading the government not to include Muslims whenever 'collective' fines were imposed on a village due to an act of sabotage: but it is also a fact that but for an odd incident the Muslims never came forward to give evidence against the saboteurs who were almost always Hindus.

In UP and other states where Hindus were in majority, the League had its strongest base but most of the leaders were not in favour of Pakistan because their part of the country could not possibly have been divided on the lines of religion. Division of opinion in Punjab and Bengal over the call for a Muslim homeland was now weakening Jinnah's hold on the League. His charismatic personality had taken him to the top of Muslim leadership but strongmen at state level often contested his instructions and, at times, even ignored them. According to some historians, "he was obliged to stand still on the side-lines claiming victories which he had not won, and denying defeats he had not suffered."

In order to further widen the rift between the communities and to create a counterpoise to Congress, Linlithgow advised Governors to explore the possibilities of forming non-Congress ministries in their provinces. This move allowed formation of League ministries in Muslim majority provinces, enhancing the League's stature in the process, and adding further to the League's ambition of an independent Pakistan. The provincial League in Assam, however, passed a resolution asking Jinnah to refrain from giving instructions on local matters of which he did not know much in any case. In Punjab, many rural Muslim MLAs resented Jinnah's dictatorial attitude and went so far as to threaten resignation from the League. Things came to such a head that the Governor of Punjab, Lord Glancy observed, 'Jinnah might make an ideal leader of a Demolition Squad, but anything in the way of constructive suggestion seems foreign to his nature.' (Glancy to Wavell, 6 April 1944)

Gandhi-Jinnah Meeting

With most of the Congress leaders in jail and the 'Quit India' movement simmering down, the Government released Gandhi in May 1944, mainly on the advice of doctors who were apprehensive that his failing health, particularly after the recent death of his wife Kasturba, could cause avoidable problems for the administration should something happen to the Mahatma. Immediately, on his release Gandhi wrote to Jinnah proposing a meeting of the two. But the meeting could not be held for a while because at that time Jinnah was convalescing in Kashmir after a strong bout of 'lung ailment'. Gandhi had agreed to call for this meeting because certain senior Congress leaders, particularly Rajagopalachari, were convinced that in order to hasten the departure of British the Congress had to accommodate Jinnah's demands. 'Pakistan is not so dreadful', was his conviction. CR's (as Chakravarti Rajagopalachari was popularly addressed) proposal was to hold a plebiscite in those districts, which had a high percentage of Muslims in order to resolve the issue of their separation from Hindustan. The application of this proposal would have certainly resulted in the partition of Punjab and Bengal, as it eventually happened. In April 1944, Rajagopalachari presented his formula to Jinnah in the hope that it would bring about a 'final settlement of the most unfortunate impasse' that was coming in the way of the country's independence. Jinnah replied that he could not accept the formula, but he would place it before his Working Committee. Knowing that this would serve no purpose CR ended the correspondence on 8th July 1944. Jinnah had his own reservations. He was not very sure of any large-scale support for Pakistan even in Muslim majority districts of the Central India because there was no way that area could form part of Pakistan. Lack of support from such a big section of the Muslims couldn't have helped the cause of a Muslim homeland. And a division of state like Punjab or Bengal would have meant massive dislocation of people if they elected to move to more secure Hindu/Muslim majority areas. Jinnah's rejection of holding a plebiscite is thus understandable, as it would have given him, to use his own words, a "maimed, mutilated and moth-eaten" Pakistan. May be he was still looking for a federal structure; and, therefore, accepted the Congress invitation to hold talks with the Mahatma. There was a great deal of expectation from this meeting because by and large both Hindus and Muslims still wanted the country to remain united. In a Press statement dated 5th August 1944, Jinnah used the term 'Mahatma' about Gandhi and appealed for calm consideration of the points of dispute between the Congress and the League. He said, "It has been the universal desire that we should meet. Now that we are going to meet, help us. We are coming to grips. Bury the past."

The two leaders met at Jinnah's residence in Malabar Hill. Jinnah was courtesy personified. He came out into his porch to receive Gandhi and at the time of his departure he escorted the Mahatma back to his car. Conversation between them continued for eighteen days. But they were nowhere near any solution to the complex problems they had sat down to resolve. Feeling of camaraderie and fellowship that was on display initially gradually vanished. Both of them became cautious and it was arranged that after each meeting their conversations should be confirmed in an exchange of letters.

Gandhi put forward his proposals to Jinnah for deliberation. The terms of the proposals were: -

- When the war ended, a commission would demarcate the "contiguous districts" in North West and East India having an absolute majority.

- In the areas thus demarcated, a plebiscite of the adult population would be taken.

- If the majority voted for a separate sovereign state, it would be given effect to, but border districts would have the option to join one of the new states.

- In the event of separation, mutual agreements would be entered into for safeguarding defence, commerce and communications.

- These terms would be binding when the British transferred full power to India.

The formula clearly conceded the principle of Pakistan, and embodied Rajagopalachari's belief that this would satisfy the Muslims and that they would, in due course of time, cease to want Pakistan. Whereas the Leaguers were happy and Muslim papers were jubilant that Gandhi had accepted Pakistan in principle, Congressmen were surprised, shaken and did not know what to make of Gandhi's attitude. The Sikhs, the Mahasabha and the Unionists were alarmed that the success of Jinnah-Gandhi parleys would prejudice their position in Punjab.

It is unlikely that Gandhi ever thought that Jinnah would accept the formula. For, as Jinnah pointed out, demarcation of boundaries on the lines suggested would relegate 11 districts in the Punjab and the same number in Bengal to Hindustan; and Karachi and Dacca would be the only ports left to Pakistan. For Jinnah the only solution of India's problem was to accept the division of India into Hindustan and Pakistan. Gandhi held the view that the Muslims could not be a separate nation by reasons of acceptance of Islam. "Will the two nations become one if the whole of India accepted Islam?" he countered.

This extremely long-drawn dialogue between Gandhi and Jinnah took place from 9th to 27th September 1944. Nothing came off it because both of them stuck to their known stands on the issues involved. Jinnah pointed out to the unrepresentative character of Gandhi at the start of negotiations. Jinnah had also been emboldened by the fact that his standing with the Muslims had been going up all the time the Congress leaders were in Jail. The war had been won and the British no longer had any reason to humour the Mahatma. Finally the talks were adjourned with two announcing to meet again, but they never did. As a senior Communist leader commented, "Gandhi failed to see freedom behind Jinnah's demands and the latter failed to see democracy behind Gandhi's conditions." Where Jinnah was concerned, the League could now claim equal status with the Congress. Cry for 'Pakistan' was gaining momentum by the day. In the words of Chaudhuri Mohammad Ali, "In giving its allegiance to the Pakistan movement, the Muslim community was not merely seeking to escape the domination of the Hindus. What filled the Muslim masses with the urge for action was the desire to recreate a truly

Islamic society in which the justice, the democratic equality, the freedom from want and the devotion to social welfare that had characterised the earliest Muslim community should again prevail". (Chaudhuri Mohammad Ali '*The Emergence of Pakistan*', p 40).

The enhancement of the League's prestige between 1942 and 1945 owed much to the British and the Congress. It is apparent that Gandhi had reconciled to the division of India 'as between members of the same family and therefore reserving for partnership things of common interest'. But Jinnah was not enamoured with either the sentiments expressed by Gandhi, or with his line of argument. He would have nothing short of two nations theory and therefore complete dissolution amounting to full sovereignty in the first instance. He wanted his Pakistan now, before the foreign rulers left India. He said separation must come first and then a treaty would settle matters of common interest between the two states. For tactical reasons, the British recognised the League's claim to speak for Muslims at the all-India level. The Cripps mission had already conceded the right of cession to the Muslim majority provinces, thereby giving some substance to the possibility of Pakistan. Like the British, Congress leaders also gave recognition to the principle of Pakistan in 1942 and 1944, not withstanding Jinnah's 'rather' shaky position in the Muslim majority provinces. They thus undoubtedly gave substance to the demand for Pakistan, and indirectly built up the stature of Jinnah and the League at all-India level because to a common Muslim the idea of a homeland where a Hindu majority wouldn't be guiding his destiny had some kind of a sentimental appeal. But call for Pakistan did not necessarily strengthen the League's hold over provincial Leaguers or Muslim groups, who were often not committed to the sovereign Pakistan of Jinnah's definition, but were interested in provincial power, which they knew would dissipate if Pakistan becomes a reality.

Footnotes

1. F Hutchins '*Spontaneous Revolution*' (Harvard, 1971) p228.
2. Ch Mohammad Ali '*The Emergence of Pakistan*', p40.

14

The Unnatural Divide

Note: Voluminous documentation on the 'transfer of power' released in recent years by the British Government gives a vivid account of happenings during 1946-47. It appears that the majority of Congress leaders, including the 'strong man' Vallabhbhai Patel, were by now reconciled to the idea of partition, and some of them even wished for it as not too bad an idea if the country could be rid of the British. Gandhi and Azad were still hopeful of a rapprochement, but the last Viceroy Lord Mountbatten had seemingly won over Nehru to the idea of partition. He told his foreign biographer, Michael Brecher, "We saw no other way of getting our freedom—in the near future, I mean". For Nehru and Patel and all the Congressmen yearning for the fruits of power, the Carrot Mountbatten dangled before their noses was too delectable to be refused. They gobbled it down, *"The Last Days of the British Rule* by L Mosley p 247)

In 1943 Linlithgow, who had been the Viceroy for a very trying eight years handed over to Archibald Wavell, who had been in Delhi since 1941 as the supreme commander of the allied forces. Churchill had no great opinion of Wavell as a military tactician, and thought he would be more useful as Viceroy than supreme commander. At a cabinet meeting attended by the Viceroy-designate, Churchill showed his utter bias and hatred for Indians when he stated, "Britain owed 800 million pounds sterling to India and that British workmen in rags were struggling to pay rich Indian mill-owners for the privilege of defending them from the Japanese." To Churchill Indians were ungrateful wretches who should be put in their place. Wavell was sent to India with instructions to utter only vague promises of constitutional reforms when the 'war was won.' And for good measure also added, 'over my dead body would any approach to Gandhi take place.' (Before coming to India as Viceroy Wavell had recommended to the British Government to release

Gandhi and Nehru and he be allowed to appoint them as members in his Executive Council. He, in fact, wanted to confer with a select group of Indian leaders including Gandhi, Nehru and Jinnah in order to arrive at a methodology for handing over power to the Indians, but only on a condition that the war must be successfully concluded. Churchill turned down the proposal with utter disdain.)

Wavell arrived back in India on 17th October 1943. According to him, during his informal briefing Linlithgow was dismissive about the famine then raging in Bengal. Linlithgow couldn't care one way or the other if the Indians kept dying of hunger. He also did not believe that any political progress was possible while Gandhi was alive. His conclusion was that the basic problem was the stupidity of the Indians and the dishonesty of the British. In contrast with Linlithgow, within six days of having been sworn as the Viceroy Wavell flew to Calcutta to study the famine and get first hand information about the prevailing situation. He also went to the worst affected districts, and saw for himself the pitiable condition of the destitute wandering around and sleeping in the streets. The sham going on in the name of 'relief operation' annoyed him no end. On return when he asked the Director General of Health to personally visit Bengal that worthy expressed his inability to do so because of some pressing urgency in Simla. The Viceroy, literally, had to order him to leave at once for Calcutta. He also appealed to the prime minister to have special shipments of foodgrain sent to India. In Churchill's own phrase he 'badgered' the prime minister and the British government endlessly for grain shipments. True to form, Churchill remained callously indifferent to the Viceroy's pleas. Wavell got his consignments only when he threatened to resign, provoking Churchill to describe him as 'the greatest failure as a Viceroy that we ever had.'

According to the available records there was enough food available within the country. If the administrative machinery had so wished people could have been fed and the misery of the population could have been minimised. There, apparently, were reasons for the British government to remain indifferent to the Bengal famine. With Bose, his INA and the Japanese having taken hold of Burma there was no way the prime minister was going to help Bengal overcome its misery.

By the end of 1944, Wavell doubted his own capability to persuade India to become a nation. The only method to restore British control was to bring in large number of own people in the Military and the government. This could not be done without damage to the infrastructure back home. Britain neither had resources nor will power for such a task. Save imperial glory there was nothing to be gained by taking recourse to any foolhardy course of action. Then the America's and the world opinion was strongly against holding on to colonies when a great war had been fought in the name of democracy. The King Emperor was still hopeful of retaining control over India, and to fulfil his cherished dream of following his father's example of being crowned on Indian soil as Emperor of India, but even Winston Churchill, the strongest proponent of continuation of Raj had by now given up hope, partly because of the Cripps mission, influence of the press and American antipathy to holding on to countries against their wish. And to hasten matters to their logical conclusion, Churchill lost the elections, Clement Atlee, the new Labour Prime Minister in his very first address to the parliament announced that British must quit India, and sooner the better.

In 1945, when the war ended, Britain was riddled with far too many problems of her own. Wheels of the Raj still creaked around, but had apparently lost almost its entire vigour. The dream of holding on to the Jewel in its crown, that is India, still existed but, in reality, the control had already passed on to Gandhi, Nehru and Jinnah. With the war's end, the promises of Montagu, Irwin, Linlithgow and Cripps had come home to roost. Wavell was already at his tether's end. His administration was too tightly stretched in dealing with the Bengal famine, unrest in certain parts of India over the likely shape of the future government, and such was the rivalry between the Indian National Congress and the minority Muslim League that the practical issue now was how to get out without leaving anarchy behind; the police force had already started showing signs of a 'confused sense of loyalty'. Biggest worry was that of a communal violence that could totally destabilize the country. There was now a sense of urgency because the crumbling administrative framework could not be expected to endure the strains any longer when the 'homeland' itself was in need of urgent reconstruction and revival. The elite Indian Civil Service, which now had more than fifty per cent Indians, was in disarray, bureaucrats were seeing disappearance of the Raj; and, with a view to safeguard their careers and personal interests, were shifting their loyalty to nationalist politicians.

In June 1945, Wavell released all members of the Congress Working Committee still in jail and called a conference at Simla to discuss constitutional change. The conference was doomed to be failure from day one; Congress and League failed to agree on who represented Muslims at the national level. The simplest course would have been to have followed the lines of the war time Cripps offer and allow the Indians to elect a constituent assembly, to which power could be handed over on a specified date. This course unfortunately was not available because of the conflict between the Indian National Congress and the Muslim League. Fully knowing for certain that Jinnah and his League had by now consolidated their hold on Muslim dominated areas, the Congress still refused to admit validity of the Muslim League's popularity among the followers of their religion. Paradoxically, Nehru and Gandhi still regarded this as a temporary effervescence encouraged by the British for the obvious reason of 'Divide and Rule.'

Wavell did try to get Nehru and Jinnah to serve together in a caretaker administration, which would prepare a federal constitution to give Hindus and Muslims self-rule in their own provinces while Defence and Foreign Affairs were reserved for the central government. It seems that the issue of equal representation in the Central Government between Congress and the League, earlier agreed to, at some stage got modified into equality of representation for Hindus and Muslims. Gandhi protested against the provision of parity between 'Caste Hindus' and Muslims in the proposed Council. To him the principle of such parity was an evil when and if accepted in the Centre and cannot be extended to provinces. Congress representatives were instructed to insist during the Conference 'that the party would not accept the right of League to nominate all the Muslim members of the new government, and would nominate individuals belonging to all communities. Wavell agreed that the Congress could nominate Muslims and Scheduled Castes, but said the principle of parity must be maintained'. Bait was thus placed before both organisations. Congress could think that Government would let it have all Hindu and some Muslim seats, and the League could think that it would get all the Muslim seats.

Both organisations failed to see through the British game. Jinnah was concerned that the Muslims would remain in a minority in the new Council because the Scheduled Castes and the Sikhs would always vote with the Hindus. Wavell tried to reassure him, and pointed out that the Viceroy and Commander in Chief would ensure fair play for the Muslims. Jinnah continued to harp on his theme that only the League had a right to nominate all Muslim members to the Council. He also wanted some guarantee that any decision which the Muslims opposed in the Council could only be passed by a two-third majority, meaning thereby that he was seeking some kind of a 'communal veto'. Wavell told him that such a condition was not acceptable to him. Even Maulana Azad's offer that Congress would agree to not nominating a Muslim in fact, but must stress on principle that it could do so, was turned down by the League.[1] Despite intensive negotiations, including a visit by Nehru and Jinnah to London, where they met the King-Emperor, this model of future governance of India did not get approval, either of Jinnah, or Nehru. On 14th July Wavell decided to close the Conference. He couldn't have accepted Jinnah's demand to have Muslim parity with all other parties combined without risking a serious and severe backlash to any such concession to the League.

In Congress eyes, the conference could not have succeeded so long as the British gave 'one party the power to veto all effort'. The Congress Working Committee never learned that the directive not to embarrass Jinnah came from the war cabinet. Gandhi did not deny that Wavell had made an honest attempt to break the political deadlock, but his blunt comment on the Viceroy's ending the conference was that "An honest attempt should have ended honestly."[2] The British Cabinet did discuss Jinnah's claims, had considered those to be unfounded and wrong, but they chose to let him get away with it. The crafty British had once again played on the age-old Hindu-Muslim distrust and animosity so that they could tell the world that Indian disagreement prevented a satisfactory political solution. They could not, therefore, hand over power to a representative Indian Government that was universally acceptable.

Jinnah was by now confident that if he could hold on to his plan a little longer he would get an entirely sovereign Pakistan. He was no more interested in being a perpetual minority in a Hindu dominated India; any sign of weakness on his part at this stage of negotiations would have alienated his followers. He urged Leaguers to 'remove from your mind any idea of loose federation.' "There is no such thing as loose federation," he told them. Continuing, he added, "When there is a central government and provincial governments, they (Central Government) will go on tightening and tightening until you are pulverised with regard to your powers as units" (Pirzada, Documents P 427). Nehru was content to blame just about everybody else, and of course the British for the impasse. He compounded his lack of foresight by telling a press conference, as the Congress President, that Congress was going into the Constituent Assembly without any prior or compulsive commitment to any group or organisation. The Constituent Assembly was, in any case, to function as a body unfettered by previous understandings between various groups and combinations. This innocuous statement of Nehru gave Jinnah the reason he was looking for to reassert his authority on the Muslims and to back out of the agreements made earlier, he could now claim that the Congress would bulldoze through the proceedings because of its 'Hindu' majority. One could, if so inclined, find some satisfaction from the fact that Jinnah, now riding on a fanatic wave, had hardened his stand so as to part ways with a Hindu majority India, but responsibility for what was happening was not his alone. There was Sapru Committee, which consisted of eminent men unconnected with the Congress or with the Muslim League, seeking solution to end the deadlock between the Congress and the League. The Committee's recommendations and Sapru's own view emphasise the fact that those outside the Congress and the Muslim League recognised that the fears of the Muslim community about its future in a free and United India were genuine, and that it was necessary to enact effective constitutional provisions which would allay those fears if the unity of India was to be preserved. The Muslim leadership felt that the British had effectively dislodged the Mughals when they took control of the country. Now that they were leaving, in their opinion it was only natural that the Muslims either had a country of their own or had constitutional safeguards where their interests were concerned once the British left India. A sense of exclusion and even persecution drove the Muslims away from any unitary solution. Hindu leaders paid little heed to the developing communal animosity. The situation allowed Jinnah to adopt an un-cooperative and non-conciliatory stand over the issue of a Muslim homeland. Hindu leadership did nothing to counter this argument. The Congress High Command, with Nehru giving the lead, was arrogant and lived in a world of make-believe and was not prepared to face reality of the situation. Somehow the Congressmen always gave the impression (particularly to the Muslims) that the Hindus being in majority were the rightful heirs of the Raj: and this trait eventually convinced the Muslims that they would always be a permanent minority in a Hindu India. Muslims thought that since the Mughals had lost the empire to the British it should legitimately revert to them. Obviously, there was enough ground for the mischief-makers on both sides to keep the flames of communal hatred alive. What was worse Jinnah was also by now convinced that he could retain and sustain the leadership of the Muslims only if he could convince the common co-religionist that he was the only one who could make Islamic aspirations become a reality. His following was growing by the day: barring Azad, CR, or some lower level congressmen, everyone of them failed to see the direction in which the political wind in the country had started blowing.

The Elections of 1945-46

Notwithstanding the turmoil in the country, the government decided to go ahead with the elections to the Central Legislative Assembly and various states. What added a sense of urgency was the return of the members of the Indian National Army—who had laid down their arms when Japan surrendered—were repatriated to India. They were welcomed as heroes. In order to set an example, the British military authorities decided in November 1945, to bring to trial three of their senior officers, a Hindu, a Sikh and a Muslim before a military court, which assembled in the Red Fort—a symbol of power and government's authority. Unwittingly, the government provided the people to come together with a fervent zeal to resent the presence of the British and this effort to punish those who had clearly been fighting for the freedom of the country. This historic trial is a subject of study and research in itself. Sir Tej Bahadur Sapru, the eminent parliamentarian Bhulabhai Desai and Jawaharlal Nehru himself, who donned his robe and wig for the occasion, and perhaps for the first time as a professional lawyer, defended the three accused. Jinnah did not offer his services, but the League joined the outcry against the trials because the Muslims formed a fairly large segment of the INA prisoners. Nehru had never supported the INA, and before the end of the war with Japan had declared, in Calcutta, that he would oppose Bose even at the head of his army. Never before any event had captured the imagination of Indians regardless of colour, creed or religion. How could Nehru possibly fail to seize this opportunity for political advancement of his own? And that of his party. The politicians were finding the issue as a godsend to rally people around against the British. It soon became difficult to differentiate between an INA rally and an election meeting.

The rallies often turned violent as the protesters became more and more restive due to lack of any positive response from the government. In Calcutta, where people felt to be closer to the INA cars, buses and lorries were set on fire, streets were blocked, trains stopped by the crowds, and there were pitched battles between police and the protesters. By the time some kind of order was restored by the army 33 people had been killed and more than 200 injured. Seventy British and 37 American soldiers were also injured and over 150 police and military vehicles were destroyed. The public reaction totally surprised the British, by now they were realising the seriousness of the mistake in putting INA officers on a public trial. By putting a Hindu, a Muslim and a Sikh on trial, the British had unified all three communities against the Raj. 'Quit India' slogans began to appear on the walls in all major towns and cities, pamphlets and posters proclaiming the INA men as 'Patriots and not Traitors' circulated widely. Agitation gained momentum all over the country with students, Sikh taxi-drivers and just about everybody joining the protest rallies. The British were horrified. Senior officials now recommended that it would be wise to hold the trials in some remote corner of the country. The Red Fort, they pointed out, was far too closely linked to the earlier eras and the revolt of 1857. But Auchinleck, who had replaced Wavell, as the Commander in Chief after the latter's elevation as the Viceroy, was of the same soldierly breed as his predecessor. He refused to stoop to subterfuge in any shape and form, regardless of the consequences of an action, which he thought to be morally and legally right. 'Once it had been decided that the trials could not be held in secret,' he wrote later, 'it would have been wrong to tuck them away somewhere where defence counsel, relations, etc, could not conveniently attend, and the Red Fort was the most convenient place from nearly every point of view.'

For a while, political controversies over the issue of trial continued to rage. Sir George Cunningham, the Governor of NWFP reported to the Viceroy that 'every day that passes now brings over more and more well-disposed Indians to the anti-British camp'. He recommended that the trial be abandoned because the issue had now become 'purely an Indian verses British affair. Nationalistic frenzy soon spread to the armed forces. At several air bases, the staff refused to carry out orders. The army remained loyal for immediate purposes but the Royal Navy, which had been established during the War, mutinied in February 1946 simultaneously in Bombay and Karachi because of the poor quality of their rations and, more importantly, against the racist posture of their officers. Vallabhbhai Patel went to defuse the situation; he succeeded in doing so; or else there would have been far too many casualties. The government in London was shaken by these events, but Wavell elected to proceed ahead with the trial. Harsh sentences were handed down to all the three officers on trial; which were later commuted.

Elections were held in three phases: in December 1945 to the Central Legislative Assembly, in February 1946 in four provinces; Assam, Sind, the NWFP, Punjab, and finally in the provinces of Bihar, UP, Bombay, Madras, the Central Provinces and Orissa. The anti-British unity shown by the Indians during the INA trial soon evaporated into usual communal disputes and rioting, especially in Punjab and Bengal. Both, the Congress and the League improved their respective positions in the Central Legislative Assembly, Hindu Nationalist Party was completely wiped out. From ten seats in 1934 it failed to win even one seat in this latest round. The Congress and the League had received full support of their respective electoral colleges. It was a clear sign of polarisation on communal lines. That the division of the two communities was complete was confirmed when the results of provincial elections came out. With 930 seats the Congress obtained majority in eight provinces, including Assam and the NWFP where the proportion of Hindus was relatively small but the influence of Abdul Gaffar Khan, better known as the Frontier Gandhi, had its impact in turning the voters against the League in the NWFP.

Nevertheless, the League had given a crushing blow to the Muslim candidates put up by the Congress. The results proved that the Muslim League dominated the Muslims as completely as the Congress dominated the Hindus. This was so because Jinnah had declared in advance that Pakistan was at stake in these elections. The election campaign was fought by the Congress on the issue of Indian unity and by the Muslim League on the issue of Pakistan, and more importantly, the right of the

League solely to represent Muslims. The results should have acted as an eye-opener to some of our leaders who would not believe that Jinnah had acquired complete hold over the Muslim masses. After all, Gandhi had elected to have long drawn discussions with Jinnah only as the representative of the Muslims, his stock had started going high after that failed parley. The polarisation these elections had manifested made the administration more and more difficult. The more Jinnah pressed his demand for Pakistan, the greater was the friction between communities. But the League had failed to secure majority in Punjab and Bengal, without which there could be no Pakistan. The League had made spectacular breakthroughs in these two states, primarily at the expense of "Confederation or the Unionists" lobby. Its appeal in the name of Islam and the Quaid-i-Azam had started bearing fruits.

Ignoring all the bickering between Hindu and Muslim leaders, Wavell set about the task of setting up a constitution-making body in consultation with the newly elected provincial assemblies. He also wanted to form a new Executive Council based on party lines. But London upset all his plans. Apparently shaken by the Royal Indian Navy mutiny and other acts of mass violence a conciliatory gesture was needed to placate Indian opinion. The Attlee government, aware of the worsening situation in India, particularly in the light of INA trials decided to send a Cabinet Mission for an on the spot study of the situation; and to make recommendations for smooth transfer of power. Unlike last time when Cripps had come to win Indian support for the war effort, the war had since been won; now the Mission's mandate was to 'discuss and explore all possible alternatives without proceeding on any fixed or rigid pre-conceived plan'. Cripps, by now an old hand at Indian affairs, along with Pethick-Lawrence and A V Alexander, who was the First Lord of the Admiralty when Churchill was the prime minister, constituted this Cabinet Mission. By sending no fewer than three of his senior colleagues to India when their services were urgently required for reconstruction and rehabilitation of a war-weary nation Attlee was establishing credentials of his government in resolving the Indian issue with all earnestness. During the parliamentary debate, which preceded the dispatch of mission, Attlee had declared, "We are very mindful of the rights of the minorities and minorities should be able to live free from fear. On the other hand, we cannot allow a minority to place a veto on the advance of the majority." To which Jinnah retorted immediately by saying that the Muslims were not a minority but a nation.

Cabinet Mission to India

Before the Mission arrived, Wavell made serious effort to bring some kind of sensibility in the Indian leaders. Drawing inspiration from the

Americans he put across the ideas of George Washington and Madison while making a broadcast to the nation on the Cabinet Mission Plan. Wavell said, "No constitution and no form of Government can work satisfactorily without goodwill and determination to succeed even an apparently illogical arrangement can be made to work. In the complex situation that faces us today there are four main parties: the British; the two main parties in British India, Hindus and Muslims; and the Indian States. From all of them change in their present attitude and outlook will be required as a contribution to the general good, if this great experiment is to succeed. To make concessions in ideas and principles is a hard thing and not easily palatable. It requires some greatness of mind to recognise the necessity, much greatness of spirit to make the concession. I am sure this will not be found wanting in India, as I think you will admit that it has not been found wanting in the British people in this offer." (*Transfer of Power*, Vol. VII pp. 611-613)

The Mission, under Lord Pethick-Lawrence came in March 1946 and spent over three months confabulating with different leaders but it did not meet with any great success in making them agree on the basic issues of the type of structure the country should have after the British left. The Cabinet Mission did make a promising start when it started meeting Indian leaders separately so as to get a first hand feel of the political situation. Cripps met Jinnah privately on 30th March and found him to be totally firm on his demand for Pakistan. Nehru was away touring Malaya; Cripps and Pethick-Lawrence had invited Gandhi to come to Delhi so that they could talk and ascertain his views on the issues involved before a formal presentation before the Mission.

Azad, who was the Congress President, presented his Party's opinion based on the notes that Nehru had prepared before leaving for Singapore. Cripps advised him to evolve his own ideas in addition to those of Nehru so that the Mission could get a total perspective of the Congress Party on the issue of Pakistan. In consultation with Gandhi and Working Committee Azad issued a lengthy public statement, setting out his personal objections to the idea of Pakistan, and outlining his and his Party's proposed solution. Totally negating Jinnah's two-nation theory, projecting formation of Pakistan as harmful to the Muslim interests, terming the whole idea even un-Islamic, Azad made a forceful plea for unity. "I am one of those who considers the present chapter of communal bitterness and differences as a transient phase in Indian life. I firmly hold that they will disappear when India assumes the responsibility for her own destiny...Differences will no doubt persist, but they will be economic and not communal. Class and not community will be the basis of future alignments...90 million of Muslims constitute a factor which nobody can ignore and whatever the circumstances, they are strong enough to safeguard their own destiny."

Azad, as President of Congress, held the view that to concede Pakistan was a defeatist policy. He forwarded, what he called a rough outline plan of action, for consideration of Gandhi and other Congress leaders on the following lines:

- The future Constitution of India must be federal, in which Central subjects only of an all-India nature are agreed upon by the constituent units.

- The units must be given the right to secede.

- There must be joint electorates in the Centre and in the Provinces with reservation of seats.

- There must be parity of Hindu and Muslims in the Central Legislature and the Central Executive till such time as communal suspicions disappear and parties are formed on economic and political lines.

Gandhi rejected these proposals out of hand. He, in fact, advised Azad to keep quiet on the subject of Hindu-Muslim parity. Efforts to ease Azad out of his presidential chair under the able guidance of the Mahatma started in right earnest (*Transfer of Power*, Vol. VI pp 155-157)

On 16th April the Mission met Jinnah again, informing him that the Pakistan that he envisioned is not acceptable to the other party. Jinnah was categorically told that he could not reasonably hope to receive both the whole of territory, much of it inhabited by non-Muslims, which he claimed and the full measure of sovereignty, which he said was essential. He was then asked if he was willing to accept the scheme, which envisaged an Indian Union consisting of three principal parts—the Hindu majority provinces, the Muslim majority provinces, and the Indian States. In this scheme the Union Government was to control such subjects as Defence, Foreign Affairs and Communications. Characteristically, Jinnah said that the Congress should make a statement first and indicate its stand on this line of action. 'Clearly, Jinnah was playing this game as a lawyer who wanted to score a triumph in a legal negotiation totally unmindful of the life and death of millions of Indians it involved:' Alexander, the only non-lawyer of the three ministers and the most sympathetic to the League, wrote in his diary that night. Alexander was absolutely right in his analysis. All along Jinnah had been telling his friends that he was a lawyer and not a politician; all that he was doing was advocating on behalf of the Muslims, fighting their fight, and his whole life revolved around winning whatever case he was fighting. Now with the most important case of his life nearing its conclusion, he could not allow himself to weaken—any concession made now without knowing what the opposition had to offer in return—would give away his bargaining strength. Trouble was that the opposition also had well qualified and adequately competent lawyers pleading its case. A deadlock was always going to be a certainty.

To make matters worse, Gandhi started feeling that the initiatives taken by Azad to resolve the impasse by propagating a three-tier system, with Muslims and non-Muslims provinces forming their own sub-federation, each with its own legislature, and a loose federal government at the centre; were not in line with the thinking of the Congress Party, and were more in tune with Jinnah's demands. Gandhi asked Azad to relinquish his presidentship of the Party. Azad agreed to do so and exercised his right to nominate Nehru as his successor who had been more sympathetic to the Azad Plan rather than Patel, who took a far more 'hard line' Hindu attitude where unity of India was concerned. Patel threatened to contest this succession but Gandhi prevailed upon him to let Nehru take over as the Party president. Gandhi, in any case, had anointed Nehru as his 'heir apparent' a long time back during Wardha meeting of the All India Congress Committee in January 1942. Azad continued to lead the negotiations while the Cabinet mission was in India. Tired of the entire goings on and with the Mission not reaching any understanding with either of the parties, and the stifling heat of Delhi not improving the atmosphere, the Mission decided to move to Simla where they were going to hold a Conference with the national leaders in order to arrive at a workable solution.

Both the rivals, Congress and the League, were also advised to send their representatives to Simla so that finer modalities could be worked out. The talks were due to begin on 2nd May, but Jinnah did not fetch up for three days, claiming to be busy with his work at Delhi. Finally when he did arrive along with his entourage, Jinnah refused to shake hands with Azad or Gaffar Khan, whom he had been castigating as 'Congress show-boys' and traitors to the Muslim cause.

Talks, finally, got under way on the 5th of May, but the impasse remained on all the key issues. Should there be a central legislature and if so what should its powers and responsibilities be? Should provinces be allowed to form themselves into groups, and if so should those groups have their own legislatures? Should the constitution-making body be set up before or after a decision on groupings, and therefore on Pakistan? Should there be one constitution-making body or two—one for Hindustan and one for Pakistan? Should the League be given parity with Congress in any interim government? Round and round they went, in ever-decreasing circles, getting nowhere. Ultimately, Jinnah showed the first signs of conceding an important point. He intimated that given enough safeguards he might be prepared to consider accepting groupings of autonomous provinces within a loose union. But Gandhi and Patel were not willing to concede even this. Nehru told the Mission that the Congress was going to work for a strong Centre and to break the Group system and they would succeed. He did not think that Mr. Jinnah had any real place in the country. The Muslim League and the Congress each represented entirely different outlook on the working of the Constitution-making body and they were bound to have strong differences in the Interim Government. (*Transfer of Power* Vol. VII, p 855)

Pethick-Lawrence had no choice but to admit failure of his attempts and closed the Simla conference. The Mission finally made a unilateral declaration about the future course of action on 16th May 1946. Inter alia, it was stipulated that in their scheme of things Britain would transfer power at the end of a transition period, which would be required for drafting the constitution of the Indian Union. During this period an interim government presided over by the Viceroy and made up of fourteen members, all Indians, representing the main communities, would rule India. To prevent any one party from overshadowing the others the mission took care to specify in a declaration, that the composition of the interim government would not prejudge the final set-up nor serve as a precedent. Lastly, it also declared that in case one of the parties felt it should not participate in the interim government, the Viceroy would proceed nonetheless to form a government "which will be as representative as possible of those willing to accept this plan of action." Wavell had already told Nehru that Britain could not hand over power to central legislature with a Hindu majority, without safeguards for the Muslims. He felt that such a move would not lead to the united India, which he assumed both, Nehru and Jinnah, wanted.

The Cabinet Mission's plan was structured around four propositions:

- A Union of India would be set up, restricted to three main functions; foreign affairs, defence and communications, as well as the authority to raise corresponding financial resources. The Union would be made up of an executive and a legislature composed by the representatives of British India and the princely states. The eleven provincial governments, grouped so that predominantly Hindu and Muslim areas could enjoy virtual self-government, would control everything else.

- All subjects other than the Union subjects and all residuary powers will vest in the provinces.

- The constituents or delegates, elected by the legislative assemblies of the provinces on the one hand, nominated by the princes on the other, would meet in a preliminary session to appoint their chairman and decide on their rules of procedure, after which they would divide up into three sections constituted in a manner that allowed representation to all the states and princely states depending on their size and population profile. To ensure uniform representation the plan clubbed together Muslim majority states in the north under one section, Bengal, Assam, Princely states and British India were also put together in one group. The groups were to be divided into sections. Section A was to consist of the Provinces of Madras, Bombay, United Provinces, Bihar, Central Provinces and Orissa in which the Hindus had an overwhelming majority. Section B was to consist of Punjab, North-West Frontier Provinces and Sind in which the Muslims had a majority of about 62:38. Section C consisted of the Provinces of Bengal and Assam, in which Muslims had a majority of 52 to 48.

- Any province, which disliked the arrangements, could opt out after ten years, provided sixty per cent of the population voted to do so in a plebiscite. This percentage was probably fixed in order to ensure that Hindu and Sikh votes were likely to turn the verdict against Pakistan.

Essentially, the proposed plan was similar to the 'three-tier' structure that Azad had been propagating. Pethick-Lawrence's apparent attempt at keeping all options open disclosed his desire to avoid taking stand on any issue. Shorn of legalese, the Cabinet Plan rejected the formation of Pakistan and proposed a federation of provinces and states possessing a greater autonomy than under the terms of the 1935 Act. Resolutely co-federal, the proposed Union could move either towards a gradual separation or develop into a more unified federation.

In principle, the Mission was giving the Muslims the benefits of Pakistan whilst avoiding its defects and drawbacks. Although the Cabinet Mission rejected Pakistan, the Mission was clear that mere paper safeguards were enough to alley the fears of Muslims in a "Hindu Raj"; and safeguards had to be provided to alley those fears. The power of Sections to form their Constitution by a majority came near to securing parity between Hindus and Muslims in their respective Sections. Everyone knew that the British meant business, but nobody liked the plan. Congress wanted to secure a strong centre before the autonomous provinces went on their possibly separate ways, while Jinnah was disappointed that it ruled out an independent Muslim state. The Sikhs, for their part, expressed alarm at being incorporated into a Muslim-ruled province.

Jinnah did not reject the plan out of hand but expressed an opinion that formation of Pakistan was the only lasting solution; wily politician that he was he left the final decision to the League Council: knowing fully well that at that point of time he was "the League", and his opinion on the subject, well known as it was, would prevail. Jinnah was keen on retaining unity of India but he also wanted an escape route if the Muslims found themselves stifled in any future dispensation. He reportedly told the Muslim League council that the Plan conceded the substance of Pakistan and provided machinery for achieving a fully sovereign state in ten years. Since defence was to remain in British hands until the new constitution was enforced, he clearly envisaged a long drawn out process of constitution making, a British presence until it was complete, and the British enforcement of their interpretation of the Mission Plan. On 6th June 1946 the Council of Muslim League passed the following resolution:

"... It is for these reasons that the Muslim League is accepting the scheme, and will join the Constitution making Body, and it will keep in view the opportunity and right to cession of Provinces or groups from the Union, which have been provided in the Mission's Plan by implication...The Muslim League also reserves the right to modify and revise the policy and attitude set forth in this resolution at any time during the progress of the deliberations of the Constitution-making body or the Constituent Assembly, or thereafter if the course of events so require, bearing in mind the federal principles and ideals here before adumbrated, to which the Muslim League is irrevocably committed." (*Transfer of Power* Vol. VII p 838)

It is hard to visualise how Nehru and the Congress would have ever agreed on the British having the last word on the constitution. Jinnah was sure that the Congress would not accept the 'grouping' of states in a manner that diluted its hold on the granary of the country-meaning Punjab, and on the princely states along with natural reserves of Bengal and Assam. The Congress under Nehru's leadership was in favour of a powerful centre. In its view, this was the only way to maintain the unity of the country, improve the condition of the masses and develop economically. Jinnah was proved right in his assessment of the Congress response. To further add to the confusion, Gandhi refused to accept the Cabinet Mission proposing the composition of an interim government. A stalemate had been reached: Exhausted, the Cabinet Mission left for London on 29th June 1946, leaving behind a Viceroy saddled with the responsibility of saving the Plan and forming an interim government when the main protagonists were in total disagreement with each other. The Congress opposition to parity and the Congress demands for the status of a Dominion Cabinet produced a result, which the Congress neither desired nor expected. This foolhardiness destroyed unity of India.

The Plan could have worked successfully retaining India's unity only if Nehru and the Congress had shown goodwill towards Jinnah and the Muslim League, giving Jinnah something that he could take to his followers as a solution of their apprehensions of a Hindu-dominated India. But it also meant sharing power with the League, something that was not acceptable to Nehru. Even earlier, on 3rd November 1945 in an interview with Viceroy, Nehru had said: "The Congress could make no terms whatever with the Muslim League under its present leadership and policy, that it was a reactionary body with entirely unacceptable ideas with which there could be no settlement." (Penderel Moon—Viceroy's Journal p 180). In spite of the fact that the League won all the thirty seats reserved for Muslims and had polled 86.6 per cent of the total votes cast in the Muslim constituencies during the December 1945 elections, Nehru remained as adamant as ever to grant Jinnah his appropriate status. He never let any opportunity slip where he could deride Jinnah or the League.

The Congress leaders had to get their stand on the Mission ratified by the All India Congress Committee, which assembled in Bombay on 7th July and was presided over by Nehru, who had been elected as the president of the party only recently on specific insistence of Gandhi. In the usual course of things the Party president would have become the Prime Minister of India when the British finally left, and Gandhi had already anointed Nehru as his heir-apparent way back in 1942; so nobody else was allowed to come up to take up the Party's leadership. If Rajagopalachari or Sardar Patel had been the Party president in 1946 what course the history and geography of India would have taken has been a matter of debate among the commoners as well as the intellectuals. But Nehru's contribution in pushing the country towards partition has hardly ever been doubted: During the debates, he did not conceal his opposition to the constraints imposed by the Plan on the future Constituent Assembly, i.e. to the groupings of the provinces. He gave the widest possible publicity to his opinions on the issue when during a press conference that he held on 10th July 1946, he said: "that by accepting to take part in the Constituent Assembly the Congress did not necessarily give its consent to the procedure of accession, i.e. to the election of the delegates, "what we do there," he declared, "we are entirely and absolutely free to decide." He made no bones about his reservations about the grouping of the provinces. He also declared that regarding the minorities the Congress would accept no outside interference, certainly not of the British. He envisaged a much more powerful central government than the one contemplated. Congress, he concluded, regarded itself as free to change or modify the Cabinet mission's plan exactly as it pleased.

Gandhi added his bit to the confusion over the Congress stand on the issue of grouping by saying, "I regard the Constituent Assembly as the substitute of Satyagraha. It is a constructive Satyagraha." Apparently, both Nehru and Gandhi had agreed to enter the Constituent Assembly to fight the battle of 'Grouping' and had planned to have issues resolved their way, something that they couldn't get from the Cabinet Mission.

Naturally, there was consternation in the Muslim League camp; the League felt that the rights and benefits promised to the Muslims under the Cabinet Mission Plan were in jeopardy due to this altered stand of the Congress. Jinnah accused the Cabinet Mission of having played into the hands of the Congress, which got a Constituent Assembly under false pretence. He was sure that the Congress would utilise its absolute majority in order to annul all the advantages that the League had obtained under the Cabinet Mission. He never had any faith in either Gandhi or Nehru and he was being proved right by, what he called 'breech of trust' by Nehru when things were moving towards a workable solution to the massive problems facing the country. He was not the only one to have this feeling.

Just about every senior (and sensible) Congress leader was also critical of these utterances of Nehru. Patel was most vocal. He said, "He, that is, Nehru has done many things recently which have caused us great deal of embarrassment. His actions, including his press conference, immediately after the AICC, are all acts of emotional insanity."[3] All the Party leaders agreed with this assessment made by the Sardar. It was a moment in history when circumspection and discretion in making public utterances should have been the order of the day. A leader who was reckoned to be the future prime minister of India should have known that there was much to be gained by silence or at least in not making speeches that could easily be construed as a deliberate effort to renege. The fortunes of the country were in the balance, and one false or indiscrete move could upset them. Nehru chose this moment to launch into what his biographer, Michael Brecher, has described as 'one of his more fiery and provocative statements in his forty years of public life. Nehru certainly did not realise that he was telling the world that once in power the Congress would use its strength at the Centre to alter the Cabinet Mission Plan as it thought fit, notwithstanding the fact that both the Congress and the League had accepted the Plan as a cut and dried scheme not open to alterations by either party. In one stroke Nehru had set in motion wheels that would destroy India, an India the British had so laboriously united into one entity taking over a hundred years in doing so. "Unfortunately, at this critical moment, when a peaceful settlement of the future was almost within sight, it was upset by some indiscreet utterances of Pandit J L Nehru", was the usual refrain.

Nehru's freedom from communal prejudices was, of course, transparent and never doubted even by his enemies. Once Sardar Patel quipped, with somewhat malicious wit, that Jawaharlal was "the only genuine nationalist Muslim in India." Nehru resented those who were busy bringing in religious sentiments into national affairs. Those from the Hindu dominated parties were not very happy with his stand on the issue. But he failed to see that 'religion' was the only weapon left with Jinnah who also nursed prime-ministerial ambitions.

Maulana Azad was also upset with the statement of the Party president; he had worked really hard on arriving at all the compromises with the League. (He recorded in his diary, "Jawaharlal's mistake in 1937 had been bad enough. His mistake of 1946 proved even more costly."(-*India Wins Freedom*, p 162 of the revised edition published after thirty years of the first edition). (Note: In 1937, Nehru had rejected the suggestion of a coalition on the theoretical ground that a Cabinet must be homogenous and that no Muslim should be admitted into the Cabinet unless he joined the Congress Party. It is now universally accepted that this penchant for theoretical as opposed to practical considerations, led, in about ten years, to the partition of India.) Clearly, the assumption of the Congress President ship by Nehru in 1946 was not in the best interests of the country. Historians who are favourably inclined towards Nehru have tried to exonerate him of the sins of impudence or lack of restraint. It is true that his remarks in public did not contradict the stand taken by the AICC, but by airing them in Public and at his level as the Party president he had given enough cause to Jinnah and the League to feel uncertain in any future dispensation where the Muslims would be in a minority; may be if Nehru had been a little circumspect Jinnah wouldn't have got the handle to negate the Plan without being blamed for the break up of the country.

Azad had a practical and constructive approach to the sensitive issues involved. As a nationalist Muslim, he was prepared to admit, what his Hindu colleagues in the Congress were not willing to recognise or to admit, that the fears of Muslims about their fate in a free and united India were genuine. He could foresee the ramifications of Nehru's stand. He called for a special session of the Working Committee, which met on 8th August. Azad highlighted the consequences of the Party president's 'thoughtless' speech. He wanted the Working Committee to issue a statement saying that the All India Congress Committee stood by its original resolution; and that no individual, not even the Congress president could change it. The Working Committee was now faced with a dilemma. To repudiate the Party president would lower his prestige; and to allow the stand taken by him to be official would mean reneging on the

Cabinet Mission Plan, which could create all kinds of complications. The Committee finally passed a resolution expressing its genuine regret that League had decided not to participate in the Constituent Assembly, carefully avoiding to make any mention of what had led to this sorry state. The resolution also pointed out that neither the Working Committee nor the All India Congress Committee ever objected to the principle of grouping, their objection was confined to the short point—whether a province can be forced to be part of a particular group against its will? Jinnah was not mollified with these half-baked overtures. He stuck to his view that Nehru's statement and Gandhi's virtual endorsement implied that the moment the British left the country, the Hindu-dominated Constituent Assembly would do away with all that the Cabinet Mission had promised to the Muslims by manipulating the 'grouping' of the provinces, and thus deny the minorities any visage of protection.

Jinnah had not yet rejected the Plan, and with Congress expressing its reservations with the Party president being mindlessly vocal on the issue where it concerned validity of Jinnah's leadership of his community he stressed that the Viceroy should now proceed to form the 'interim government' with only those who had accepted the long term Plan without reservations. He had already extracted a promise from Wavell that if the League accepted the proposed plan and the Congress did not, then the Viceroy would invite the League to form a government. Based on this premise the League members had already given their 'go-ahead' to Jinnah, who now started badgering the Viceroy to stand by his commitment. Trouble was that the British could not have sidelined Congress at that point of time: in order to avoid offending Nehru and Gandhi the government dilly-dallied; and in the process the British destroyed whatever little faith Jinnah had in the 'so-called British fair play'. Jinnah felt let down. Sulking over this obvious partisanship of the Imperial government Jinnah took the decision to break off all talks, and wrote to Attlee about the partisan attitude of the delegation, saying that the happenings have shaken the confidence of the Muslims, and shattered their hopes for an honourable and peaceful settlement and was therefore no longer interested in continuing with on going negotiations. He had no other option; else the charged up members of the League would have abandoned him in no time. That he could get the Muslims their own homeland was his only USP. Nehru and his uttering had given him reason to abandon unitary aspirations he had been nurturing during the earlier phases of the freedom struggle. In any case, Muslims in Punjab and Bengal were by now seeing their dominant status returning in the regions after a gap of almost two hundred years, and they were in no mood to let any political manipulation deprive them of the 'glorious future,' which was expected to bring back the helicon days of the

'Mughal Empire'. On 27th July the League finally rejected the Cabinet Mission's May Plan. The stage was now set for break up of the country.

(Note: The large number of official documents leave no doubt that the Congress was not interested in working the Plan in the spirit in which it was intended to be worked. Its opposition to parity and its demand for a Dominion Cabinet, if granted, would have enabled the Congress to get hold of real power over the Government of India as well as over Provincial Governments, and thereby settling the Hindu-Muslim issue on its own terms. This was never going to be acceptable to Jinnah and the League. Of course, in allowing the Congress to persist in its rigid stand Cripps and Pethick-Lawrence played a major role when they were seen to be regularly hobnobbing with Gandhi, Nehru and Patel while not giving same importance to Jinnah. Both these gentlemen were great fans of Gandhi. At the formal meeting, Wavell was 'horrified at the deference shown' to Gandhi by Pethick-Lawrence and Cripps. 'They stood up when he entered, and when Gandhi wanted a glass of water the secretary to the Mission was sent to fetch the same instead of sending for a peon; on there being some delay, Cripps himself rushed off to see about it,' Wavell wrote later.) In spite of all the courtesies and deference shown to Gandhi, neither Cripps nor Pethick-Lawrence could make him shift his stand on the issue of Pakistan, which he termed was 'an untruth', and 'a sin'. Gandhi reiterated his belief that the two-nation theory was dangerous. Sticking to his demand of independence first; with the constitution to be drawn later, he demanded an 'absolutely national government immediately, even if it meant asking Jinnah to lead it: and if he does not accept the offer then let the Congress form a Government.' There is little doubt that Gandhi was asking the Viceroy to stop seeking agreement between Congress and the Muslim League and to hand over power to Congress, but instead of saying so straightforwardly, he gave it the moral wrapping of mentioning the Muslim League first.

Britain had emerged victorious from the war, but its power was greatly reduced during those six years, both in terms of trained manpower and financial resources. It was no longer in a position to rule India and all the concerned parties knew it. Any threat of a 'direct action' by Congress would have posed a serious threat to the Government, to top it all the British Government was in no position to alienate Congress. The end of the World War two and emergence of a strong and solid 'Communist block' had changed power equation in the world. 'Cold War' that had set in between America and her Allies—especially Britain—on one side; and Soviet Russia and its satellites on the other; had both the Americans and the British worried. India was a major area of trade and investment, and a large contributor to the costs of imperial defence.

It was a fair field for the employment of British civil and military officers. In mid 1946 the Labour Cabinet resolved that in the context of the cold war it must retain imperial control over India. Those British leaders, who had hithertofore been egging Jinnah along to persist with his demand for an independent 'Muslim Homeland' so that they could prolong their stay in India, even while on the surface professing for India to remain united were now suddenly getting jittery. Their worries were valid. Strategically, Attlee, and his American counterparts were strongly of the opinion that a divided India would provide only a weak defence against Russian ambitions in the region, particularly when the Indians were not likely to allow retention of British Military bases on their soil after independence. Nehru was already showing signs of his growing fondness for a 'Socialist' India after the British left. India's two most vulnerable frontiers had always been the northwest and the northeast, the routes taken by invaders since time immemorial. In case Pakistan came through both these routes would be in that country, which Pakistan could not defend without active cooperation of India, or material help from the Western Bloc. They also had to bear in mind that in any future war they should be in a position to have recourse to India's industrial and manpower potential and to use its territory for operational and administrative bases. It was, therefore, necessary that there should be coordinated machinery for defence of geographical India, and that there should be a common defence authority with whom His Majesty's Government could deal. For them a Congress government for all India was the preferred option because the party was most likely to retain its membership of 'Commonwealth', thereby allowing Britain to preserve its supremacy in the region.

Trouble was, that they also knew that Muslims were not likely to accept independence under a Hindu-dominated Congress. So, in their view the option was for either Britain to hang onto India till some kind of settlement had been arrived between the two antagonists or hand over power to the most vociferous party. Both solutions were obviously unworkable in the given circumstances. This assessment was proved to be correct when Cripps received a letter from Gandhi castigating the Commission for even having thought of putting British troops in India. The Mahatma wrote, "I would put on record my conviction that Independence in fact would be a farce, if the British Troops are in India even for peace and order within or danger from without...If the position about the Troops persists, 'Independence next month' is either insincere or a thoughtless cry. Acceptance of 'Quit India' by the British is unconditional, whether the Constituent Assembly succeeds or fails...As to the Interim Government, the more I think and observe, the more certain is my feeling that a proper National Government responsible in fact if not in law, to the elected members of the Central Legislative Assembly should precede the summons for the election of members of the Constituent Assembly.[4] To say that both, the Viceroy and the members of the Commission were shaken on receipt of this letter would be an understatement. Alexander was convinced that Gandhi not only wanted to humiliate the British Government but also wanted to secure power without a constitution coming into being and so as to abandon the just fears and claims of the Muslim League. Wavell agreed with him; and both of them wanted to send an equally terse reply; telling Gandhi 'he had to take it or leave it' on the Plan. However, they agreed with Cripps to send a more reasoned reply which Cripps had drafted, reaffirming that independence must follow not precede the coming into operation of the new Constitution, and the paramount status of the Empire must remain until independence. Gandhi dismissed the Mission's letter as another example of the imperialistic notions of the British.

Two days after the Muslim League had passed a resolution withdrawing its acceptance of the Plan, Wavell pressed Nehru to give an assurance to the Muslim League about grouping as intended by the Plan. Nehru told him that if the Congress had reservations about certain clauses of the Plan so did the Muslim League. The Viceroy pointed out that the League's reservations were 'long term' on a possible Pakistan a number of years ahead, whereas the Congress reservations were short term affecting the immediate future of the country. Wavell's arguments, persuasions and even oblique threats cut no ice with either Nehru or Gandhi. In their scheme of things Jinnah was irrelevant to the country's future. Why these two refused to see the harm that their stand would do to the unity of India continues to remain an enigma: unless of course, one agrees with the theory that Congress could remain a dominant force only when Punjab and Bengal were divided.

Jinnah now faced an unpalatable choice. Muslims could remain in a weakly federated Indian union under the domination of Congress, or a partition of the sub-continent could be pressed for. He was by now totally convinced that Islam constituted a sufficient basis for separate nationhood; that British India actually comprised two nations whose destiny could not be attained except as independent of both Britain and each other. Having warmed up to this view he now flung himself energetically into attaining Pakistan for the Muslims. By now just about every Muslim leader was convinced that formation of Pakistan was only a matter of time. Too much communal tension, fear and hatred had been built amongst all the protagonists. It was now turning into a situation where holding of nerves and not blinking first was going to decide who wins. Till the very last Jinnah continued to propagate that Hindus and Muslims must remain united. But anyone could see that he was only hedging his bets and keeping his options open because the 'endgame' had not been dealt as yet and no one was sure of the final act in this drama of tremendous significance for the people of this country. During a debate on the Cabinet Mission Plan he said, "...I believe there is no progress for India until Muslims and Hindus are united. Let not logic, philosophy and squabbles stand in the way of your bringing that about." Continuing, he said that he had been put into a corner by arrogance of Nehru and unreasonableness of Patel and others. He didn't say so but did imply that in order to retain his hold on the League he had to do something dramatic and inspiring for his flock to remain with him at that crucial stage.

Tragically for India, and particularly for the Hindus and Sikhs of Punjab and Hindus of Bengal response from the Congress Party continued to be devoid of any mature statesmanship that could be construed as a formula which would allay Muslim fears about their safety, security and progress when India became free. Instead, it preferred "logic", "philosophy" and "arithmetic" in order to score debating points totally impervious to the tense communal situation then prevailing in the country. This, when in these areas the Muslims had already started adjusting the demographic structure to suit their convenience. Congressmen encouraged by Nehru's tirades against Jinnah's call for parity continued to oppose and deride Jinnah's plea, concurrently pressing for a dominion status on their terms.

Footnotes

1. Recalling India's Struggle for Freedom by Hiren Mukerjee pp 138-39
2. Quoted by Pyarelal, Mahatma Gandhi, The Last Phase, and Vol. 1 part 1. p 132
3. Sardar Patel's Correspondence Vol. 3 p 154
4. Quoted in 'The Proudest Day' page 387-88

15

Jinnah's Gamble

Call for Direct Action

Jinnah was normally a man who was more inclined to use constitutional methods to achieve his goals. He considered himself an Indian nationalist as late as 1938. The Congress had contemptuously rejected Jinnah's modest proposals in 1928, spurned his offer of co-operation in 1937 and 1939 and sabotaged the compromise plan for a united India in 1946. Till 1937, he made no appeal to religious sentiments of the Muslims in order to consolidate his position among his co-religionists. He had joined the Congress as a nationalist Muslim, and dominated that organisation as well as a fledging Muslim League in 1916. But he had been gradually finding himself isolated from Congress inner circle. His efforts to get along in the larger interests of the country were seen as a sign of weakness by Nehru and others. This was a situation that was not acceptable to Jinnah. When the League did not make a particularly impressive performance in the provincial elections he started looking for a compromise formula so that both Hindus and Muslims could co-exist. In a public statement, shortly after the elections of 1937 he declared, 'nobody will welcome an honourable settlement between the Hindus and Muslims more than I and nobody will be more ready to help it'. He followed it up with an appeal to Gandhi to help resolve the issues involved. It was only when Nehru proclaimed that there was no such thing as Hindu-Muslim question or the minority question in India; and with Gandhi harping on his theory that divine intervention would resolve whatever differences the two communities had once the British left, Jinnah felt that the time to assert had come. Although he did realise that 'Direct Action' against the British by Congress had given a lot of mileage to that organisation, he did subscribe to the thought that direct action by the masses would lead to large-scale violence at that point of time because the divisive forces were already at work all over India. He knew that any call of this nature would provoke both Hindus and Muslims to go for each other's throat egged on by the unruly members belonging to both the communities, and with the British stoking the flames in their own interest the common man had no chance.

Congress refusal to contemplate parity in the 'Interim Government' or the compulsory grouping of provinces for constitution making put the cat amongst pigeons. The British Government played along with this sentiment because nobody wanted to antagonise Nehru or Gandhi. Surprisingly, the Imperial government had not as yet come to the conclusion that where Muslims of the sub-continent were concerned Jinnah's grip was virtually total. It appears that presence of a fairly large number of eminent Muslims in the Congress fold created a picture where Jinnah's leadership of his community was still a matter of conjecture where either·the government in London or Nehru-Gandhi combine were concerned. The overwhelming victory of the Muslim League candidates in Muslim-dominated areas in the 1945-46 elections, and total defeat of nationalist Muslims in the Central Legislature, showed that the Muslim League was an effective representative of an overwhelming majority of Muslims. Congress could no longer rationally claim that that it represented the whole of India. Neither Gandhi nor Nehru realised that the issues involved were not theological but political needing political solution. What is worse, the solution offered by Azad, which also conformed to the Cabinet Mission Plan was also not given the importance it deserved. May be in the opinion of Gandhi and Nehru the Nationalist Muslims had by now lost their relevance as the League had clearly established that the Muslims were by and large now with the League.

Unfortunately for India, and to Jinnah's discomfiture the Labour Government felt that in the post-war scenario in an independent India, Britain's interests would be best served by enlisting Congress cooperation. This seemingly one-sided approach put Jinnah into a quandary. He had to come up with something dramatic enough so as to continue with his hold on the Muslim flock. He called for a meeting of his followers in Bombay on the same day. There he launched a proper fight against the dishonesty of the British, against the Cabinet Mission, which, he said, had allowed itself to be tricked by the Congress and above all against the Congress leaders who had 'neither decency, nor honour, nor courage'. Accusing the British of appeasing the Congress, he thundered: "The Congress was bent upon setting up Caste Hindu Raj in India with the connivance of the British." He called on the Muslims to resort to 'Direct Action' to achieve Pakistan...to get rid of the present British slavery and the contemplated future 'Caste-Hindu domination'. As a protest against 'their deep resentment of the attitude of the British', the League called upon Muslims to renounce the titles 'conferred upon them by the alien government.' The faithful were exhorted to give a fitting reply to the British-Congress 'treachery'. Jinnah concluded with the famous words: "Today we have said good-bye to constitutions and constitutional methods. Throughout the painful negotiations, the two parties with whom we bargained held a pistol at us; one with power and machine gun behind it, the other with 'non-cooperation' and the threat to launch mass civil disobedience. This situation must be met. We also have a pistol."[1] In the excited mood of the audience, a single word from Jinnah would have sufficed to trigger off a total 'Jihad'. However, he was satisfied to proclaim "a direct action day" for August 16, 1946. May be he still had hopes of some mature response from Congress leaders. Mr Liaquat Ali Khan when asked what he interpreted as 'direct action', replied, "Direct Action" means any action against the law. Sardar Abdul Rab Nishtar was more specific when he said that Pakistan could only be achieved by shedding blood and, if opportunity arose, the blood of non-Muslims must be shed, for "Muslims are no believers in ahimsa." (GD Khosla- *Stern Reckoning*).

For the unfortunate Punjabis, Bengalis and all those throughout the rest of India who were forcibly uprooted as late as 27th January 1946 Nehru was propagating that the Muslims were incapable of launching any 'direct action' movement. 'Transfer of Power' documents reveal that it was Congress that was actually holding a threat of this kind of action if the party did not have its way. This arrogance and lack of political foresight led to a situation where Jinnah was forced to give his 'direct action' call. His followers were getting restless and more and more aggressive by the day. Nehru and his Party decided to ignore these tidings. Neither Gandhi nor Patel made any effort to fathom the damage that could be caused to the country's unity by their obstinate approach to the issues raised by Jinnah who was fully aware of the sway Nehru held over Hindus, some Muslims and of course the British. Congressmen continued to sit on a moral high ground, knowing fully well that Jinnah wasn't entirely wrong in his assessment of the prevailing situation where a majority rule would have meant Hindu Rule unless there were some kind of checks and balances incorporated to safeguard Muslim interests. This lack of pragmatism, maturity and political sagacity on the part of Gandhi, Nehru, Patel and others, particularly from the majority community, destroyed unity of India. Not withstanding the prevailing situation, Jinnah still had a hope for, what he thought, was a fair deal for the Muslims. On 6th July 1946, Jinnah, in a strictly private communication addressed to Attlee, wrote:

"I therefore trust that the British Government will still avoid compelling the Muslims to shed their blood, for, your surrender to the Congress at the sacrifice of the Muslims can only result in that direction. If politics are going to be the deciding factor in total disregard of fair play and justice, we shall have no other course open to us except to forge our sanction to meet the situation, which, in this case, is bound to arise. Its consequences I need not say will be most disastrous and a possible settlement will then become impossible." (*Transfer of Power*, Vol. VIII, pp 106-107).

To this letter Attlee's reply, dated 23rd July 1946, to put it mildly, was evasive. The reply said, *inter alia*, "As regards the Congress statement on the issues involved, it has clearly left something to be desired. But I must point out that the Muslim League in their resolution of 6th June also made certain reservations." The prime minister gave no statesman-like response, which could assuage Jinnah's apprehensions about the future of his community in a free India. Attlee clearly wanted to please Gandhi and Nehru because this kind of approach seemed to suit British interests. By now Jinnah was convinced that a fight with the Congress would be unequal unless he too adopted the means that Gandhi had used so successfully in arousing the emotions of the country against the British. Having exercised all options which could safeguard Muslim interests in a free India and failed; and seeing no future for himself unless he too came up with something as dramatic as Gandhi's calls over the years Jinnah elected to be as melodramatic as the Mahatma. It was on 29th July 1946, that Jinnah declared that for the first time in its history, the Muslim League had abandoned constitutional methods in order to achieve its goal.

That Jinnah was playing on the Muslim sense of persecution at the hands of Hindu Congress if 'parity' was not granted did not worry anyone but Azad. Gandhi took the stand that: " When two parties cannot agree, and both are sincere in their respective conditions, it is clear that one of them must be wrong. Both cannot be right. The world must be arbiter in that case. It dare not withhold judgement." We all know that very often parties holding opposite views are partly right and partly wrong. Political sagacity and wisdom demanded that the gap between opposite views be narrowed by negotiations. Hindu leaders made no effort in this direction. Azad, who did try was at once marginalised and even removed from the Party president's post. Wavell made all kinds of efforts to appeal to the nobler sentiments of Congress leaders but they had shut themselves out of any option other than a "Majority Rule"—a condition totally unacceptable to Jinnah and the Muslims who apprehended that they would be reduced to the status of second class citizens in a Hindu domination once the British left.

Worried over the consequences of the call for Direct Action, the British cabinet advised Wavell to see Jinnah as soon as possible and to press him to allow Muslim Leaguers to join the Interim Government. The British did not want to get into a situation in which both Congress and the League were in opposition; and the government had to be carried on by the Viceroy indefinitely. Wavell tried to persuade Nehru to seek rapprochement with Jinnah because Jinnah had evidently reacted to what Nehru had said about him and the League. He wanted Nehru to show real statesmanship and maturity of thought and action by giving the League appropriate assurances so that Jinnah could be brought back to the negotiations table once again. Nehru was reluctant to discuss any assurances to be given to the League. He ended this meeting with the Viceroy by saying that 'if there was any dispute over the interpretation of the Cabinet Mission proposals, the same could be referred to the Federal Court', knowing fully well that there was neither time, nor energy nor patience with any of the concerned parties for any such move. The only other test he said, "was the test of battle." Clearly, it was a veiled threat to the Muslim League, given from a position where one was in majority and was fully aware of this strength. Wavell then tried to prevail upon Jinnah to participate in the Interim Government. Jinnah agreed for the sake of the country's unity. But he had to contend with those Muslim leaders who were by now seeing a country of their own. He had to have an escape route if parity was not ensured. Seasoned lawyer that he was he created a situation which allowed him to change his mind if the final scenario did not suit his demands and if he had ample reasons to scuttle the whole thing at some stage. He did this by nominating a 'Scheduled Caste' as the League representative.

Jinnah was hedging his bets. He knew that the Congress would never accept this poaching on its territory. And that is what actually happened. Congress refused to consider any such nomination. Jinnah had clearly decided on a course of action from which he could not retract without serious trouble with his Muslim followers. Nehru met Jinnah on 15th August 1946 in order to seek some kind of a compromise formula so that the unity of the country could be retained. But the fact that the Congress had accepted Viceroy's invitation to form interim Government on 6th August 1946 without even trying to find out if the League was likely to change its stand must have weighed heavily on Jinnah's mind—the meeting between the two leaders failed to produce any positive result.

Hindu-Muslim Riots

This tendency towards fragmentary parochialism, with leanings towards intolerance towards each other and emerging political conservatism was not something that was new to India. Hindu-Muslim riots had been far too frequent; of late, these had grown in frequency and intensity. Now with Jinnah, seemingly, giving his blessings to the

Muslims to show their muscle the Hindus and the Sikhs also started giving an equally violent response. What the law-makers and jurists had been unable to resolve after years of bickering was decided by arson, looting and murder. What the most eminent political leaders had been unable to establish through the exercise of reason, the ordinary folk took on to do so by force. The common man had, obviously, decided that the politicians were not likely to end the long drawn uncertainty about the country's future. Restive and restless members of both the communities took to streets challenging each other for a fight to finish. During the summer of 1946, the enmity between the Hindus and the Muslims exploded into vicious and bloody riots, which—by a chain reaction—spread right across the sub-continent.

16th August, Friday, was declared to be a holiday in Bengal and Sind, the two provinces ruled by the League so that people could participate in a 'peaceful' demonstration and show solidarity with the Quaid-i-Azam. But continued violence of the past few months suddenly manifested itself in a mass fury and the two warring communities went totally berserk. There is no doubt that Suhrawardy, the Chief Minister of Bengal, was directly involved in inciting the Muslims in Calcutta. In an intelligence report, the General Officer Commanding Eastern Army Command was informed that while addressing a huge Muslim crowd at the Ochterlony monument, the Chief Minister had said, "I will see how the British could make Mr. Nehru rule over Bengal, and the Direct Action Day would prove to be the first step towards the Muslim struggle for emancipation." He then urged the crowd to return home early and be ready for teaching Hindus a lesson. He also told the Muslim crowd that he had already arranged with the police and military not to interfere with the Muslims. The anti-social elements in the crowd needed no second invitation to indulge in violence, arson and loot. As soon as the meeting ended, most of them surged towards Hindu shops and houses, looting them and setting on fire what could not be taken away. Hindu gangsters retaliated wherever they were in a secure majority; soon a free for all followed. Some members of the two communities in the police and para-military forces also saw this mayhem as a chance of a lifetime to settle old scores. SG Taylor, then Inspector General of police in Bengal, recollects:

The attitude of the Chief Minister during the rioting was reprehensible. During the height of the disturbances he drove round Calcutta with the local Army Commander to assess the situation. As they drove the Army Commander said that in the Army Hindus and Muslims live and work happily together." To this the Chief Minister replied: "We shall soon put an end to all that." Suhrawardy ordered Taylor that all Muslims who had been arrested in the 24 Parganas district for rioting be released.

When Taylor refused to do so because it was beyond his authority, the Chief Minister directed that in future when any number of Muslims is taken in custody for rioting and arson, the same number of Hindus be also arrested, whether they had committed any crime or not.

With such political patronage to the rogue Muslim elements Hindus and Sikhs of Calcutta had no chance of matching the communal fury of the rampaging mob. Army was called in but even nine battalions of troops proved to be ineffective in the face of raging riots. The city alone reported more than four thousand killed and ten thousand wounded. Soon the ripple effect of these happenings felt all over India. Massacres in Calcutta and Bihar claimed thousands of victims, in Punjab hundreds or possibly thousands were killed. Clearly, the country had reached a stage of suppressed civil war.

Reaction of the national leaders to the happenings in Calcutta, to say the least, was palpably lacking in any wisdom or thought for the hapless masses caught in the crossfire of this carnage. When journalists asked Nehru if the troubles in Calcutta were going to make him change his plans, he replied: "Our programme shall not be upset if a few people 'misbehave' in Calcutta.[2] Liaquat Ali Khan, the secretary general of the League asserted in an interview to *T10he Statesman*, that the "communal" arrogance and the spirit of violence fostered by the Congress were exclusively to blame for the troubles. It was doubtful if the British administration was capable of controlling the situation, or containing the violence. The Viceroy visited Calcutta from 25th to 27th August for an 'on the spot' study of the situation. Before leaving Delhi, on the 24th he announced the names of the interim government, which was to take office at the beginning of September. Nehru wanted to fill all the five Muslim seats with non-League Muslims; but the Viceroy, still hoping that Jinnah might eventually come around, filled only three seats with Congress nominees, hoping to fill the remaining two with Jinnah's candidates. The carnage in Calcutta convinced him that an agreement between the League and Congress was essential if further communal carnages were to be prevented.

On return from Calcutta, Wavell wrote to the Secretary of State saying: "I see no hope at all of avoiding further and more rioting in Calcutta and elsewhere in India unless there is some settlement at the Centre. With this end in view, and ostensibly encouraged by some Muslim leaders that Jinnah could still perhaps change his mind the Viceroy met Gandhi and Nehru in Delhi. He gave out his plan of action to stem the violence then rocking the country. The Viceroy's proposals were:

- The principle of the grouping such as it had been set out in the Plan of 16th May be accepted,

- To constitute coalition governments at the Centre and in Bengal, with the League as a partner,

- Failing the above, he, the Viceroy, would not call the Constituent Assembly.

Trouble was, Wavell had already invited Nehru to form an interim government, an announcement to this effect had also been made on the radio and the press had also been informed. Now his fresh proposals seemed to be backing out from a major decision on the future of the country, a situation that was not acceptable, either to Nehru or to Gandhi. They were not willing to concede any such grouping with the League in the face of its intransigence and instigating violence in Calcutta. Nehru followed it up with a written reply next day: conveying that they i.e. the Congress Party was shocked at this sudden change of the Viceroy's attitude, and the party had no reason to modify the position defined earlier by its leadership.

Wavell took their reaction as justification for Jinnah's doubts about Congress; 'convincing evidence' that the Congress always meant to use their position in the Interim Government to destroy the grouping scheme which was the only effective safeguard for the Muslims. Wavell rightly believed that if the Congress and the League joined the Interim Government, the need for them to work together and in harmony in order to solve pressing problems then facing the country could produce a friendly atmosphere. But the issue of nationalist Muslims joining the interim Government continued to be a stumbling block. The Viceroy tried to sidestep the issue by not nominating any nationalist Muslim to the proposed Executive Council of fourteen members. Thereafter, Wavell knew that he had lost all credibility with the Congress and resultantly with his own government, which had asked him to tread carefully where it concerned Gandhi, Nehru and Congress.

Wavell could not believe that Jinnah, as 'a highly intelligent man, is sincere about the "two nations theory". He was right in this assessment because Jinnah had not been able to answer awkward questions raised by various experts about implications of Pakistan. Where Jinnah was concerned, Pakistan consisted initially of Sind, Baluchistan, the NWFP, Punjab, Assam and Bengal. Where sovereignty of these provinces was concerned only the Muslim residents in them were to decide; other inhabitants had no say in the matter. The Viceroy wanted to find out as to how Jinnah expected Calcutta, one of the most important cities in the East and predominantly a Hindu constituency, to become a part of

Pakistan. There was no answer coming from the Leaguers on these serious issues. Churchill was more than happy with this situation. 'The stalemate between the Congress and the League was a gift that would ensure continuation of the Raj', the Prime Minister concluded. The situation gave him hope that the pledges and promises that the Government had to make in order to ensure cooperation of the Indians because of the war may not have to be fulfilled because the natives had serious differences among themselves. The common man was not as politically and philosophically savvy as the leaders were, nor was he that confident of his security and safety in an environment where he was in a minority. Neither the Congress, nor the League had worked out this aspect in their respective strategies. What was worse—frequent and violent communal riots—also hadn't made the two parties any wiser about the 'majority' community's treatment of a minority community in its area of influence.

Constituent Assembly Sworn In

On 2nd September 1946, Wavell swore in the new ministers. The occasion was historic for more than one reasons: it was the first time in the country's history that a representative government encompassing the whole of India had been formed. Nehru, as vice-president of the Executive Council under the Viceroy was, to all intents and purposes, the prime minister and foreign secretary of India. Patel was member, in charge of police and internal security. Defence, with responsibility for the army, went to Baldev Singh—the solitary Sikh member. But the Muslim representatives were only those who had Congress affiliation. The League, and therefore, the Muslim majority was not represented in this dispensation.

Efforts were still on to somehow retain unity of India and for this purpose Gandhi and Jinnah met once again, perhaps for the last time. On 4th October 1946, Gandhi and Jinnah agreed upon a formula to resolve the deadlock. They signed an agreement which stipulated: "The Congress does not challenge, and accepts that the Muslim League now is the authoritative representative of the overwhelming majority of Muslims of India. As such, and in accordance with democratic principles, they alone have today the unquestionable right to represent the Muslims of India. But the Congress cannot agree that any restriction or limitation should be put upon Congress to choose such representatives as they think proper, from amongst the members of the Congress as their representatives." (*Transfer of Power*, Vol. VIII, p 673). Finally, and after so much of turmoil Congress accepted that Jinnah had the sole right to represent the Muslims according to democratic principles.

Further negotiations were left for Jinnah and Nehru to work out a solution that would be acceptable to both sides. With this agreement giving equal status to Jinnah and the League a hope got generated that India might remain united. But Nehru, never fond of Jinnah, immediately extinguished all such hopes when on 6th October 1946 he wrote to Jinnah, *inter alia*, saying: "...we feel that the formula is not happily worded.... the League should recognize the Congress as the authoritative organisation representing all non-Muslims and such Muslims as have thrown in their lot with the Congress...We would suggest, therefore, that no formula is necessary and that each organisation may have its candidates on merit." In substance Nehru repudiated the formula agreed to between Gandhi and Jinnah. At the back of Nehru's mind was his fixed belief that if he approached the Muslims without the League's interference, he could reverse the verdict of the 1945-46 elections in provinces where Congress had not been able to win majority. Jinnah did not agree with Nehru's version of Jinnah-Gandhi accord. Gandhi himself claimed that he had signed without carefully reading the text and the sub-text because the time was short and he was over-strained.

Muslims were not at all pleased with this turn of events. Millions of Muslims marked the eve of the new government's inauguration by flying black mourning flags from their homes. In Bombay, the black flag demonstration turned into a communal riot. Soon enough riots spread through the length and breadth of the country, with more and more killings taking place day in and day out. In Noakhali, in the hinterland of Bengal, and in areas around Calcutta violence was far too ferocious. Gandhi decided to embark on a mission to restore peace and communal harmony, which from 7th November 1946 to 2nd March 1947 kept him away from the Centre. May be, the Mahatma did not want to be anywhere near Nehru and Patel who were at the time having their own difference of opinion over the issue of 'leftist or rightist' leanings when freedom came, he did not want to be taking side with either of them. Killings, rioting and arson carried on; Hindus and Muslims began to form militia and arm themselves for a final parting of ways.

On 9th December, the Constituent Assembly met in Delhi without the League, and without any communal incident; the princes were also absent. It elected Rajendra Prasad as its president. On 13th December, Nehru rose to move that "This Constituent Assembly declares its firm and solemn resolve to proclaim India as an Independent Sovereign Republic". In a confidential note to the AICC dated 4th December 1946, Gandhi opposed its meeting without the League, for such a Constituent Assembly was being held without agreement among Indians themselves, and under cover of British arms. Nehru and Patel disagreed with Gandhi and decided to ignore his missive. On the 8th of December, that is a day before the Constituent Assembly met in the House of Commons, Winston Churchill, speaking for the Opposition had issued a sombre warning, which was to prove to be prophetic a few months later :

"I must record my own belief...that any attempt to establish the reign of a Hindu numerical majority in India will never be achieved without a civil war, proceeding, not perhaps at first on the fronts of armies or organised forces, but in thousands of separate and isolated places."[3]

The assembly had been adjourned until 20th January 1947 with a view to allow various parties to come to some kind of a solution to waxing communal problems. Hectic parleys went on at various levels but the Congress ensured that the League remained as evasive as ever by announcing that 'there must be no compulsion on any province or part of any province, and that the rights of the Sikhs in the Punjab must not be compromised in any way'. (To add to the confusion already prevailing the resolution passed by the All India Congress Committee on 6th January 1947 accepting the British Government's interpretation of "grouping" added a rider, which effectively nullified that acceptance:

"It must be clearly understood however that this must not involve any compulsion of a province and that of the rights of the Sikhs must not be jeopardized. In the event of any attempt at such compulsion, the province or part of province has a right to take such action as may be deemed necessary in order to give effect to the wishes of people concerned." (*Transfer of Power* Vol. IX p 463). Jinnah treated this resolution as a repudiation of the Plan.)

This stand of the Congress was at variance with the original 'Cabinet Mission' Plan. The League demanded that since, neither the Congress, nor the Scheduled Castes, nor the Sikhs were subscribing to the Plan the Government must be sacked. In turn, Patel declared that it was the League, which was coming in the way to smooth transfer of power. Therefore, either the League members be removed from the Assembly, or the Congress will withdraw in protest. As usual, there was a stalemate. Fact of the matter was, by now Congress had also come to realise that there was no alternative to partition. Saner elements in the Party conceded in private that by not accepting the Cabinet Mission Plan the Party had made a great mistake. If the same terms were offered now the Congress would have gladly accepted those but a great opportunity had been lost, this realisation had come too late in the day. The Congress, actively assisted by Pethick-Lawrence, Cripps and the Viceroy had been treating Jinnah and the League with utter disdain, and the Plan which would have been accepted by them in 1946 became wholly unacceptable in 1947, level of mutual distrust had by then gone too high for any meaningful rapprochement. Now it seemed certain that the Indians would rather have total chaos. Cleverly, the British had thrown the final responsibility for the solution on the Indian leaders themselves.

King George VI showed a surprising understanding of the situation. "We have plans to evacuate India," he noted in his diary "but we cannot do so without leaving India with a workable constitution. The Indian leaders have got to learn that the responsibility is theirs and they must learn how to govern."

Breakdown Plan

Wavell read the situation to be serious enough and ripe for a 'civil war'. He was convinced that to make the Congress and the League work together within the same government was an impossible task. For him the time to pull out of the whole mess had come; now the priority for him was to ensure that the British and Anglo Indians were not subjected to sufferings the Hindus and Muslims were going through because their leaders had failed to agree among themselves. He was encouraged by his advisers to work out a kind of plan that would ensure that the British citizens now serving in India came to no harm or got caught in the cross-fire when the Hindus and Muslims went for each others throat with ever increasing ferocity. His reaction to the political turmoil then raging in the country was to organise an orderly retreat for the British; leaving Indians to their own devices and fate in the event of a total breakdown not only of negotiations but that of public order as well. In consultation with his military and civil advisers, Wavell worked out what came to be known as the 'Breakdown' Plan. The salient features of this plan were:

* Withdraw with minimum disorder,
* Maintain cohesion of the Armed Forces,
* Administer shock and pressurise political leaders to adopt pragmatic outlook,
* Progressively reduce the British responsibility in India but at the same time, and at each stage, strengthen position in the remaining territory.

Wavell now wanted to put his 'evacuation plan' in motion. He wanted South India to be evacuated first, holding north till such time the British community could be taken out of the country latest by 31st March 1948. He drew up a plan on these lines and presented the same to London as the only viable option remaining if the British interests in India were to be safeguarded. Assuming that the British administration had only eighteen months before the curtain came down on the Raj; Wavell had worked out a time frame for his planned withdrawal from the country. He wanted Indians to be given six months to sort their affairs out; that is, till 30th March 1947, after that within one year the British civilians and military manpower was to be progressively taken out of the country.

The Cabinet in London refused to accept Wavell's evacuation plan as the only option available. However desirable it might be to leave the two warring parties to solve their problems in their own way, Attlee could not countenance a policy of scuttle, leaving India in chaos with no guarantees for the minorities. He was worried that such an approach could give the impression that His Majesty's Government was no longer capable of governing India. He also apprehended that to leave India before a constitution had been framed would be regarded as an act of weakness and it would seriously undermine Britain's international position. With a Soviet Bloc having come into existence after the War there was no way the British could abandon India to its own fate, which could easily put the "Jewel in the Crown" in the Communist lap. It was also essential to keep India in the 'Commonwealth Defence System' as India's cooperation was necessary for the maintenance of Britain's strategic interests in the Middle and Far East, such an arrangement would also have allowed Britain to use India's army and economic resources for military purposes in the future. Attlee knew that only an amicable transfer of power would make that possible. He also wanted to show to the world that they were leaving India not under circumstances of ignominy, but were going freely and not under any compulsion.

Wavell Sacked

Wavell was recalled. In fact, Attlee sacked him rather unfairly, and far too ungraciously. In his letter of 31st January 1947, Attlee informed him that his appointment was a wartime appointment, he spoke of a need to make a change in the Viceroyalty when ushering in a new policy which would prove exacting for Wavell. For practical and political reasons Attlee had found his 'evacuation' plan to be too ignominious an end to 200 years of British involvement in India. To him Wavell's plan was more of a military retreat rather than a solution to a political problem. He felt that the Plan was 'defeatist': "and I am not a defeatist but a realist, he told his friends." He was of the opinion that power must be honourably and peacefully transferred as soon as possible to one successor state or, if the worst came to the worst, to two. But he accepted Wavell's view that 31st March 1948 should be fixed for the withdrawal of British power in India in a phased manner. Technically, he was saying the same thing as Wavell but he doubted if Wavell could display enough of political savvy at that stage which would ensure that the two warring parties retained friendly feelings towards the British after the Raj had wound up. How much chaos and bloodshed Wavell's plan would have caused and whether it would have been greater or lesser than what actually happened is a matter of conjecture.

Footnotes

1. Pirzada Foundation of Pakistan Vol. II p 560.
2. Nehru quoted by *The Statesman* of 18th August 1946, front page.
3. P Moon Wavell: The Viceroy Journal p 341.
4. Parliamentary Debates, House of Commons, 5th series Vol. 431 p 1360.

16

Raj—The Last Lap

"Quit India" movement took important Congress leaders away from the centre-stage. This allowed the Communists, Muslim League and hard-core Hindu leaders to fill the vacuum. Unfortunately, hardly any one of them had the vision to think of India as a whole. And with Savarkar and others like him stoking the Hindutva flames, Suhrawardy in Bengal and leaders in Punjab reminding Muslims that Islam was in danger, there hardly was any option left for the British but to let the two communities sort out their affairs. It is evident that one of the reasons why the issue of Transfer of Power was getting prolonged was that the decision-makers in London were in no hurry to quit India, they wanted to prolong their hold for as long as possible. The official stand had been that "the British were not in India to teach the art of self-government but to safeguard British investments in the country". It was only due to the 2nd World War and the tremendous amount of men, material and money that the War consumed had weakened Britain so much that it was no longer in a position to hold on to this great asset. In a bid to lengthen their rule they had been directly or indirectly encouraging the Muslims and the princes to put their respective spanners in the nationalist movement for freedom. However, by the time this wisdom dawned the British found that it was now totally impossible to keep the country united. There were by now too many vested interests involved wanting to have their share of the 'Indian pie'. Hindu and Muslim leaders just could not agree on anything and people paid a very heavy price in terms of millions of lives lost, property destroyed and created permanent enmity between the two countries.

In a last ditch effort to keep the country united the prime minister invited Nehru, Jinnah, Liaquat Ali and Baldev Singh to London for finding some way to prevent partition. In an aside to Baldev Singh, Jinnah offered any guarantee the Sikhs might require. 'If you can persuade the Sikhs to join hands with the Muslim League we will have a glorious Pakistan, the gates of which will be near about Delhi, if not in Delhi itself,' Jinnah told Baldev Singh. But the Sikhs were too distrustful and wary of Muslims, so the gambit failed. The London conference, from 2nd December to 6nd December 1946 did not bring about any compromise or solution.

Attlee now had to find a Viceroy who could have enough of guile, political savvy and élan to meet the Imperial government's goal of getting out of India with minimum damage to British prestige and do so in a hurry. By now Congress had also come around to the conclusion that the Muslim majority provinces would be a perennial source of trouble unless these were divided. In the Punjab, both Hindus and Sikhs began to favour partition of the province as their only safeguard. Patel was also convinced that it was far more beneficial for the Congress if power were transferred to two central governments on the basis of dominion status. He was hopeful that dominion status would allay the fears of the princes about their future, and make them willing to come to the negotiating table.

The prime minister presented the position of the British government in the House of Commons on 20th February 1947; he announced that the transfer of power would take place before 30th June 1948. The prime minister also declared, "If it should appear that the Indians had not been able to formulate a Constitution worked out by a fully representative assembly by that date then His Majesty's Government will have to consider to whom the powers of the central government for British India should be handed over on the due date; whether as a whole to some form of central government for British India, or in some areas to the existing provincial Governments, or in such other ways as may seem most reasonable and in the best interests of the people of India." As regards the princely states, the statement reiterated the principle laid down by the Cabinet Mission, i.e. "powers and obligations would not be handed over to any government of British India but would return to its source, meaning, to the princes themselves. That the British prime minister was confused about his next course of action is clear from this statement. His proposal to revert power to the princes meant that the country would be fragmented into a huge number of entities, without any responsibility towards a central government. This was not a solution to the problems of communal harmony or lack of it then facing India. Both, Punjab and Bengal were under Muslim majority governments and Hindus were uncomfortable due to an uncertain future. Ever since the provincial elections, the Muslim League had been deriding the government of the Unionist Khizar Hyat Khan, and doing all that it could to scare the Hindus and Sikhs out of Punjab. In January 1947, Khizar tried to ban the National Guards of the League and Hindu RSS. The League took to the streets and launched a full-scale 'direct action'. Khizar panicked and withdrew his ban, but it was too late. By now the League had smelt blood and was in no mood to relent. The Hindus warned Khizar that if he failed to suppress the Muslim agitation they would take matters into their own hands.

Political uncertainty led to massive killings for the next three days. Attlee's statement of the 20th February added to the pressure on Khizar because the League now was in a tearing hurry to alter the demographic structure of the province. Armed bands of Muslims attacked the Hindu and Sikh localities of Rawalpindi, Multan, Lahore, Sialkot and Amritsar. Sikhs were targeted more specifically because the Muslims saw them as the most resolute adversaries and they wanted them to leave as quickly as possible. The Sikhs had a reason to forcefully safeguard their interests; their holiest of the holy shrines were in the areas, which were Muslim dominated and their fertile lands were located in the West Punjab. Initially taken by surprise by the ferocity of the League gangs, they soon regrouped and started responding to violence with violence.

On 3rd March, Master Tara Singh of the Akali Party in Punjab raised the Cry for a holy war. He exhorted his followers: "O Hindus and Sikhs! Be ready for self-destruction...If we can snatch the Government from the British, no one can stop us from snatching the government from the Muslims...Disperse from here on the solemn affirmation that we shall not allow the League to exist...I have sounded the bugle. Finish the Muslim League."

Khizar resigned after ten days of total turmoil. Governor Jenkins went through the motion of inviting the League to form a government, but he knew that there was no chance of Hindus or Sikhs supporting the League, which did not have a majority in the province. Jenkins, in fact, described the situation in Punjab as a 'war of succession' where both the claimants were no longer interested in seeing reason. Jinnah once again offered to the Sikhs a province within the State of Pakistan. Master Tara Singh on 5th April 1947 agreed to enter into negotiations with the Muslim League on the basis of division of Punjab. The British Administration was clearly siding with this scheme of Jinnah because no tangible effort was being made to quell riots and killings of the Hindus and Sikhs; perhaps the British aim was to let the state be destabilised as much as possible so that the Sikhs could be scared into agreeing to Jinnah's offer and thus create a buffer between the Hindu Punjab and the Muslim Punjab. There was resentment among some of the Sikh leaders over this horse-trading and the Hindus of the province were equally upset with these developments. Tension and consequent rioting continued unabated.

The Governor took complete control of Punjab, managed to restore some kind of uneasy peace for a while. He informed the centre that if the state were to be divided then he would not be able to hold on without a heavy presence of the Army. Central government did not have any troops for Punjab, certainly not enough to control and contain spreading communal violence. Trouble soon spread all over Punjab, Hindus were forcefully pushed out of Muslim dominated districts and the Muslims were hastened out of Hindu majority districts with equal force. The Congress observed that it was astonished to see that the British government was incapable of restoring law and order. To which Jenkins replied that he was facing a "communal war of succession" in which all political parties were actively participating.

Jenkins still had some military means—although insufficient—he no longer had the administrative, police and judicial means at his disposal, without which the sheer force of the army became ineffective and even dangerous. Often policemen, soldiers, even the administrators themselves were a party to the crimes being committed under their eyes. Refugees started pouring in from both sides with tales of atrocities, killings, raping and arson. There virtually was no government in Punjab at that point of time. Having been neither anticipated nor organised, the migration of Hindus and Sikhs towards the East, of Muslims towards the West, took place in most gruesome conditions. Before reaching the border, these pitiful caravans were attacked and looted. Railway stations became places of ambush, and trains became slaughterhouses. The refugees, while moving towards their part of the divide, further spread the hatred that had been simmering for years. Killings and arson spread to Rajasthan, Delhi, Kashmir and other parts of the country. India was an inferno with no immediate end to this mayhem in sight.

Under the clouds of misery, deteriorating law and order and killings, Congress Working Committee met in the first week of March to consider the British Prime Minister's statement in the Parliament. After hectic parleys lasting more than three days, the Party adopted a series of resolutions on 8th March 1947. In addition to accepting the Cabinet Mission Plan, it also invited the Muslim League to discuss with it the modalities for peaceful transfer of power. More significant was its resolution concerning troubles in Punjab. The Working Committee suggested that the Punjab be divided into two parts according to the Muslim or non-Muslim population. On 9th March, Nehru forwarded the document to Lord Wavell, adding that the same formula be applied in Bengal as well. Jawaharlal Nehru and Sardar Patel had come to the conclusion that there was no alternative to, at least, a temporary partition of the country. They hoped that once the British left and the dust settled down, the country could be reunited. ("I have no doubt whatsoever that sooner or later India will have to function as a unified country. Perhaps the best way to reach that stage is to go through some kind of a partition now," Jawaharlal Nehru said to a friend in a letter he wrote on 29th April 1947).

The Congress party's apprehensions about a federal structure leading to a weak Centre were somewhat justified. If Punjab (granary and the sword-arm) and Bengal (intellectually superior to most regions, and with its natural and mineral reserves) had an option to opt out of the Confederation at any time then Congress will not be able to establish its total hold on the country with any authority with only UP, Bihar, Orissa and other generally backward states supporting the Party. No Congressman was saying it, but fact of the matter was that unless Punjab and Bengal were weakened by a Partition, in a Confederation Congress virtually had no future. May be, if Patel and Nehru had listened to Rajagopalachari in 1942 and then again in 1944, the country could have been saved such a heavy loss of life and property. Their arriving at the same conclusion, which that visionary had suggested five years ago, was now too late to implement in a conciliatory and peaceful manner. Troublemakers belonging to both the communities had by now tasted blood, and were also encouraged by the factionalists to go the whole hog. The British were also in a hurry to get out as their homeland was reeling under all kinds of problems that had come in the wake of the 2nd World War. They had no time to play politics; and if the Hindus and Muslims were busy exterminating each other then so be it.

Mountbatten Replaces Wavell

Wavell was replaced by a much more flamboyant Mountbatten. Attlee had already offered the Viceroyalty to Mountbatten on 18th December 1946 without giving any inkling to Wavell that he was on his way out. A cousin of the King, a royal person who possessed unusual diplomatic talents, Mountbatten was eminently suited for the assignment particularly when the princes and their selfish agendas had to be considered while resolving the crises then raging in India. All along having pandered to the idiosyncrasies of the native rulers, some of whom were now seeing themselves to be sovereign in their own right, was adding to the headaches then being faced by the government. The problem was that all along the government had been lavish and rather indiscriminate in making all kinds of promises to the princes without any distinction between great and small, full-powered, or small principalities. Now the rulers of Bhopal, Travancore and Hyderabad had already declared that on the departure of British they intended to set themselves up as independent sovereign states. Congress certainly would not have allowed this kind of balkanisation of the country. Such self-created tangles by the British government did need 'royalty' to negotiate with the princes.

Initially Mountbatten was not keen on the assignment. He apprehended that a failure might ruin his naval career and be the death-knell of his life-long ambition to become First Sea Lord. Wily character that he was, he started making demands and seeking guarantees about his future and also a free hand to deal with the Indian situation. He wanted to be taken back into the navy after his India assignment in a post that was equivalent to that which he would leave. Admiralty objected but was over-ruled by the government.

Above all, he wanted plenipotentiary powers. Mountbatten was aware of what Wavell had suffered from backseat driving in London. He told the prime minister that he could not have Whitehall ministers breathing down his neck. Before leaving England he laid down two conditions before the prime minister: that he be given an entirely free hand to deal with the Indians—something that Wavell had never obtained—and that a final date for withdrawal be announced by London, to take effect fifteen months after his taking up office. This period should be announced publicly stressing that thereafter the British would leave the country. In his opinion, seventeen months should have been adequate to achieve the desired results. The Atlee administration accepted his suggestions and sent him out to India with this as his mandate. It was not entirely different from what Wavell had recommended but in the instant case it was having political rather than military connotations.

How Attlee agreed to give a free hand to someone who was not an astute politician is a matter of conjecture. May be Attlee had run out of options where getting out of India with minimum of 'collateral damage' was concerned; aware of Mountbatten's professional inadequacies he did want to saddle him with Cripps so that the political situation did not get out of hand. When it was suggested to Mountbatten that he accept that Sir Stafford Cripps, with his long experience of having dealt with the Indian politics and politicians, come to India to lend him a helping hand, he flatly refused because Cripps could have easily overshadowed him, and that was not in keeping with his future plans for his advancement in the Royal Navy. He had set his heart on becoming the First Sea Lord, an honour that had been taken away from his father earlier because of his German origins. Very diplomatically he suggested to the prime minister that Cripps would be more valuable back home, as his expertise would come in handy to the prime minister when any critical issue arose demanding immediate action based on awareness of events and situation prevailing in India. But he did insist that the Government set a definite date for terminating the British Raj before he left for India; he thought that such an announcement might induce Congress and the League to come to some kind of understanding about the future of the country.

While the Government was busy working out final modalities for leaving India, Mountbatten went about recruiting his key staff members who were to accompany him on this mission. He selected General Ismay, now retired, but an old India hand as his principal staff officer. Not only was Ismay born in India, his grandfather had been military secretary to Lord Hastings. Other key members were from his former team during his Kandy days. An important member was Alan Campbell-Johnson, a former Royal Air-force Public Relations Officer who had been with Mountbatten since July 1942 and had more than a big hand in 'building up' a larger than life image of the Viceroy designate.

Not known for any military brilliance, Mountbatten had risen in the navy purely on the strength of his manipulative skills and royal connections. His official biographer, Philip Zeigler, writes that 'his vanity, though child-like, was monstrous, his ambition unbridled. The truth in his hands was swiftly converted from what it was to what it should have been. He sought to rewrite history with cavalier indifference to the facts to magnify his own achievements'. In 1943, his accelerated promotions over many brilliant commanders during the war finally saw him anointed as the supreme Allied Commander, South-east Asia. Mountbatten set up his headquarters at Kandy, in Ceylon (now Sri Lanka); and virtually sat out the rest of the war. Logically, he should have set up his office in Delhi but he knew that with professional soldiers like Wavell and Auchinleck already stationed in the Indian capital there was virtually no chance of his getting any prominence or importance. Secondly, by then Delhi was fast becoming a hotbed of nationalist politics and freedom movement, naturally these happenings did not suit futuristic plans of the Viceroy designate. What takes the cake is the fact that Mountbatten took no part in the campaigns that recaptured Burma; militarily speaking he was too incompetent to make any meaningful contribution: Legendary William Slim and Sir Oliver Leese were doing all the fighting, but this lack of any active participation did not deter him from styling his viscountcy and later earldom 'of Burma'. Sir Alan Brooke, the chief of the Imperial General Staff, regarded Mountbatten as an 'over-promoted nuisance'. At the end of the war he recorded: 'Seldom has a Supreme Commander been more deficient of the main attributes of a Supreme Commander than Dickie Mountbatten.' According to those who knew Mountbatten intimately, his own words were never the most reliable source of information—he habitually garnished events and conversations to highlight his own importance and contribution totally overlooking the fact that his effort in matters military were of doubtful merit. He would give different versions to different people depending on what suited his selfish interest at a particular point of time.

Field Marshal Sir Claude Auchinleck, the C-in-C, was of the opinion that Mountbatten was eminently unsuitable for this sensitive assignment at such a critical time for the following reasons:

- He had an inflexible German mind, and his professional grooming in the Royal Navy had not prepared him for slow and patient negotiations.

- A novice in politics he had no idea of complex Indian situation where intricate inter-racial, religious and political currents guided the judgment of the local leaders.

- Mountbatten wrongly thought that he knew India and the Indians just because he had visited Delhi on some occasions when he was the Supreme Commander.

- And lastly a member of the Royal Family could never become a politician because nobody had trained him for such a profession.

Notwithstanding the professional opinion of the senior military commanders of the times, Mountbatten had many qualities: he had great warmth, social skills, a quick mind and tremendous energy. He was always self-confident, a quality that made his subordinates always look up to him whenever there was a problem: this trait alone made him a natural leader of men. To put in correct perspective, Mountbatten had the right amount of theatrics to take on the 'Indian Greats' like Gandhi, Nehru and Jinnah. Attlee also believed that Mountbatten would be better placed to deal with the princes because of his royal connections: some of the princes had been disdainful of Wavell because he was a mere soldier, and therefore much below their station in life. By sending Mountbatten in place of Wavell, who was more practical than charismatic, an effort was being made by the British Government to ensure smooth transfer of power; or at least, to make it as smooth as possible under the circumstances.

Having been the Supreme Commander of the Allied forces in South-east Asia during the war with his headquarters in Ceylon (now Sri Lanka), Mountbatten was generally familiar with the ground realities. He had drive, he could be ruthless and he was not unsympathetic to the general policies of Atlee where these concerned winding up the Raj. Another of his leading characteristic was charm and a gift of persuasion, which he could put to good use when interested in having a solution to his way of thinking. The biggest plus he had was, farsightedness. Earlier in life he had exploited his royal connections—however remote—for professional advancement; now he was ready to serve the Empire by 'winning friends' for the 'Crown'. One incident that highlights this trait is the way he treated Nehru when the later visited Malaya and Singapore in 1946 for an 'on the spot study' of the conditions of the local Indian population. The inputs received from various quarters had indicated that the people of Indian origin were sulking, were hurt with the treatment meted out to them by the British during the war; and had a large number of grouses against their rulers. Wavell had grudgingly allowed Nehru to go because he wasn't too sure of his responses to the situation then prevailing there. In order to somewhat restrict the Indian leader local officials decreed that Nehru's movements would be strictly limited, and no official transport would be provided for him to see things for himself.

Mountbatten saw Nehru's visit as an opportunity to win confidence and restore goodwill of the Indians. He was still supreme commander in South-east Asia based in Singapore, and insisted on treating Nehru as though he were already prime minister of an independent India. He entertained him at Government House as if a Head of free country's government was on a visit; in addition to providing to Nehru all the trappings usually meant for such dignitaries he also lent him his personal car and driver. Nehru visited places of his choice in style and enjoyed the hospitality extended by Mountbatten. Wherever he went the official machinery ensured that Nehru received all the courtesies and ceremonies entitled to a leader of stature. When Nehru visited YMCA forces' canteen, Mountbatten and his wife Edwina, accompanied him, sitting alongside Nehru in the open car. Seeing their leader being given so much respect and dignity by the Supreme Commander, local Indians, who were so far a defiant and bitterly anti-British mob, suddenly turned into an exuberantly happy crowd with definite pro-British sentiments. There was virtually a stampede when people rushed forward to meet and touch their leader, Edwina almost got trampled by default but managed to crawl out safe and sound. Nehru continued his tour, virtually as head of free India's Government, with full support of the Supreme Commander and his staff; and Mountbatten continued to generate friendly feelings for the Empire among the local Indians by his thoughtful gestures towards Nehru whom the people recognised as their future prime minister once the British left their homeland. In a nutshell, Mountbatten was that kind of a British who had originally come for trade to India, befuddled some selected natives, won over with their charm those who were circumspect in a manner that allowed the Empire to expand without even wanting to do so.

Mountbatten Arrives

Mountbatten arrived in India in March 1947. Before accepting the assignment he had made a large number of pre-conditions, which were largely accepted by the prime minister—primarily because of his royal connections, and the then prime minister had run out of viable options because Wavell being a professional soldier to the core was not up to political intrigues that were required to manipulate Indian thinking that would safeguard British interests even after they had left the sub-continent. The mandate given to Mountbatten was:

- To obtain a unitary government for British India, and the Indian States.

- If possible the Government should be within the British Commonwealth, through the medium of a Constituent Assembly.

- To set up and run the country in accordance with the Cabinet Mission's Plan.

Mountbatten was given until 1st October 1947 to try and persuade the main parties to accept the package in totality. If, by that time there was no prospect of agreement, he was to report back to the British government with his recommendations for how to hand over power on the due date. This was flexible to within one month but he should aim at 1st June 1948, as the effective date for the transfer of power.

Soon after arrival Mountbatten went to work like a man in a hurry to get the unpleasant task done as fast as possible. First thing he did was to have decided that the Congress and the Muslim League must be given an ultimatum to arrive at a solution to the vexed issues involved and there must be a timeframe for them to do so. He started his tenure by inviting different leaders for one to one talk. The first meeting was with Nehru; it lasted for over three hours. During the course of their discussions, Mountbatten asked Nehru what he thought of Jinnah, encouraging him to be frank, as it would help the Viceroy in planning his strategy for dealing with Jinnah. Nehru was at his vitriolic best. Jinnah, he said, was a man to whom popular acceptance of his community had come very late in life, at over sixty: before that he had not been a major figure in Indian politics—an assertion that ignored the fact that as early as the First World War Jinnah had been one of the great hopes of both Congress and the League. He was, Nehru said dismissively, a successful lawyer but not a very good one. He had succeeded in politics only by taking up a permanently negative attitude, and could never stand up to constructive criticism. (As recorded by Campbell-Johnson). Mountbatten's next appointment was with Liaquat Ali, an aristocrat and an Oxford graduate, but the Viceroy did not find him to be as articulate, intelligent and quick-witted as Nehru. By the end of March, Mountbatten had held individual interviews with every member of the Indian Cabinet. Thereafter, he invited a large number of people to a number of garden parties and lunches to make a personal assessment of the general Indian opinion. It was a brilliant public relations exercise that created a lot of goodwill for the Viceroy.

But Mountbatten had still not met either Gandhi or Jinnah, two men who held the destiny of the country in their hands. Gandhi was still in Bihar and Jinnah was recuperating in Bombay after yet another bout of sickness. Finally, Gandhi arrived on 31st March for a meeting with the Viceroy. The talks lasted for two and a half hours. They met again the next day when Gandhi made a unilateral suggestion to Lord Mountbatten saying, "let Jinnah be the Prime Minister with his own Cabinet, which might be all Muslims, all non-Muslims or whatever if that could ensure that India remained united." The Congress would pledge itself to collaborate with him freely and sincerely", he promised. For good measure, he went on to add that the British must face the consequences of their historic policy of divide and rule. Mountbatten told Gandhi that he found his suggestion of inviting Jinnah to govern 'attractive', and agreed to consider it sympathetically if Congress accepted it. Taking it to be a tacit approval of the Viceroy, Gandhi went into action to make a detailed plan for implementation of his proposal. Both Patel and Nehru were horrified when they heard of the offer made by the Mahatma. They prevailed upon him to immediately withdraw his offer and to accept the realistic solution: 'partition'.

Gandhi should have appreciated that the politicians of the country did not share with him his spirit of renunciation and moral sacrifices. Therefore, no politician, not even Jinnah would have accepted such a deal, particularly when he was seeing his Pakistan on the horizon. That late in the day such gestures and sacrifices had lost all their meaning. Mountbatten quickly came to the conclusion that this was not a practical politician with whom he could reach pragmatic and workable agreements. Congress was also finding the Mahatma's idealistic approach to various vexing problems then facing the country to be embarrassingly out of tune with the ground realities. The Working Committee, particularly Nehru and Patel, started ignoring the Mahatma. They did not even tell Gandhi; much less consult him, about the Working Committee's resolution calling for the partition of Punjab and Bengal. They had also not conveyed to him that they had decided to remove the problem of the Muslim League by accepting the principle of Pakistan. Mountbatten reported that in the course of an interview with Gandhi on 1^{sr} April

1947, "Gandhi urged me whatever happened, to have courage to see the truth and act by it, even though the correct solution might mean grievous loss of life on our departure on an unprecedented scale." (*Transfer of Power*, Vol. IX, p 259). That is, by now Gandhi was resigned to the fact that the hardening of stand taken by the two protagonists could eventually lead to a large-scale destruction all over India, and he was mentally prepared for it.

On 5th April 1947, Mountbatten finally got to meet Jinnah; but was put off because he could not thaw the great man with his much-publicised charm. 'My God, he was cold', he told Campbell-Johnson afterwards. 'It took most of the interview to unfreeze him.' But finally Jinnah did succumb to Mountbatten's charm and technique of encouraging his visitors to talk freely about their opponents, so that he could show sympathy for their views and be seen as a friend. Jinnah was neither a gossip, nor given to running down his opponents as Nehru was; but he did supply a sharp analysis of the Congress and its leadership. Taking the example of Gandhi who nobody listened to, he established that there was not even one Congress leader who spoke for the whole party. In contrast, he said, in the League he was the only one to deal with. If the League did not ratify any decision he made, he said, he would resign and that would be the end of the League. From 5th to 10th April, Mountbatten met Jinnah everyday trying to persuade him to come to some kind of a compromise solution that could prevent partition. But Jinnah continued to be adamant. He then tried to prevail upon Liaquat Ali but found him to be equally unresponsive to anything short of Pakistan. In his personal report of 17th April 1947 addressed to the Prime Minister he stated, ' until I had met him (meaning Jinnah) I would not have thought it possible that a man with such a complete lack of administrative knowledge or sense of responsibility could achieve or hold...so powerful a position.' But he did come around to share Jinnah's apprehensions that Congress did not intend to implement the Cabinet Mission Plan in a fair manner. After his meeting with Sardar Patel on 25th April where the Sardar emphatically stated the Congress would not accept any suggestion for a further degree of parity for the present Central Government, and if the Muslim League did not accept the Cabinet Mission's Plan, Congress desired partition, Mountbatten came to the view that Jinnah might be right in his belief that Muslims would not get a fair deal if Congress was allowed to have its way in any future dispensation. In his report to London after this meeting with Patel, Mountbatten informed the prime minister that as per Patel Congress would never accept "parity" in the Central Government. But Mountbatten continued to keep a close watch on the thinking of Hindu leaders, particularly Nehru so as to decide on his future strategy.

Mountbatten started toying with the idea of granting dominion status immediately, either to an Indian union, or to three dominions—India, Pakistan and the Princely States—all to be linked by a common centre and with himself as a 'Constitutional Viceroy.' In this thought process he was also inspired by Krishna Menon, a close associate of Nehru who was not keen to remain in Commonwealth once the British left. Mountbatten had tried to prevail upon Nehru that membership of Commonwealth was essential if British officers were required to lead the Indian army; seen as a necessity at that time because Indian officers had not attained adequate experience or seniority to run what was known as the world's best fighting machine. Mountbatten sent Menon away to think about ways and means of making Nehru change his mind on the issue of remaining in Commonwealth. But he dropped this idea at once when Ismay pointed out to him that in such a scenario he would cease to have any personal power or any control over the armed forces. Mountbatten kept on with his hard sell. He was conscious of the fact that if a united India was not going to be part of the Commonwealth as Nehru had been hinting at then the British interests could only be served if the partition was allowed to come through. He now started meeting those leaders of the Congress who in his opinion could mould the Party's stand on the issue of remaining in Commonwealth. He told Defence Minister Baldev Singh of the advantages that would accrue to Pakistan because of having agreed to remain in the Commonwealth as it would be able call on British officers for all services, send its own officers for training at British establishments, and receive secret military hardware and information; resultantly, Pakistan's armed forces would soon be immensely superior to those of Hindustan.

With Nehru insisting on a strong centre and with Jinnah clamouring for his Pakistan, and communal riots raging throughout the country, Mountbatten was at the end of his tether. To add to his worries, Suhrawardy began pressing for an independent 'Bangladesh' with Calcutta as its capital. Jinnah welcomed the prospect; but Nehru and Patel were averse to any such arrangement because a Muslim dominated Bangladesh would finally start leaning towards Pakistan, and thus affecting security of residual India. Clearly, there were too many vested interests in the country, and Mountbatten with all his charm, negotiation skills and expertise in 'managing people' had finally run out of options that could allow the British to leave India without acrimony, and in a shape that suited long term imperial interests.

In the meanwhile, retaliatory strikes by both the communities were assuming alarming proportions; massacre for massacre, arson for arson became the order of the day. In the Punjab, RSS militants and Sikhs had by now readied themselves to respond to the League gangs. For what took place in Lahore against Hindus and Sikhs was responded with equal ferocity against the Muslims in Amritsar. Soon, entire villages started moving out from West Punjab towards East Punjab bringing tales of atrocities committed by the Muslims. Concurrently, Muslim refugees started moving towards Pakistan carrying their stories of woe at the hands of Hindu and Sikh gangs. By 19th April, convinced that civil war was in the making, Mountbatten came rapidly to the conclusion that circumstances demanded an immediate partition because the Hindu-Muslim divide had gone too far for any reconciliation between the two communities. Jinnah continued to disagree with just about everything the Viceroy said or did to sustain the unity of India unless Congress agreed to the 'parity factor'. Mountbatten considered Jinnah to be 'a psychopathic case'.

Mountbatten was more than keen to get under the skin of Hindu leadership. Therefore, when Nehru agreed to grant an interview to a prominent British journalist he virtually had certain leading questions planted in order to make his assessment. The details of questions put through Norman Cliff and answers given by Nehru were immediately cabled to the Prime Minister in London.

Pt. Nehru's interview with Mr. Norman Cliff

Memorandum by the Secretary of State for India Office on 31st March 1947 was forwarded in order to indicate thinking of Hindu leadership on the subject of future relations with the British government. Following points were highlighted:

1. The conception of the Cabinet Mission Plan is that parts of India can opt out of the Union now instead of at a later date. This would involve the partition of Punjab and Bengal. Those parts that opt out can deal directly with the Union of India in regard to future relations and common subjects. Though this phrase is consistent with partition into two States it could also be consistent with the idea of small units standing out separately and having individual relations with the Union as opposed to the States of Pakistan and Hindustan.

2. The flat refusal to contemplate Bengal remaining united unless it stays inside the Union.

3. Referendum—Nehru's reply may indicate that Congress will demand a referendum everywhere or nowhere.

4. India and Commonwealth—Nehru emphasises in reply to a question whether there will be a temporary association that

India is going to be a 'Republic' but that the form of its relations with the Commonwealth cannot be defined now.

5. Bases—Nehru makes it clear that the establishment of British bases in Pakistan would adversely affect relations with Hindustan.

6. Division of the Army—If any division takes place it will be fatal and weaken the Central authority in the area it controls.

(*Transfer of Power*—Volume XI refers)

It is obviously clear that Congress had its own and convenient interpretation of the Cabinet Mission Plan. It did not accept the 'grouping' provisions that were crucial to the Muslim League's acceptance of the Plan. There is no doubt that Nehru and Patel did not want to share power with the Muslims by accepting 'parity' and these leaders were willing to have the country broken up so that Congress could rule over the 'residual. India'. Thereafter, there was no other course open to Mountbatten but to go along with Congress because he had also been advised by the prime minister to keep Nehru and Gandhi in good humour. To this end he would consult with, show his communications with the Government in London to Nehru so as to obtain the 'reactions' of the Congress leadership; but he never felt the necessity of giving the same status to Jinnah. Unfortunately for India, Jinnah was too astute a politician and a lawyer to miss the significance of this deliberate slight to his status as a leader of the Muslims. Mountbatten's clever moves to placate the Hindu leadership would thus make Jinnah more and more resolute and determined in seeking his goal—that is either a partition or parity for the Muslims. It was now clear that the situation in India had reached a saturation point where a division of the country was the only course open if the sentiments of Jinnah and lust for power of the Congressmen had to be accommodated.

One thing perhaps could have helped: if Dr. Jal R Patel, who had diagnosed that Jinnah was suffering from pulmonary tuberculosis and didn't have long to live, had made this information available to the leaders of the country. This input could have changed everything; for, Jinnah alone personified the League and none other than him could have forced the issue of dividing the country on communal lines. Certain historians stipulate that Mountbatten was aware of Jinnah's terminal sickness. According to them, he even had a copy of the doctor's report in his possession. But he sought to rewrite India's history with cavalier indifference to the prevailing situation. This way alone he could magnify his own achievements in bringing Raj to an end with speed and élan. Loss of Indian life and Indian property, the agony and torture suffered by millions of Indians had no meaning for him. May be, if Mountbatten had stuck to his original timeframe of eighteen months the things could have sorted themselves out on their own. But that was not to be. Circumstances helped him in executing his macabre plan. Sporadic and intense rioting, looting and killing demanded that the date of British withdrawal be brought forward. For him the solution now was 'rush tactic'. (In his book *Mission with Mountbatten*, Allen Campbell-Johnson wrote: "India in March 1947 was a ship on fire midstream with ammunition in the hold, By then it was a question of putting out the fire before it reached the ammunition. There was in fact no option before us but to do what we did.").

Mountbatten now asked his staff to work on an alternate plan if what was known as 'Plan Union' based on the Cabinet mission proposals did not find favour with the Indian leaders. This plan, known as 'Plan Balkan', allowed for power to be demitted to the provinces or sub-provinces, which would be free to join together in groups; the states could join the groups if they so wished; the interim government would remain until June 1948; Muslim and non-Muslim members of the assemblies in the Punjab and Bengal would vote separately on partition of their provinces, which would take place if both sections voted for it; the predominantly Muslim district of Sylhet in Assam could choose to join the Muslim part of Bengal; and there would be fresh elections in the NWFP to enable its people to decide for themselves where they wanted to go. Jinnah had no violent objection to Plan Balkan. He opined that power be transferred to Provinces as they existed and they could group together or remain separate. When Mountbatten asked his views on keeping Bengal united at the price of remaining outside Pakistan he replied: 'I should be delighted. What is the use of Bengal without Calcutta; they much better remain united and independent. Jinnah could afford to be magnanimous; his Pakistan had nothing to lose by such an arrangement. But things could get difficult for the residual India.'

NWFP had an election just a year back and the majority had expressed its opinion by voting for Congress Government. This was not acceptable to Jinnah; for, how could he have justified a Muslim Pakistan when in his backyard existed Congress Government in what primarily was a Muslim dominated region. There was an urgent need to correct the situation. The methodology adopted was the same, as had been done in others parts of the country where there was a fair chance of creating a Muslim majority by using muscle power. The League started infiltrating its volunteers in a large number in the province and was busy in creating a turmoil that was leading to breakdown of administration. Aim of the League was to establish that the legally and constitutionally elected government had lost people's mandate. The Governor of the Frontier, Olaf Caroe, also gave credence to the League propaganda by stating that the Congress Government of the province had lost people's confidence, and that there was a need for a fresh round of elections so as to ascertain people's wish. The Viceroy played along because if (and it certainly would have) NWFP opted for India then there would be a permanent source of trouble in the region, particularly when the Afghans were already taking more than normal interest in the NWFP knowing that India could not hold on to a province that was not contiguous to the rest of the country. So a referendum was mandated for the province. The idea was to allow the Indian people to make their own decisions on partition, so that the British could not be blamed if things went wrong. Ismay was sent to London to present this fresh plan to the government. Mountbatten asked for Cabinet approval by 10th May, so that he could present it to all the political leaders at Simla one week later.

But the Plan did not find favour with the Indian leaders. Jinnah's negative reaction was followed by protests from the Congress Working Committee over the clause dealing with fresh elections in NWFP where a Congress led government was in power. With the League having established a strong base in the state in the interim it was almost certain that the Congress ministry led by Dr. Khan Sahib, brother of Abdul Gaffar Khan would be wiped out. Mountbatten liked the idea of a referendum in the NWFP instead. The proposal upset Jinnah who demanded that elections should follow referendum—this alternative was not acceptable to Nehru and the Congress. Squabbling started all over again. Finally, Mountbatten coerced Nehru and Patel to agree to this line of approach to resolve the issue. Cleansing process gained momentum; leaders in NWFP, Punjab and Bengal went into an overdrive to ensure victory in a referendum or election by increasing their vote base by hastening the departure of the rival communities from their strongholds. Congress leaders had clearly shown a lack of vision by agreeing to a referendum in the NWFP when the same process was not to be followed in other Muslim majority provinces. Congress leaders eventually just abandoned Badshah Khan and his Pakhtoons to their fate.

Khan, in order to avoid further bloodshed, decided to boycott the referendum because a large number of non-Muslim populations had already fled the province, and the League had managed to intimidate most of the Muslim population. Congress made a half-hearted effort to have the option of independence also included in the terms of referendum but gave up the idea when the Viceroy drew attention to the fact that the Congress was not willing to give such an option to any other province. To Mountbatten it looked as if Nehru was mobilising his forces to frustrate the partition. On 2nd June 1947 Mountbatten held a meeting with the

Indian leaders where he stressed upon urgency to transfer power as soon as possible. The only objection, which he could see to such an early transfer of power, was a likely accusation that the British were "quitting" on their obligations. He considered that it was the duty of the British to continue to help—not to rule—India. They would stay at the disposal of the Indians for as long as the latter wished. Concurrently, he also started marketing his plan that would allow the British to cause as much mischief as possible so as to render India perennially weak after independence.

Seeing that the Cabinet Mission Plan had not made much headway with the Indian leaders, Attlee and his colleagues gave their approval to the fresh proposals forwarded by Mountbatten with minor modifications, which were seemingly semantic and were not expected to influence the basic idea. The approved version of official plan (Plan Balkan) was cabled from London on 10th May. An exuberant Mountbatten announced to the press that on the 17th of May he would present the Government's final decision to the Indian leaders. However, soon he started to have doubts because what appeared to be minor improvements to the original document could also be interpreted as fundamental changes. The whole plan was now totally different not only from the Cabinet mission plan but even deviated from the one, which he had forwarded for approval. Beset with doubts, Mountbatten elected to let Nehru have a look at what the Cabinet had approved with a clear understanding that the latter would only advise as a friend of the likely response of the Indian leadership. Nehru was aghast; the approved plan encouraged Balkanisation of the country by allowing individual provinces such as Bengal and the NWFP to break away as independent sovereign states, rather than forming groups as had been originally contemplated. As for the princes, the revised plan was a direct invitation to them to remain independent kingdoms, thereby creating a situation where there could be hundreds of mini countries, all needing British help to survive. How Attlee hoped such a plan to be accepted by the Indian leaders has never been answered successfully.

Mountbatten was rattled by Nehru's reaction; he would have been severely embarrassed if he had gone ahead with his planned conference on the seventeenth. He was clearly at his tether's end, but was also relieved that he hadn't held his 'conference' as announced. Rejection after an official announcement would have been too embarrassing for the government and could have effectively and terminally damaged his chances of becoming the First Sea Lord; a job he had been pining for, manipulating for and stepping on toes all his life to attain that goal. V P Menon, the seasoned bureaucrat and a close confident of Patel, now came to his rescue with yet another plan, which envisaged early transfer of power would essentially retain unity of India, while allowing Pakistan to secede. Knowing that Jinnah had by now reconciled to the idea of a truncated Pakistan, Mountbatten wanted Menon to quickly work out the details so that Nehru's opinion could be obtained before he left Simla for Delhi. He also cabled Ismay in London, telling him to hold everything as the draft plan had been cancelled and a newer version was in pipeline. Mountbatten conveyed to Ismay that he had good reason to believe that both sides would accept dominion status if power were to be transferred earlier than June 1948. Campbell-Johnson was asked to think of a plausible lie for cancellation of the impending press conference that was to follow formal announcement of the 'approved future of India.' All that Campbell-Johnson could think of was to inform the press party that owing to imminence of the Parliamentary recess in London, it has been found necessary to postpone H.E. the Viceroy's meeting with the Indian leaders announced to begin on 17th May, until 2nd June 1947. On return to Delhi, Mountbatten found prime ministerial summons waiting for him to come personally to London and explain why the whole thing had gone out of control when the Viceroy had all along been telling the Government that the situation was well within his grasp. The prime minister also wanted to be reassured that the latest plan did have the approval of the Indian leaders. Before leaving for London he decided to have a final meeting with the Hindu leaders. The confusion amongst the Indian leaders was total. Jinnah wanted his Pakistan. Patel and Nehru wanted India to remain undivided but on their terms.

The British Parliament swiftly implemented the decision to partition India. In London, Atlee introduced on July third the India Independence Bill, which without opposition was rushed through all its constitutional stages in one week. The Bill set up India and Pakistan as self-governing dominions, on the same lines as Canada and Australia. It was recognised that dominion status would only be a temporary condition. Once the two new countries had the control of their own affairs they would decide for themselves their form of government.

Pragmatism and prevailing situation demanded that the transfer of power to the two dominions be undertaken in two stages if the whole exercise had to be peaceful. The first stage should have been confined to ascertaining the views of the Assemblies of Punjab, Sind, Bengal; and the referendum in NWFP and Sylhet in Assam; to be followed by demarcation of areas as recommended by the Boundary Commission. Alongside, notional division of the armed forces, civil services, assets etc should have been undertaken. This stage should have culminated with the establishment of two fully independent governments in the two

Dominions ready to start running the administration. In the second stage, a central authority composed of leaders from both the countries and ideally under a common Governor General could have worked out the modalities of a smooth transition. As there were a large number of British forces still stationed in India and the communal virus had not yet bitten the native soldiers it would have been possible to ensure that the decisions taken by the central authority were implemented without any hesitation. The interim period between the formation of two independent countries and 30th June 1948, the date originally set for the British to leave, would have given adequate time for the things to settle down. But this did not happen.

For generations past the stress in Indian politics had been all on freedom of the country. Now that the freedom was in sight, the balance had swung over to the other extreme and unity of the country had once again become a major problem, just as it was when the traders from overseas had started taking control of the country. No lessons had been learnt in the interim. In 1946 Jinnah had been prepared to find the Pakistan demand realised, at least, temporarily, by the grouping of the six provinces within the Union of India. In 1947 he was willing to see the demand satisfied by the separate dominion-hood of provinces. But Congress leaders who wanted a dual transfer of power to a single truncated Pakistan dominion and a single Indian dominion frustrated him.

Footnote

1. GD Khosla Stern Reckoning p 100.

17

Formation of Pakistan

'The British are a just people. They have left India in exactly the same state of chaos as they found it—in utter chaos'. So said a Magistrate (The Making of Pakistan by Richard Symonds)

On 9th March 1947 in an interview with the Associated Press of America at New Delhi, Vallabhbhai Patel asserted that the political impasse would be broken at once if power is transferred to the Central Government "as it stood" with the "Viceroy standing out". In that event, "immediately there would be peace in the country". He further said, "If there were conflicts in the Cabinet on any question, the majority will rule. (*Transfer of Power* Vol. X pp. 716-717). Patel further reiterated his stand when during an interview with Mountbatten on 25th April 1947 he said, "Congress would not accept any suggestion for a further degree of parity for the present Central Government and if the Muslim League did not accept the Cabinet Mission Plan, Congress desire partition because the Congress had reached the maximum limit of their concession." When Mountbatten brought out that the thing that most worried Mr Jinnah was the prospect of a Centre permanently dominated by the Hindus, the Sardar replied that he would never consider parity in the Central Government. Mountbatten was now absolutely clear that the Cabinet Mission Plan was dead, and partition of India was the only solution. With the assistance of V P Menon and other advisers he set about evolving a plan for division of the country that could be acceptable to the Congress and the Muslim League.

In a meeting on 3rd June 1947 Mountbatten tried to persuade Congress that it would be valueless for them to have in their own territories a large section of population, which was bitterly hostile to them. This would only be embarrassing to their own development. He, however tried to score brownie points by making sanctimonious statements like, "He was as much opposed to the partition of the Provinces as he was to the partition of India as a whole, but nobody who had seen the communal bitterness prevalent in the country with riots, bloodshed, massacre and torture could believe that this strong feeling could be healed. It was no good appealing to logic or reason. The only way where the peoples of India could eventually live together would be to split them now and start afresh. The only way power could be handed over in the immediate future was on the basis of 1935 Act with Dominion Status and the British would remain as the servants of India as long as they were wanted." Congress leaders were at their wit's end. They knew that by dilly-dallying for so long over and by negating the options made available hithertofore they had lost their advantage. Even Mahatma Gandhi, who had earlier been saying that partition would come over his dead body, had come to the conclusion that circumstances had arisen which made partition unavoidable. Mountbatten used his famous manipulative skills to the hilt. He told Nehru that divided Punjab and Bengal would make Pakistan politically so insecure, economically so weak and militarily so unsafe that it would never pose any threat to India. To further lay it thick and strong he also prophesied that eventually Pakistan might even rejoin India. Nehru bought this line of thought in totality. "Let Jinnah have Pakistan", he declared: "By cutting off the head we will get rid of the headache."

An elated and obviously relieved Mountbatten immediately informed the prime minister of his latest 'coup'. The main thing on his mind was not to give Indian (Hindu) leaders any time for a rethink, understand the enormity of what they were getting into and be provoked to change their stand. Therefore, on the evening of 3rd June itself he made a Radio Broadcast to the nation where he announced future plans of the British government with regard to what lay in store for Indians when the foreign rulers finally left the country. Before they could marshal their resources and regroup Mountbatten struck. He unilaterally decided to transfer power on 15th August because he felt that was in the interest of Indians not to delay. (A book on Mountbatten reports him as having told its authors, "The date I chose came out of the blue...I hadn't worked it out exactly then...Because it was the second anniversary of Japan's surrender. Larry Collins &Dominique Lapierre—*Mountbatten and the Partition of India*). Later, he tried to give a different set of his reasons, but nothing absolves him from the fact that his haste and hurry only added to the problems that were already burning the country.

In order to establish that there was a commonality of thinking among the Imperial government and the leaders of more prominent communities in the country, he wanted the Hindu, Muslim and Sikh leaders to also broadcast their messages so as to assuage feelings of fear and uncertainty about the future of citizens who were likely to be caught on the wrong side of the impending divide. As per an earlier agreement with the Indian leaders Pandit Nehru also broadcast an address to the nation after the Viceroy. He, *interalia,* agreed with the Viceroy that the country needed to be divided on communal basis. (Note: Full text printed in *"Independence and After-A* Collection of more important speeches of Jawaharlal Nehru from September 1946 to May 1949," Government of India 1949).

Jinnah in his broadcast laid stress on the proposed referendum in NWFP. He kept his options partially open by stressing that the final decision would be taken by All India Muslim League that was to meet on 9th June 1947. But he did let slip in his rhetoric for the NWFP Muslims to unite and forcefully opt for joining Pakistan. (Jinnah actually told the Viceroy that he could only speak for himself. He would like Viceroy to consider that, in order to give a definite answer, it was necessary to make the people understand stressing that Muslim League was a democratic organisation. In order to lay it thick he emphasised that " he and his 'Working Committee' would have to go before their masters, the people, for a final decision.")

Patel took offence to Jinnah's abuse of this facility when he exhorted NWFP Muslims. Patel immediately wrote to Mountbatten conveying his feelings that Jinnah had committed a sacrilege by making a political, partisan and propagandist broadcast and had turned All India Radio into a Muslim League platform by appealing to League persuasion.

Baldev Singh followed these principal participants with his address to the Sikhs. Largely he stuck to Nehru's line and tried to calm nerves of the Sikhs who were agitated over likelihood of their being uprooted from West Punjab. But nobody was taken in by his speech. Instead, the Sikhs elected to give credence to Master Tara Singh who had all along been painting a dismal picture where his community was concerned.

On 3rd June 1947 in the Durbar Hall of the Viceroy's House, Mountbatten announced the full Partition Plan, making it public for the first time. The salient features were:

- Division of the subcontinent into India and Pakistan.
- Pakistan to be truncated—on the basis of 'contiguous areas' of population. Armed forces to be divided along with all the assets.
- Referendum in NWFP and Assam.

- Establishment of two Constituent Assemblies if the existing one is not acceptable to both the parties.

- Establishment of a Boundary Commission in Punjab and Bengal to demarcate the boundaries on the basis of contiguous majority areas of Muslims and non-Muslims that will also take into account certain other factors.

- Independence for the Indian States, but these were advised to accede to one or the other dominion.

- Grant of Dominion status to India and Pakistan.

Anticipated date for handing over to be some date in 1947 itself.

Notwithstanding the carnage that was being experienced by the Indians, Mountbatten went ahead with his designated date of 15th August. And so the blow fell on the country's integrity. Our leaders had failed to agree on how to put our house in order. May be they were chary of the reaction of the people who were already fed up with the ongoing turmoil and were now reconciled to whatever the fate willed, provided calm and peace could be restored at the soonest.

One mitigating circumstance for this indecent haste to get out is the fact that between March and May 1947, Jinnah was perpetually propagating formation of a League ministry in Punjab so that the whole province could eventually be absorbed into Pakistan of his vision. This was something the Viceroy could never have allowed to happen because a unified Punjab would have made Pakistan too strong an entity for Britain to manipulate; such an arrangement would have also caused grievous hurt to Sikh sentiments, a community that had served the Empire with such a distinction during the two great wars. Mountbatten had no option but to speed up the process of transfer of power before Jinnah and his League could further muddy the already deteriorating situation in the country, a situation that Mountbatten had partially helped to create by advancing the date for withdrawal of the British from India.

The utter turmoil confronting the Indian leadership made Nehru and his colleagues in the Indian National Congress to insist that Mountbatten continued as the Governor General of the newly created dominion of India. They failed to see that all along Mountbatten had been building up a case for this demand to come from the Indian leaders. British government floated the idea that Mountbatten should also perform the same role for Pakistan till the situation could be brought under control. Megalomaniac that he was, Mountbatten had already conveyed to the Government that his popularity was such that there should be no difficulty in his becoming the Governor General of both,

India and Pakistan. He was confident that as both the parties looked up to him as their messiah it would be easy enough to meet this requirement. He had after all given Jinnah his Pakistan: there was no reason to suspect that the latter would not reciprocate. The prime minister and his cabinet colleagues were, in any case, so enamoured with him that they gave Mountbatten virtually a free hand to proceed along his planned agenda for division of the country, its assets and liabilities in any manner that he deemed fit. He started behaving as an independent head of state rather than as the personal representative of the King. But to his horror and surprise Mountbatten found that Jinnah would have none of it. All his efforts to sell the idea of a common Governor-General with its (perceived) advantages cut no ice with Jinnah. He wanted to be the Governor General of Pakistan himself. When Mountbatten, to discourage him, brought to his notice that the Governor-General had less power than a prime minister, Jinnah retorted: "In my position it is I who will give the advice and others will act on it." That Jinnah could not be persuaded against taking up the Governor-Generalship of Pakistan ruled out any hope of eventual unity between the two dominions and signalled that India and Pakistan would be what Jinnah had always intended once he had decided to pitch for a Muslim homeland eight years ago. Hereafter the two nations would have no link with each other except by treaty. Nehru, who was leader rather than founder of India, was content to be just the prime minister.

Having failed to secure Jinnah's concurrence for his continuation as the Governor-General of both the countries Mountbatten decided to teach a lesson to the ungrateful Indians. In June, after three months in India and in consultation with the Atlee Cabinet, Mountbatten announced that to wait until June 1948, was too long a wait. Jinnah had now come up with another demand; he wanted undivided Punjab and Bengal and a corridor linking East and West Pakistan. There was a very little chance of this demand finding favour with anyone, but it did manage to convince Nehru that partition was now totally unavoidable.

Instead of planned seventeen months the date of British leaving India was changed, it was brought forward to 15th August 1947: at the same time a Paper on the "Administrative Consequences of Pakistan" was also circulated. In a press conference held on 4th June 1947, Mountbatten gave reasons for pre-poning the date of departure of the British from India. He said that once a decision (to transfer power) had been made there was no point in delaying its implementation. In any case, Indian leaders were anxious to assume their full responsibility (Note: According to *the Statesman* of 5th June 1947 this passage read, " Waiting would only mean that I should be responsible ultimately for law and order and the general conduct of the Government. In point of fact, however, much you might use Interim Government; it would never be the same thing unless they were legally in control of the responsibility). The Viceroy also announced at that press conference that the transfer to two dominions could be affected on 14th/15th August. His declaration left only three months for the creation of two new administrations, for dividing the Armed forces and for defining the frontiers of two new states. The treaties between the King-Emperor and hundreds of princely states were unilaterally abrogated, thereby ensuring that without the British support they would inevitably have to opt for either India or Pakistan. Now Mountbatten was in a hurry to get out because the circumstances were leading to a civil war, which the British could not contain or suppress; soldiers and policemen were already shifting their loyalty according to their religion and thus could no longer be trusted to side with Britain if the government decided to use force to quell the riots then raging all over the country. And clever as he was, Mountbatten did not want the British to be blamed by history for the mess they had created in the sub-continent. The British also wanted to leave India too weak to be of any consequence during polarisation of nations in the West and the Communist (or the East blocks) in the aftermath of the 2nd World War. Nehru had already given his mind on the subject and it wasn't in the best interest of His Majesty's Government.

All through Mountbatten had kept his ear to the ground. He had been constantly gauging reactions of Indian leaders and that of the common men. He was aware of the fact that Gandhi was not particularly happy with the idea of partition; and he was also aware of the fact that the Mahatma was powerful enough to sway emotions of the people, both Hindus and Muslims, and thus could spike his plans for speedy exit with minimal collateral damage to the British interests in India.

On learning that Gandhi was upset with impending partition and might voice his opinion during his next prayer meeting, Mountbatten invited Gandhi for a meeting where he told him that although many newspapers had christened it a "Mountbatten Plan" they should really have christened it as a "Gandhi Plan" since Gandhi himself suggested all the ingredients to him.

As per Mountbatten:

- Mr Gandhi advised me to try and get the Cabinet Mission Plan or any other Plan retaining the unity of India accepted by all the leaders provided it did not involve coercion or violence. I had bent every effort to follow the first part of his advice; but when no agreement could be reached I had followed the second part of his advice and not insisted on a Plan that would involve coercion with its attendant risk of violence.

- Mr Gandhi had advised me to leave the choice of their own future to the Indian people. It was, therefore, he who gave me the idea of letting the Provinces choose, and the method proposed seemed simplest and fairest way of carrying out his suggestion.

- Mr Gandhi had told me that the British should quit India and transfer power as soon as possible and not later than the end of the year. I told him that this had been the most difficult idea of his to carry out, and I was very proud to have found a solution.

- I told him that I had understood that in his earlier days he had not been averse to dominion status. Mr Gandhi was kind enough to say this was indeed so, and that even during the War he had expressed himself as not being against it, and he later sent me an extract from *Harijan* dated 16th December, 1939 in which appeared the words "Similarly, I have said to a friend that if Dominion status was offered I should take it, and expect to carry India with me."

(*Transfer of Power Papers*, Volume XI page 131-132).

Seemingly, Gandhi was convinced that Mountbatten had honestly tried to follow his advice and that he had taken a far greater part in shaping the future of India than had at first sight appeared to him from the way the Plan was worded. It appears that having appreciated that unless India broke up his protégé was not likely to have much of a future in a "united India" Gandhi played along with Mountbatten's game plan which suited just about every body but the poor citizens of the country who were going to suffer the consequences of partition. Gandhi apparently abandoned the idea of criticising Mountbatten and his Plan during his any forthcoming Prayer meeting. That, utter confusion, chaos and killings had manifested themselves with the freedom looming large on the horizon obviously bothered neither the Viceroy nor the future prime minister of India; nor for that matter, the father of the nation who had already ensured his Nirvana by being a Mahatma. If you and I suffered this indifference then so be it.

The new country of Pakistan, organised evidently in an indecent haste, consisted basically of the western Punjab and eastern Bengal, together with Baluchistan and Sind adjoining the Punjab. It was to contain about 80 million of the 400 million of the sub-continent's population. Over a thousand miles of Indian Territory separated these two segments of Pakistan. Soon after the announcement defining the areas, which were to form Pakistan, was made, a sort of cleansing process started. Muslims started expediting Hindu departure by setting fire to their houses in Lahore, Dacca and elsewhere, and Hindus responded by doing the same to Muslim property. In the weeks before and after August 15th, millions of people fled from their homes to seek refuge in territory that was to be in control of their own religion. With just about no one to control the situation, there were massacres of innocent people across the divide. Stories of atrocities spread from province to province, multiplying in horror as they were retold, and whole communities of Hindus and Muslims sought bloody revenge. Exactly how many died has never been computed—it certainly ran into hundreds of thousands, and may well have been over a few millions. India suffered destruction on a scale similar to that which Europe had just gone through in the course of the Second World War. Only difference is that in Europe people have again come together because they saw an economic necessity in doing so, but the bitterness of this calamity still lingers in India and Pakistan.

18

Who Made Me A Refugee?

Britain's involvement in the 2nd World War and build up of the opinion of America and other democracies for India to be free, could have allowed this country to remain one, but the Mahatma was too far gone to think differently from his already propagated thoughts and opinions on the subject of majority opinion versus minority aspirations. Things apparently of no significance sometimes matter deeply, and it is strange that Nehru was a party—and Abdul Ghaffar Khan also—to the ceremonial opening in the late thirties of a temple to Mother India, 'Bharat Mata Mandir' in Varanasi, on the walls of which are engraved, along with a relief map of India, the alphabets of all major languages of India with exception only that of Urdu on account of foreign origin of the script. How this kind of thoughtless affront to important elements of our own people could pass muster seems nearly inexplicable (*Recalling India's Struggle for Freedom*, Hiren Mukerjee, p-130).

Lord Wavell, who was more of a soldier than a politician made a last ditch effort to save the country's unity when he invited Gandhi in order to persuade him to make Congress Party see reason and accept the Cabinet Mission Plan which had taken some kind of a final shape after prolonged and often painfully long-drawn deliberations. But the attempt failed because Gandhi made a distinction between "right" and "duty". "If it was the 'right' of the Congress to nominate a nationalist Muslim it could be waived, but if was a 'duty' owed to the nationalist Muslim the matter was different," he said. During the argument, which took very acrimonious turn, the Viceroy told his visitor that he was not a trained lawyer like Nehru, Gandhi and Jinnah but a plain and simple soldier who had seen enough death and destruction to seek peace at all costs. Gandhi banged on the table saying: "If India wants its blood-bath, it shall have it."[1] (A dramatic account of this session is available in

"The Last Days of the British Raj" by Mosley pp. 37-42). Gandhi followed it up with a letter to the Viceroy where he was rather admonitory. He told the Viceroy, "as representative of the King you cannot afford to be a military man only, nor to ignore the law, much less the law of your own making. You should be assisted, if necessary, by a legal mind enjoying your full confidence." Gandhi, as always, blamed the communal troubles entirely on the British presence, and repeated his demand for the immediate withdrawal of the British army, leaving its peacekeeping role to Congress. 'Quit India', he reiterated, was unconditional. But it appears that the Mahatma was gradually getting convinced that the Hindu-Muslim issue was not going to be resolved without a fight between the two. In a conversation he had with one Major Wyatt on 13th April 1946, the apostle of peace pontificated: "There may well have to be a blood-bath in India before its problems are solved. He would urge non-violence on Congress but does not expect them to observe it, The only thing he expects from Congress in the event of civil war is that they will fight decently and take one tooth for one tooth, and not a hundred teeth for one tooth as the British do." (*Transfer of Power* Vol. VII, pp 262) Penderel Moon in the 'Epilogue' of his 'Viceroy's Journal' observes: "If it was not for Gandhi's last minute intervention, the Congress would have accepted the Mission's proposal for an Interim Government, and, with a Congress-League Coalition Government installed in office at the beginning of July, the communal outbreaks of the next few months would never have occurred."

In a discussion, which, Attlee held on 10th December 1946 with a number of his Cabinet colleagues, he said: "...Pandit Nehru's present policy seemed to be to secure complete domination by Congress throughout the Government of India. If a constitution was framed which had this effect, there would certainly be strong reactions from the Muslims. Provinces with a Muslim majority might refuse to join a Central Government on such terms at all; and the ultimate result of Congress policy might be establishment of that Pakistan which they so much dislike. The situation might so develop as to result in civil war in India with all the bloodshed that would entail. There seems to be little realisation among Indian leaders of the risk that ordered government might collapse." (*Transfer of Power*, Vol. IX p 319). In view of all that had happened till then it would have been extremely unlikely that Jinnah and his League would accept any solution that could compromise Muslim aspirations.

May be, like Gandhi, Nehru too was convinced that once the British left and a 'progressive' government took over the religious antagonism would disappear: Clearly a naive and unconvincing reading of the situation, having known what Jinnah wanted at that point of time. The problem was that Jinnah, a liberal by conviction, was hostile to state control through centralisation and planning, something that Nehru had been propagating as a future policy for a free India. On top of everything else Jinnah's strategy was totally dictated by his perception of the power equation between the League and the Congress. There was hardly a meeting ground between these two widely divergent views on India's future. Not surprisingly, Jinnah refused to participate in the Constituent Assembly. He wanted his Pakistan: he also assured other Hindu leaders that the Hindu minority would be safe and secure in Muslim dominated states just as he expected the Muslims to be cared for in the Hindu majority states. The partition of the country suited the British very well. Having tasted slavery at their hands for so long and having experienced all kinds of manipulations engineered in London and Calcutta/Delhi the Indians were not likely to be suitably inclined to foreign relation policies that were currently being pursued by the British Government. Nehru had already been expressing his opinion about the wisdom of a 'socialist model' for an independent India; this effectively meant that in all possibility he was going to be more inclined towards the Soviet Bloc.

Another plausible reason could be that Jawaharlal's political philosophy, his impatience with religion, his contempt for communal politics and his emphasis on economic rather than political character of nationalism was not understood properly by his peers in the Congress who saw in themselves as the rightful successors of the Raj, nor by those who wanted to be seen as protecting Muslim rights. While writing his "Autobiography" in the middle thirties, Jawaharlal Nehru had noted: "We have to deal not with Communism" – to which he was definitely attracted at the time- " but with the addition of an extra syllable, with communalism. And communally, India is in Dark Age..."[2] With such a vision and apparent aversion for anything communal Nehru failed to see that the Congress stand vis-à-vis Muslim League was eventually going to put Jinnah on the defensive. He not only condoned his party men's slighting of Jinnah he actually encouraged it. By 1946 Jinnah had been prepared to have his demand for Pakistan realised, even temporarily, by the grouping of the six provinces within the Union of India. In 1947 he was willing to see the demand satisfied by a separate dominion-hood of provinces. But Congress leaders who wanted a dual transfer of power to a single truncated Pakistan and a single Indian dominion frustrated him.

The publication of Maulana Azad's autobiography 'India Wins Freedom' in a complete version in November 1988 provoked much controversy. This edition, among other things, fixes responsibility for the partition of India at one place on Nehru, and at another place on Vallabhbhai Patel by observing that 'it would not perhaps be unfair to say that Patel was the founder of India's partition'. The Working Committee resolution of 8th March 1947 had been passed without consulting Gandhi. He was at the time in Bihar on a mission to restore communal harmony. On his return he asked Nehru and Patel to explain their rationale behind the resolution because he himself was against partition of the country. Patel replied on 24th March that the resolution had been adopted after 'deepest' deliberations...you have expressed your views against it. But you are, of course, entitled to say what you feel is right. Nehru in his letter of 25th March argued that the resolution had been passed 'so that reality might be brought into picture'. Clearly, by then, and having enjoyed power, both Nehru and Patel had come to the conclusion that Gandhi was no longer relevant. At his prayer meeting on 1[sr] April, a hapless and apparently saddened Gandhi said, 'my writ runs no more... No one listens to me any more'.

Why did Nehru and Patel accept partition is one question that has been intriguing the historians all these years? Ram Manohar Lohia, the famous Socialist leader, explains that the ageing, tired and power-hungry Congress leaders had by then become so impatient with all these impediments that were coming in their way to grabbing the riches of office that they collectively agreed to let Jinnah have his Pakistan so that they could get to rule over the country's dismembered parts. Another explanation is that the Congress leadership had neither the temperament nor enough mental strength to face a likely civil war. This is where Nehru and Patel failed the nation. Abraham Lincoln faced a much worse situation in 1860 when people in the north and south America went to war over slavery and the situation took such a turn that even preservation of the union came under threat. Lincoln stuck to his principles and his stand over the issues involved. He did not let his advisers or his cabinet to influence his judgment at any stage saying that regardless of whatever the price north has to pay unity of the country would have to be sustained. For over four years and against all odds Lincoln insisted that 'if we fail it will go to prove the incapacity of the people to govern themselves'. In the civil war millions of Americans on either side died, Lincoln himself was assassinated but he ensured that the unity of the country was preserved. Either Nehru or Patel, or may be both, could have taken a stand on the issue of break up of India; but they did not do so. Nehru was smelling power; and in a united India Jinnah would not have allowed him to rule as he wished to. The British could not have accepted an India that was not likely to remain in their sphere of influence; Nehru was already singing praises of the Soviet model. The English had to help division of the country in a manner that would leave both sides unsatisfied and fighting over territory for generations to come. That, it would also dissipate India's economic and industrial energy while trying to contain Pakistan's ambitions, and thus weakening it for a long time to come was an added bonus. The Congress had already shown its negative stance by isolating itself from the war effort. A united India was no good where the British and American interests in the post-war world were concerned was an obvious conclusion where our rulers were concerned.

It could not have been unknown to the Congress leaders that Jinnah developed his fixation about Pakistan late in life, after many jolts to the secularity to which he had long tried to cling, though in his own way. After Subhas Bose, as Congress President (in 1938) corresponded with Jinnah without success, Jawaharlal's personal qualities seemed to make Jinnah thaw a little and correspondence followed in 1939. In retrospect, it appears strangely thoughtless that Nehru virtually threw away unequalled opportunities of an approach at least to an understanding. He wrote repeatedly of so-called "psychological barriers", wondering even "what purpose will be served by our discussing with each other". It is a pity that Jawaharlal, normally so conscious of his own personality and its diverse and complicated pulls, was insensible of analogous, if dissimilar, intricacies in the mental make up of the older man. (*Recalling India's Struggle for Freedom*, Hiren Mukerjee p-131). On 18th October 1939, Nehru wrote to Jinnah: "I am ashamed of myself in so far as I have not been able to contribute anything substantial to the solution of the Hindu-Muslim problem in a friendly way." This acceptance of failure does not behove a leader of that stature, particularly when he had not cited any compelling reasons or compulsions for his lack of action to ensure that the country remained united—fatal deficiency in a leader who aspired to be a nation-builder, and was far too well educated and exposed to the modern world to be a pragmatist and a realist.

There was a clear example of a thriving democracy in America where a wide range of divisive and divergent views had been accommodated in order to ensure unity of a newly founded country. Why was Congress not willing to take a leaf out of the American Constitution will forever be an enigma. George Washington's famous words when certain states were trying to remain out of the American union because of powerful vested interests: "...the Constitution we now present, is the result of amity and that mutual deference and concession which the peculiarity of our political situation rendered indispensable," should have given Nehru and Patel an idea of what the Americans had done to manage conflicts and thus created a great country. But realism was never a favourite with the Congress leaders, they allowed themselves to unwittingly become instruments in the hands of fundamentalists of different hues. It was in the interest of the British to string both Hindu and Muslim leaders along. Nehru was seeing prime ministership of India coming his way sooner than he had anticipated and if that broke up the country then so be it. To be fair to him it must be stated that throughout his life Nehru was distinctly secular in his deeds, actions and decisions. He was trusted and loved by Muslims in India, they reposed much more faith in him and his fairness than what they did even in Gandhi. And yet, he failed to grapple with the spectre of partition. His share in the country's failure to overcome machinations of selfish politicians and clever businessmen from England is consequently much more than anyone else. In spite of an absolutely clear understanding of the issues involved and an abundance of goodwill he had earned over the years from both Hindus and Muslims, he failed. It was this failure of his, which allowed the British, and more specifically Mountbatten, to get away with this crime against humanity where they made partition of this country on the grounds of religion appear a most natural meeting the aspirations of the people of this sub-continent, a division that continues to cause ill-will and unfriendliness, not among the common people of both the countries but respective governments.

A reading of official documents, hithertofore classified, leave no doubt that the Congress was not interested in working the Cabinet Mission Plan in the spirit in which it was intended. Its opposition to Jinnah's call for parity and its demand for a Dominion Cabinet, if granted without resolving Muslim apprehensions, would have enabled the Congress to get hold of real power over the Government of India as well over the Provincial Governments and would have allowed it to settle all the issues on its own terms. In this Cripps and Pethick-Lawrence, who had been mandated to keep both Nehru and Gandhi in good humour, directly or indirectly encouraged the Congress leaders to hold on to their stand where Muslim aspirations were concerned. More importantly, the Mission was giving contradictory and confusing assurances on grouping of the Provinces to both the parties, all the time hoping that something would turn up. On 16th May 1946, Pethick-Lawrence and Cripps explained their rationale for the grouping and functioning of the Groups to the Muslim representatives: and, on 24th June 1946 explanations given to Gandhi were contrary to those given earlier to the Muslims. Wavell repeatedly pressed the Government to make a categorical statement on the subject, but his advice was not taken seriously. (Wavell wrote… "The Congress will not seriously negotiate with the Muslim League so long as they can get what they want by pressure on H.M.G." He said further, "I am confident that H.M.G can only succeed by stating quite openly and firmly what they intended by their Plan as to the method of drawing groups and provincial constitutions…" (*Transfer of Power* Vol. 1X pp 241-242). This unwillingness to state firmly to both the parties what the Plan meant for each one of them, ultimately lead to its failure. It was only after Jinnah's call for Direct Action and consequent bloodshed and likelihood of a civil war that the His Majesty's Government felt compelled to act.

Any pragmatic study of the events leading to India's freedom reveals that the partition of the country was not inevitable. It became inevitable because Hindu leaders, including a leader as well-intentioned and liberal in his thinking as Nehru failed to realise that by 1946 the Muslim League dominated the Muslims as the Congress dominated the Hindus: And the fact, that in any future dispensation the two would have to live and work together if India was to remain united never got registered with any one of them except perhaps for Azad. The lesson that an appeal to religious sentiment to secure political goals was dangerous to the unity of India was not learnt, is obvious from what followed in the years to come. Nehru, Patel and Gandhi were great leaders in their own ways. But none of them had either the vision or the courage to take risks in the larger interests of the country. Even Abraham Lincoln's example of having stood for his principles and unity of America inspired no concrete plan among these visionaries which could save India's unity when all along it was clearly known that Jinnah's call for Pakistan was primarily a bargaining point for garnering some specific concessions for the Muslims. (Jinnah, in fact, admitted as much to a close friend. He told his friend that he was only a lawyer whose brief was to get a 'fair deal' for the Muslims in any future dispensation. And as a lawyer he had been all along using constitutional means towards this end till he felt that the Congress was bent upon using a 'Hindu majority' to stifle Muslim aspirations.) Throughout the 1920s and for a long while thereafter his political ambition remained at the all-India level, he along with his liberal allies cooperated with the Congress Swaraj Party in demanding introduction of political responsibility for the Indians. However, by then demands of Muslim political interests had also escalated; both in Punjab and Bengal. The regional leaders had started talking of Muslim majority independent states. Their Hindu counterparts were equally vociferous in negating any such call. Senior Congress leadership made no effort to quell such divisive calls, or made any gestures that could convince the Muslim leadership that in an independent India both Hindus and Muslims would co-exist as equals. Jinnah in order to retain hold on his flock gradually fell in line with the demands of the 'separatists.' He never really expected that such brilliant Hindu leaders would agree for a break up of the country in such a manner and that a Pakistan would be carved out which would be totally disconnected.

Pakistan was the outcome of this lack of vision, statesmanship and rigid approach of the Congress and other Hindu leaders till it was too late to reverse the trend. Always underestimating the seriousness of the call for a sovereign Pakistan if parity was not accorded, neither the British nor the Congress had formulated any strategy to challenge or resist this call. It is difficult to see how Jinnah could have agreed to a united, secular India in which he would have had to play a likely second fiddle to Gandhi or Nehru. (In an interview he gave to Louise Fischer in 1942 Jinnah said, "I have been in this movement for thirty five years. Nehru worked under me in the Home Rule Society, Gandhi worked under me. I was active in the Congress Party....My goal was Hindu-Muslim Unity...So it was until 1920 when Gandhi came into the limelight. A deterioration of Hindu-Muslim relations set in...I had the distinct feeling the Unity was hopeless, that Gandhi did not want it. It disappointed me." (Fisher in his book on Gandhi, pp 150-151). Obviously, a major factor that led to the break up of India was the 'personality clash' between Jinnah and Gandhi all through the freedom struggle.

For the Congress to refuse to think in terms of coalition, to attempt to undermine the leadership of the minority community by means of mass contact movements, to insist to the end that Congress alone represented the whole of India may have been necessary for the rhetoric of nationalism and bargaining with the British, but it had serious consequences for India's plural society. This aspect was never understood by the party leadership, for that matter even Mahatma failed to appreciate the significance of divisive developments, which had made serious inroads in the Indian political psyche with the introduction of separate electoral colleges in the 1920s when the process of seeking freedom from the British effectively took off. Gradually and along with the freedom movement gaining momentum a situation arose where the main Indian parties failed to identify any method of governing the 'now united Indian Empire.' They could not agree upon any solution that could have retained the country's identity. The price of freedom became partition. The Partition holocaust does not justify Gandhi's lofty claim that the freedom was free of bloodshed. Ask the refugees from both sides, ask those who saw their dear ones slaughtered on either side of the divide and ask those whose women were raped and houses plundered if Gandhi had any reason to gloat over his strategy; or if Nehru had any reason to be proud of what he and his party did to this country. That these leaders were aging and were in a hurry to see India free in their lifetime is no justification for what price the common Hindu, Sikh or Muslim paid for their foolhardiness.

The Hindus had the power to keep the sub-continent under one government if they had the sagacity and the wisdom to decentralise power to the Provinces and had allowed for the Muslim sentiments to be respected wherever the community felt threatened due to lack of adequate representation. Whenever any benefit was conceded to the Muslims it was always given with great reluctance and the gesture was always too late to have any positive impact on the commonality of the issues involved. The Hindu leadership lost three great opportunities of keeping India together: the first when they refused to form Coalition Ministries in the provinces in 1937; the second when they refused Cripps' offer of the steps to be taken towards self-government in 1942 and finally when they rejected the Cabinet Mission Plan in 1946. All these rejections stemmed from a misplaced feeling that Hindus were in a position where they could control the destiny of every other community. Leaders like Nehru and Gandhi treated Jinnah indifferently. In 1928 Jinnah was worsted by the forces of Hindu orthodoxy when he sought accommodation with Congress on an all-parties constitutional scheme. Seeing this negative attitude of these leaders the lower rung leadership and the Congress following also derided Muslim efforts to establish an identity of their own. Congress leaders were unwilling to accept Jinnah's assertion that he was *The Spokesman* of the Muslims. Nehru, in fact, took great pains to run him down at every opportunity. As is clear from Patel's assertions recorded in the Volume X Transfer of Power papers, Nehru and Patel were front-runners in this game plan. Nehru had the decency to admit that the people of India could 'justly' censure him for inability to perform many of his promises. The other Hindu leaders were generally content with the trappings that come with power.

The partition was definitely a failure of the politicians. The events leading to the freedom had been issuing periodic warnings of what might happen if they did not show sagacity, maturity and farsightedness in resolving their mutual differences. How could Nehru and Jinnah overlook the passion a Punjabi had for his land and his honour. How could Nehru be unaware of the feelings of the Sikhs for their shrines; as a national level leader he should have known that to a Sikh what comes first is his religion, his honour, his family and the country, in that order. In Jinnah's case, a total lack of empathy on the part of Congress, particularly a total lack of understanding of his compulsions by Patel and Nehru left him with no choice but to pitch for a place where his community will not be a 'permanent minority'.

Gandhi was no longer an effective leader of the Congress when the events were heading towards this painful end, but he had a tremendous following among all the communities and there should be no reason to assume that if he had put his foot down or demanded a particular course of action from the Congressmen that could have helped this country remain one he would have succeeded. No one, just no one could dare defy him. But he had set his heart on Nehru becoming an undisputed leader when the British left. This was not acceptable to Jinnah unless some safeguards for Muslims were included in the final deal. The Mahatma was either too naive or out of touch with the ground realities; for, he totally failed to read the situation which demanded that the Muslim sentiments had also to be taken into consideration before any final solution was implemented. Having made harmony between Hindus and Muslims the main object of his public prayer meetings, he now appeared as a traitor to both Hindus and Sikhs. His long march seemed to be ending in a failure, which now appeared to be beyond any remedy. Finally, one Nathuram Godse— a Hindu Brahmin—shot him down in cold blood on 30th January 1948 while he was going for his prayer meeting at 5 PM.

Another aspect of this sorry saga was the Hindu leadership's reluctance to respect Muslim sentiments on issues that concerned only the Muslims. The only time the Hindu leadership showed any proactive stance was when Gandhi lent support to the Khilafat Movement in the twenties. Many historians are of the opinion that it was a mistake because this allowed the Muslim clergy to attain prominence at the expense of secular Muslims, thus negating any positive impact such a gesture could have had in ensuring the country's unity. According to K M Munshi (*Pilgrimage to Freedom*) Jinnah warned Gandhi not to encourage fanaticism of Muslim religious leaders and their followers.

(Note: According to Mr Richard Casey, then Governor of Bengal, Gandhi informed Casey "Jinnah had told him that he (Gandhi) had ruined politics in India by dragging a lot of unwholesome elements in Indian life and giving them political prominence, that it was a crime to mix up politics and religion the way he had done." (Transfer of Power Vol. VI p 617))

Gandhi-Jinnah: A Clash of Personalities

Gandhi's confrontationist approach all through the freedom struggle, and his non-cooperation movements were at a complete tangent to Jinnah's constitutionalism. Gandhi and Jinnah were two absolutely different kinds of leaders. Gandhi preferred a "bottoms up" approach. He liked to carry masses along in whatever he did. Jinnah, on the other hand was a leader to whom all that suited was "top down". (In an article written for "*Time and Tide*" issued from Delhi on 13th February 1940 Jinnah expressed the opinion that Western Democracy was totally unsuited to

India, and that its imposition was a disease in the body politic. ('Quoted by G D Khosla in his book Stern Reckoning'.) The basic premise on which Gandhi and Nehru could have talked with him i.e. a 'democratic structure' for the country itself was seemingly too far from Mr Jinnah's perception where India's future was concerned. However, if somehow these two thought processes could have been harmonised then may be the Indian history would have had a happier ending to its glorious 'freedom struggle'. Some well-meaning and highly respected people still express the opinion that what India needed was a "benevolent dictator". The root of the partition clearly was a 'personality clash', which had nothing to do with any specific ideological differences between the two. B R Ambedkar described the situation thus: "The first thing that strikes me is that it would be difficult to find two persons who would rival them for their colossal egotism, to whom personal ascendancy is everything and the cause of the country a mere counter on the table. They have made Indian politics a matter of personal feud. Consequences have no terror for them; indeed they do not occur to them until they happen...they choose to stand on a pedestal of splendid isolation. They wall themselves off from their equals, are very happy to be fawned upon. ...Politics in the hands of these two great men has become a competition in extravaganza. These two will never meet, except on preposterous conditions. Jinnah insists that Gandhi should admit that he is a Hindu. Gandhi insists that Jinnah should admit that he is one of the leaders of the Muslims....they make long and interminable speeches, like lawyers whose trade it is to contest everything, concede nothing and talk by the hour." (B R Ambedkar quoted in 'Jinnah by Asiananda'- page 138-139). As to why the bitterness of Gandhi-Jinnah feud, which virtually started during a reception in honour of Gandhi by the Gujrati community thirty years before the break up of India, has not been critically analysed is somewhat intriguing. May be their departure from the scene soon after the partition had something to do with this.

Mountbatten Lets India Down

In the highly inflamed communal atmosphere the orderly transfer of power in Punjab and Bengal depended entirely on the Boundary Commission award defining areas that would form part of East and West Bengal, East and West Punjab. Redcliffe did not attend a single hearing of the concerned parties personally. Only the reports of the proceedings were sent to him every day. After all the "hearings" were over he held discussions with the members of the Commission and then communicated his decisions or Award to the Viceroy (*Stern Reckoning* - G D Khosla). How this ham-handed approach to such a serious subject could have done justice to any of the contending parties is a matter of conjecture. Indication of distinct boundaries of the two countries would have allowed people some time to collect whatever of their belongings they could and shift base to areas most conducive to their religious leanings. This could have brought some kind of order when killings were mounting. There was a consensus of opinion among Jenkins, the Punjab Partition Committee and Mountbatten that every day's delay in publication of the Punjab Award would greatly increase the risk of disorder in Punjab: yet, he elected to sit on it. Mountbatten was duty-bound to exercise his full control and authority over all the resources available to him at least till the midnight of 14th August 1947 and to use these to protect the people of this country. He had the means, in the form of army and air force, to provide adequate cover and protection to the hapless people who were shifting from one part of the country to another due to its impending division. He, virtually, abdicated that duty. The Viceroy elected to let things drift. Minutes of the Staff Meeting held on 9th August 1947 (69th Staff Meeting) clearly reveal that Mountbatten was more concerned with his reputation and that of the British Government. As a representative of the British Government he shirked accepting responsibility of putting down the disturbances, which would have unquestionably followed publication of the awards. All the riots and carnage then going on would have ultimately reflected on His Majesty's Government if it were established that mass-migration had been hastened because the State had not taken adequate precautions to protect the common man when Redcliffe had already defined division of Punjab. Where Bengal is concerned, on hearing that the Chittagaon Hill Tracts had been given to Pakistan by the Bengal Award, the Viceroy conveniently accepted the advice that the announcement on both the Awards should be withheld till after the Independence Day. According to Campbell-Johnson, the Viceroy did not want to mar the celebratory aspect of the independence because neither India, nor Pakistan was likely to be totally happy with the end result.

Mountbatten should have taken Nehru and Jinnah in his confidence about the award so that these two could take steps to ensure that all those who wished to cross over to the other side could do so when there was still time and there was still one central authority having resources to enforce peaceful and orderly transfer of people by employing 'still undivided' armed forces. The Governor of Punjab, Jenkins even appealed to Mountbatten that, "Even a few hours warning would be better than none as the nature of the award would affect the distribution of police and troops." Since, Mountbatten was to be the Governor-General of only dominion India on the mid-night of 14th August 1947 authorised to act only on the advice of a 'council of ministers' thereafter, with no control on the Army and the Air force it was incumbent on him to wisely employ resources available to him before that crucial date. He failed to do so. Mountbatten decided to abdicate his duty towards the citizens of India. The gravest reproach to Mountbatten's sense of duty, responsibility and, sense of values is that he placed the celebration on Independence Day much higher than the lives of the people of India because it definitely satisfied his "monstrous vanity." Nehru was giving him a chance to present himself in his full military regalia to the people of India and Mountbatten was not the type that would let such a 'marketing' opportunity go by when he desperately wanted to be the 'First Sea Lord' of the Royal Navy. As to why Mountbatten actually sat on such crucial Reports, and was he doing it at the behest of someone will only be known as and when the last volume of 'Transfer of Power' is declassified and made available to the public.

Mountbatten betrayed India by sitting on Redcliffe's award for six crucial days when the 'award' was already in his hand on 9th August 1947. Contrary to his boast that he would use Army and even Air force to quell riots he did nothing of the kind, and took no steps to prevent, or to confine within the narrowest possible limits, murder, butchery, mutilation and defilement of Muslims and Hindus, and to take steps to protect the hapless and helpless people who had been forced to flee their homes. He failed in the most elementary duty of the Government, which was to protect life, liberty and property of His Majesty's subjects. The King, and for that matter Attlee would never have wished that the last days of the British Raj should be branded with infamy, and be stained with the needless spilling of blood. Machiavellian Mountbatten later shamelessly claimed credit for having accomplished, in less than two and a half months, one of the 'greatest administrative operations' in history. Hundred of thousands of Hindus, Muslims and Sikhs who got slaughtered in the process of this accomplishment had no meaning for this soulless representative of the British Raj. India's 'communal madness' undoubtedly contributed to the holocaust; but the grievous effects of that madness could have been contained if Mountbatten had exercised his immense powers and had taken drastic steps to, at least, minimise the slaughter of innocent Indians during those last days of the Raj. To cap it all, on his return to UK in June 1948, he claimed that the transition period had been relatively peaceful. In support of this contention he noted that only three per cent of the population were involved in the disturbances. That the three per cent meant ten million or one in every thirty-five Indians was never considered to be catastrophic enough by him. Jinnah's personality and arrogance of the Congress helped him to conceal these realities from the world till the "Transfer of Power" papers were declassified by Harold Wilson in 1967 instead of keeping them locked up till 1999 as was originally envisaged. (Volumes

X to XII *Transfer of Power* are quite graphic about vanity and immaturity of Mountbatten while dealing with the complex situation then prevailing in India).

Division of Armed Forces

It was a mischievous ploy on the part of the British to keep the issue of division of the armed forces hanging till the very end. Now, in the middle of a political upheaval, chaos and disorder to envisage division of the Armed forces was a sure call for further deterioration of the situation. The C-in-C, the Air C-in-C and the Naval Chief all pleaded with the Viceroy that the partition of the Armed forces was not possible in such a short time frame. Any effort to do so would inevitably lead to anarchy. Auchinleck wanted to hand over properly organised and fully functional Armed forces to the two dominions. Mountbatten overruled his military advisers, saying that the division had to be done irrespective of the consequences. By giving such a short timeframe to the emerging Dominions the Viceroy was also ensuring that Britain would continue to play a major role in the affairs of the sub-continent; and the British Government hoped to bring about cooperation between India and Pakistan under its aegis and would thus be able to manipulate both India and Pakistan for a long time to come.

The Partition of the Forces was to be in two phases. In the first phase there was to be a rough and ready division of units and sub-units on the basis of religion. That is, the units, which already had a distinct Hindu and Muslim identity, were to be allocated to the two dominions straightaway. The next phase was to comb out the units themselves on the basis of a voluntary transfer. Also, the Muslims who hailed from the areas, which had now been identified as part of Pakistan, were not to be given any option of serving with the Indian army. Similarly, non-Muslims from the rest of India now serving in the Armed forces would not have the option of joining the Armed forces of Pakistan. To further add to the confusion it was also decided that all the existing Armed forces of India would remain under a single administrative control until sorted out into two distinct forces and the two governments were in a position to administer them.

So, where Clement Attlee and Mountbatten are concerned, the sore of Partition could be their "parting kick" to the ungrateful Indians who had the temerity to seek freedom from such a 'benevolent' and progressive Raj. A united and strong India was not conducive to the British global interests in the 'cold war' that had already started between America and her allies on one side and the Communist bloc on the other. With so many loose ends and disputes between the two dominions left in the course of a hurried partition Britain had ensured that the governments and the people of these two, now independent, countries would expend time, energy and effort in resolving these 'inherited' problems for a long time to come. The dreadful cost the British made us pay before transfer of power to divided India has lessons for posterity to register and for us to ensure that these are not forgotten. Freedom has extracted from us a very heavy and exhausting price; a price we still continue to pay—as if a usurious moneylender of the past keeps collecting only the interest with the principal remaining intact. In the instant case it is in the form of a perpetual and perennial sore of an unnatural divide that is keeping the pot of mutual hate boiling.

Dominique Lapierre and Larry Collins in their 'run away' best-seller *Freedom at Midnight'* have been more than incongruous and uncharitable to the history of the sub-continent when they write: "This disaster was no accident of history. At the time of their birth both India and Pakistan were two Siamese brothers tied to each other by a cancerous tumour, Punjab. The British had cut off the tumour and separated the twins but had not succeeded in clearing out the cancerous cells." But the surgeon was a bad one. Mountbatten played the main villain in this tragic operation. One can easily conclude that he sought to rewrite India's history with cavalier indifference to the prevailing situation. His sole aim was to magnify and glorify his own achievement, which in any case were of doubtful merit.

It seems extraordinary in retrospect that Jinnah should have argued that Hindus and Muslims constituted two nations and still expected Pakistan to include undivided Punjab and Bengal with their substantial Hindu and Sikh minorities. To be fair to the man; it must be stated that until 1947 itself, Jinnah visualised Pakistan in terms of greater autonomy or independence for existing provinces of British India rather than a strict redrawing of boundaries according to religion. As the Pakistani author Saad Khairi has argued in his *'Jinnah Reinterpreted'*, the presence of non-Muslims was an integral part of Jinnah's Pakistan. Their presence was in fact a guarantee of safety for the Muslims left behind in India. As late as mid 1947, Jinnah was still investing in shares and property in India and according to his solicitor in Bombay, he even had a plan to retire to Bombay after completing his tenure as the Governor General of Pakistan. He left his house fully furnished there; in 1947 he saw nothing illogical in the thought. Apparently, it was the killings and riots and the exchange of population, which set the seal on the new divided sub-continent and left Jinnah with a great sense of bitterness and betrayal. It is also beyond dispute that immediately before partition Jinnah gave his blessings to efforts by Suhrawardy and Sarat Bose to float the idea of an independent and united Bengal. It was a sure sign that even in the last stages of the transfer of power he was not opposed to a future for the Bengalis built around their ethnic rather than religious identity. It is another matter that the prospect of permanent subordination to a Muslim majority was not acceptable to many Congressmen and Hindu leaders and Bengal had to be divided along with Punjab. Jinnah left India for Pakistan on 7th August 1947, with an appeal to both Hindus and Muslims to "bury the past", wishing India success and prosperity. The next day Patel said in Delhi. "The poison had been removed from the body of India." The sentiments were never likely to or expected to improve relationship between the recently divided family.

The separation of the 'twins' continues to have an impact: in the memories of millions of individuals, and families affected by communal carnage and ethnic cleansing, in the continuing dispute over Kashmir, and in the costly military and nuclear standoff between the two countries—a situation which neither of them can afford. The British are definitely culpable in creating a situation where both the countries are busy diverting their scarce resources away from human development; and this is so when the common man is willing to forget and forgive. How devious and cunning the British were needs no further explanation. The battle over India's history is far from over; the contest between the two protagonists is still on.

Epilogue

"Public opinion has preened itself on British virtue in withdrawing voluntarily from India.... It may be hard to disentangle whether the British action was based on high principle or on less glorious desire to retreat to shelter before the storm broke."

Manchester Guardian, 11th October 1947

After a detailed study of the period under British rule one is convinced that 'initially' the official policy was not to disturb the native structure in any manner: no interference in the religious, social, cultural, or domestic affairs was either allowed or envisaged by the Company. Indians themselves, with their propensity for mutual conflicts and greed, allowed the British to become reluctant rulers initially. Thereafter, particularly after 1857, they had all the reason to be ruling this country. But resentment against them was virtually concurrent to consolidation of the Empire. One major mistake that the British made was to treat the natives as second-class citizens: Indians were not invited to share the power of the Raj, but only feel it. In the fear that familiarity would breed contempt, Company servants and those who came in after India was declared as a Colony of the Empire, held themselves aloof from the natives, they feared that any physical or friendly contact would only reduce the awe in which the natives held British demi-gods. Trouble was that the Indians were far too ahead of their British masters in intellectual capabilities, no way the Raj could have gone on and on. British generally left Indians to their own devices so long as nothing threatened the Raj. On hindsight this policy was relatively prudent because every time they touched the existing set up, they burnt their fingers, the partition of Bengal and its after-effects is a case in point. The government composed of White Sahibs who were totally out of touch with the ground realities of the times adopted the weapon of repression to nip in infancy the rising tide of resentment against the foreign rulers but failed to make any lasting impression. Yet, it is also a fact that the hundred years of British rule formed the only time when India was effectively linked together as an entity. Fact of the matter is that the British remained strangers in the land and never really understood or properly appreciated what they called the 'jewel in the crown'.

Lord Elphinstone observed: "In due course the British would leave India. Better to have an early separation from a civilised people than a violent rupture with a barbarous nation." That all such views were more paternalistic and sanctimonious is given: fact of the matter is that they all believed that the British power rested not on popularity but on power. This analysis is confirmed when one reads '*The History of British India*', in seven volumes written by John Mill, the father of famous philosopher John Stuart Mill, wherein he stipulates, "Only the provision of firm government could lead the natives out of a swamp of superstition into the modern age and only useful knowledge would civilise them." To an extent he was right, priest-craft and superstition, between them, had rendered Indians, in mind and body, the most enslaved segment of the human race. Not unnaturally, Mill's History encouraged the servants of the Company to 'reform' India, and to bring her quickly into the modern age so that she could share the benefits of progress. A lot was done to rid India of some of her religious curses, curses like Sati, but all that was done without proper education of the masses who generally lived in villages and were not too sure of the intentions of the Whites. Things like land consolidation in the hands of a few faithful further alienated the common man.

In the early part of the last century just about everyone thought that the British Empire in India could last for generations. This assessment of the prowess of the Empire was not without rationale. At the end of the First World War, the British government controlled well over a quarter of the world's land surface. The British Empire contained 450 million people, comprising representatives of practically every race and religion in the world. In terms of numbers, the predominant religion was Hinduism, followed by Islam, the third was Christianity; thereafter, there were splinter groups of various other faiths. The land area of 14 million square miles stretched to all the five continents, it was the Empire 'upon which sun never set'. At almost any hour of the day there was some place on this earth where the Union Jack was being hoisted at dawn. In geographical terms of direct authority, it exceeded anything achieved by any other power in history. Keeping India in her grip had become a cornerstone of global British policy. India, after the loss of the North

American colonies, gave Britain the extra-territorial weight for domination of the world trade in the power struggles of the times. They had no option but to hang on to this acquisition at any cost. There can be no denying that when India became free, when the "brightest jewel" no longer bedecked the British Crown, when the chain of world imperialism broke at its most significant link, it meant that the entire climate of world politics was no longer the same. It meant that the winds of change were soon to blow, as they did all over Asia and Africa. It signalled a new Era in History, for over areas of the earth's surface, long labelled dark and underdeveloped, the deprived and the disinherited had begun to come into their own.

That a small western power should come to India from a distance of thousands of miles and subjugate this vast continent full of martial races and illimitable resources is an astounding phenomenon in Human history: that it was made possible by the endemic weakness of its opponents is also a fact of history. Just as a play needs an audience, the last two decades of British rule in India had world interest, particularly because of the striking contrast between the intentions and personalities of the protagonists. International events, especially the Second World War and American opinion, raised the importance and heightened the tension of these years as both the Indian leaders and the British went on to design their respective strategy with a mind towards international acceptability. The means of mass disobedience chosen by Gandhi and the Congress Party and the British action to counter this strategy had now become newsworthy internationally. This heightened the universal appeal of the Indian drama, and added an additional dimension to this presentation of a difficult subject. India's struggle for political emancipation was manifesting itself throughout the British rule in spasmodic outbursts but never a continuous affair. For the first time in Indian history Britain had imposed a foreign domination and the concomitant mechanism of exploitation. First the East India Company and afterwards the government which succeeded it, did nothing extraordinary to either supersede or replace the existing native machineries of governance.

The lower ranks of the colonial bureaucracy were mostly corrupt. The police habitually used torture and were left to their devices because it was convenient for the British to do so. Since a dishonest and corrupt official could be relied upon to carry out anti-nationalist directive of his superiors, sometimes with relish, a blind eye was turned on their activities. No serious effort was ever made to stamp out these evils from the administrative system. Sycophants and anti-India officials were rewarded for the enthusiasm they showed in crushing the activities of the freedom fighters at various levels. Penderel Moon, a highly respected ICS officer, considered British policies in India to be directly responsible for keeping the Indian peasants in absolute poverty and reducing them to a stage of bondage. In his view the introduction of the English legal system with its emphasis on the inviolability of contract where the majority was illiterate meant a subjection of the peasant to the moneylender and ensured ruthless exploitation by the landlord. Naturally, every time the British tried to do something, which was thought to be an improvement on the fragile native infrastructure and latent distrust of the common man of the white ruler did not let them succeed. One thing the British failed to appreciate was that neither the Mughal nor the British Empire was powerful enough to subvert the structure of Indian society founded on caste and village. The source of survival and native wealth was village, each with its headman, its immutable cycle of sowing, monsoon and harvest, changing little as Empires rose and fell. For centuries India had had a sophisticated network of 'people's courts, bankers and moneychangers. This network ensured that the social and economic structure of the country did not disintegrate with the disappearance of the Mughals and consolidation of the British Raj. The caste system prized exclusiveness, aloofness, and self-reliance, which in the context of the political struggle for independence became a national expression of a local truth under the guidance of the Mahatma.

A study of the British rule in India exhibits a strange connection between agitation and reforms. The fierce Bengal agitation against the partition of the state resulted in reforms of 1909; the Khilafat movement coincided with Montagu-Chelmsford reforms of 1919; the Congress non-cooperation campaign heralded the reforms of 1935; and the Congress sponsored 'Quit India' movement brought Sir Stafford Cripps post-haste to India for negotiations. One reason could be that awareness generated by modern education during the later years of the nineteenth century, and the fact the Indians were increasingly getting convinced that the primary aim of British rule in India was to serve British interests only, that John Bull at home was no better than John Bull abroad, and that neither Conservative Party nor Liberal Party could be relied upon to do justice to India made leaders of those respective generation realise that the grip of the British on India was far too strong to be shed off with one heave. They had to move by stages. The British relented, often under duress, but generally because people like Morley were there to realise that the 'mighty Raj' was a historic travesty, Britain was too far away from India and there were too few British people to let this unnatural condition survive for an indeterminate length of time. Keeping this aspect in mind Morley wrote to Minto on 15th August 1907; "...how intensely artificial and unnatural is our mighty Raj, and it sets one wondering whether it can possibly last. It surely cannot, and our business is to do what we can make the next transition whatever it may turn out to be, something of an improvement... Morley to Minto (Minto Papers M1007 No. 48) Trouble was that whenever the Raj tried to devolve responsibility to Indians, first at the provincial and subsequently at the national level—the way it handled Muslim mindset, even in early twentieth century while formulating Reforms, it is clear that the aim of the exercise was to play on the Muslim insecurity vis-à-vis Hindu majority and thus prolong their own hold over the country. With the nationalist leaders playing to their tune because either they lacked political maturity or sagacity to understand the trader from England, it became obvious that in due course of time the Muslim community would regard separation as the only salvation to their aspirations. What added to this analysis was the fact that the Congress could never have safeguarded the interests of Muslims the way they wanted it without alienating its majority community supporters. As Nehru put it, 'Whatever offer we make, however high our bid might be, there is always a third party which can bid higher, and what is more, give substance to its words.' (Jawaharlal Nehru *'An Autobiography'* p 137)

Alongside the 'reforms' the government also brought in repressive legislations like the Rowlatt Act, which actually stirred the otherwise simple and unsophisticated Indian masses into expressing their resentment in a manner that eventually changed the course of the British rule in India. The time-tested policy of left-handed concessions and right-handed repression clearly failed. Realising the gravity of the situation the King-Emperor did try to sooth the feelings of hurt in his Indian subjects over the misdeeds of his representatives in the country by issuing a royal proclamation and even sending his son to express 'royal grief' after the Jallianwala Bagh massacre but he had kept it too late.

Nothing was ever done by the British to encourage or advise the princes to bring their states into constitutional harmony with their neighbouring provinces. In fact the British failure to deal decisively with all the tall claims some of the more powerful princes had been making over the years created a political anachronism that had a tremendous impact on the political situation then prevailing in the country. Consequently, the future unity of India turned into a question whether the princes and the Muslims would accept an increasingly dominant and essentially a Hindu Congress.

May be if the British had been less arrogant, less socially stand-offish, less racially contemptuous while they ruled India, the history of the sub-continent would have been different. But nobody had equipped or groomed them to deal with a people with culture older than their own. It has also got to be recorded that India arrived at independence with one of the largest cotton goods industries in the world, mostly in Indian hands, structures for the exploitation of her mineral wealth, and internal and external communications serving a thriving export trade— India overall did quite well materially out of British investment in the country in the form of; firstly, making it a single entity; and more importantly, in providing the country with an administrative infrastructure that has withstood the test of time. The British left behind railways, schools, universities, and statues of Queen Victoria and sundry Governor Generals and Viceroys, industries, a legal system and much more. What they couldn't leave behind was their culture; alien, itself exhausted, trivial and shallow.

Main fly in the ointment was that the British did not rule India by love, but by fear. It was a theme Gandhi was to develop with devastating eloquence in due course of time. The failure of the British to understand the subtle Hindu mind, forsaking it for the mercenaries from the Punjab and other parts of India who were faithful to any overlord who offered them a good fight and adequate wages; and the conservative, at times reactionary, support of Muslims, was the ultimate failure of British rule. The capacity of the learned Indian to live in two cultures, sometimes more than that, put him in an intellectual class, which was way beyond the comprehension of a normal British official who had set foot in India to rule on behalf of the crown. In simple language, the average Indian was far too intellectually superior to an average British.

Jawaharlal Nehru once said, "Whatever the limitations of our freedom struggle it has, by and large, steered clear of certain trivialities, which often mar such phenomena. This is a claim, though not indisputable where hard-nosed and 'often biased' experts are concerned, has tremendous merit. Apart from the mutiny of 1857 very few Europeans lost their lives at the hands of Indians, whether criminals or 'freedom fighters'. History, "a cruel goddess" as Friedrich Engels once called her, will of course pronounce her verdict without pity, and her votaries, plunging into the record, choose, wherever thought fit to denigrate men and events.

How does one describe the events of August-September 1947? Once the religious genie was out of the bottle, there was no returning it; for, religion proved a more potent stimulus to nationalism than secular politics. Hindus and Muslims had been at each other's throat for over three years and there was no end to this mayhem in sight. So, was it genocide? The word defines use of violence at a very large scale. But genocide is usually a premeditated act, that is to say the result of a decision emanating from a central power. That is how the International Tribunal at Nuremberg had defined it while trying Nazis for their 'war crimes'. That is how Pakistan interpreted the word when it made its representation to the Security Council on 15th January 1948. But if it was genocide it was reciprocal, and no central power had 'seemingly' sanctioned it. It was the reaction of a population driven to despair by the failure of its leadership. Partition was not the irruption of an "ethnic" violence aroused by hatred of the other. Hindus, Muslims and Sikhs are of the same stock, the same colour and they speak the same language. They do practice different religions, but religious difference is no more than difference in social status of individuals, their life styles and caste or culture.

Mercifully and in general perception, our freedom struggle and especially its leaders, and more importantly lay protagonists largely do manage to survive this test of history. Their sacrifices, in the face of all kinds of adversity, merit recording. This, not withstanding the fact that even more than fifty-eight years after independence we are far removed from the goals originally set by the founding fathers, is in itself a kind of indictment of the system we elected to adopt after independence. This inadequacy of the choices that we made in 1947 and thereafter should not be allowed to colour our perception of the freedom struggle in itself." More than fifty years after the British left India we are ranked *138th* in the list of 179 countries in the Development Programme of the United Nations. Over 400 million of our citizens are illiterate and live in the direst poverty, and 200 million have no access to safe drinking water. This situation is a clear reflection on the kind of governments we have had. A country like India, long weighed down by history and a culture that was in place when the White man had still not left his caves, needs to be read and absorbed in its correct perspective.

The principles, ideologies, and the values the old guard cherished have disappeared because these have become outdated in today's materialistic world, or the present generation finds it to be too cumbersome to live up to them. Either way, it is necessary that the same be redefined taking stalwarts of our freedom movement as role models for the purpose. It is important to do so because among the literati, the Indian educated class of the later years of the British rule, a feeling persists that the British perhaps were on the whole motivated by a desire to be benevolent to the people of this country when they did what they did to ensure continuance of their Empire. Not without reason, the older people often consider that the things were better during the 'Raj'. But that should not be a reason for anyone of us to negate the fact that a hard won freedom deserves to be studied and respected. Fighting for the liberation of the country was a difficult task, but given the present circumstances it is still more difficult and tenacious affair to preserve it.

Mutual jealousies and conflicts made the country an easy prey to organised invasions in the past. It is not certain if very many lessons have been learnt from that experience. Lack of vision and trust among our leaders, mutual bickering, one up man ship and sundry grievances destroyed all that the Raj had achieved for this country in unifying India into one entity.

Delving into History is like shining a torch into a cave. You cannot see the whole cave, but as you play the beam of the torch around, a collage of shapes is revealed. One interprets this incomplete information about the contents of the cave any which way. History tells us about the intricacies and events of a particular era, their impact on the key players who welded those events into historic milestones. History is, primarily, a guide and help to the social understanding of a particular era and a study of the imponderables and those factors that influenced events of that period keeps life going. An ancient country like India has far too long a past; and our history is the source from which we must constantly draw our inspirations for the present and the future. If we have not been wise before the event, let us learn from a study of the past so that we can be wise at least after the event. It is always difficult to obtain real historical truths behind events that shaped a particular course of action. To be fair and objective, history requires to be written again and again, a recurrent task whose definitive shape will always remain elusive, notwithstanding the fact that the period covered in this effort of mine is far too recent, but the lessons of this eventful period have got to be registered, acknowledged and be taken as a guiding beacon before the current trends in our country's politics wean us away from a progressive society that the leaders who withstood the British onslaught had dreamt of.

Lord Dufferin's warning of 1887 that British attempts to 'Divide and Rule' would recoil on them rang true in 1947. In August 1947, the Muslim League was the only party to achieve what it wanted.

Bibliography

The Amritsar Legacy by Roger Perkins.

The Amritsar Massacre by Rupert Furneaux

Amritsar—The Massacre That Ended the Raj by Alfred Draper

The Proudest Day by Anthony Read & David Fisher

Towards Freedom by Jayaprakash Narain

Muslims and India's Freedom Movement by Shan Muhammad

Eminent Muslim Freedom Fighters by G Allana

The History of British India by PE Roberts

The Indian Army by Stephen P Cohen

The Springing Tiger by Hugh Toye

The Fall of the British Empire by Colin Cross

The Long Afternoon by William Golant

Ghadr by Khushwant Singh and Satinder Singh

Recalling India's Struggle for Freedom by Hiren Mukerjee

Stanley Wolpert Transfer of Power

Pirzada Foundation of Pakistan

P Moon Wavell: The Viceroy Journal

Freedom at Midnight Dominique Lapierre and Larry Collins

KM Panikar—Imperialism in Practice and Theory

Strangers in the Land (The Rise and Decline of the British Indian Empire)
Roderick Cavaliero

India in Transition by Aga Khan

India and the Passing of Empire by Sir George Earle

Inside India by Halide Edib

The British in India by Sir Percival Grifith

The Awakening of India by J Ramsay MacDonald

The Sole Spokesman by Ayesha Jalal

Strangers in the Land by Roderick Cavaliero

Prelude to Partition (The Indian Muslim and the Imperial System of Control) by David Page

The Origins of the Partition of India by Anita Inder Singh

Legend and Reality by HM Seervai

The Demand for Partition of India by Syed Ali Mujtaba

Jinnah—A Corrective Reading of Indian History by Asiananda

Stern Reckoning by GD Khosla

The Transfer of Power Papers Volumes I to XII

Index